CRIMINAL LITIGATION

CRIMINAL LITIGATION

Craig Osborne BA, MA (Econ), Solicitor

Senior Lecturer in Law, Manchester Metropolitan University

BLACKSTONE
PRESS LIMITED

First published in Great Britain 1993 by Blackstone Press Limited, 9-15 Aldine Street, London W12 8AW.
Telephone: 081-740 1173

ISBN: 1 85431 294 4

British Library Cataloguing in Publication Data
A CIP catalogue record for this book is available from the British Library.

Typeset by Montage Studios Limited, Tonbridge, Kent
Printed by Livesey Ltd., Shrewsbury, Shropshire

CONTENTS

CONTENTS

16 Committal Proceedings

17 The Crown Court: Preparation and Trial

18 Sentencing and Procedures after Conviction

19 Juveniles in the Criminal Process: The Youth Court

20 Appeals in Criminal Cases

21 The European Convention on Human Rights

PREFACE

This book is intended to be a 'legal resource book' for the new Legal Practice Course in criminal litigation. It deals with all aspects of the written standards produced by the Law Society for that course but it is my intention to go well beyond them. It is intended to be a legal resource book in the fullest sense, being a full and self-contained treatment of the relevant aspects of mainstream criminal practice. It includes not merely details of criminal procedure but also the law of evidence and practical and tactical considerations in dealing with clients and the criminal courts. Students will of course derive advantage from referring from time to time to other sources, in particular, the statutes or cases referred to in this text.

The subject matter of a book on criminal litigation is perhaps considerably less contentious than the equivalent on civil litigation, where strong differences of opinion may arise as to what should or should not be included at a certain level. I have included a chapter on the European Convention on Human Rights and Fundamental Freedoms which the Law Society, rightly, stress as being a vital part of the armoury of all litigation practitioners. Notwithstanding that at present the contribution of cases under the Convention to the annual fee income of the average practitioner is minimal, its importance as a last resort and a means of righting injustices, particularly for those caught up in the criminal justice system, cannot be over-emphasised.

In complying with the Law Society's written standards, I have decided that a thorough and relatively academic approach to the law of evidence is necessary. Evidence, more than most other subjects, is difficult to convey accurately, and comprehensibly, in a brief form and if some of the chapters on evidence are found lengthy and discursive it is because it is my view that in order to explain the working of evidence in practical situations it is necessary to understand the rationale of the common law rule or legislation. If the chapters on evidence are found heavy this is my defence, or if it is no defence, my mitigation.

My own slowness in submitting this work to the publishers, which has unfortunately occasioned them some loss of sleep, has worked to my advantage in that I have been able to substantially revise the text at proof stage to take into account amendments incorporated in the Criminal Justice Act 1993 which mainly comes into effect late August.

I have been very grateful throughout for the enthusiasm, commitment and professionalism of the publishers and particularly to Mandy Preece the workaholic and long suffering managing editor of this series.

I am very grateful to the Magistrates' Association for permission to produce the two forms on sentencing guidelines incorporated at the end of **Chapter 18**.

Craig Osborne
August 1993

TABLE OF CASES

ONE

AN OUTLINE OF CRIMINAL PROCEDURE: EARLY STAGES

1.1   The Course of Criminal Proceedings

In order to show in simple form the course of criminal proceedings, a very brief preliminary outline of the progress of a criminal prosecution will be given here.

1.1.1   POLICE INVESTIGATIONS

After a crime has been committed it will be investigated by the police and unless the offender has been apprehended at the scene of the crime, detection work of various kinds may occur until the police have a suspect. They have powers of arrest and search and the right to interrogate. They may also, for example, hold an identity parade, obtain fingerprints, and so on. We will then assume that they consider they know who committed the offence.

1.1.2   PROSECUTING THE SUSPECT

The police then have an option to proceed against the suspect in one of two ways:

(a)   causing a *summons* to be issued against the suspect; or
(b)   *charging* the suspect.

The first option would be more likely in the case of routine or trivial crime such as driving offences. In such situations the accused may well have been apprehended at the scene of the crime. He will usually be released there and then and told that he may later be prosecuted. Subsequently, the police will adopt a procedure known as *laying an information* before a magistrates' court and a summons will be issued against the suspect. The prosecution will then be taken over by the Crown Prosecution Service (CPS) and will come before the courts where it may be dealt with on the first occasion or adjourned for a variety of reasons depending on which course the case takes.

Alternatively, the accused may have been arrested by the police and actually *charged* at the police station. In this case the charge sheet which notifies the charge will specify the date on which the accused is to appear before the magistrates' court. The decision on whether or not to charge is normally that of the arresting and investigating officers, sometimes after consultation with the CPS. A charge is the appropriate form of prosecution for more serious offences.

1

1.1.3 PROCEDURE IN THE MAGISTRATES' COURT

With very few exceptions, not relevant at present, all prosecutions commence in the magistrates' court. Offences may broadly be classified into three types for procedural purposes:

(a) Those that are triable *purely summarily*, i.e. those of relative triviality where only a magistrates' court has jurisdiction (e.g., careless driving).

(b) Those triable only *on indictment* in the Crown Court before a judge and jury, i.e. those offences too serious to be tried by magistrates (e.g., murder, rape).

(c) Those offences which may be more or less serious depending on a variety of circumstances including inter alia the degree of violence (e.g., assaults) or the amount involved (e.g., theft). These offences are known as '*either way*' offences.

In the case of these latter offences there needs to be a decision as to which court, magistrates' court or Crown Court, will try the case.

In the case of purely summary offences, when the accused person appears before the magistrates' court it is unlikely that the case will be dealt with at the first appearance if the accused is pleading not guilty. This is because of the expense of calling witnesses and preparing the case fully which can be avoided if the accused pleads guilty. Thus if he pleads guilty he will be dealt with then and there, if he pleads not guilty the case will be adjourned for trial at some later date. In the case of some offences (mainly motoring offences) the accused may be offered the opportunity to plead guilty by post without attending court.

In the case of an offence triable either way the court has to decide on the *mode of trial*. It will hear representations about what factors relevant to the offence make it more suitable that the accused should be tried in either the magistrates' court or the Crown Court, and the magistrates' court will then decide. However, whilst the magistrates' court may decide to send the case to the Crown Court for trial, if it decides that it is willing to try it then, in the case of 'either way' offences, the accused always has the power to overrule the court and insist on the right to jury trial.

In the case of offences which are triable purely on indictment or those triable either way which are being taken to the Crown Court, there is a preliminary stage known as a *committal hearing* at which the magistrates may make a preliminary examination of the case. Thereafter they either dismiss the case (if there is shown not to be sufficient evidence on which to commit to the Crown Court) or allow the case to go to the Crown Court for trial.

At any stage of this procedure, questions of bail, legal aid and adjournment may arise. The magistrates' court has the power to adjourn a case at any time and when it does so it will sometimes be required to consider how to deal with the accused during the adjournment, for example, whether or not to allow him bail. The magistrates' court will also often have to decide whether an accused is entitled to legal aid.

The accused will be tried in the magistrates' court or committed for trial to the Crown Court. At the end of his trial in either court, if he is convicted, matters of sentencing and mitigation will arise.

1.2 Professional Ethics

1.2.1 DUTIES OF THE PROSECUTOR

In principle a prosecutor has a duty to act as a minister of justice and to see that all relevant facts and law are before the courts. He should not strive for a conviction at any price and should indeed even present matters favourable to the defendant. Other aspects of this principle are that the prosecution generally play no part at the sentencing stage and do not as in other countries press for any particular sentence or for the defendant to be dealt with severely; nor do they present facts in emotive language.

The prosecution have a specific duty to make available to the defence any evidence which they have obtained which is favourable to the defence, and to inform the defence of any material inconsistency in witness statements obtained by the prosecution, e.g., where a witness having given one version of events subsequently gives a significantly different version. This is by virtue of guidelines issued by the Attorney-General which appear at [1982] 1 All ER 734. In addition there is a Code for Crown Prosecutors published by the CPS which sets out various considerations appropriate for a Crown Prosecutor in respect of the commencement and course of a prosecution including evidential and ethical matters.

1.2.2 DUTIES OF THE DEFENCE SOLICITOR

The defence solicitor has a basic duty to do what is best for his client but in addition has an overriding duty not to mislead the court. Within these confines however he must act as vigorously as possible in his client's interests even if he privately believes him to be guilty.

It is appropriate here to consider a number of aspects of the defence solicitor's duties.

1.2.2.1 Confidentiality

A solicitor may not reveal anything which the client has told him while the solicitor-client relationship exists, without the client's proper authority. One aspect of this is that a solicitor is under no obligation to give the prosecution any advance warning of the nature of his client's defence to a charge. He is entitled to maintain the secrecy of this, in principle until the defence case opens, although usually it will be necessary to indicate the nature of the defence case when cross-examining prosecution witnesses. To this principle there are three exceptions where the prosecution are entitled to some notice of matters relevant to the defence case.

(a) Under s. 81, Police and Criminal Evidence Act 1984, a person who proposes to rely on *expert evidence* in a criminal trial must give advance disclosure of this to the opposition.

(b) In the case of an *alibi* defence. In the case of trials on indictment, details of an alibi defence must be disclosed no later than seven days after the committal proceedings (s. 11, Criminal Justice Act 1967).

(c) *Matters of law*. As is common throughout the criminal and civil processes, authorities to which a party intends to refer ought in principle to be disclosed to the opponent before trial.

Finally, it will be noted that unlike in the case of civil legal aid there is no requirement as such to report to the legal aid authorities, e.g., if one considers one's client is behaving unreasonably. It may be a prudent step to obtain prior authority for the incurring of major items of expenditure but even where a solicitor personally feels that his client's case is hopeless, if the latter persists in pleading not guilty there is no duty to report the matter and the solicitor may continue to represent him and do his best for him.

1.2.2.2 A client who admits his guilt

Where a client admits his guilt a solicitor may continue to act for him even on a not guilty plea to a limited extent. A solicitor may permit the client to plead not guilty and thereafter may do everything possible during the prosecution case, for example cross-examine their witnesses as vigorously as possible (provided this does not involve advancing any untruthful version of events) and in particular, if the prosecution case depends on a confession, he may make every appropriate attempt to have the confession ruled inadmissible. Thereafter he may make a submission of no case to answer.

If however the case is not dismissed at that stage then a solicitor may not permit his client to go into the witness box or call perjured evidence. Accordingly if a client does admit his guilt it is vital to point out to him that you may continue to act for him even if he pleads not guilty, but only if he agrees not to call evidence.

1.2.2.3   Knowledge of a client's previous convictions

What if a client has previous convictions and the solicitor is aware of this but the court is not? As indicated previously a solicitor would not be permitted to let his client assert in the witness box that he was a person of good character nor could the solicitor's conduct of the case take that path. More commonly the problem will arise after a guilty plea or conviction. When mitigating for such a client if the prosecution have not got proper details of his criminal record or think that he has no offences recorded against him, then whilst his solicitor may not positively stress his good character he can do everything possible otherwise by way of mitigation. The solicitor can therefore leave the court to conclude that his client is of good character from the absence of criminal record but must not positively state that this is so. If on the other hand the client has adopted a false name, address or date of birth in order to deceive the court by making it difficult to link his criminal record to him, the solicitor must advise his client to give his identity properly and if there is a refusal he must withdraw from the case.

1.2.2.4   Client who gives inconsistent instructions

Clients often change their instructions. They may significantly change their version of much that has occurred. Here the solicitor is essentially in no different a position from when acting for a party in a civil case who gives different versions of events. So long as he is not absolutely sure that the client is positively trying to invent some version, he can still continue to act although it may be appropriate to give the client advice with regard to his plea and the risk of conviction for perjury. It is of course perfectly proper to attempt to argue that some aspect of the facts provides a defence for the client. What the solicitor must never do however, is to suggest to the client what facts might constitute a defence and thus to encourage a change of story by the client which accords with those more favourable facts.

1.2.2.5   Interviewing prosecution witnesses

There is no property in a witness and it is perfectly proper to interview prosecution witnesses. In the course of interviewing them no attempt should be made to put words into their mouths nor should one misrepresent whom one is, for example, by giving the person the impression that one might be a prosecution solicitor. Apart from this however, no court is likely to conclude that a respectable solicitor is trying to pervert the course of justice. It is sometimes thought appropriate to warn the prosecution of one's desire to interview their witnesses. It is doubtful whether there is any rule positively requiring this. Certainly in the converse cases when the police are checking on defence alibis they do not trouble to give the defence solicitor a chance to be present.

1.2.2.6   Conflicts of interest

It is very important when acting in a criminal case to ensure that there is no conflict of interest between co-accused. This is particularly so because in most courts where legal aid is granted to the accused there is an attempt to assign the same solicitor to each of the accused in the interest of saving time and costs. Sometimes if there is only a slight possibility of conflict of interest in such a situation and the matter is proceeding to the Crown Court, matters may be satisfactorily resolved by briefing separate counsel for each of the accused.

In criminal cases however one should always be aware of the possibility of a conflict of interest suddenly arising. If, having taken on two clients, a conflict of interest does arise then generally it will be impossible to continue to act for either. This is because you will have received confidential information and will wish to use it in the conduct of client A's case against former client B. This might particularly be so where one of two clients changes his plea and pleads guilty, perhaps even subsequently testifying for the prosecution. In such a situation, if you would have wished to cross-examine former client B in a very vigorous manner, you would be unable to do so without breaching the duty of confidentiality and you would be hopelessly hamstrung in the conduct of client A's defence.

It should also be borne in mind that a conflict of interest may arise at the mitigation stage although there is nothing apparent at the stage when guilt is still being contested. Thus, for example, if faced with two clients who are aged say 18 and 28 and the latter has a bad criminal record, then when mitigating for the younger should they both be convicted, it might well be appropriate to suggest that he has been corrupted and led astray. This is clearly not possible if also acting for the elder.

Therefore, great care should always be taken to beware of a conflict of interest in a criminal case and to act appropriately where such arises. If assigned to act on legal aid for two or more co-accused you should always interview them separately. If it is then apparent after seeing the first accused that there is a possibility of conflict arising you can decline to act for the other accused then and there. If there is no such apparent conflict then you can interview the second accused. If it transpires from *his* version of events that there is a conflict, confidential information will now have been obtained from both and you cannot act for either.

Finally, you should not overlook the possibility that you may have acted for both of two co-accused on previous occasions. If there now seems to be any possibility of a conflict arising then everything will depend upon the nature of the confidential information which was obtained on those previous occasions. If the information could in any sense be used against B to A's benefit you cannot act for either.

1.3 Preliminary Considerations

In this section, we shall consider the matters which are likely to arise in the course of routine criminal proceedings. In the case of civil proceedings, there is generally no particular urgency about the issue of the writ. If the limitation period has not yet expired, then you would generally be well advised first to collect all the information relevant to liability, and possibly information relevant to quantum. In the case of civil proceedings, it may of course be possible to obtain a negotiated settlement at a very early stage, or even without the issue of proceedings at all. There is nothing that corresponds to those features in criminal practice. In criminal practice, the solicitor will usually only be consulted after proceedings have been instituted, and he has no control over when the client is likely to be brought before the court.

The one obvious exception to this is the case of a client who is suspected of an offence and may already have been interrogated at a police station but has not yet been charged. He might require advice about, say, the nature of police bail, about whether, if he returns to the police station as he has been requested to or bailed to do in a few days' time, he should consent to having his fingerprints taken or to taking part in an identity parade, and so on. More experienced criminal clients who are well aware of their right of silence may wish to discuss whether they should maintain silence, or whether the giving of some carefully prepared exculpatory statement, or even the giving of some limited assistance to the police in enquiries, might result in their not being charged at all. In this sense, therefore, you might act for a client to help him achieve the best outcome without there needing to be any court proceedings as such. (For further consideration of this see **1.3.2** below.)

In the mainstream of cases, however, the prosecution will already have been instituted and the solicitor's duty is to do the best for his client as defendant. We shall therefore consider steps to take in the conduct of a normal case, although some individual tactical considerations, e.g., whether to opt for summary trial or Crown Court trial where that choice arises, will be dealt with separately under the relevant aspects of procedure.

There are two essential preliminary matters which are likely to need consideration. The first is bail and the second is legal aid.

If, when the client comes into your office, having been charged, he has already been granted police bail, then you can generally anticipate that there will be no objection to his having continued bail from the court. This is the reality, although one can never entirely rely on it. The courts are given a broad mandate to enquire into the question of bail and the absence of a prosecution objection may not always be treated as conclusive, although cases where it is not are rare.

Exceptionally even where the police have released someone on bail, they may find, after having done so, good reason to object to bail at the first hearing. Such a case might well be where the alleged victim expresses terror at the continued freedom of the accused, or the police become suspicious that the accused may have committed offences other than the one which they were initially investigating. So bail must always be considered. However, where an accused has been released on bail, then the date of the preliminary hearing might well not be for some time.

It ought to be mentioned here that one common trait of persons charged with criminal offences is that they are not always as well organised, or systematic, as they might be, and despite the fact that they may well have been charged weeks ago they may only get around to making an appointment with a solicitor the day before the first hearing. There may thus be very little time to take preliminary steps before that hearing. This is a well-known facet of criminal litigation with which all practitioners learn to cope. It may be appropriate in cases where there seems any possible doubt to telephone the prosecution to get confirmation that no objection to bail will be raised.

The second matter that needs to be considered is legal aid. The initial interview can be given under the Green Form Scheme if the client qualifies, and a full legal aid application will need to be completed and sent to the magistrates' court, or perhaps taken round by hand if the case is to be heard in the immediate future. If the case is, for example, to be heard the next day, then it is for the solicitor to decide whether he is prepared to risk legal aid being refused, or not dealt with in time, and to continue with the case.

An option might be to send the client down to court to ask for an adjournment for the purpose of obtaining legal aid but many consider it unwise to do this. First, there is always the fear of the policeman involved in the case 'persuading' the unrepresented accused to see sense and plead guilty for his own good, and secondly, there is always the risk that the court might insist on dealing with the case, particularly if there has already been one adjournment, and might instruct the accused to seek the assistance of the duty solicitor, or some other solicitor who is within the precincts of the court, and therefore the client will have been lost.

Of course, many busy criminal solicitors who practice most of the time at the same court may well be in that court the next day in connection with other matters and therefore there will be no great risk of lost costs if one agrees to see the client there to pursue his legal aid application orally if need be. Normally, if one can get the legal aid application down to the court at least a day before, that will be long enough for it to be dealt with in most urban courts.

We now turn to the other important aspects of preparing the case.

1.3.1 THE FIRST INTERVIEW

If this takes place in a police station or in custody just before a first appearance, this will inevitably be rather hurried. All one may have time to do is to find out matters relevant to a bail application. But whatever the outcome of that first meeting, subsequently there will be an opportunity to interview the client in complete privacy and at greater length. If the bail application has been successful, or no objection to bail has ever arisen, this will be in one's own office; if the bail application has been unsuccessful, it will be in the remand centre or prison. There are a number of important matters which need to be discussed with the client. These are as follows.

1.3.1.1 An objection to bail

If it is clear that there is to be an objection to bail, then the first issue, and certainly the one uppermost in the client's mind, will be this question. One must have regard to the grounds for refusing bail and the facts to be used in assessing those grounds. (For further details see in particular **6.5.**) The client's first proof of evidence therefore, whilst dealing with the background to the alleged offence in as much detail as seems appropriate, should concentrate on matters relevant to bail. If it is anticipated that the main objection is on the basis that the client is likely to abscond then details of his current address, term of residence there, other ties in the area, present work record, family ties, financial position and the like will be relevant. If the objection is that he will commit further offences, then his previous record when on bail, the nature of his previous criminal record generally, together with other factors to do with his family and work situation will be relevant. If the objection is that he will interfere with witnesses, then one must concentrate on the precise nature of the allegation that will be made and see what matters can be brought up to deal with it, in particular in this case the suggestion of bail conditions. The client should in such a case be asked what he knows about the suggestion of potential interference and what conditions he would be willing to submit to in order to avoid being remanded in custody.

Relevant to any objection to do with bail are more general details of his personal life and history. These must be obtained together with telephone contact numbers for persons who might assist with bail, e.g., friends, relatives or his employer.

Having dealt with obtaining the preliminary information for a bail application, it is then appropriate to deal with the charges brought against the client and the question of how, if he were unfortunately to be convicted, the court might deal with him. This is equally relevant whether or not the client has been given bail by the police.

1.3.1.2   The precise charges

If the client has come in to see you in your office it is commonly the case that he will have forgotten or lost his charge sheet, in which case a duplicate will need to be obtained. In such a situation you should never rely on a client's recollection of what offence has been charged. 'Theft' will all too often prove to mean 'robbery' in such circumstances. The charge sheet ought also to reveal whether he has been charged with other people, which it is vital to know.

1.3.1.3   Details of the charge

Personal details should be taken from the client and then he should be invited to give his account of the incident resulting in the charge. This is as important in the case of a criminal client as it is with a client in a civil case, or a witness in either case. The more fresh the events are in the mind of the accused, the better the statement will be. This is particularly so where some fast moving or interlinked series of events is what needs to be described, for example, precisely how a fight started, or the precise course of events at work which led to the accused being charged with theft of the employer's property. It may be that something will be thrown up which can immediately be investigated to good effect.

Many clients in criminal cases give vague or apparently unconvincing accounts of incidents. This may be because of lack of intelligence or natural diffidence. Every attempt should be made to draw the client out about his case. In some instances, kindness and sympathy may be needed for this, in others it may perhaps be better to attempt to put the client through a cross-examination about the vaguer or apparently more improbable features of his version. Everything will depend upon the circumstances and the personality of the client.

1.3.1.4   Details of the plea

All the foregoing assumes that the client is intending to plead not guilty. If he is pleading guilty, then circumstances and details relevant to a plea in mitigation need to be considered. Indeed details of these matters must also be taken from a client who denies the charge, although the collection of evidence relevant to mitigation is often left until somewhat later in the case. It must be remembered however that the likely sentence to be imposed is an important factor in a bail application. In the case of a client pleading not guilty, which is what we are primarily concerned with, once the solicitor has tested the client's own story and looked for possible leads to further avenues of enquiry (e.g., other witnesses who could be contacted), this is perhaps as much as can be done at this stage. The client should be asked to give any account he can of his own criminal record, if he has one, but as we shall see below it is most unwise to rely on this.

There will inevitably need to be another full interview with the client to discuss matters in the light of what you subsequently manage to find out about the prosecution evidence, or about lines of investigation that you have yourself pursued. If the client requires advice about how to plead it may be possible to give this at this stage or it may need to be postponed until a later stage.

1.3.1.5 Writing to the prosecution

In contrast with the position in a civil case, in a criminal case one is entitled to a certain amount of assistance from one's opponent. The prosecution is supposed not to press for conviction at any price in the full adversarial manner, but rather the Crown Prosecutor, whether solicitor or counsel, is supposed to act as 'a minister of justice' presenting facts and law impartially and fairly to the court. In the heat of the action it may be sometimes difficult for the accused or his advocate to discern this in the manner in which the Crown Prosecutor seems to be conducting the case, and one may feel that on occasions a somewhat indecent enthusiasm for the fray for its own sake may colour the Crown Prosecutor's attitude. However, at this stage anyway, the prosecution are obliged to assist the defence solicitor and a letter should be written requesting the following:

(a) A copy of the client's criminal record, if any.

(b) A copy of any written records required to be kept under the Police and Criminal Evidence Act 1984, e.g., custody records.

(c) A copy of any statement made by the client under caution.

(d) The criminal record of any co-defendant.

(e) The criminal record of any prosecution witnesses.

(f) The names and addresses of any persons interviewed whom the prosecution do not propose to call at trial. It should be remembered that the prosecution are obliged to inform the defendant of any evidence that comes into their possession which is favourable to the defence.

(g) If the client has been interviewed on tape then one should ask for a copy of the tape. Many police forces prefer to supply a so-called 'balanced summary' but experience shows that these are often not an accurate reflection of the whole course of the interview and it is best to insist upon having the tape to listen to oneself.

Some of the above, especially items (e) and (f), may not be made available until much later, but there is no harm in making the formal request at this stage. If the case is proceeding to the Crown Court for trial on indictment there will inevitably be committal proceedings. Almost invariably, the prosecution, unless quite exceptionally they have themselves decided on a so-called 'full' committal where most of their witnesses are brought before the court, will wish the defendants to agree to a short form committal under s. 6(2), Magistrates' Courts Act 1980, in which case written statements of their evidence are served on the defendant in advance.

Furthermore, if the matter is proceeding as a summary trial and concerns an offence such as theft (i.e., an 'either way' offence — for definition see 5.3.3), then advance information as to the facts and matters on which the prosecution propose to rely must be given to the accused, in accordance with the Magistrates Court (Advance Information) Rules 1985. This must include a copy of the statements of the witnesses who are going to be called by the prosecution, or a summary of the evidence in those statements.

Moreover, even in the case of summary offences, then, depending upon the defending solicitor's relationship with the prosecution, the Crown Prosecutor may well be willing to let the solicitor look at copies of his witness statements in advance, no doubt in the hope that, when seeing the overwhelming nature of the case against the accused, the accused can be persuaded to plead guilty.

1.3.2   'NEGOTIATIONS'

When reasonably full information about an alleged offence and offender has been obtained, it may be appropriate to approach the prosecution to see whether they might be willing to reconsider the decision to prosecute. The Code for Crown Prosecutors to which we have already referred sets out some of the criteria on which a prosecution should be based. Thus the following factors may be relevant:

(a) *Triviality* of the offence such that, even if there is a successful conviction, the offender is bound to be dealt with leniently so that the cost of the proceedings is hardly worth the time and trouble.

(b) *Staleness*, e.g., if the offence occurred a considerable time ago then a prosecution may be oppressive.

(c) *Youth* or *old age and infirmity* of the offender.

(d) *Mental illness* and *stress*.

(e) In sexual offences the *ages* of the relevant participants and the question of consent, or corruption.

(f) The *complainant's attitude*, e.g., if the complainant is clearly reluctant.

In addition to these factors you may attempt to argue that there is insufficient evidence or that the public interest, for some other reason, does not require a prosecution. You can then concentrate on the above factors suggesting perhaps that the accused is a young adult who could be dealt with by caution rather than prosecution, that the client is elderly or infirm or that the strain of criminal proceedings may lead to a considerable worsening in the accused's mental health.

It may be that you will be able to supply the prosecution with information to support your argument, e.g., information that, say, a middle-aged defendant who appears to have acted significantly out of character was suffering a serious illness, or had experienced recent bereavement. If all or any of these things can be advanced it may be possible to persuade the prosecution to reconsider.

It may also be possible, although this is usually left until later in the procedure, to argue that a certain charge should be reduced to one of less seriousness (e.g., that what is presently charged as a robbery really only constituted theft even on the prosecution's version).

1.3.3   REINTERVIEWING THE CLIENT AND ADVISING ON PLEA

Thus in many cases you should have found out the substance of the prosecution evidence. It is then necessary to see the client again to get his comments on this evidence. At this time, it may be appropriate, in the light of all that is known about the prosecution case, to suggest to the client lines of questioning which will be put to him in cross-examination, so that he can consider how he might deal with them. This is not in any sense with a view to inviting him to think up glib answers well in advance, but genuinely to see whether he does have answers to the points that will be raised.

It may be that when the full weight of the prosecution evidence is known, the case will appear overwhelming against the client. In such a situation, the client should be questioned carefully to see whether he might not wish to plead guilty. An advocate has a difficult and delicate task here. A client ought to be given the advantage of having explained to him that a plea of guilty might, in a borderline case, make the difference between going to prison and not going to prison, especially if the nature of his defence involves a frontal attack on the truthfulness or integrity of prosecution witnesses, e.g., policemen. Such advice, however, to a client who is at the moment maintaining a not guilty plea must be tempered with the very strongest affirmation that he should not consider pleading guilty unless he actually is guilty. In other words, no attempt should be made to bully a person into pleading guilty but this must be combined with the realistic advice on sentence previously referred to.

It is at this stage, where the whole of the evidence is being reviewed, that the client should be taken through any previous convictions and be asked to explain something of the background to each of the offences, or those which are most recent. We will return to this in the section on sentencing and mitigation later, but the point is that it may well be that something can be said to make an apparently bad criminal record look at least a little better. For example, some of the offences may have occurred at a time when the accused had a drug addiction, since cured, and stole to finance the habit. This is obviously a matter which might, in the eyes of some courts, present some explanation for an apparently consistent course of criminal conduct.

1.3.4   OTHER STEPS

In the light of all the information obtained from the accused, and it is very much a matter of 'feel' whether one does this immediately after the first interview or somewhat later in the light of having seen some of the prosecution evidence, one will need to consider other steps. These may briefly be summarised as follows:

(a)   Consider interviewing other witnesses as soon as possible. If these are prosecution witnesses already, as previously indicated, it is normally considered courteous to inform the prosecution that you propose to do this, although there is in fact no property in a witness and it ought not to be considered an attempt to interfere with the course of justice to want to interview a witness.

(b)   Consider whether expert evidence (e.g., a psychiatrist's report on the accused) is needed. This is unlikely in a routine case.

(c)   If the location where an event happened is material, visit it so that you can gain a clear picture. It may even be desirable to take photographs or make a plan. For example, if a fight broke out in the confines of a crowded public house, then a plan of the layout of the public house might assist. If the matter is a driving offence, just as in the case of a civil action involving a road accident, it may be appropriate to make plans, or take photographs of the scene, to enable the court to get a full picture of the layout of the road junction etc. In this connection also, you should ask the accused to show you his driving licence to ensure that actual endorsements correspond to his criminal record.

1.3.5   CALLING WITNESSES

It is perhaps useful here to summarise the ways in which witnesses may be called before magistrates' courts and the Crown Court.

(a)   In the magistrates' court, a *witness summons* is obtained from the clerk to the justices. This is done by attending in person, or writing a letter requesting the issue of the summons. A summons can, in principle, only be issued if the clerk (or a magistrate) is satisfied that a witness at a summary trial or committal proceedings will not attend voluntarily. This requirement is contained in s. 97 of the Magistrates' Courts Act 1980.

Individual courts and clerks vary in the enthusiasm with which they require this condition to be fulfilled. Many will issue a witness summons simply on a request from a solicitor and his assurance that it seems in all the circumstances likely to be required. Others, more pedantically, require some positive assertion that the witness will not attend voluntarily. Indeed, they may require there to be a first attempt to have the witness attend voluntarily, and only if he does not will a summons be issued. This can be highly inconvenient and is arguably very foolish in view of the difficulties in efficiently arranging the listing of criminal cases. The time of many people may be wasted if the trial cannot go ahead because a clerk has insisted that there be some evidence that the witness will not attend voluntarily before a summons can be issued. It is a fact of life that even witnesses who have given an assurance of attending voluntarily often fail to do so because they wish to avoid the inconvenience, possible expense and loss of earnings of attending court proceedings. It is for this reason that it is prudent in every case in *civil proceedings* to subpoena witnesses.

(b)   In the Crown Court there will be a committal before a Crown Court trial at the end of which 'full' or 'conditional' *witness orders* will be made in respect of prosecution witnesses. For defence witnesses, a witness order may be obtained on request from the Crown Court under the Criminal Procedure (Attendance of Witnesses) Act 1965. This is achieved by lodging a simple form of request and there is no need in this case to assure the court that the witness will not attend voluntarily.

(c) Finally, consideration ought to be given in the case of the evidence of apparently uncontroversial witnesses to the serving of the evidence in the form of a statement prepared under s. 9 of the Criminal Justice Act 1967 (or s. 102 of the Magistrates' Courts Act 1980 for committal proceedings). The use of these sections will be considered in due course in the context of committals, and in the section on evidence (see **16.3** and **9.12.1**).

TWO

FINANCING CRIMINAL LITIGATION

2.1 Introduction

The need to ensure that the financial basis of the relationship between the litigation client and the solicitor is clearly established applies as much in criminal as in civil litigation. Thus, subject to obvious individual exceptions (e.g., a wealthy regular client on a driving charge), it is prudent, indeed essential, to obtain payment in advance for work done in criminal litigation. Whilst the criminal case will not run for as long as the average civil case, there are, for obvious reasons, even greater risks of non-payment by the clientele.

Private-paying clients are, however, considerably rarer than in civil litigation. We shall now therefore consider the question of legal aid. As we shall see, there are important differences from civil legal aid in the manner of application, criteria for eligibility and other ancillary matters.

We will then briefly examine the principles for the award of costs in criminal proceedings.

2.2 Legal Aid and Advice

2.2.1 THE GREEN FORM SCHEME

The Green Form Scheme can be used just as in legal aid in civil proceedings. Legal advice and assistance on any matter of English law can be given to a person who qualifies on a financial eligibility test. Financial eligibility is worked out with the aid of a 'key card' and if, after taking into account certain permissible deductions, the client is left with a disposable income of no more than £61 per week, Green Form assistance can be given. Naturally, criminal matters come within the scope of this scheme. Work up to a total value of two hours' fees can be done by a solicitor for a client and this would cover such things as taking the first statement, filling in application forms for legal aid proper and perhaps some preliminary collection of evidence.

2.2.2 ADVICE AT THE POLICE STATION

If a client is at the police station, and this applies whether he is in custody or attending voluntarily in connection with assisting the police with their enquiries into an offence, a person is entitled to free legal advice and assistance from either his own solicitor or the duty solicitor (see **2.2.4**) up to an initial limit of £90 worth of work. Unlike the Green Form Scheme, this scheme is not means tested in any way so even the wealthy are entitled to assistance under it. The claim for fees is made to the Legal Aid Area Office on a prescribed form.

2.2.3 ASSISTANCE BY WAY OF REPRESENTATION (ABWOR)

Neither the Green Form Scheme nor the police station scheme referred to above cover actually taking a step in proceedings (i.e., representing the client in court). For this, in general, full legal aid is required. However there is an exception, namely under reg. 7 of the Legal Advice and Assistance (Scope) Regulations 1989, which provides for assistance by way of representation (ABWOR) in the criminal courts in certain circumstances. This scheme is means tested in a similar way to the Green Form Scheme. Unlike the Green Form Scheme however, where if one has an income of more than £61 per week assistance cannot be given, there is a sliding scale of contributions above that figure. Between the figures of £61 and £147 net income assistance can be given but the client must pay a contribution of one-third of his net disposable income above £61. The scheme is available to cover representation for a defendant who does not have full legal aid but has not been refused legal aid where the magistrates' court:

(a) is satisfied that the hearing should proceed on the same day;
(b) is satisfied that the party would not otherwise be represented; and
(c) requests a solicitor who is within the precincts of the court to represent that party.

This might come about if a person, newly taken into custody or otherwise, happened to be before the court without legal representation and it appeared that a solicitor was available and the matter seemed relatively straightforward and brief (e.g., a plea in mitigation after a guilty plea). If a solicitor was present in the precincts of the court for the purpose of representing somebody else and was able to come to represent this client then the court can authorise such representation under the ABWOR scheme. In fact many courts deal with applications for legal aid proper very swiftly, and in such cases there would be no advantage in granting assistance by way of ABWOR as opposed to considering a full legal aid application, except the saving of such time as it takes to fill in a full legal aid application form. The use of the ABWOR scheme therefore varies considerably from court to court.

2.2.4 DUTY SOLICITOR SCHEMES

Duty solicitor schemes originated nearly 20 years ago in schemes run in some parts of the country on a voluntary basis, whereby solicitors experienced in criminal work would attempt on a rota system, either at a police station or in magistrates' court cells in the early morning before the day's sittings, to give advice and assistance and to represent persons in custody (or in some cases also persons not in custody who came to court and were in need of assistance and were unrepresented) on such matters as a preliminary bail application or a plea in mitigation.

The method of remuneration was sometimes by the Green Form or in some cases by the prompt grant of legal aid, and the persons attending as duty solicitors were, if the client wished, entitled to act for the client for further stages of the proceedings. These voluntary schemes have now been replaced by a formal duty solicitor scheme under the Legal Aid Board Duty Solicitor Arrangements 1989. The duty solicitor scheme has two principle aspects.

2.2.4.1 At the police station

Under this scheme persons who are at a police station, whether under arrest or voluntarily, are entitled to free legal advice and assistance up to an initial limit of £90 from a duty solicitor or, if they prefer, from their own solicitor. The main point of duty solicitor schemes however is that they operate throughout the night and therefore there ought in principle always to be a duty solicitor available whereas the client's own solicitor may well not be willing to come out, even if the client knows his home telephone number.

The remuneration for duty solicitors under this scheme is by a combination of fees for various elements of the duty, e.g., for being 'on duty' overnight, and a fixed fee per telephone call to persons in custody where the duty solicitor does not attend at the police station, together with various other fees calculated on a time basis for actual work at police stations. Duty solicitors in this scheme are volunteers in ordinary private practice with experience of criminal cases, who participate on a rota basis.

2.2.4.2   At court

The court duty solicitor will see persons before they go before the court for the first time and may represent them at that stage. Many courts now deal only with bail applications on the first occasion where the duty solicitor is acting, though others may deal with pleas in mitigation after a guilty plea. If the case goes past that first hearing then the defendant must apply for legal aid proper.

2.3   Legal Aid Proper

The Legal Aid Act 1988 allows application for legal aid at any stage in criminal proceedings. The most important and significant differences from civil legal aid are:

(a)   Application is made not to the Legal Aid Board but to the court before whom the accused is to appear, whether it is a magistrates' court or the Crown Court; and

(b)   There is no time for an exhaustive and thorough investigation of means as occurs in civil proceedings. Often the accused is in custody and the case ought for that reason to proceed very swiftly, but in any event the delays of some weeks which are common in deciding on financial eligibility in civil legal aid applications would clearly be out of the question in criminal cases. Accordingly, the courts both assess the applicant's means and decide whether or not the person should receive legal aid in principle.

2.3.1   CRITERIA FOR THE GRANT OF LEGAL AID

There are two criteria for the grant of legal aid in a criminal matter. By s. 21 of the Legal Aid Act 1988 legal aid must be granted when:

(a)   it appears that the applicant's *financial resources* are such that he requires assistance in meeting the costs of the proceedings; and

(b)   it is *desirable* to do so *in the interests of justice*.

2.3.1.1   Applicant's financial resources

A person applying for legal aid, as we shall see below in a moment, has to provide some evidence as to his means. This is done by filling in a legal aid application form giving details of income and capital. The court will then assess his means. This will be done very swiftly indeed, often on the same day on which the legal aid application is received by the court, or indeed, if application is made at the court in the course of proceedings, there and then.

The accused's financial eligibility is worked out on a sliding scale in a somewhat similar way to the computation in civil proceedings. An individual who is in work will be expected to produce recent wage slips to the court together with any appropriate evidence of capital. However, he is not subject to cross-examination or interview about these matters.

As in the case of civil legal aid, a person whose disposable income or capital are below a certain amount will receive legal aid without contribution; those above certain prescribed maxima will have legal aid refused on financial grounds; and between the two a legal aid contribution order will be made on a sliding scale which will require the person to make some contribution toward the cost of his legal representation. The contribution may either be required in one lump sum, if it is from capital, or in instalments over a period of six months if it is from income.

The court is required to assess the approximate likely cost of the case, which is naturally somewhat difficult in view of the fact that the case may take several different courses, e.g., the costs may be multiplied many times by the defence electing a full committal hearing (see **16.2**). The recent introduction of 'standard fees' for many cases will make this assessment somewhat easier.

Legal aid may be reassessed throughout the course of the case should the client's means change.

If a legally-aided person subject to a contribution order fails to pay any instalment of contribution, the court may revoke the grant of legal aid (s. 24(2)). An accused must be given the opportunity to make representations on the matter.

2.3.1.2　**'In the interests of justice'**

We turn now to the second criterion that of 'desirable in the interests of justice'. This naturally confers a discretion on the court, and regard must be had to s. 22 of the 1988 Act in deciding on whether the interests of justice make it desirable for an accused to have legal aid. This section lays down that legal aid should be granted in particular whenever one of the following factors applies:

(a)　the offence is such that if proved it is likely that the court would impose a sentence which would deprive the accused of his liberty, or lead to loss of his livelihood or serious damage to his reputation;

(b)　the charge may involve consideration of a substantial question of law;

(c)　the defendant has inadequate knowledge of English, or suffers from mental illness or physical disability;

(d)　the defence will involve the tracing and interviewing of witnesses or the expert cross-examination of a prosecution witness;

(e)　legal representation is desirable in the interests of someone other than the defendant.

It is now appropriate to consider these matters.

(a)　*The offence is such as might lead to the defendant losing his liberty, livelihood, or suffering serious damage to his reputation.*　A client's liberty will obviously be at risk if the charge is serious in itself; if there are serious aggravating circumstances, e.g., breach of trust of some kind; if the accused already has a bad criminal record, especially if the accused is already under a suspended sentence; and possibly if the accused will be in breach of a probation order if convicted.

Loss of livelihood might be particularly relevant in the case of a driving offence which might lead to the loss of a driving licence in the case of someone who needs it for his job. Thus, an offence which is disqualifiable in itself, or disqualifiable under the 'totting-up' procedure, would be an example of an offence which might lead to loss of livelihood, and this might be so even where the actual offence charged is not a particularly serious one, e.g., speeding, if the points allotted for the offence might lead to the defendant being disqualified and the loss of his job. This would also be applicable in the case of other offences which are not sufficiently serious to merit a custodial sentence. For example, in the case of someone whose job requires them to handle money and of whom utter financial probity is required, e.g., a bank clerk or a cashier, any conviction for an offence of dishonesty may be sufficiently serious to lead to dismissal.

Finally, there is a separate ground where an offence would cause serious damage to reputation but is not in itself serious enough to be likely to lead to a custodial sentence; an example would be where the person accused had a certain standing in the community such that a conviction would cause grave embarrassment, e.g., a vicar charged with shoplifting some trivial item.

The suggestion of risk of loss of reputation can sometimes be prayed in aid even for a client who has a criminal record if the kind of offence with which he is now charged is significantly different, e.g., where previous convictions were for, say, trivial public order offences but the present charge involves some element of dishonesty.

With the introduction of the Criminal Justice Act 1991, which provides a strong presumption in favour of offenders being sentenced only to 'community orders' which do not in themselves involve loss of liberty, a number of magistrates' courts declined to grant legal aid even in respect of relatively serious offences. That basis for a decision to refuse legal aid was considered improper by the Divisional Court in a recent case which has not yet been fully reported. The Court held that although the likelihood of a community order was not specified in the Legal Aid Act 1988 as one of the grounds for grant of legal aid, s. 22 of the Act is not exhaustive and the likelihood of a community order was a further ground upon which legal aid could be granted.

(b) *The charge raises a substantial question of law.* If the facts of the offence are such as to raise a difficult matter of law, e.g., there is a conflict of authority on some relevant matter, then this ground may apply. The defendant clearly will need the assistance of a solicitor in saying whether or not this is the case.

(c) *Inadequate knowledge of English or suffers from mental illness or physical disability.* This ground needs little explanation. If legal aid would otherwise normally be refused on the basis that the particular case was sufficiently minor or straightforward for the person to be able to represent himself, then this might be appropriate.

(d) *The defence involves the tracing and interviewing of witnesses or expert cross-examination of a prosecution witness.* In other words, the case needs a lawyer's special skills and a layman could not do these things for himself.

(e) *Legal representation is desirable in the interests of someone other than the defendant.* An example commonly given is the case of a sexual offence against a young child where it is undesirable that the defendant should personally conduct the cross-examination of the child which might distress the latter. This example would, of course, be covered also by the first of the criteria.

It must be noted that these criteria are not in themselves exhaustive. Moreover, there is specific provision that, where a doubt exists about the granting of legal aid, the doubt should be resolved in favour of the applicant.

In addition to the more general criteria for the grant of legal aid in s. 22 of the 1988 Act, there are four separate situations where a legal aid order *must* be made subject to means. These are:

(a) where an accused is committed for trial on a charge of murder;
(b) where an unrepresented accused who wishes to be represented appears before magistrates following an earlier remand in custody by them, was unrepresented on the earlier occasion and is at risk of a further remand in custody to the Crown Court;
(c) where an offender is remanded in custody by a magistrates' court or the Crown Court with a view to reports being prepared on him prior to passing sentence;
(d) to a successful appellant in the Court of Appeal whose case has been taken to the House of Lords by the prosecution.

2.3.2   METHOD OF APPLICATION

A legal aid application is made in writing to the magistrates' court on Form 1, together with a prescribed form of information about means and resources (Form 5). In principle, legal aid cannot be granted until Form 5 has been lodged duly completed. The application should be taken or sent to the magistrates' court as soon as possible. Generally it will be dealt with very swiftly, perhaps even the same day, and the result telephoned through to the solicitor's office. The solicitor will then be sent a legal aid order together with a form of 'Report on Case' on which the eventual application for fees must be made. The application forms when received are dealt with by a magistrates' clerk, or referred to the magistrates.

It will be observed that the 'interests of justice' criteria do not require as such that the accused is likely to *win* the case, which is (roughly speaking) the criterion for the grant of civil legal aid. Indeed, one may obtain legal aid even though the accused always intends to plead guilty.

If the magistrates' court refuses to grant legal aid, then a further application can be made and this will be referred to a different magistrate or bench of magistrates, and therefore there will in effect be fresh minds considering the application. In principle, this can be done any number of times. Moreover, even if previously refused, a further oral application can be made to the magistrates at the start of the hearing to which the application relates. It may be possible then to amplify the grounds upon which the application is made.

In fact refusal of legal aid is often because the solicitor has not given sufficient information as to why legal aid is required in the interests of justice. For example, in the case of a person with a bad criminal record who might be under a suspended sentence at present, the solicitor might merely have put 'accused may receive custodial sentence' on the application form without giving details. If the application is refused, it is likely to be because the magistrates are unable to see that there is a real possibility of a custodial sentence. It goes without saying that, since in the application form it may often be appropriate to disclose a client's past criminal record, the same magistrates who consider the written legal aid application form, or hear an oral application, will not then go on to deal with the trial of the accused if he is pleading not guilty.

Magistrates' courts making a legal aid order may make one just for the magistrates' court proceedings, or in the case of an indictable offence may make a so-called 'through' order which will cover the accused for the proceedings when they reach the Crown Court. In fact, it makes very little difference which is granted because, at the end of committal proceedings, if one has not obtained a 'through' order, one simply applies to the court to extend the legal aid to cover the Crown Court proceedings. Moreover, if, for any reason that was not done, application may be made to the Crown Court itself in writing on a prescribed form.

2.3.3 WHAT IF LEGAL AID IS REFUSED?

First, as has previously been stated, a person who is refused legal aid can always make another application to the court, either in writing or at the hearing itself. Second, under regs 15 to 17 of the Legal Aid in Criminal and Care Proceedings (General) Regulations 1989 (SI 1989 No. 344), a person who has been refused legal aid in the case of an indictable offence, including an offence triable either way (that is triable either in the magistrates' court or the Crown Court), may apply to the Legal Aid Area Committee. This Committee is a body composed of practising solicitors and barristers who sit part-time on a rota basis. Application on a prescribed form may be made as follows:

    (a)   in the case of offences which are purely indictable or triable either way;
    (b)   where the refusal has not been on the grounds of means alone;
    (c)   where application is made within 14 days of receiving notification of refusal;
    (d)   where the original application for legal aid was made at least 21 days before the proposed hearing date of the case, whether committal or summary trial, assuming that such a date had been fixed at the relevant time (which is unlikely). The relevant information must be sent on Form CRIM 9. The Area Committee will then review the case and may grant legal aid.

2.3.4 LEGAL AID BOARD GUIDELINES FOR THE GRANT OF LEGAL AID

The Legal Aid Board has issued guidelines in an effort to regularise the practice of magistrates' courts, many of which have remarkably different rates of grant for legal aid in respect of similar offences. The guidelines are intended merely to be starting points after which each case must be considered on its particular merits by reference to the proper criteria.

The guidelines indicate that offences which are triable only on indictment always merit legal aid; and they give a list of the more common either way and summary offences where legal aid may be appropriate. In addition they give a number of offences for which legal aid should normally be refused unless there are exceptional circumstances. Examples of the latter include drunk and disorderly conduct; prostitution; television licence offences; urinating in the street; and most road traffic cases, including driving with excess alcohol, unless such cases fall within the statutory criteria (e.g., where loss of livelihood might result from conviction and disqualification).

2.3.5   WHAT DOES LEGAL AID COVER?

Legal aid covers preparation for and the conduct of proceedings in the court that grants it, whether magistrates' court or Crown Court. As explained in **2.3.2,** in the magistrates' court a 'through' order may be made which will also cover proceedings in the Crown Court. Once legal aid is granted, then usually the conduct of the case is not reviewed in the same way as might be the case for civil legal aid. A solicitor who bona fide chooses a particular course of action which may be considerably more expensive than its alternative will not be subject to criticism or refusal of fees. For example, one crucial stage at which a defence solicitor has a choice which may involve considerable expense is the case of the decision whether or not to insist upon a full committal where the charge is eventually going to be tried in the Crown Court. A solicitor who chooses to have a full committal will not be subject to review, criticism or disallowance of fees. Although 'standard fees' are currently in force (see below) these will not be expected to cover the conduct of a full committal.

Legal aid orders in the magistrates' court do not usually cover representation by counsel, unless specific approval has been given by the clerk to the justices. Legal aid may be specifically granted for representation in the magistrates' court by both solicitor and counsel only where the offence is indictable and the court considers it to be unusually grave and difficult. If such an application is refused, the solicitor concerned may apply again to the court or to the Legal Aid Area Committee. It should be understood that this does not mean that in those cases where barristers are seen in the magistrates' court acting for legally-aided defendants that each is concerned with an indictable offence which is unusually grave or difficult. The individual advocacy resources of any given firm may mean that the firm is unable to cover all the criminal cases which are coming up on any given day. In such a case it is always open to the firm to instruct counsel on any particular case, but the allocation of fees payable will be affected in that the maximum fee to be paid would be that which would be appropriate if a solicitor had conducted the case. Consequently the fees to the barrister and the solicitor will be apportioned in accordance with what is reasonable.

Legal aid in the Crown Court usually consists of representation by solicitor and counsel. Exceptionally, if the person is before the court and unrepresented, legal aid may be ordered to be by counsel alone, e.g., for a plea in mitigation. Counsel will take instructions direct from the client in such a case.

There is one other vital difference between legal aid in civil and in criminal proceedings. Legal aid certificates are never retrospective in civil cases. Any work done for the person before legal aid is actually granted cannot be paid under the legal aid certificate. In *criminal cases* however, practice has recognised that it is often necessary for a solicitor, not only in his client's interest, but also in the interests of the smooth running of the court itself, to take instructions and take some action before the legal aid application can be considered.

For example, suppose that an accused person came into one's office the day before a charge was to be heard. One would use the Green Form to complete a legal aid application and for a preliminary interview with the client, but suppose that some further work was done in the way of contacting witnesses and trying to get them to court for the next day. All this would be done in expectation of legal aid eventually being granted. In such a case, if legal aid is in fact granted, then work done in urgent circumstances can be paid for even though the work was done before the grant of legal aid (reg. 44(7), Legal Aid in Criminal and Care Proceedings (General) Regulations 1989).

Legal aid orders also cover preliminary advice on the giving of notice of appeal from the magistrates' court to the Crown Court, but further steps in connection with the appeal will not be covered and you will be required to apply to the Crown Court itself for legal aid for the conduct of the appeal. Legal aid orders granted by a magistrates' court do however cover the conduct of one application for bail to a Crown Court judge in chambers where the magistrates have refused bail.

2.3.6 PAYMENT OF FEES UNDER LEGAL AID

The question of payment of legal aid fees is at present in a state of some uncertainty. In Crown Court cases a bill on the prescribed form must be lodged with the taxing officer of the Crown Court and the costs will in that case be paid direct from the Crown Court itself. There are standard fees for most kinds of work done in Crown Court cases, which do not directly relate to time expended on the matters. There is a discretion to allow fees in excess of the standard fee where appropriate.

Until June 1993 payment in criminal cases in the magistrates' court, which is made by the Legal Aid Board, was by submitting a claim to the Legal Aid Board on the prescribed form of 'report on case', indicating the amount of time spent on preparatory work, travelling, waiting and advocacy. Payment was then allowed at certain hourly rates. Under proposals currently in force the Lord Chancellor has replaced that with a system of standard fees somewhat similar to those which apply in the Crown Court. The standard fees are meant to be an incentive to practitioners to conduct criminal litigation in a well-organised and efficient way and so, it is said by the Lord Chancellor, reasonable profits can be made for firms which are properly organised. The lawfulness of these provisions has been unsuccessfully challenged in the Divisional Court, it being contended that the basic requirement under the Legal Aid Act 1988 to offer fair and reasonable remuneration is breached by a system which must inevitably involve a 'swings and roundabouts' approach whereby solicitors will inevitably run some cases which are more difficult or time-consuming at a loss to be made up by those that can be processed more efficiently.

Many practitioners consider that the rates provided do not allow fair remuneration even on a 'swings and roundabouts' basis and indeed that all criminal work can now only be done at a loss, or at least in such a way that serious risks are taken with clients' interests by cutting corners. In particular it is suggested that a good deal of the preparatory and other crucial work on cases may need to be carried out by low paid and unqualified staff in order for a solicitor's firm to make reasonable profits on such work.

The standard fees scheme set by the Lord Chancellor's Department provides for three major types of case: guilty pleas, not guilty pleas, and 'paper' committals. All other types of case, including 'full' committals and cases involving a barrister being assigned, are outside the scheme. If a trial is listed as a not guilty plea but in fact the client decides to plead guilty at the start, then the solicitor is paid as if it were a not guilty case because the level of preparation will have had to be much the same.

In each category there are two levels of standard fee: a lower fee covering an estimated 70 per cent of all cases and a higher fee covering the next 20 per cent of cases, with the most expensive 10 per cent of cases outside the scheme. Those cases remain subject to the full legal aid assessment on an hourly basis as formerly. The fee structures are different for London cases than for those outside London.

2.3.7 WHAT HAPPENS WHEN A LEGALLY AIDED PERSON IS ACQUITTED?

In such a case, whether in magistrates' courts or the Crown Court, it is usually inappropriate for there to be any order for costs between the parties or from central funds. The normal order is that, if the legally aided person has not had to pay any contribution, then no order for costs will be made; if he has had to pay a contribution, then the order will be that the contribution be returned to him and any unpaid parts of his contribution be remitted. This is the usual practice, although it is not invariably the case (e.g., if it appears to the court of trial that the accused has been acquitted on some unmeritorious technicality).

2.3.8 LEGAL AID FOR APPEALS BY WAY OF CASE STATED

This is considered to be within the civil jurisdiction and consequently application is for civil legal aid to the Legal Aid Board.

2.4   Orders for Costs

2.4.1   ON CONVICTION

If an accused is convicted the court has a discretion to order that he pay all or some part of the prosecution's costs in addition to any penalty it imposes (s. 18(1), Prosecution of Offences Act 1985). This applies both in the magistrates' court and in the Crown Court and the amount to be paid must be specified in the order.

2.4.2   ON ACQUITTAL

If an accused who is not legally aided is acquitted then the matter is governed by ss. 16–21 of the Prosecution of Offences Act 1985 and by a Practice Direction entitled *Practice Direction (Crime: Costs)* [1991] WLR 498. This indicates that the normal consequences of an acquittal on indictment should be the making of an order for defendant's costs, that is costs out of *central funds*, which are funds established for this purpose by the government. Such an order should only be refused if

(a)   the defendant was at fault in bringing suspicion on himself and misleading the prosecution into thinking the case against him was stronger than it actually was; or
(b)   he was acquitted on a technicality but there was ample evidence to support a conviction.

Similar principles should be applied in the magistrates' court. Where an accused is entitled to costs then he is also entitled to an allowance for travel and subsistence just as if he were a witness (reg. 23, Costs in Criminal Cases (General Regulations) 1986).

2.4.3   UNNECESSARY OR IMPROPER ACTS OR OMISSIONS

The court may make an order that costs incurred by one party as a result of 'any unnecessary or improper act or omission' by another party shall be paid by that other party (s. 19(1), Prosecution of Offences Act 1985). This would only be appropriate as a final order in the case of a prosecution which has been unreasonably brought. It may however be appropriate as a means of obtaining the costs of a given part of the hearing, e.g., where an adjournment has been occasioned because the prosecution were not ready then the costs of that day's adjournment may be ordered to be paid to the accused, and this applies even if he is ultimately convicted. However, magistrates' courts are particularly reluctant to make orders for costs against the prosecution believing that this implies criticism of the conduct of the CPS or the police in bringing the prosecution.

2.4.4   IMPROPER CONDUCT

The Courts and Legal Services Act 1990 inserted a new s. 19A into the Prosecution of Offenders Act 1985. This gives the court power to order a solicitor or barrister to meet the whole or part of costs wasted 'as a result of any improper, unreasonable or negligent act or omission' by the representative or his staff. It is well established in the case law from the same words in civil cases that oppressive or improper conduct is not required and all that is needed is simple negligence. Thus if a trial is prolonged by the arguing of hopeless points of law, by the calling of unnecessary witnesses or by proceedings being brought in an improper form, a wasted costs order may be made against either prosecution or defence legal representatives.

It is obvious that this sanction is more likely to be applied in respect of improper conduct by the defence. Since improper conduct by the prosecution is more susceptible to control during the course of the trial (e.g., a judge may be reluctant to interfere with the defence's right to call as many superfluous witnesses as it wishes because of the risk of appeal, but the same consideration does not apply to the prosecution). In any event if the prosecutor is sufficiently guilty as to be culpable within the section, such an order may be made, and this is especially the case if the accused is not legally aided.

THREE

MANAGING A CRIMINAL LITIGATION PRACTICE

3.1 Introduction

In this chapter we shall be considering some important features of managing a criminal litigation case load including office administration and organisation, file management and some practical considerations about the building up and organisation of a criminal law practice.

3.2 Keeping Time Records

It is essential for the efficient management of all legal work that a proper time recording system exists so that fee earners can identify what work they have done and for which clients. The extreme importance of this in civil litigation is stressed in the corresponding **LPC Guide: Civil Litigation** at **3.3**.

In civil litigation one will need to know how much time has been expended on a client's business in order to be able to charge that client a fair and reasonable sum. The eventual charge reflects not merely the time expended, although that is an essential preliminary ingredient in the computation, but also factors such as the importance of the matter to the client, the urgency of the matter, the amount of work involved, the number of documents written or perused, and so on. In civil litigation it is necessary to have accurate information not merely for the purpose of charging the client but, in the event of success in the litigation, in order to be able to justify the fees to the court at the taxation of costs and obtain as much as possible from the losing opponent. In civil litigation moreover it makes no difference whether the client is or is not legally aided when considering the importance of keeping time records.

In criminal litigation a very much higher proportion of work will inevitably be for legally aided clients, save in all but the most specialist practices. With the growing importance of standard fees it may at first sight appear that it is unnecessary to keep proper time records since more or less the same fee will be obtained however fast or slowly a case is processed. This would however be a bad misjudgement for a number of reasons. In particular:

(a) Only by having efficient office systems can a full criminal litigation case load be properly managed, and time recording is an essential part of this, quite apart from its use to justify the fees charged.

(b) There will still be many cases, in the average busy criminal practitioners' case load, where standard fees are not appropriate and the habit of proper time recording must therefore become ingrained.

(c) Some cases in a criminal context may go to the Divisional Court of the Queen's Bench Division which, in matters of taxation of costs, applies civil procedures so that bills in a civil format under RSC ord. 62 will be required. The practice of the Supreme Court Taxing Masters is to require full itemised bills together with time-based attendance records.

Time recording is therefore essential, and proper information must be retained on dedicated forms rather than odd scraps of paper. In particular, accurate records are essential to indicate:

(i) telephone calls and letters, ingoing and outgoing;
(ii) attendances with the client, witnesses and others;
(iii) conferences with counsel and time spent in drafting the brief to counsel;
(iv) other preparation time on the case;
(v) travelling time to and from court or to interview witnesses;
(vi) waiting time at court;
(vii) actual advocacy on one's feet in court both at trial and at every preliminary stage.

Only by keeping scrupulously accurate records can each case be charged for as appropriate.

3.3 Other Aspects of Office Management

The extreme importance of keeping accurate records and updating diaries in civil litigation cannot be overstressed. Missing the Limitation Act date is a fatal form of negligence; but there are others, in particular missing time limits for one or other of the vital procedural stages, or simply letting a case 'go to sleep' for so long that one's opponent becomes able to apply to strike out the case for want of prosecution. Quite apart from such obvious consequences of bad administration, there are other effects, for example if you are acting for a plaintiff and your opponent has the feeling that you are slipshod, incompetent, do not know what to do next, or are simply not eager to press on as fast as possible to trial, that opponent is put in an immeasurably better position, and frame of mind, for negotiations. The importance of brisk compliance with all relevant time limits for practical and tactical purposes is stressed in the **LPC Guide: Civil Litigation, 4.5.3.**

In criminal litigation, since the readers to whom this guide is addressed are likely to be acting for the defendant, it is possible to take a passive line. It is initially up to the police and prosecution to decide whether to charge at all and in what format to proceed and the first appointment at court will be fixed by a procedure over which the defendant has no control. As to subsequent hearings, when dates for major events such as a full committal or summary trial are being canvassed at a first hearing, your own diary commitments can be taken into account by the justices' clerk. Thereafter it is vital to keep a proper diary both in relation to court appointments and in relation to key dates for specific preparatory steps, in particular:

(a) Service of alibi notice.
(b) Following up the client's proof of evidence and obtaining witness statements.
(c) Ensuring replies to letters written to the prosecution seeking the information described at **1.3.1.5** (i.e. witness statements, criminal record, custody record, copy of tape-recorded interview, etc.);
(d) Custody time limits. By s. 22 of the Prosecution of Offences Act 1985 there are regulations which lay down custody time limits for trials on indictment. In particular the following are the maximum periods for which an accused can be held in custody:

(i) 70 days between first appearance in the magistrates' court and committal;
(ii) 70 days between first appearance and summary trial for an offence triable either way;
(iii) 112 days between committal for trial and taking plea on his trial in the Crown Court.

If these times are exceeded, the accused has an absolute right to bail no matter how serious the offence with which he is charged. The prosecution may however apply for an extension of the time limit. See also **16.2.10.3**.

(e) After the final action in any case the appropriate date for appeal and delivery of bill.

3.4   File Management

Files are likely to run for a good deal less time and be less bulky than in civil cases. They may well therefore take less management. This is of course subject to major exceptions. In substantial cases, in particular in cases of commercial fraud, there may be several trolleys full of relevant documents; very bulky documentation will be sent to you by the prosecution quite apart from the documents which your own case has generated. The same aspects of case and file management then become necessary as in civil cases.

Even in factually more simple crimes such as serious cases of violence, the number of depositions collected by the police, irrelevant or marginally relevant though most of them are likely to be, may involve cupboards full of documents. There must be adequate accommodation in order to deal with such cases.

With regard to other documents which will constitute your own file, it is vital to keep proper receipts for disbursements and other material relevant to your own bill separate from such things as correspondence, witness statements and the like.

3.5   Office Personnel

The relatively small number of firms which handle large commercial fraud and 'white collar' criminal cases are so organised as to be able to devote considerable personnel resources to such cases. Relatively large teams are put together, often involving one or more partners, a number of assistant solicitors and other fee earners, and sometimes, if appropriate, specialists from outside the criminal law, e.g., company lawyers, accountants and the like. If these cases are for private-paying clients then substantial sums should be taken on account and interim bills delivered, the sums held on account being topped up so that one is always ahead just as in the case of civil clients. If such cases are run on legal aid there are provisions for obtaining interim payments as the case goes along, both for substantial disbursements (such as for accountants' reports) and for profit costs. Such cases would not of course be remunerated on a 'standard fees' basis.

Many of the bigger firms of solicitors employ their own enquiry agents, often ex-policemen, for purposes including finding witnesses and taking witness statements. Where more delicate enquiries are concerned it is probably better for a solicitor to employ an outside enquiry agent so as to keep his firm at one remove from the sometimes unorthodox tactics adopted by such persons to obtain useful information.

No matter how a team might be constituted, whether for a big case or a more modest one, it is vital that someone be designated to supervise the whole process and that the client should know with whom he has to deal.

3.6   Relations with the Client

A client on a criminal charge is entitled to every bit as much consideration and courtesy as any other client (and indeed arguably more so, given that he is likely to be under greater strain than most other clients). In particular you should remember that:

(a)   It is unprofessional conduct not to discuss legal aid with a client even if it seems obvious on the face of it that he is unlikely to qualify. If he is a private-paying client then where possible a fixed fee or a best estimate must be given for the work together with a quotation of the hourly rate. In such cases the estimate must be regularly reviewed and the client must be made aware of other factors that might increase costs which are outside the solicitor's control (e.g., that the prosecution might insist on a full committal). An appropriate 'client care' letter must be written to the client explaining the charging basis and confirming the hourly rates. Payments on account will be obtained and interim bills delivered as discussed above.

(b)   Practice Rule 15 applies to criminal clients as much as to any others and clients must be informed whom to approach in the event of any problem and what the firm's complaints handling procedure is. This involves letting the client know, preferably in writing, the name and status of the person responsible for the day-to-day conduct of the case and the person responsible for its overall supervision (if different).

(c)   The client should be kept fully informed in writing of each material development and of each stage of the case and reminded about key dates. Merely because a client has a criminal record one should not assume total familiarity with the criminal justice process. Despite the client's apparent knowledge of the various options available at every stage, in many cases you should bear in mind the possibility that much of what is said, and the 'underworld slang' in which it is expressed, is often mere bravado. The story is probably apocryphal of the client who on being charged said 'I am saying nothing until you get me my copy of Archbold!'. (Now such a client would obviously instead demand his copy of *Blackstone's Criminal Practice* ('A snip at £95 — a goldmine of information for the busy criminal' — per 'Nosher' Thribb, Cell 231, E Wing, Durham Prison.).)

3.7   File Keeping

Within the file a full record should be kept of all relevant material. It is dangerous to keep material facts in one's head because of the possibility of urgent situations arising whilst one is away or unavailable. The files should be interchangeable within the office as far as possible; this is of course the virtue of having more than one person employed on a given file, although clearly run-of-the-mill matters will not merit such duplication of effort.

In particular, in practices which cover a number of courts, it may well be that the requirements of sensible management mean files, at least for preliminary stages such as paper committals, mode of trial hearings and the like, have to be exchanged between members of staff so that, for example, the advocate who is attending Barchester Magistrates' Court that day will deal with all matters there whilst his colleague at Middlemarch Magistrates' Court will deal with all matters there. If this is not done and each one deals with every aspect of his own file no matter where the cases are, there will be a remarkable amount of effort in duplicated travelling time hurtling between courts.

Moreover, the indulgence of the magistrates or their clerk in holding back cases for the convenience of late arrivals can never be guaranteed. Sensible practice management therefore usually means that all work in a given court is given to the same advocate. For that reason there should be a pro forma usually pinned to the inside of the file giving details of important aspects of the case; in particular the client's name, address, telephone number and contact address in the daytime if possible, any police or CPS reference number with telephone number, a box to be completed with details of the next hearing date, and the nature of that hearing. These are key things which need to be picked up at a moment's notice.

Other important but more basic information, in particular to do with costs, disbursements and the like, should also be kept somewhere in the file.

In firms with a substantial criminal litigation department, there must be a supervising partner of the whole advocacy resources of the firm so as to ensure that fee earners are efficiently used between several courts. It will be up to such a person to consider the requirements for advocacy in the week ahead in deciding whether it will be necessary to use counsel to supplement the in-firm advocates where the latter are stretched over too many cases or too many courts.

3.8   Managing the Practice

It is important that the firm should be flexible enough to cope with slumps and peaks in workload since this may ebb and flow in criminal litigation. Having said that, it is notoriously difficult to combine a criminal litigation practice with any other field of work. This does not of course mean that a firm which deals with criminal litigation cannot deal with any other areas of work, simply that individuals or departments dealing with criminal litigation will find it hard to fit in much else; the calls on one's time are so unpredictable given the fact there is no fixed listing system in magistrates' courts. At the time of writing, attempts are being made to introduce some form of listing so that, at least for routine applications, advocates need not attend before a certain time each day.

Unfortunately the nature of clients in the criminal litigation process makes it difficult for criminal courts to run even as efficiently as civil courts, fallible though procedures in the latter may be. Some large urban courts may have 20 criminal courts in action at the same time and it is possible for them to be flexible so as to take cases from one court to another to be dealt with expeditiously. However, in much smaller courts in rural locations there may only be two courts sitting simultaneously in the same building. Although no courts are so capricious as to take full contested summary trials before shorter matters such as guilty pleas, bail, mode of trial hearings and the like, it is not unknown to arrive at 9.30 a.m. and not have one's case dealt with, short though the point may be, before mid-afternoon.

Sadly, in some locations the clerks, who, sometimes in conjunction with the CPS, choose the order of cases, may well play 'favourites', with local solicitors who often appear before them having priority in getting their cases dealt with. Thus if one is appearing in a strange location one may be left until towards the end of the list. For this reason one can never be entirely sure when one will be back in the office even if one only has one or two simple matters to deal with in court. It is thus unsafe for criminal advocates to book in any appointments much before mid-afternoon.

It may therefore be that preliminary action on new cases, such as completing legal aid applications and taking statements, is left to other fee earners within the department, and that those solicitors who wish to do so virtually specialise in advocacy. With magistrates' court advocacy it may even be difficult to combine it with other aspects of criminal practice, such as the time-consuming preparation of major trials for the Crown Court, and some specialist criminal practices have quite separate sections dealing with Crown Court cases.

3.9   Use of Counsel

There is nothing in the magistrates' court which should be beyond the scope of a competent solicitor advocate, even the conduct of a full committal in the case of very serious offences, although in such a case counsel is sometimes briefed as a tactical step. Thus one should rapidly become perfectly competent to conduct bail applications before magistrates, a Crown Court judge or indeed a High Court judge in chambers; all aspects of other preliminary hearings such as adjournment requests; mode of trial hearings and short form committals; full committals; and summary trial. In addition there are at present limited rights of audience in the Crown Court on appeals from magistrates' courts where one has acted below. A good solicitor will want to take every opportunity early on to polish and improve his advocacy technique in all or any of these forums. In Crown Court trials on indictment however, at present solicitors have no rights of audience and therefore counsel will need to be involved. In such cases it may be that a conference with counsel of your choice is desirable quite soon after you obtain instructions, so as to plan your tactics and consider, for example, matters of oral evidence, documentary evidence received from the prosecution, the possibility and usefulness of a full committal, and the like. In cases which involve expert evidence, rare though these are by comparison with civil cases, counsel may be able to advise on the appropriate expert to use in terms, for example, of psychiatrists, other doctors, document analysts, forensic accountants, etc.

It is important to establish that one is in funds to instruct counsel at the outset, or to ensure that legal aid is available.

In principle one will wish to select competent and experienced counsel of appropriate seniority for the case in hand. The much vaunted 'cab rank' principle of the Bar provides that a barrister is obliged to accept any brief in a court in which he usually practices for a form of work which he usually does, provided that he is available to do the case and the fee is reasonable. The Bar's Code of Conduct insists that, by definition, a legal aid fee is always reasonable and therefore counsel may not refuse a legal aid case.

One does not have to be an extreme cynic however to appreciate that much of the expertise of a barristers' clerk lies in ensuring that barristers who can be more profitably employed elsewhere are often 'unavailable' for run-of-the-mill legal aid Crown Court cases. There is, nonetheless, a large number of highly competent specialist barristers in all major trial centres whose practices are mainly built around criminal work, in the main out of personal preference notwithstanding that it is not the most remunerative of fields, and who are satisfied to be remunerated at legal aid rates for a great deal of the time. Such barristers generally alternate defence with prosecution work and the CPS generally pay standard fees similar to the going rate for legal aid cases.

3.9.1 INSTRUCTING COUNSEL

When preparing instructions to counsel, which are likely to be either to advise on plea or evidence or on some practical or tactical matter, it is important to give the matter your full professional attention and deal with it in as thorough and comprehensive a way as possible. All relevant documents should be included, namely relevant prosecution statements and other evidence received, where necessary the tape of the recorded interview, and proofs of evidence of the defendant and his witnesses. It is unwise however to send counsel original documents for he is quite likely either to lose them or to return them bearing marmalade, ketchup or coffee stains.

The brief should contain full and detailed information and should be more than a mere recital of the statements. It should contain the solicitor's own analysis of the situation and, where appropriate, the result of his own researches or knowledge on matters of law, practice and evidence. It is always worthwhile for the solicitor to bring his own intelligence to bear on a case so that two minds can be working to the client's advantage rather than one.

3.9.2 CONFERENCES WITH COUNSEL

In substantial cases a conference with counsel is often desirable. If the client is on bail this will be at counsel's chambers or if he is in custody it will be at the remand centre or prison. Counsel may well wish to take the client through his proof of evidence and test him on possible inconsistencies or implausibilities in it. This is not with a view to suggesting a better story, which would be quite unprofessional; it is with a view to highlighting difficulties so that counsel may know how best tactically to approach the case.

It may be that specific advice needs to be given to the client about his plea if his version is transparently untruthful and counsel feels that there may be significant advantages to the client in pleading guilty (e.g., an indication of contrition may mean the difference between a custodial and a non-custodial sentence). The work of both barrister and solicitor in advising the client in such a situation is extremely onerous and delicate and must be undertaken with great care so that the client is not, in any sense, bullied into pleading guilty when he insists he is not.

The advantages of having a conference with the barrister include the fact that it makes the client feel more part of the team and should increase his confidence. Unfortunately, due to the unpredictability of the length of criminal trials, the listing system in the Crown Court is also somewhat haphazard and it is very common for the barrister of one's choice not to be available on the day. Moreover, this may even be the case if the barrister has actually represented the client in court before. For example, in the Crown Court many cases are listed 'to plead' and a plea is taken so that the Crown Court can know roughly how long a case will take. The case may then be adjourned for some days, or weeks. It may therefore be that a client has seen his own barrister on one or several occasions and naturally he will be very disappointed if his own barrister is unable to attend the trial itself. Learning to cope with a disgruntled client in that situation, especially if after the trial the client is convicted, when he will attribute his conviction to the change of barrister, is an important part of a solicitor's skills.

3.9.3   BRIEFING COUNSEL FOR THE TRIAL

The subject of preparation for the trial is dealt with more specifically in **Chapter 17** at **17.8**.

3.10   Building a Criminal Litigation Practice

Criminal litigation is one of the fields where it is perhaps easiest to build a practice from scratch. Even a new sole practitioner opening an office in the High Street may attract a reasonable number of clients, especially if he is qualified to get on the police station and court duty solicitor rotas. The onerous nature of being available throughout the night, especially when one's turn arrives at a weekend, makes the police station rota relatively unattractive to many solicitors. Such work usually falls to the most dedicated, which often means relatively young solicitors who still have their early enthusiasm. In some areas of the country there are so few solicitors on these rotas that one's turn may come round once a fortnight or indeed more often. The remuneration, whilst hardly adequate for those in large firms with substantial overheads, can be attractive for small firms, including sole practitioners of the kind previously mentioned.

If one is already a competent advocate, having worked for two or three years for some other firm, then one may well build a good clientele on the basis of enthusiasm, personality, and personal recommendations. There will undoubtedly be larger well established firms in the area with whom one is competing for clients. Such firms often have apparently unfair advantages and one will often find in the early stages that one mysteriously loses clients to such firms. Sometimes, and disappointingly, this even happens where one has, against the odds, secured bail for a client in the face of strenuous CPS opposition. Often these changes of solicitor come about for bizarre reasons. Sometimes it is claimed that the police or prison officers actually recommend persons in custody to take a particular solicitor. In most walks of life such a recommendation from people who are, in effect, the opposition, would be viewed strangely, but a surprising number of criminal clients seem to accept such 'advice' seriously. If the client is in custody he may well mix with other prisoners and ask them for their recommendation. Many criminal clients do remain faithful to the solicitor of their choice and thus may be prepared to recommend him to others, to the detriment of the client's present solicitor who may be relatively unknown in the field. This appears to be so no matter how deplorable the performance of the other solicitor often is, criminal clients being particularly prone to adopt a 'better the devil you know' approach in these matters. Some solicitors retain their popularity with their clients by the regrettable expedient of taking them small presents such as smarties, jelly babies, or books of poetry (Sylvia Plath is a particular favourite in Strangeways) whilst they are on remand. Nonetheless, despite these difficulties, competence and enthusiasm will eventually acquire a criminal practice for those who are so inclined.

FOUR

POLICE POWERS AND ADVISING THE CLIENT IN THE POLICE STATION

4.1 Introduction

In this chapter we shall be considering the early stages of the investigation of an offence and the powers of the police in relation to:

(a) Arrest
(b) Search
(c) Taking fingerprints and photographs
(d) The detention of a suspect
(e) Interrogation of a suspect
(f) Identification procedures.

In legal theory the police have no greater powers than the ordinary citizen save where such powers are expressly conferred by statute or have been deemed to exist at common law. The law has constantly striven to strike an appropriate balance between the liberty of the citizen to come and go as he pleases without being impeded by officers of the state and the realistic need to confer upon police and other investigative agencies limited powers to interfere with the freedom of citizens for good cause in the general interest of the suppression of crime.

The law at present is largely contained in the Police and Criminal Evidence Act 1984 (the '1984 Act') and in Codes of Practice issued under s. 66 of that Act. In some cases the 1984 Act merely restates the previous law with some additional refinements but in other cases express new powers are conferred. We shall now go on to consider the various stages of the investigation process and police powers in relation to it.

4.2 Arrest

4.2.1 ARREST WITH A WARRANT

If the police know the identity of a suspect whom they wish to arrest they will lay an information in writing on oath before a magistrate. This is commonly done orally. The warrant of arrest then obtained may be endorsed for bail which would authorise the police to release the suspect once having arrested him and after they have made the decision whether to charge him. Alternatively the warrant may not be endorsed for bail, in which case the suspect must be brought before the court. Such warrants may only be issued where:

(a)   the offence is triable on indictment or punishable with imprisonment; or

(b)   the defendant's address is not sufficiently established for him to be subject to the alternative procedure of a summons being sent to him (s. 1(4), Magistrates' Courts Act 1980).

Arrest with a warrant is now somewhat unusual. As we shall see shortly, the police have such wide powers to arrest without a warrant that it will only be exceptionally that a warrant is required. We turn now to the more common procedure for arrest, namely arrest without warrant.

4.2.2   ARREST WITHOUT A WARRANT

The power to arrest without warrant is now contained in s. 24 of the 1984 Act which broadly restates the law previously contained in s. 2 of the Criminal Law Act 1967 with some refinements. It provides a power of summary arrest, that is immediate arrest without prior formalities, for the police in the case of arrestable offences. 'Arrestable offences' means:

(a)   Offences for which the sentence is fixed by law (e.g., murder).

(b)   Offences for which a first offender of 21 years or over may receive a prison sentence of five years or more. This therefore means that certain offences are always arrestable offences. Thus theft is one such offence since it carries a maximum penalty of seven years. It is irrelevant that for the purposes of the offence with which one is concerned there is no prospect whatsoever of the arrestee receiving a prison sentence of five years. Thus for example a person suspected of shoplifting some small item may still be arrested under these powers notwithstanding that there is little prospect of him going to prison at all, still less for five years.

(c)   Sundry other offences listed in sch. 2 to the 1984 Act which are expressly made arrestable offences notwithstanding that they do not carry a maximum penalty of as long as five years, e.g., offences of indecent assault on a woman.

(d)   Certain other offences which the statute creating the offence expressly made arrestable notwithstanding that they did not carry a penalty as long as five years, e.g., the offence of taking a vehicle without the owner's consent under s. 12 of the Theft Act 1968.

By s. 24(6) and (7) of the 1984 Act a constable has the following powers:

(a)   if he has reasonable grounds for suspecting that an arrestable offence has been committed he may arrest without a warrant anyone whom he has reasonable grounds for suspecting to be guilty of the offence;

(b)   to arrest without a warrant anyone who is about to commit an arrestable offence or anyone whom he has reasonable grounds for suspecting is about to commit an arrestable offence;

(c)   to arrest without a warrant anyone who is in the act of, or whom he has reasonable grounds for suspecting to be in the act of, committing an arrestable offence.

In addition, by s. 25 of the 1984 Act, where a constable has reasonable grounds for suspecting that any offence which is *not* an arrestable offence (e.g., careless driving) has been committed or attempted or is being committed or attempted, he may arrest the relevant person if it appears to him that service of a summons is impracticable or inappropriate for any of the reasons specified in s. 25(3) of the 1984 Act, for example:

(a)   that the name of the relevant person is unknown to and cannot be readily ascertained by the constable; or

(b)   the constable has reasonable grounds for doubting whether a name furnished by the relevant person as his name is his real name; or

(c)   the relevant person fails to furnish a satisfactory address.

In these latter cases, therefore, a policeman who stops someone whom he believes to be committing a driving offence which is not arrestable would be entitled to arrest the person concerned if he felt that he was not being given a true name and address so that criminal proceedings could be instituted through the summons procedure which, as we shall see shortly, does not usually involve the preliminary arrest of the suspect.

Quite apart from this, certain other statutory powers of arrest are expressly preserved, for example, that in s. 7 of the Bail Act 1976 for the offence of absconding.

4.2.3 PROCEDURE ON ARREST

On arrest a person is to be cautioned in the following words: 'You do not have to say anything unless you wish to do so, but what you say may be given in evidence.' In addition, under s. 28 of the 1984 Act an arrest is unlawful unless at the time, or as soon as is practicable thereafter, the person is informed of the ground for the arrest and this applies whether or not it is obvious what the ground for the arrest is. This does not mean that a suspect must be told in technical language what the offence is, still less need reference be made to the section of the statute under which he may eventually be charged, but the circumstances said to constitute the offence must be clearly indicated to him.

4.3 Search

4.3.1 STOP AND SEARCH

By s. 1 of the 1984 Act a police officer has the power to detain and search any person or vehicle for stolen or prohibited articles. 'Prohibited articles' are:

(a) offensive weapons;
(b) articles made or adapted for use in, or intended for use in:

(i) burglary;
(ii) theft;
(iii) offences of taking away a motor vehicle under s. 12 of the Theft Act 1968;
(iv) obtaining property by deception under s. 15 of the Theft Act 1968.

It will be seen that this is a fairly wide power. A constable, however, must only use this power if he has reasonable grounds for suspecting that he will find stolen or prohibited articles. It has been stressed that searches must not be carried out simply on the basis of the racial origin of the person or because the person is found in an area in which offences of a certain kind are relatively common. There must be a specific reason for suspecting the individual concerned. The notes for guidance accompanying the Code of Practice which supplements s. 1 warns that the degree or level of suspicion required to establish the reasonable grounds justifying stop and search is no less than the degree of suspicion required to effect an arrest.

4.3.2 POWERS TO ENTER AND SEARCH PREMISES

The police have the following powers:

(a) To enter and search any premises with the written permission of the occupier.
(b) To enter and search any premises to (inter alia):

(i) execute a warrant of arrest or commitment to prison;
(ii) arrest a person for an arrestable offence;
(iii) save life or limb or prevent serious damage to property (s. 17, 1984 Act).

(c) To search premises where an arrest took place for evidence relating to the offence for which the person has been arrested, but only to the extent that the power to search is reasonably required for the purpose of discovering any such evidence (s. 32).

(d) In the case of arrestable offences only, to search premises occupied or controlled by the person arrested for evidence relating to that offence or connected or similar arrestable offences.

Thus in this latter case a general fishing expedition is not permitted but no doubt a search will be easy enough to justify unless all the stolen property has been recovered and there can be no conceivable grounds for thinking that the individual was involved in other similar offences. A full record of any searches made under this provision must be made and entered on the individual's custody record (see below).

(e) Finally, a search may be executed under a search warrant which may be issued on application to the magistrates in certain circumstances.

In none of these cases do the police have powers to seize items subject to *legal privilege*. Such items include the contents of a solicitor's files or solicitor/client communications unless they could be regarded as coming into existence with the intention of furthering a criminal purpose (e.g., communications between a solicitor and a client constituting a conspiracy).

4.3.3   SEARCH OF PERSONS AFTER ARREST

4.3.3.1   Away from a police station

This is governed by s. 32 of the 1984 Act.

An arrested person may be searched upon arrest away from a police station if the constable has reasonable grounds for believing that the arrested person may present a danger to himself or others, or has reasonable grounds for believing that a person might have concealed on him anything which might:

(a) be used to assist him to escape from lawful custody; or
(b) be evidence relating to an offence.

However, the search may only take place to the extent that it is reasonably required for the purpose of discovering such things and in any event the constable may not require a person to remove any of his clothing in public other than an outer coat, a jacket or gloves.

4.3.3.2   At the police station

Under s. 54 of the 1984 Act a custody officer may order the search of an arrested person if he considers it necessary to ascertain or record property that that person has in his possession when he is brought to the station.

4.3.4   FINGERPRINTING

Previously the police had no power to take a person's fingerprints before he was charged with an offence unless he consented. However, now, under s. 61 of the 1984 Act, a person who gives his consent must give it in writing but if he does not consent an officer of at least superintendent rank may authorise the taking of fingerprints:

(a) before the individual has been charged where it is believed that fingerprints will tend to confirm or disprove his involvement in the commission of a particular offence; or
(b) after he has been charged or informed that he will be prosecuted for any recordable offence (that is an offence which, on conviction, will be recorded in national police records).

4.3.5   PHOTOGRAPHING

A person's consent in writing must be provided for the taking of photographs before charging, but after he has been charged with a recordable offence he may be photographed without his consent.

4.3.6   MISUSE OF POLICE POWERS

So far we have considered in very brief outline police powers in relation to the preliminary conduct of an investigation. The description given is hardly adequate as a full treatment of the law and practice. There is, however, a reason for this which is that the nature of this text is essentially practical. We are only concerned with police powers and conduct in the context of the criminal process. In any of the cases previously described, breach of the law or misuse of powers may be a police disciplinary offence. Moreover, in many cases misconduct would also give rise to liability in tort, e.g., an arrest that was unlawful would be false imprisonment; entry of premises in improper circumstances would be trespass to land; and taking fingerprints forcibly in situations where it was not appropriate would be battery. We are not, however, for present purposes concerned with the consequences to the individual police officers or the police force of complaints or actions in tort. We are concerned with the effect of any abuse of process on the criminal prosecution. What then is the effect of any such misuse of police powers? The answer is likely to be that so far as the criminal prosecution is concerned, misconduct by the police, at least in relation to search and entry will have very little effect.

As we shall see later when dealing with the law of evidence, on the basis of the case law before the 1984 Act there was no power for the court to exclude evidence; it could merely indicate disapproval of the way in which it was obtained. Therefore if a prosecution were commenced by an unlawful arrest and involved obtaining evidence by unlawful entry and seizure and the wrongful obtaining of fingerprints, these things would have had no effect whatsoever on the criminal process. Whatever the consequences (if any) in terms of disciplinary action against the police or action in tort, misconduct would not have given grounds for excluding the evidence thus unfairly or illegally obtained.

The present law is now contained in s. 78(1) of the Police and Criminal Evidence Act 1984 which provides:

> In any proceedings the court may refuse to allow evidence on which the prosecution proposes to rely to be given if it appears to the court that, having regard to all the circumstances, *including the circumstances in which the evidence was obtained*, the admission of the evidence would have such an adverse effect on the fairness of the proceedings that the court ought not to admit it.

The effect of this remains uncertain but, in the context of search and entry anyway, it is widely considered to make little change to the previous law. It will be noted that the trial judge has to have regard to whether or not the conduct will have an effect on the fairness of the proceedings. 'Fairness' relates to the question of whether the jury will be adversely affected not by the item of evidence concerned but by the circumstances in which it was obtained. It is suggested that the way in which evidence is obtained by search or seizure will not in itself usually affect the fairness of the proceedings, however 'unfair' in general terms police conduct may have been. If evidence is relevant it will still be admissible. Accordingly it is suggested that for the purposes of the criminal prosecution, misconduct by the police in arrest, search, fingerprinting etc. will not have a great effect.

4.3.7   CONFESSIONS

It ought to be stressed, however, that if the police are relying on a *confession* then by virtue of s. 76 of the 1984 Act the court needs to investigate the circumstances in which the confession was obtained to see whether it is admissible, that is whether it was obtained by *oppression* or whether there is anything in all the surrounding circumstances which might render it *unreliable*. Therefore it could well be that the conduct of the police generally, which might include unlawful search, seizure or arrest, might have had such an effect on the mind of the person that it could be said to contribute to the unreliability of his confession. These matters will be discussed subsequently in the section on confessions (see **10.1**).

Under s. 78 of the 1984 Act a confession may be excluded even if it is not *unreliable* if the circumstances in which it was obtained lead to the conclusion that the admission of the evidence would have an adverse effect on the fairness of the proceedings. The occasions when ss. 76 and 78 together have most frequently led to the exclusion of confessions have mainly been connected with police misconduct or omission in the course of detention and interrogation, a stage of procedure at which the suspect is clearly vulnerable to improper pressures with direct consequences for the outcome of his trial.

We shall now discuss the rules in relation to detention and interrogation.

4.4 Detention

4.4.1 THE CUSTODY OFFICER

Part IV of the 1984 Act creates the post of custody officer, who is a police officer of at least sergeant rank who has various responsibilities at 'designated police stations'. Designated police stations are those which have sufficient accommodation and facilities for the purpose of detaining arrested persons.

In principle the custody officer takes formal charge of arrested persons on the premises and has the duty of supervising the detention and interrogation of such persons. He must also keep a 'custody record' which records details of the course of a suspect's detention and interrogation.

When a person is brought to the police station after arrest he must be brought before the custody officer who will at that stage decide whether there is sufficient evidence to charge him with the offence for which he was arrested. If there is he should be charged forthwith. He may then be released on bail (with deposit of security or provision of sureties if appropriate) unless:

(a) his name or address cannot be ascertained or the custody officer has reasonable grounds for doubting whether a name or address furnished by him is his real name or address;

(b) the custody officer has reasonable grounds for believing that the detention of the person arrested is necessary for his own protection or to prevent him from causing physical injury to any other person or for causing loss of or damage to property; or

(c) the custody officer has reasonable grounds for believing that the person arrested will fail to appear in court to answer bail or that his detention is necessary to prevent him from interfering with the administration of justice or with the investigation of offences.

Thus where the person is charged the custody officer must consider bail. It will be noted that the matters which he has to consider correspond approximately to some of those contained in the Bail Act 1976. The Bail Act itself however does not apply at this stage. The Bail Act governs the grant of bail *by a court*.

If the individual is not released on bail he must be brought before a magistrates' court as soon as practical and in any event not later than the first sitting of the court after he has been charged with an offence.

What however if the custody officer decides that there is as yet insufficient evidence to charge? The suspect must then be released unless detention is necessary to secure or preserve evidence relating to an offence for which he is under arrest or to obtain such evidence by questioning him (s. 37 of the 1984 Act). A written record of the grounds for detention must be made in the presence of the person arrested and the grounds must be conveyed to the person.

There are further limits on detention before charging namely:

(a) There is an overriding duty on the police to charge an individual as soon as there is sufficient evidence to justify a charge.

(b) No person may be detained for more than 24 hours from the time at which the arrested person is brought to the police station save where the offence being investigated is a *serious arrestable offence*.

Serious arrestable offences are a special category of offences. Where a serious arrestable offence is concerned the police have greater powers than they have in the case of other offences. Serious arrestable offences comprise:

(a) Certain offences which are always serious, e.g., murder, manslaughter, rape, kidnapping, certain other sexual offences and various Firearms Act offences.

(b) Any other arrestable offence if its commission has led or is intended or likely to lead to certain serious consequences as defined in s. 116 of the 1984 Act. The serious consequences are:

(i) serious harm to the security of the state or public order;
(ii) serious interference with the administration of justice or the investigation of offences;
(iii) the death of any person;
(iv) serious injury to any person;
(v) substantial financial gain to any person; or
(vi) serious financial loss to any person.

In relation to the last of these, it should be noted that there is a subjective criterion for establishing whether the offence involves 'serious loss'. By s. 116(7) 'serious' means 'serious for the person who suffers it'. Thus theft, e.g., of a person's welfare benefit Giro cheque might well qualify even though the amount involved is modest.

In the case of serious arrestable offences the police have the right to detain the suspect for longer than the basic 24 hours. However, even in such cases the total period of detention must not exceed 36 hours and requires authority of an officer of at least superintendent rank. This officer should have reasonable grounds for believing that it is necessary to detain that person without charge in order to secure or preserve evidence or to obtain such evidence by questioning him, and that the investigation is being conducted diligently and expeditiously.

The concept of the serious arrestable offence allows the police other greater powers. If the police do require to detain a person beyond 36 hours they must apply on oath by way of information to a magistrates' court for a *warrant of further detention* and the person must be present at the hearing and has the right to be legally represented. Detention may then be authorised until up to 96 hours from the 'relevant time', i.e. from the time at which the person first came to the police station.

In every case where a person is detained reviews must be made of his detention (whether charged or not) no later than six hours after the detention was first authorised by the custody officer and thereafter every nine hours to ensure that the reasons justifying detention still exist. The review officer is an officer of inspector rank who must not have been directly involved in the investigation (in cases where the arrested person has not been charged) or the custody officer if he has. If the criteria for continued detention are not satisfied then the arrested person must be released.

4.5 The Conduct of Interrogation

Interrogation is now governed by Code of Practice C, issued under s. 66 of the 1984 Act, concerning the detention, treatment and questioning of persons by the police. We shall consider this shortly, but meanwhile it is important to note two specific powers provided in the statute itself, namely:

(a) By s. 58 of the 1984 Act a person arrested and held in custody in a police station is entitled to consult a solicitor privately at any time if he so requests. Any such request must be recorded in the custody record. The consultation may be in person or by telephone and may be with his own solicitor, if he has one, or with a duty solicitor. A delay in compliance is permitted only where the detainee is being held for a serious arrestable offence and an officer of at least superintendent rank has authorised the delay, and delay is in any event only permitted if the officer has reasonable grounds for believing that receiving such legal advice would:

(i) lead to interference with evidence of an offence or to interference with, or physical injury to, some third person;

(ii) lead to persons suspected of an offence being warned that the police are looking for them; or

(iii) hinder the recovery of the proceeds of an offence.

(b) Under s. 56 of the 1984 Act a person has the right not to be held incommunicado. Section 56 of the 1984 Act provides that a person under arrest at a police station shall be entitled on request to have one friend, relative or other person likely to take an interest in his welfare informed of his arrest and of the station where he is being held. Delay in permitting the person to exercise this right is only permitted in the circumstances where the right to legal advice may be delayed or refused.

Finally, an individual held in custody has the right to read the relevant Codes of Practice. However, a person arrested is not entitled to cause unreasonable delay to the investigation while he reads the Codes.

4.5.1 CODE OF PRACTICE C

Unfortunately the full text of this Code of Practice runs to nearly 30 pages and it is not practical to set it out here. The most important parts are ss. 11 and 12 and those sections appear in full towards the end of this chapter (see 4.8) for ease of reference. It is only possible here briefly to summarise some of the most important provisions. The Code in particular provides that:

(a) There is a basic duty to inform a person arrested of certain rights.

(b) Where there are grounds to suspect a person of an offence he must be cautioned in the same terms as those of the caution upon arrest. Further, where there is any break in questioning, the suspect should be recautioned when it resumes or he should be reminded that he is still under caution. Moreover, a detailed record must be made of the conduct of the interrogation; of meals and refreshment breaks; of complaints; and of any reasons for delaying a break in the interview.

A person must be charged as soon as the prosecution have sufficient evidence on which to charge him. In other words the prosecution having already obtained such evidence may not delay charging merely because they wish to collect further information from the suspect. Having charged the suspect he may not be further questioned with regard to the offence except:

(a) where necessary for the purpose of preventing or minimising harm or loss to some other person or the public; or

(b) in order to clear up an ambiguity in a previous answer; or

(c) where it is in the interests of justice that he should have put to him, and have an opportunity to comment on, information concerning the offence which has come to light since he was charged.

In the latter case he should be cautioned again before questioning is resumed. He should not be referred to any written statement made by another person or to the contents of any interview with such person without first being cautioned and then shown the statement or interview record without any further comment being invited by the officer who tenders the statement etc. to him.

The temptation for the police to delay charging, so as to be able to continue interrogating, is therefore considerable but is in part alleviated by the provisions referred to above. As indicated at the outset, breach of these provisions is likely to be considerably more relevant to the criminal process in terms of the admissibility of evidence than breach of the provisions with regard to arrest and search.

A suspect will now be in the confines of a police station and unless he is already well used to custody he may have little idea of his rights (and the average suspect is unlikely perhaps to obtain much benefit from reading the 1984 Act and the Codes with which he may be supplied). He may have no idea about how long the police can keep him, what their powers are whilst he is there, or what they may be doing at his home or with his family meanwhile. He is therefore in a very vulnerable situation. The provisions requiring the keeping of exhaustive custody records are meant in part to ensure that the police thoroughly rationalise and justify each of the steps they propose to take with regard to the way in which they treat the suspect or the reasons why they are keeping him in custody or prolonging his custody. They also ensure that the police themselves keep their actions under review in the light of the fact that the custody record may come up for examination in court and they may be asked then to justify exactly why they behaved in the way in which they did.

Thus, for example, suppose that a suspect was arrested on a Saturday night and put in a cell before questioning started some hours later. It would be easy enough at the trial for the police to say that due to the volume of activity in the police station on the Saturday night it was impossible to question the suspect immediately. In fact they may very well have left him in the cell for a few hours as part of a well recognised softening-up process so as to make him more amenable to questioning later. Whilst the keeping of records does not prevent this kind of practice, the police will need to be very sure that they can justify it at the time they are writing up the custody record.

Interrogation procedures now involve a careful review of the case not by the investigating officer but by the custody officer, and in some cases by a review officer who also is not connected with the case. In both cases it is intended that the officers concerned will be sufficiently aware of the need to preserve their personal reputations and integrity to ensure that they do their job efficiently and do not merely succumb to the enthusiasm of their colleagues involved in the investigations who may wish to conduct matters in a certain way. It will be noted that both the custody officer and the review officer may well be of inferior rank to the investigating officers whose procedures they may be charged with supervising.

The process of interrogation may be vital for the success of the eventual prosecution. No matter what evidence the police already have, they are likely to try to obtain a confession from a suspect if at all possible, thinking it will then be harder for him to plead not guilty and a great deal of time and cost may well be saved. Breaches of the Codes or of the substantive sections of the 1984 Act, e.g., ss. 56 and 58, are not in themselves matters which invalidate a confession. They will, however, be seriously taken into account in considering whether in all the circumstances the confession is *unreliable*.

4.5.2 TAPE RECORDING OF INTERVIEWS

The tape recording of interviews is now dealt with as Code of Practice E, issued under the authority of s. 66 of the 1984 Act. The Code is too lengthy to set out in full. Interviews at a police station should now be tape recorded in the case of indictable offences, including those triable either way. If for any reason an officer decides not to tape record an interview there may be comment in court (and indeed consequences in respect of any confession allegedly obtained). The officer concerned should therefore be prepared to justify his decision in each case.

In principle the consent of the suspect is required though the police may carry on with tape recording even in the event of objection if they think it appropriate. To do so, however, might involve them in adverse comment in court. The following are the main features of the tape-recording process:

(a) The tape recording must be done openly and not without the knowledge of the suspect.
(b) Two tapes must be used on a twin deck machine; one of these will be the 'master tape' which is sealed at the end of the interview and will not be opened until the court proceedings.
(c) A balanced summary of the relevant parts of the interview will be prepared from the 'working' copy of the tape and this balanced summary will be sent to the defence. If the defence require it they may insist on listening to the whole tape.
(d) A transcript of the tape may be prepared for use in court to avoid the time needed to set up the recording and playing equipment. Naturally the tape may in some situations be played in court in order to resolve difficulties; to indicate authenticity; or so that the full picture can be conveyed to the court in terms of pauses, breaks, tone of voice, etc.
(e) Any interview which is not tape recorded must be contemporaneously recorded in note form whether or not the interview takes place at the police station. At the end of the interview an arrested

person must be given the opportunity to read the interview record and to sign it as correct or to indicate in which respects he considers it inaccurate.

(f) The tape or interview record must indicate where the interview took place, where it began and ended, any breaks in it, and the persons present. This will usually be done by the interrogating officer giving details at the start and end of the interview.

This tape will be an essential tool for challenging the admissibility of any confession on the grounds of unreliability or unfairness. For further discussion of these aspects see **10.1.7.2** and **10.1.7.3**.

4.6　Identification Procedures

The Court of Appeal in *R* v *Turnbull* [1977] QB 224 laid down important guidelines as to the need for a jury or magistrates to exercise caution in convicting in a case depending wholly or substantially on disputed identification evidence. The normal case will be where an eye-witness at the scene of some incident believes he can recognise the perpetrator who is not apprehended at that time, and subsequently a suspect is found.

At one time the suspect might have been tried and the identifying witness would have seen him for the first time since the crime sitting in the dock and would purport to identify him then and there. There are clearly grave dangers in this course. The witness may feel sure that the police will have the right man and even if he entertains doubts may identify the man in the dock simply because he is there. Accordingly for a very long time now 'dock identifications' have been disapproved and identity parades have been used.

An identity parade is an opportunity for a witness to see the suspect as soon as possible after the crime and to test the witness's ability to pick the suspect out of a group of people of similar appearance. The guidelines for the conduct of identity parades are now contained in Code of Practice D, issued under s. 66 of the 1984 Act.

Where the police have a suspect and the evidence on which they base their case is wholly or substantially that of identification they should hold an identity parade. They must give the suspect the right to refuse to take part. If, however, he does refuse there are two important points to note and these will generally mean that it is prudent for a suspect to consent. If he refuses:

(a) The refusal may be given in evidence at any subsequent trial and may be subject to comment.
(b) Some less satisfactory method of identification, such as group identification or identification by video of the suspect and others, or even confrontation (that is one to one with the witness), or allowing the witness to see the suspect and a few other prisoners in the cell, may be adopted. Generally speaking a properly conducted identity parade gives the suspect a better chance. The full Code of Practice D is too lengthy to set out in this text but Annex A, which deals with the conduct of the parade, and part of Annex B, which deals with video parade identification, are set out for reference at the end of this chapter (see **4.9** and **4.10**). We shall however now summarise some of the more important features of Code D.

4.6.1　CONDUCT OF AN IDENTITY PARADE

The following conditions must be complied with when conducting an identity parade:

(a) Certain information must be given to the suspect in a written 'notice to suspect'.
(b) The suspect may have a solicitor or friend present at the parade unless the parade officer reasonably considers that this cannot be arranged without causing unreasonable delay having regard to the lawful period of detention.
(c) The parade must be conducted by a uniformed officer of at least inspector rank who is not personally involved in the investigation. The point of this is to ensure that the procedure is

scrupulously carried out and that the officer charged with organising the parade has no personal interest in the case which might lead him to shortcut any procedures.

(d) The parade must consist of at least eight persons other than the suspect who are so far as possible of the same age, height, general appearance and position in life as the suspect. The suspect may choose his own position in the line, and may change positions if he wishes in between inspections by identifying witnesses if there are more than one.

(e) It is vital to ensure that the witnesses are segregated from the parade so that they do not see any member of the parade beforehand, and are not prompted by any photograph or description of the suspect or given any clues, or communicate with each other or with any witness who has already seen the parade.

The procedure on the parade is that the witness is brought into the room where the members of the parade are and walks past them. It is important that each witness is told before the parade that the person involved may or may not be in the parade and that he has no obligation to make a positive identification. This is to avoid any pressure the witness might feel under to pick someone since the witness is aware that the police are now looking for vital evidence. The witness will make the identification by saying at which number in the line the person is standing.

The witness may ask, if he wishes, for any member of the parade to speak, move, or adopt any posture. If this suggestion comes from the witness then the officer in charge of organising the parade is required to remind the witness that the parade has been selected on the basis of physical appearance not, for example, similarity of voice and the officer must specifically ask the witness whether he is capable of identifying any person on the basis of appearance alone. However, thereafter the witness's request may be met.

4.6.2 THE USE OF PHOTOGRAPHS

Annex D to Code D sets out rules for the use of photographs. This Annex is set out for reference at the end of this chapter (see **4.11**) but it is convenient to summarise it and indicate some of the more important considerations here:

(a) Photographs should not be used where there is a suspect already available. At this stage one should go straight to an identification parade. Clearly an identification parade is preferable to photographs and moreover if photographs have been used they substantially detract from the value of any subsequent identity parade so far as that witness is concerned. This is because the witness who may have seen an incident for some few seconds and is able to pick out a photograph on the basis of his recollection of that incident will obviously clearly remember the features in the photograph should any subsequent identity parade be held. There is thus one vital further remove between the crime and the parade and a witness who has an opportunity of studying a photograph at leisure is unlikely to fail to pick out that person at the parade. Nonetheless the requirements of the Code are that if a witness has identified a suspect from a photograph he should still go on to confirm this at an identification parade.

(b) A witness must be shown at least 12 photographs at a time and, as far as possible, they should be of a similar type and with a resemblance to the suspect.

(c) If one witness makes a positive identification then there should be no further showing of photographs, and an identity parade should be held for other witnesses involved.

In the exceptional case where a witness attending an identification parade has previously been shown a photograph or photofit picture, the suspect and his legal representative must be informed of this fact before committal proceedings or summary trial.

To summarise therefore one can say that photographs should only be used where there is no suspect at all. Thus if for example some offence is committed in a large city and the police have little idea who might have committed it they will first look in criminal records for persons who have a propensity to that type of crime and who live locally. They will then show photographs of such suspects to one eye-witness in the hope that a lead can be obtained. If the eye-witness then identifies someone, an identity parade will be held with that suspect (if he is willing) for the first witness and subsequently any other eye-witnesses involved.

4.6.3 IRREGULARITY IN IDENTIFICATION PROCEDURE

What if there is irregularity in the showing of photographs or conduct of identity parades? The answer depends on the degree of the irregularity:

(a) Any deliberate leading of a witness, e.g., by showing only one photograph, or indicating which is the suspect in a parade, ought to invalidate the whole of the identification evidence thus obtained from the witness concerned.

(b) If there is some lesser breach of the rules, for example, if a parade had two individuals in it who did not look very much like the suspect, or was one person short of the required number, then that would be a matter within the discretion of the trial judge. He might very well rebuke the prosecution for these deficiencies but it is most unlikely that he would rule the evidence out entirely, although he ought to comment that because of the defects in procedure the evidence might be less reliable.

The problems of defects in the holding of an identification parade and the subsequent exclusion of identification evidence are discussed at **12.8.3.4**.

Occasionally if a suspect has a very unusual appearance, for example in terms of height, hairstyle, etc., it may be impossible to organise a proper parade. In these circumstances there may be no alternative to group identification or simple confrontation, i.e., letting the witness see the suspect at the police station. It should be noted however that if a suspect wishes there to be an identification parade he has the right to one, and failure to accord him this right is likely to be fatal to the evidence (see **12.8.3.3**).

Finally, it is important to note that, unless exceptionally the defence wish them to do so (e.g., to explore the procedure involved so as to point to impropriety), the prosecution must not lead any evidence before the jury of the use of photographs. This is because the reference to police photographs is tantamount to telling the jury that the accused has a criminal record.

4.7 Advising a Suspect at the Police Station

We shall now consider some general aspects of assisting a suspect at the police station. Recent research has demonstrated the poor quality of legal advice and assistance often given to suspects at police stations. Some firms of solicitors send unqualified and inexperienced staff for this work partly because it is not well paid and partly because it is often required at inconvenient or unsocial hours or on very short notice and disrupts the working day. Clearly if a telephone call is received to say that a client is in custody within office hours and that the police are intending to interview him shortly, a difficult decision has to be made as to whether to drop everything, including possibly cancelling appointments with other clients, to attend the police station or to decline to assist thus losing the client. If the telephone call indicating that a client is in custody comes outside office hours, the disruption to personal life may be equally extreme. Nonetheless a firm which holds itself out as undertaking a substantial amount of criminal work ought to have the resources to send competent lawyers to assist at what, as recent case law shows, is often the most vital stage of all in the criminal justice process, where things may go seriously wrong for a defendant.

4.7.1 OBTAINING INSTRUCTIONS

You could be called out through the duty solicitor service, by the client direct if the police have permitted him to telephone, by the police themselves, or, quite often, by a third party such as the suspect's spouse who indicates that he has just been arrested. In the latter case you may have to ring around to see which police station he has been taken to. If it is possible that he may have been taken to one of several police stations it is important to ensure a record is made of the telephone call to each police station. The level of co-operation that can be expected may vary greatly. Sending a fax message is excellent evidence of any communications which are made and of the relevant times.

On arrival at the police station you should insist on a private interview with the client. In principle, by s. 58 of the 1984 Act, a suspect is entitled to consult his solicitor privately unless access may properly be delayed in the case of a serious arrestable offence and such delay is authorised by a superintendent. That delay may only be exercised on appropriate grounds set out in s. 58(8) of the 1984 Act and a solicitor should ask at the time what the grounds are and record the answer given to him. Section 58(8) provides as follows:

> An officer may only authorise delay where he has reasonable grounds for believing that the exercise of the right conferred by subsection (1) above at the time when the person detained desires to exercise it—
>
> (a) will lead to interference with or harm to evidence connected with a serious arrestable offence or interference with or physical injury to other persons; or
> (b) will lead to the alerting of other persons suspected of having committed such an offence but not yet arrested for it; or
> (c) will hinder the recovery of any property obtained as a result of such an offence.

Very commonly the ground chosen is that access to a solicitor 'will lead to the alerting of other persons suspected of having committed a serious arrestable offence, but not yet arrested'. The real reason is often that the solicitor might advise the suspect not to co-operate or answer questions.

It may be possible in the course of discussion to reassure the police officers concerned or even to convince them that they are wrong in believing the alleged crime to be a serious arrestable offence. Where a refusal is maintained despite any argument that one can put forward, one should note the name and rank of the officer making the decision and check that a record of the refusal is made in the custody record.

On the assumption that one has been able to speak to the client, the following matters are worthy of attention.

(a) Full records should be made of everything that happens at the police station. These can be useful for comparing with or challenging the custody record. The timing of arrival and departure and all relevant incidents within that time, especially the more formal ones such as participation in interviews or identification parades, should be noted. One must insist that the interview is in private and well out of hearing of others; it should take place in a closed room and not in a corridor or some area to which the public or other police have general access. As much information as there is time to obtain from the suspect should be gathered. At this stage one would have an eye to the possibility or probability of either an interrogation and/or identification and therefore the background facts to the alleged incident are what is material. Bail of course will need to be considered shortly but for the time being it is important to get the facts of the case.

(b) If one is advising a suspect before he is going to be interviewed, then the advice will vary with the circumstances. By far the best course is to advise the suspect to say nothing whatsoever during interview until one has a thorough picture and can give informed advice. Once one has obtained all the background then, at least with a suspect of some intelligence, one may form the view that he will have little to lose by giving his version, for example if he has an apparently complete defence such as an alibi and you are confident that he is telling the truth and thus is not giving hostages to fortune by advancing it at this stage.

(c) The suspect's criminal record, if you do not already know it, should be checked so far as possible. This may be relevant to the likelihood of him having committed the offence itself, to the way in which the police will be inclined to treat him and, at a very early stage, to the possibility of bail. One should never however rely on the version of his criminal record given by one's client. Criminal clients have a strange tendency to tell their solicitor what they think the solicitor wants to hear, i.e. that they are of previous good character even though this will very shortly be exposed as totally untrue.

(d) If, having considered everything, it seems inappropriate to put forward the suspect's case at this stage, then firm advice to remain silent should be given and the suspect should be told the reasons for this and why answering questions may be undesirable. It is unfortunately true that many habitual criminals are not very intelligent. They are often also not aware of their limitations and may feel confident of their ability to exchange badinage with interrogating officers and talk themselves out of their predicament. Clients should be discouraged from this. The interview will be tape recorded and any smart answer or throwaway remark given by the suspect may sound much less impressive when played back to a jury at trial in six months' time. It can always be forcefully pointed out to the suspect that if the police had a cast-iron case against him they would hardly be bothering to ask him questions to improve it. This is not in fact entirely true, or logical, but it often strikes a chord with clients.

(e) It is of course always important to remember that what the client is really interested in is obtaining the best possible outcome. If he admits guilt to you it does not follow that you are obliged to advise him to plead guilty. It may be that the prosecution will have an extremely hard time proving their case especially in the face of his silence and you are entitled to give him that advice.

As indicated earlier (see 1.2.2.2), you must not be a party to him putting forward any untruthful version in court nor in interview, and therefore you must advise him to remain silent at all stages, leaving the police to decide whether they have sufficient evidence on which to charge. One should bear in mind however that obtaining the overall best result for a client may involve looking ahead to sentence as well as issues of guilt and innocence. There is no doubt that a prompt admission, especially one showing contrition, and co-operation with the police, especially to the point of assisting in the recovery of stolen goods, or even, if he is so inclined, assisting in the apprehension of his accomplices, will be powerful factors in mitigation. In this connection it is also important to discuss one other matter namely the possibility of a caution.

4.7.2 CAUTIONING

Cautioning is an important way of keeping minor offenders out of the courts and in some cases reducing the risk of them reoffending. A Home Office Circular No. 59/1990 provides police with guidance on cautioning offenders as an alternative to prosecution.

The caution may be given in the case of any criminal offence, including road traffic offences. A caution is a serious and formal matter which is recorded by the police and it is likely to influence the police in any decision about whether to prosecute if the person concerned should offend again. Evidence of the caution may be given in subsequent court proceedings. A caution is appropriate where:

(a) The offender has admitted the offence.

(b) The offender consents to be cautioned rather than charged (though very few are likely to refuse).

(c) The public interest has been considered, in particular the nature of the offence, the likely penalty if the case was taken to court, the offender's age, state of health and previous criminal history, and the offender's attitude towards the offence.

(d) There is a presumption in favour of a caution particularly in the case of juveniles and the elderly or infirm. The Home Office Circular stresses however that there is no presumption that a caution is inappropriate for other groups, e.g., adults in good health.

(e) The views of the victim ought usually to be obtained and his or her consent to a caution asked for, although it is not fatal to cautioning that consent is refused.

It is therefore obvious that there may be an opportunity for what one might describe as 'negotiations' with the police on a suspect's behalf. The question of the procedure to be followed, a release on bail pending further investigations, the precise charge, the nature of the interview, and the possibility of caution might all arise. The negotiating skills necessary in civil litigation may be equally appropriate here.

4.7.3   THE CONDUCT OF THE INTERVIEW

Following the case of *R* v *Chandler* [1976] 3 All ER 105 (confirmed more recently in *R* v *Dunn* [1990] Crim LR 572) your presence during the interview may lead to adverse inferences being drawn from the exercise of the right of silence. It is possible also that the presence of a solicitor can rectify defects in an interview which might otherwise have been fatal to its admission as evidence. One must also bear in mind that it is usually tactically unwise for the suspect to reply to some questions and not others, and it is better either to attempt full co-operation or to remain silent throughout.

The investigating officer must be allowed to conduct the interview at his own pace and in his own way. You are allowed to intervene, for example where the officer is not asking questions but making statements or where the questions are offensive, oppressive or impossible to answer (e.g., they contain several muddled questions all rolled into one). You should remember throughout that by virtue of paragraph 6D of Code of Practice C, a solicitor is *not* guilty of any misconduct if he seeks to challenge improper questions to his client or the manner in which questions are put, if he advises his client during the course of an interview not to reply to particular questions or if he wishes for an adjournment to give his client further legal advice. A solicitor should not be asked to leave an interview unless his interference with its conduct goes beyond what is proper. Misconducts may include such things as answering questions on the client's behalf, prompting the client orally or giving him written replies to read out. If at any stage a solicitor feels that an interview is getting out of hand he should ask for it to be interrupted so that he may give further advice in private. That advice will usually be to say nothing more.

It is important that a solicitor maintains his own records of the times and events of the interview. You may think that it is pointless to try and make a transcript because the tape will eventually be available but you may not obtain access to that tape until some months later and it may be that the note is required earlier than that, for example to consider the facts fully or for a bail application.

At the end of the interview the police should be asked what the position is with regard to continued detention, further interviews and the like. If it is apparent that they are likely to reinterview and perhaps the hour is already late and you are very tired, then you should see whether other resources are available within your firm to ensure that the client has representation at the subsequent interview. This will not be as satisfactory as remaining or coming back yourself, because the element of continuity will be lost but it is certainly better than nothing.

4.7.4   IDENTIFICATION CASES

You must be prepared to give the client full advice about identification parades. In principle the decision is the client's but it is usual to attempt to cajole him towards the best tactical view which is that an identification parade gives him the best chance. A suspect has the right to a parade if it is practicable. The case law shows that the police must extend reasonable co-operation here so that a delay even of some weeks may be appropriate in order for the solicitor to attempt to obtain similar looking members of the public to participate in the parade (e.g., as in *R* v *Britton and Richards* [1989] Crim LR 144, where the suspect had dreadlocks and his solicitor felt that the co-operation of members of the West Indian community could be obtained to put on a parade).

You should of course check the details of the parade to ensure that Code D is respected. It may be necessary to inspect the physical layout of the area where the parade is to take place to ensure that witnesses are brought in properly and by a route which will not involve them speaking to each other. Likewise you should ensure that the suspect and witnesses do not arrive at the police station at the same time. If your client has a unique feature, e.g., a scar, everyone in the parade should wear a sticking plaster over the place of the scar; if he wears glasses so should everyone else in the parade or he should take them off. Your client should be advised to remain silent at all times during the parade so as not to assist unnecessarily in any form of voice identification — this being notoriously suspect. Although a witness may ask for a voice identification there is no obligation on a suspect to co-operate.

If less satisfactory forms of identification are to be used, for example a group identification, perhaps in the street, then you should closely observe all aspects of it. It may for example be possible, if, as is increasingly common, the suspect is invited to walk down the street past the witness, to make a video of the event in case of any unfair procedure, for example where the client was the only black person walking down the street at the time.

For the same reason as with interrogations, records should be made showing precise dates, times and significant events.

Eventually the client will either be charged, released without charge, released on police bail pending further enquiries or asked to return at a given time to participate in other interviews or identification parades.

4.8   Code of Practice C, ss. 11 and 12

11.   Interviews: general

(a)   Action

11.1   Following a decision to arrest a suspect he must not be interviewed about the relevant offence except at a police station (or other authorised place of detention) unless the consequent delay would be likely:

(a)   to lead to interference with or harm to evidence connected with an offence or interference with or physical harm to other persons; or
(b)   to lead to the alerting of other persons suspected of having committed an offence but not yet arrested for it; or
(c)   to hinder the recovery of property obtained in consequence of the commission of an offence.

Interviewing in any of these circumstances should cease once the relevant risk has been averted or the necessary questions have been put in order to attempt to avert that risk. For the definition of an interview see Note 11A.

11.2   Immediately prior to the commencement or re-commencement of any interview at a police station or other authorised place of detention, the interviewing office should remind the suspect of his entitlement to free legal advice. It is the responsibility of the interviewing officer to ensure that all such reminders are noted in the record of interview.

11.3   No police officer may try to obtain answers to questions or to elicit a statement by the use of oppression or shall indicate, except in answer to a direct question, what action will be taken on the part of the police if the person being interviewed answers questions, makes a statement or refuses to do either. If the person asks the officer directly what action will be taken in the event of his answering questions, making a statement or refusing to do either, then the officer may inform the person what action the police propose to take in that event provided that that action is itself proper and warranted.

11.4   As soon as a police officer who is making enquiries of any person about an offence believes that a prosecution should be brought against him and that there is sufficient evidence for it to succeed, he should ask the person if he has anything further to say. If the person indicates that he has nothing more to say the officer shall without delay cease to question him about the offence. This should not, however, be taken to prevent officers in revenue cases or acting under the confiscation provisions of the Criminal Justice Act 1988 or the Drug Trafficking Offences Act 1986 from inviting suspects to complete a formal question and answer record after the interview is concluded.

(b) Interview records

11.5   (a) An accurate record must be made of each interview with a person suspected of an offence, whether or not the interview takes place at a police station.

(b) The record must state the place of the interview, the time it begins and ends, the time the record is made (if different), any breaks in the interview and the names of all those present; and must be made on the forms provided for this purpose or in the officer's pocket-book or in accordance with the code of practice for the tape-recording of police interviews with suspects.

(c) The record must be made during the course of the interview, unless in the investigating officer's view this would not be practicable or would interfere with the conduct of the interview, and must constitute either a verbatim record of what has been said or, failing this, an account of the interview which adequately and accurately summarises it.

11.6   The requirement to record the names of all those present at an interview does not apply to police officers interviewing persons detained under the Prevention of Terrorism (Temporary Provisions) Act 1989. Instead the record shall state the warrant number and duty station of such officers.

11.7   If an interview record is not made during the course of the interview it must be made as soon as practicable after its completion.

11.8   Written interview records must be timed and signed by the maker.

11.9   If an interview record is not completed in the course of the interview the reason must be recorded in the officer's pocket book.

11.10   Unless it is impracticable the person interviewed shall be given the opportunity to read the interview record and to sign it as correct or to indicate the respects in which he considers it inaccurate. If the interview is tape-recorded the arrangements set out in the relevant code of practice apply. If the person concerned cannot read or refuses to read the record or to sign it, the senior police officer present shall read it over to him and ask him whether he would like to sign it as correct (or make his mark) or to indicate the respects in which he considers it inaccurate. The police officer shall then certify on the interview record itself what has occurred.

11.11   If the appropriate adult or the person's solicitor is present during the interview, he should also be given an opportunity to read and sign the interview record (or any written statement taken down by a police officer).

11.12   Any refusal by a person to sign an interview record when asked to do so in accordance with the provisions of this code must itself be recorded.

11.13   A written record should also be made of any comments made by a suspected person, including unsolicited comments, which are outside the context of an interview but which might be relevant to the offence. Any such record must be timed and signed by the maker. Where practicable the person shall be given the opportunity to read that record and to sign it as correct or to indicate the respects in which he considers it inaccurate. Any refusal to sign should be recorded.

(c) Juveniles, the mentally disordered and the mentally handicapped

11.14   A juvenile or a person who is mentally disordered or mentally handicapped, whether suspected or not, must not be interviewed or asked to provide or sign a written statement in the absence of the appropriate adult unless Annex C applies.

11.15   Juveniles may only be interviewed at their places of education in exceptional circumstances and then only where the principal or his nominee agrees. Every effort should be made to notify both the parent(s) or other person responsible for the juvenile's welfare and the appropriate adult (if this is a different person) that the police want to interview the juvenile and reasonable time should be allowed to enable the appropriate adult to be present at the interview. Where awaiting the appropriate adult would cause unreasonable delay and unless the interviewee is suspected of an offence against the educational establishment, the principal or his nominee can act as the appropriate adult for the purposes of the interview.

11.16   Where the appropriate adult is present at an interview, he should be informed that he is not expected to act simply as an observer; and also that the purposes of his presence are, first, to advise the person being questioned and to observe whether or not the interview is being conducted properly and fairly, and, secondly, to facilitate communication with the person being interviewed.

Notes for guidance

11A   An interview is the questioning of a person regarding his involvement or suspected involvement in a criminal offence or offences. Questioning a person only to obtain information or his explanation of the facts or in the ordinary courses of the officer's duties does not constitute an interview for the purpose of this code. Neither does questioning which is confined to the proper and effective conduct of a search.

11B   It is important to bear in mind that, although juveniles or persons who are mentally disordered or mentally handicapped are often capable of providing reliable evidence, they may, without knowing or wishing to do so, be particularly prone in certain circumstances to provide information which is unreliable, misleading or self-incriminating. Special care should therefore always be exercised in questioning such a person, and the appropriate adult should be involved, if there is any doubt about a person's age, mental state or capacity. Because of the risk of unreliable evidence it is also important to obtain corroboration of any facts admitted whenever possible.

11C   A juvenile should not be arrested at his place of education unless this is unavoidable. In this case the principal or his nominee must be informed.

12.   Interviews in police stations

(a)   Action

12.1   If a police officer wishes to interview, or conduct enquiries which require the presence of, a detained person the custody officer is responsible for deciding whether to deliver him into his custody.

12.2   In any period of 24 hours a detained person must be allowed a continuous period of at least eight hours for rest, free from questioning, travel or any interruption arising out of the investigation concerned. This period should normally be at night. The period of rest may not be interrupted or delayed unless there are reasonable grounds for believing that it would:

(i)   involve a risk of harm to persons or serious loss of, or damage to, property;
(ii)   delay unnecessarily the person's release from custody; or
(iii)   otherwise prejudice the outcome of the investigation.

If a person is arrested at a police station after going there voluntarily, the period of 24 hours runs from the time of his arrest and not the time of arrival at the police station.

12.3   A detained person may not be supplied with intoxicating liquor except on medical directions. No person who is unfit through drink or drugs to the extent that he is unable to appreciate the significance of questions put to him and his answers may be questioned about an alleged offence in that condition except in accordance with Annex C. [See note 12B]

12.4   As far as practicable interviews shall take place in interview rooms which must be adequately heated, lit and ventilated.

12.5   Persons being questioned or making statements shall not be required to stand.

12.6   Before the commencement of an interview each interviewing officer shall identify himself and any other officers present by name and rank to the person being interviewed, except in the case of persons detained under the Prevention of Terrorism (Temporary Provisions) Act 1989 when each officer shall identify himself by his warrant number and rank rather than his name.

12.7   Breaks from interviewing shall be made at recognised meal times. Short breaks for refreshment shall also be provided at intervals of approximately two hours, subject to the interviewing officer's discretion to delay a break if there are reasonable grounds for believing that it would:

   (i)   involve a risk of harm to persons or serious loss of, or damage to, property;
   (ii)   delay unnecessarily the person's release from custody; or
   (iii)   otherwise prejudice the outcome of the investigation.

12.8   If in the course of the interview a complaint is made by the person being questioned or on his behalf concerning the provisions of this code then the interviewing officer shall:

   (i)   record it in the interview record; and
   (ii)   inform the custody officer, who is then responsible for dealing with it in accordance with section 9 of this code.

(b)   Documentation

12.9   A record must be made of the times at which a detained person is not in the custody of the custody officer, and why; and of the reason for any refusal to deliver him out of that custody.

12.10   A record must be made of any intoxicating liquor supplied to a detained person, in accordance with paragraph 12.3 above.

12.11   Any decision to delay a break in an interview must be recorded, with grounds, in the interview record.

12.12   All written statements made at police stations under caution shall be written on the forms provided for the purpose.

12.13   All written statements made under caution shall be taken in accordance with Annex D to this code.

Notes for guidance

12A   If the interview has been contemporaneously recorded and the record signed by the person interviewed in accordance with paragraph 11.10 above, or has been tape recorded, it is normally unnecessary to ask for a written statement. Statements under caution should normally be taken in these circumstances only at the person's express wish. An officer may, however, ask him whether or not he wants to make such a statement.

12B   The police surgeon can give advice about whether or not a person is fit to be interviewed in accordance with paragraph 12.3 above.

4.9 Code of Practice D, Annex A: Identification Parades

(a) General

1.   A suspect must be given a reasonable opportunity to have a solicitor or friend present, and the identification officer shall ask him to indicate on a second copy of the notice whether or not he so wishes.

2.   A parade may take place either in a normal room or in one equipped with a screen permitting witnesses to see members of the parade without being seen. The procedures for the composition and conduct of the parade are the same in both cases, subject to paragraph 7 below (except that a parade involving a screen may take place only when the suspect's solicitor, friend or appropriate adult is present or the parade is recorded on video).

(b) Parades involving prison inmates

3.   If an inmate is required for identification, and there are no security problems about his leaving the establishment, he may be asked to participate in a parade or video identification. (A group identification, however, may not be arranged other than in the establishment or inside a police station.)

4.   A parade may be held in a Prison Department establishment, but shall be conducted as far as practicable under normal parade rules. Members of the public shall make up the parade unless there are serious security or control objections to their admission to the establishment. In such cases, or if a video or group identification is arranged within the establishment, other inmates may participate. If an inmate is the suspect, he should not be required to wear prison uniform for the parade unless the other persons taking part are other inmates in uniform or are members of the public who are prepared to wear prison uniform for the occasion.

(c) Conduct of the parade

5.   Immediately before the parade, the identification officer must remind the suspect of the procedures governing its conduct and caution him in the terms of paragraph 10.4 of the code of practice for the detention, treatment and questioning of persons by police officers.

6.   All unauthorised persons must be excluded from the place where the parade is held.

7.   Once the parade has been formed, everything afterwards in respect of it shall take place in the presence and hearing of the suspect and of any interpreter, solicitor, friend or appropriate adult who is present (unless the parade involves a screen, in which case everything said to or by any witness at the place where the parade is held must be said in the hearing and presence of the suspect's solicitor, friend or appropriate adult or be recorded on video).

8.   The parade shall consist of at least eight persons (in addition to the suspect) who so far as possible resemble the suspect in age, height, general appearance and position in life. One suspect only shall be included in a parade unless there are two suspects of roughly similar appearance in which case they may be paraded together with at least twelve other persons. In no circumstances shall more than two suspects be included in one parade and where there are separate parades they shall be made up of different persons.

9.   Where all members of a similar group are possible suspects, separate parades shall be held for each member of the group unless there are two suspects of similar appearance when they may appear on the same parade with at least twelve other members of the group who are not suspects. Where police officers in uniform form an identification parade, any numerals or other identifying badge shall be concealed.

10.   When the suspect is brought to the place where the parade is to be held, he shall be asked by the identification officer whether he has any objection to the arrangements for the parade or to any of the other participants in it. The suspect may obtain advice from his solicitor or friend, if present, before the parade proceeds. Where practicable, steps shall be taken to remove the grounds for objection. Where it is not practicable to do so, the officer shall explain to the suspect why his objections cannot be met.

11.   The suspect may select his own position in the line. Where there is more than one witness, the identification officer must tell the suspect, after each witness has left the room, that he can if he wishes change position in the line. Each position in the line must be clearly numbered, whether by means of a numeral laid on the floor in front of each parade member or by other means.

12.   The identification officer is responsible for ensuring that, before they attend the parade, witnesses are not able to:

(i)   communicate with each other about the case or overhear a witness who has already seen the parade;
(ii)   see any member of the parade;
(iii)   on that occasion see or be reminded of any photograph or description of the suspect or be given any other indication of his identity; or
(iv)   see the suspect either before or after the parade.

13.   The officer conducting a witness to a parade must not discuss with him the composition of the parade, and in particular he must not disclose whether a previous witness has made any identification.

14.   Witnesses shall be brought in one at a time. Immediately before the witness inspects the parade, the identification officer shall tell him that the person he saw may or may not be on the parade and if he cannot make a positive identification he should say so. The officer shall then ask him to walk along the parade at least twice, taking as much care and time as he wishes. When he has done so the officer shall ask him whether the person he saw in person on an earlier relevant occasion is on the parade.

15.   The witness should make an identification by indicating the number of the person concerned.

16.   If the witness makes an identification after the parade has ended the suspect and, if present, his solicitor, interpreter or friend shall be informed. Where this occurs, consideration should be given to allowing the witness a second opportunity to identify the suspect.

17.   If a witness wishes to hear any parade member speak, adopt any specified posture or see him move, the identification officer shall first ask whether he can identify any persons on the parade on the basis of appearance only. When the request is to hear members of the parade speak, the witness shall be reminded that the participants in the parade have been chosen on the basis of physical appearance only. Members of the parade may then be asked to comply with the witness's request to hear them speak, to see them move or to adopt any specified posture.

18.   When the last witness has left, the identification officer shall ask the suspect whether he wishes to make any comments on the conduct of the parade.

(d)   Documentation

19.   If a parade is held without a solicitor or a friend of the suspect being present, a colour photograph or a video film of the parade shall be taken. A copy of the photograph or video film shall be supplied on request to the suspect or his solicitor within a reasonable time.

20.   Where a photograph or video film is taken in accordance with paragraph 19, it shall be destroyed or wiped clean at the conclusion of the proceedings unless the person concerned is convicted or admits the offence and is cautioned for it.

21.   If the identification officer asks any person to leave a parade because he is interfering with its conduct the circumstances shall be recorded.

22.   A record must be made of all those present at a parade or group identification whose names are known to the police.

23.   If prison inmates make up a parade the circumstances must be recorded.

24.   A record of the conduct of any parade must be made on the forms provided.

4.10   Code of Practice D, Annex B: Video Identification

(a)   *General*

1.   Where a video parade is to be arranged the following procedures must be followed.

2.   Arranging, supervising and directing the making and showing of a video film to be used in a video identification must be the responsibility of an identification officer or identification officers who have no direct involvement with the relevant case.

3.   The film must include the suspect and at least eight other people who so far as possible resemble the suspect in age, height, general appearance and position in life. Only one suspect shall appear on any film unless there are two suspects of roughly similar appearance in which case they may be shown together with at least twelve other persons.

4.   The suspect and other persons shall as far as possible be filmed in the same positions or carrying out the same activity and under identical conditions.

5.   Provision must be made for each person filmed to be identified by number.

6.   If police officers are filmed, any numerals or other identifying badges must be concealed. If a prison inmate is filmed either as a suspect or not, then either all or none of the persons filmed should be in prison uniform.

7.   The suspect and his solicitor, friend, or appropriate adult must be given a reasonable opportunity to see the complete film before it is shown to witnesses. If he has a reasonable objection to the video film or any of its participants, steps should, if practicable be taken to remove the grounds for objection. If this is not practicable the identification officer shall explain to the suspect and/or his representative why his objections cannot be met and record both the objection and the reason on the forms provided.

8.   The suspect's solicitor, or where one is not instructed the suspect himself, where practicable should be given reasonable notification of the time and place that it is intended to conduct the video identification in order that a representative may attend on the behalf of the suspect. The suspect himself may not be present when the film is shown to the witness(es). In the absence of a person representing the suspect the viewing itself shall be recorded on video. No unauthorised persons may be present.

(b)   Conducting the video identification

9.   The identification officer is responsible for ensuring that, before they see the film, witnesses are not able to communicate with each other about the case or overhear a witness who has seen the film. He must not discuss with the witness the composition of the film and must not disclose whether a previous witness has made any identification.

10.   Only one witness may see the film at a time. Immediately before the video identification takes place the identification officer shall tell the witness that the person he saw may or may not be on the video film. The witness should be advised that at any point he may ask to see a particular part of the tape again or to have a particular picture frozen for him to study. Furthermore, it should be pointed out that there is no limit on how many times he can view the whole tape or any part of it. However, he should be asked to refrain from making a positive identification or saying that he cannot make a positive identification until he has seen the entire film at least twice.

11.   Once the witness has seen the whole film at least twice and has indicated that he does not want to view it or any part of it again, the identification officer shall ask the witness to say whether the individual he saw in person on an earlier occasion has been shown on the film and, if so, to identify him by number. The identification officer will then show the film of the person identified again to confirm the identification with the witness.

12.   The identification officer must take care not to direct the witness's attention to any one individual on the video film, or give any other indication of the suspect's identity. Where a witness has previously made an identification by photographs, or a photofit, identikit or similar picture has been made, the witness must not be reminded of such a photograph or picture once a suspect is available for identification by other means in accordance with this code. Neither must he be reminded of any description of the suspect.

(c)   Tape security and destruction

13.   It shall be the responsibility of the identification officer to ensure that all relevant tapes are kept securely and their movements accounted for. In particular, no officer involved in the investigation against the suspect shall be permitted to view the video film prior to it being shown to any witness.

14.   Where a video film has been made in accordance with this section all copies of it must be destroyed if the suspect:

   (a)   is prosecuted for the offence and cleared; or
   (b)   is not prosecuted (unless he admits the offence and is cautioned for it).

An opportunity of witnessing the destruction must be given to him if he so requests within five days of being cleared or informed that he will not be prosecuted.

(d)   Documentation

15.   A record must be made of all those participating in or seeing the video whose names are known to the police.

16.   A record of the conduct of the video identification must be made on the forms provided.

4.11   Code of Practice D, Annex D: Showing of Photographs

(a)   Action

1.   An officer of the rank of sergeant or above shall be responsible for supervising and directing the showing of photographs. The actual showing may be done by a constable or a civilian police employee.

2.   Only one witness shall be shown photographs at any one time. He shall be given as much privacy as practicable and shall not be allowed to communicate with any other witness in the case.

3.   The witness shall be shown not less than twelve photographs at a time. These photographs shall either be in an album or loose photographs mounted in a frame or a sequence of not fewer than twelve photographs on optical disc, and shall, as far as possible, all be of a similar type.

4.   When the witness is shown the photographs, he shall be told that the photograph of the person he saw may or may not be amongst them. He shall not be prompted or guided in any way but shall be left to make any selection without help.

5.   If a witness makes a positive identification from photographs, then, unless the person identified is otherwise eliminated from enquiries, other witnesses shall not be shown photographs. But both they and the witness who has made the identification shall be asked to attend an identification parade or group or video identification if practicable unless there is no dispute about the identification of the suspect.

6.   Where the use of a photofit, identikit or similar picture has led to there being a suspect available who can be asked to appear on a parade, or participate in a video or group identification, the picture shall not be shown to other potential witnesses.

7.   Where a witness attending an identification parade has previously been shown photographs or photofit, identikit or similar pictures (and it is the responsibility of the officer in charge of the investigation to make the identification officer aware that this is the case) then the suspect and his solicitor must be informed of this fact before the identity parade takes place.

8.   None of the photographs (or optical discs) used shall be destroyed, whether or not an identification is made, since they may be required for production in court. The photographs should be numbered and a separate photograph taken of the frame or part of the album from which the witness made an identification as an aid to reconstituting it.

(b)   Documentation

9.   Whether or not an identification is made, a record shall be kept of the showing of photographs and of any comment made by the witness.

FIVE

COMMENCEMENT OF PROCEEDINGS AND MODE OF TRIAL

5.1 Introduction

With very few exceptions, not relevant for our purposes, all prosecutions are commenced in a magistrates' court. They may be commenced by one of two methods, namely, the laying of an information which leads to the issue of a summons by the court, and by charging. We shall shortly consider these two methods but before doing so it is necessary to say a few words about some preliminary matters.

5.1.1 TIME LIMITS

In criminal cases there is in principle no statute of limitation comparable to that which applies in civil proceedings. There is thus no time limit within which a prosecution must be commenced. However, in the case of purely summary offences, that is those triable only before a magistrates' court, there is a provision that an information must be laid within six months of the date of commission of the offence. This provision is not applicable to an either way offence, however the statute creating such an offence may itself lay down a time limit for prosecution (although this is rare). An information is laid for these purposes when it is received by the clerk to the justices of the magistrates' court concerned.

By s. 1 of the Road Traffic Offenders Act 1988, in the case of certain driving offences, including dangerous driving, careless driving and driving in excess of the speed limit, there is an additional provision. In these cases a defendant may not be prosecuted unless he was given notice of intended prosecution either orally at the time of the alleged offence or in writing within 14 days of the offence. However, where an accident occurs at the same time or immediately after the offence, provided the defendant was aware that the accident occurred there is no requirement to give him notice of intended prosecution.

5.1.2 GEOGRAPHICAL RESTRICTIONS

Magistrates' courts have jurisdiction to try *summary offences* committed within their respective counties. Additionally, a magistrates' court has jurisdiction over offences committed outside its county:

(a) Under s. 2(6) of the Magistrates' Courts Act 1980 where in addition to an offence (either summary or triable either way) which is alleged to have been committed in the court's county the accused is charged with any other summary offence wherever committed.

(b) Under s. 2(2) of the 1980 Act where it is 'necessary or expedient' that a person is charged or tried 'jointly or in the same place as' another person.

(c)   Under s. 3 of the 1980 Act offences committed within 500 yards of the county border and continuing offences begun in one county and completed in another may be treated as having been committed in either of the relevant counties. A similar rule applies in the case of offences against persons or property committed in a moving vehicle which at the time crossed a county boundary.

These provisions are common sense. They allow the convenient joinder of offences and offenders and save difficulty in cases where it is not entirely clear where a substantive offence occurred because of closeness to boundaries (county boundaries are in any event often notoriously hard to define).

However, these rules as to jurisdiction apply only in the case of purely summary offences. In the case of an offence *triable either way* (e.g., theft), the magistrates' court does not have this limit on its jurisdiction. In effect therefore the prosecution have the choice of courts in the case of an offence triable either way and may seek to commence proceedings in the court most convenient to them.

5.2   Commencing Proceedings

5.2.1   PROCEDURE BY INFORMATION

The laying of an information fulfils two distinct purposes:

(a)   it is the charge to which the accused must plead at the commencement of a summary trial, and
(b)   it is the procedural device which leads to the issue of a summons in those instances where the accused's first appearance before the court is secured by summons.

An information may therefore come about in three ways:

(a)   By the prosecutor delivering a signed written allegation against the accused to the court. The information must describe only one offence in ordinary language and must cite any relevant statutory provision. It may however allege, in the alternative, different ways of committing the same offence. Reasonable particulars must be disclosed but it is not essential that every legal element of the alleged defence be described. An information may be laid against more than one person. If it is required to bring more than one charge against an accused, separate informations must be delivered to the court.
(b)   As an alternative to the above, an applicant may appear in person before a magistrate or magistrate's clerk who then reduces an oral allegation to writing. Following the laying of an information in this manner the court decides whether or not to issue a summons requiring the accused to attend the court. Although often a relatively automatic process, this procedure is nevertheless judicial in nature and case law provides that the question whether or not to issue a summons must be considered judicially by the court concerned. If the summons is issued it is then served on the accused and the contents of the information are embodied in the summons. A single summons may cover more than one information, i.e. may contain several different charges. A summons may be served personally or by post on the accused.
(c)   An alternative to the above procedures applies where a defendant is not in custody at the time of laying the information, the police may proceed by arrest without warrant and charge. In these cases the police will have arrested the defendant and charged him at the police station. They will subsequently either release him on bail until the date specified in the charge for his appearance at court or bring him before the magistrates' court in custody, normally within 24 hours of charging. In these cases the charge sheet serves as the information and no separate summons is issued.

The charge sheet will be read over to the accused and he will be given a copy, whether he is released on bail or kept in custody by the police pending his first appearance. In the case of a release on bail the charge sheet will specify when he is to surrender to his bail at court.

Cases therefore commence in one of the ways previously described. The question of defects in, and amendments of, a *summons* will shortly be described. In the cases of *charges* these may similarly be amended, however it should be noted that if the case is going to be dealt with in the Crown Court, the form of the *indictment* which will constitute the final charges which an accused has to face at his Crown Court trial will not be drafted until the end of the committal proceedings. This is because it is open to the magistrates to commit on different charges from those originally brought by the prosecution and on any charge disclosed by the evidence they have heard. In a case of complexity the form of the indictment itself may need to be drafted by counsel before the Crown Court trial commences.

5.3 Classification of Offences and Choice of Court

For procedural purposes, criminal offences are classified into three categories, namely those triable only summarily; those triable only on indictment; and those triable 'either way'. Figure 5.1 on p. 58 gives examples of these.

5.3.1 PURELY SUMMARY OFFENCES

These offences are those that can only be tried by a magistrates' court. They include almost all motoring offences and the vast bulk of regulatory offences. Good examples are the offence of driving a vehicle without due care and attention under s. 3 of the Road Traffic Act 1988 and taking a conveyance under s. 12 of the Theft Act 1968. Although in principle these are triable only summarily, that is they can be dealt with only in the magistrates' court, they can be added as extra counts to an indictment where connected offences are being tried by the Crown Court, see **16.2.9**.

5.3.2 OFFENCES TRIABLE PURELY ON INDICTMENT

These are the more serious offences at the opposite end of the spectrum which can only be tried before a judge and jury in the Crown Court. They include murder, rape and robbery.

5.3.3 EITHER WAY OFFENCES

This group of offences consists of crimes which may be tried either in a magistrates' court or in the Crown Court. These are offences whose nature and seriousness is not necessarily indicated merely by the name of the offence. Thus, for example, 'theft' can cover a whole spectrum of behaviour from shoplifting a tin of peaches to stealing a Leonardo da Vinci.

If a defendant appears before a magistrates' court charged with an either way offence, there will be a *mode of trial* hearing. The practice of the courts varies as to when this takes place. It may sometimes happen at the very first appearance of the accused before the court, but more commonly will happen at an adjourned hearing. Before the mode of trial hearing, the court should be satisfied that the defendant is aware of the requirement on the prosecution under the Magistrates' Courts (Advanced Information) Rules 1985 to disclose certain advance information about the nature of the prosecution case. We shall return to this shortly.

5.4 Procedure at a Mode of Trial Hearing: ss. 18-21, Magistrates' Courts Act 1980

First, the charge is read to the defendant but he is not at this stage asked to plead to it. Then the prosecution and the defence each has an opportunity to make representations as to mode of trial. If the prosecution is being carried on by the Attorney-General, Solicitor-General or Director of Public Prosecutions and he applies for trial on indictment, the magistrates must comply with his wishes. In other cases however it will usually be the case that the prosecution in a marginal matter will for considerations of cost and speed favour the magistrates' court. Their representations will often consist of no more than saying something along the lines of 'there seems nothing special about this case to warrant the time of the Crown Court and it would appear that the magistrates' sentencing powers are adequate'. The prosecution will take the opportunity to explain to the court the background features

COMMENCEMENT OF PROCEEDINGS AND MODE OF TRIAL

Type of Offence	Triable only on Indictment	Triable Either Way	Triable only Summarily
1. Offences against the person	Murder Manslaughter Attempt to procure an abortion Causing grievous bodily harm with intent	Inflicting grievous bodily harm Unlawful wounding Assault occasioning actual bodily harm Assault with intent to resist arrest	Common assault Assault on a police constable in the execution of his duty
2. Sexual offences	Rape: Intercourse with a girl under 13 Buggery Incest	Unlawful sexual intercourse with a girl under 16 Indecent assault Living on the earnings of a prostitute	Soliciting
3. Theft Act offences	Robbery Aggravated burglary Blackmail Assault with intent to rob Burglary comprising commission of, or intention to commit, an offence only triable on indictment Burglary of a dwelling with threats to occupants	All Theft Act offences not being in the other two categories	Taking a motor vehicle without consent Taking a pedal cycle without consent
4. Criminal damage	Damage or arson with intent to endanger life	Damage where the value involved is over £2,000	Damage where the value involved is less than £2,000
5. Road traffic	Causing death by dangerous driving	Dangerous driving	Most other traffic offences, e.g: Speeding Failing to report an accident Driving while disqualified Driving without insurance Drunk in charge of a motor vehicle Failing to stop at a red traffic light
6. Miscellaneous	Perjury Attempt to pervert the course of justice Possessing a fire arm with intent to endanger life Using a firearm to resist arrest Carrying a firearm to commit an indictable offence Collecting, communicating, etc. information intended to be useful to an enemy Riot	Making false statements on oath not being in judicial proceedings Carrying a loaded firearm in a public place Shortening a shot gun Having an offensive weapon in a public place Using, communicating, etc. information entrusted in confidence to a person holding office under the Crown Violent disorder Affray Stirring up racial hatred All offences under the Forgery & Counterfeiting Act 1981 Offences under Misuse of Drugs Act 1971	Interference with vehicles Being drunk and disorderly Obstructing police Using threatening words or behaviour Dropping litter Failure to pay TV licence All offences under Factories Act 1961

Figure 5.1

of the case where the charge itself does not make it apparent, e.g., where the charge does not describe the seriousness of the assault or the value of the goods.

The defence will have already decided which mode of trial they prefer and will now present their arguments. For example, if the prosecution are contending that there is something very serious about the matter so that it should be tried in the Crown Court, then the defence may need to meet this by suggesting to the magistrates that it is less serious than it may appear and that the magistrates' sentencing powers are adequate should they convict. If the defence have already decided to ask for trial at the Crown Court, they will then make their representations as to why this should be so. A number of factors which might make the Crown Court preferable are suggested below.

Thereafter, the magistrates consider the matter and, by s. 19 of the Magistrates' Courts Act 1980, they have to take into account the following:

(a)   the nature of the case;
(b)   whether the offence is of a serious character; and
(c)   whether the punishment which a magistrates' court would have power to inflict for it would be adequate;
(d)   any other circumstances which make the case more suitable for one method of trial rather than the other.

The court should also take into account the further considerations set out in *Practice Direction (Mode of Trial: Guidelines)* [1990] 1 WLR 1439 (often referred to as the 'National Mode of Trial Guidelines'). These further considerations are that:

(a)   The court should never make a decision on the grounds of convenience or expedition.
(b)   The court should assume for the purpose of deciding mode of trial that the prosecution version of the facts is correct.
(c)   Where cases involve complex questions of fact or difficult questions of law the court should generally consider committal to the Crown Court for trial.
(d)   In considering whether its sentencing powers are sufficient and whether the offence is of serious character, the court should have regard to the likely sentence for the defendant on the basis that he will be convicted eventually and that he is at present of good character. In this connection they should look at specific features of the offence charged which might make it more serious than the run-of-the-mill offences.

A number of named offences are described in the Mode of Trial Guidelines and relevant aggravating factors described in respect of each. The presence of such a factor might make them appropriate in principle for committal to the Crown Court. So, for example, in the case of a charge of theft the fact that it was allegedly committed in breach of trust, i.e. by a person in authority, or has been committed or disguised in a sophisticated manner, or is committed by an organised gang, or the victim is particularly vulnerable, e.g., the elderly or infirm, or the property has not been recovered and is of high value may justify committal to the Crown Court. In the case of driving offences the fact that dangerous driving is alleged to have occurred and involved, for example, grossly excessive speeds or racing on a public road or that alcohol or drugs have contributed to it would be exacerbating features. In these kind of cases therefore magistrates should look closely at the possible eventual sentence as a factor in their decision about mode of trial.

At this stage the court does not have the defendant's previous convictions before it and therefore it must act on the basis that it is dealing with a person who is of previous good character. The reason for this is that in principle the magistrates may proceed from the mode of trial hearing to the trial of the offence itself and they should not of course be aware of any criminal record of the accused. In fact, more commonly, there will be an adjournment whatever they decide, in one case for summary trial and in the other for committal proceedings. The reason for this need to adjourn is simply the saving of time and costs. The prosecution would be foolish to call their witnesses to court in the expectation of summary trial if it might in fact be the case that the accused will elect trial on indictment, in which case he might also be willing to accept short form committal proceedings under s. 6(2) of the Magistrates' Courts Act 1980.

The magistrates retire if necessary and return to announce their decision. If the magistrates consider that trial on indictment is more appropriate, the accused is then told of their decision and committal proceedings take place, either then or more probably at some later date. The accused has no choice in the matter. The question of bail may arise again at this stage if the accused has hitherto been refused bail or if some new matter has arisen which leads to the police now objecting to bail (e.g., it is suggested he has tried to intimidate a prosecution witness in the interim).

If the court decides that summary trial is more suitable, then there is an obligation on the clerk of the court to give the defendant certain information. The clerk must carefully explain to the defendant personally (even if he is legally represented) that he has a choice as to which court he may be tried in but that, if he does consent to summary trial, is found guilty by the magistrates and, then in the light of certain factors, the magistrates consider that greater punishment should be imposed than they have power to inflict, they may commit him to the Crown Court to be sentenced. In other words, the accused is being told that, if his only reason for preferring the magistrates' court is his knowledge that the maximum sentence that they can normally inflict is six months' imprisonment for any one offence, then he need not think that is conclusive. If he is convicted, the magistrates may still after further consideration commit him to the Crown Court for sentence and there he may receive the maximum which the Crown Court is empowered to impose. This is by virtue of s. 38, Magistrates' Courts Act 1980 as inserted by s. 25, Criminal Justice Act 1991. The procedure on committal for sentence after summary trial is described at **15.8**.

Thereafter, the accused is asked where he wants to be tried and he has a final say. He may say that he prefers to be tried in the Crown Court or that he is content to accept magistrates' court trial.

Why bother making representations to the magistrates if the accused has already made up his mind to 'overrule' the magistrates, no matter what, and opt for Crown Court trial? Frankly, many consider that there is little point in making detailed submissions in favour of Crown Court trial where the accused has already decided (on legal advice) to opt for Crown Court trial whatever the magistrates' preliminary decision is. However, there is one advantage in doing so. If the case does go to the Crown Court, let us say on a relatively trivial shoplifting charges, and one has successfully managed to persuade the magistrates themselves to choose that as the more appropriate forum (let us say because of some alleged difficulty in a matter of evidence which can be more satisfactorily dealt with before the higher court) then if the accused is convicted in the Crown Court the record will reveal that it was the magistrates themselves who decided to send the case there. The accused will not then be subject to any criticism.

Suppose, however, that one had not tried, or, having tried, had failed to persuade the magistrates themselves to send the case to the Crown Court for trial and had in fact 'overruled' the magistrates' preliminary decision to try the case themselves. In those circumstances, the Crown Court judge may feel that it was wrong for the accused to overrule the magistrates' decision and involve the higher court's time in a trivial matter. Although it is certainly wrong in principle for him to impose a greater *sentence* to take into account his disapproval of this course of action, he is perfectly entitled to make the order which he imposes in respect of *costs* reflect his view of the waste of time of the higher court. He will therefore probably impose a higher costs order than he would otherwise have done.

Section 25 of the Magistrates' Courts Act 1980 allows the court to change from summary trial to committal proceedings and vice versa. This may either be on its own motion or on the application of either party. What was a summary trial may become commital proceedings at any time before the close of the prosecution case. The most common example is likely to be, however, where the accused having previously consented to summary trial, perhaps on an occasion when he was unrepresented, now in the light of legal advice wishes to elect in favour of trial on indictment. In such a case the magistrates have a wide discretion as to whether or not to permit the change of election for trial. It will only very occasionally arise that after hearing prosecution evidence in a summary trial the nature of the offence seems to take on a greater seriousness than formerly, so as to merit the magistrates wishing of their own motion to send the case to the Crown Court. This should only happen rarely because of the opportunity which the prosecution had at the outset to stress factors which made the offence more suitable for trial on indictment.

An accused who has elected trial on indictment may also wish to change his election. The magistrates may permit this change, if proper. Again, it is more likely to occur before any kind of hearing has started given that the vast majority of committal proceedings are in the form prescribed by s. 6(2) of the Magistrates' Courts Act 1980, i.e. short form committals. An example might be where an accused now wishes to change his plea to guilty and would naturally wish to stay in the magistrates' court with its lesser sentencing powers. It is important to remember that a mode of trial hearing will still be necessary in the case of an either way offence even though the defendant intends from the outset to plead guilty.

5.4.1 MORE THAN ONE ACCUSED

If there is more than one accused then the previous practice under which where any of them opted for trial in the Crown Court that election bound the rest is now not followed. In such a situation the magistrates are entitled to take into account the wishes of each co-accused. In *R v Brentwood Justices ex parte Nicholls* [1992] 1 AC 1 the House of Lords held that the court need not necessarily be influenced by the fact that one of the accused was electing Crown Court trial, and might still try summarily any accused who elected summary trial. The reason for this is that the proper interpretation of s. 20(3) of the 1980 Act gives the right of election to each accused individually.

5.5 Choice of Court

We have so far described the procedure by which the magistrates' court makes a preliminary decision as to which court will try the case. As we have seen, in cases of offences triable either way, the accused is always in a position to ensure that he has jury trial, either by persuading the magistrates to choose trial on indictment themselves or by overruling their preliminary decision against it. We will now consider the factors which his solicitor will take into account in advising an accused on choice of court.

5.5.1 FACTORS IN FAVOUR OF THE CROWN COURT

5.5.1.1 Acquittal rate

Despite somewhat inconclusive statistical evidence and local variations there is no doubt that many lawyers feel that in certain kinds of case the accused stands a much better chance of acquittal from a jury than in a magistrates' court. The magistrates are believed to become 'case hardened' in certain types of case. An example is shoplifting where the likely defence is that the accused forgot to pay or put the object into the wrong basket. Magistrates will have heard such defences on dozens of occasions and may generally be disinclined to believe them because the frequency with which they are advanced appears to make them improbable in any individual case. A jury is very likely to be hearing such a defence for the first time and to take the judge's direction on 'proof beyond reasonable doubt' more to heart when considering the case. Juries are thus more open minded (or perhaps more naive!) and, with this kind of offence anyway, the accused would generally seem to have a better chance before a jury.

It is also sometimes suggested that, particularly in some locations, magistrates have a belief in the invariable truthfulness of policemen which the ordinary layman no longer has and therefore that on a jury of 12 people, there are likely to be a higher proportion of sceptics about police evidence.

Allied to these points there is also the undoubted factor that 'sympathy' verdicts are not impossible. This means a verdict based on the personalities involved, on the jury's regard for the personal circumstances of the accused, or on some other legally irrelevant matter. An example is generally thought to be the trial of the civil servant Clive Ponting on Official Secrets Act charges in 1986 where, in the face of a clear direction from the judge on the issues, the jury chose to acquit the accused. In such cases a feeling that the accused has been oppressively treated by the State, be it the police or even sometimes the harsh treatment an accused may have received when testifying from prosecuting counsel, may contribute to this possibility.

5.5.1.2 Matters of law or evidence

In a case which involves difficult legal points, many lawyers doubt whether magistrates, even with the expert assistance of a clerk, really do grasp the legal niceties involved. There are no such problems in the Crown Court where the judge will certainly be capable of grasping them. More important still is the question of evidence. As we shall discuss below at **7.1** the device of having a judge and jury with separate functions in relation to evidence proves to be a very happy one in the common law system. Thus, the fact that matters of admissibility are generally dealt with by the judge with the jury excluded from court means that the jury never hear evidence which is excluded.

In the magistrates' court, there is unfortunately no equivalent to this and one needs to make submissions about admissibility which inevitably involve discussing, describing or hearing the evidence in question in front of the very magistrates whose minds may well be affected by it even if they do rule in favour of exclusion.

There are other cases where in the magistrates' court matters of evidence have to be dealt with in what is, at best, a clumsy manner. Applications to cross-examine the accused on his criminal record under s. 1(f)(ii) of the Criminal Evidence Act 1898 (see **13.3.3.2**) are necessarily difficult. In the Crown Court, the judge might, having considered the application in the absence of the jury, refuse it, or perhaps limit cross-examination to certain parts of the accused's record. In the magistrates' court, merely to make the application for leave to cross-examine under s. 1(f)(ii) tells the magistrates that the accused does have a record. There can be no equivalent of letting the prosecution cross-examine on only part of the record, since the magistrates themselves will need to see the record to rule on any such application.

Likewise, the fact that directions about evidence are given to the jury in open court, e.g., on corroboration, etc., must inevitably be more favourable to the accused than the somewhat bodged counterpart in the magistrates' court where the defence advocate in effect tells the magistrates what rules of evidence they ought to apply and how, and hopes that his submission is understood and remembered and perhaps repeated by the magistrates' clerk.

These procedural distinctions together constitute most significant factors favouring Crown Court trial in any case where a matter of evidence arises.

5.5.1.3 Knowing the prosecution case in advance

Formerly, this was perhaps the greatest factor in favour of the Crown Court, namely that the committal proceedings meant that the prosecution had to disclose their evidence before trial. In the magistrates' court, it was sometimes possible if one had a reasonable relationship with the prosecuting solicitor to persuade him to let one look at the prosecution statements in advance, but this would inevitably be only shortly before the trial and the position was considered much less satisfactory.

Now, however, this has been resolved by the bringing into force of the Magistrates' Courts (Advance Information) Rules 1985. Before the court considers the mode of trial, the defendant or his representative may request that the prosecution furnishes him with advance information and on receipt of such request, the prosecution shall, as soon as practicable, furnish either:

(a) a copy of those parts of every written statement which contains information as to the facts and matters which the prosecution propose to adduce in evidence; or

(b) a summary of such facts and matters.

In fact, since it is obviously quicker and more convenient to send a simple photostat of the statements, this will often be what the prosecution do, rather than separately preparing a summary of the relevant matters. If only a summary is provided then it can later be a source of disputes, in that it would be open to the defendant to suggest that vital matters had been omitted from the summary. It seems, however, that, despite the extra work involved, in many areas of the country Crown prosecutors supply summaries, and brief ones at that, rather than copies of their witness statements. In any event, in every case of an offence triable either way, whether proceeding in a magistrates' court or the Crown Court, there will now be prior disclosure of the prosecution case. However, although this is now a neutral feature, it does lead to another matter which is in favour of the Crown Court, namely committal proceedings.

5.5.1.4 Committal proceedings

Committal proceedings in essence give one two bites at the cherry in that one might get a weak prosecution case thrown out at an early stage. It will be seen in due course when we discuss committal proceedings that committals can be either *short form*, where the accused consents to being committed for trial, or *long form*, which involves a full examination of parts (or perhaps the whole) of the prosecution evidence. In this latter case, prosecution witnesses are called and will give their evidence just as in a trial proper and will be subject to cross-examination. To see the impression which prosecution witnesses make on the court can often be invaluable in helping to plan a strategy for the Crown Court trial and there is also the possibility of getting the case dismissed at that early stage. A discussion of the tactics involved in conducting a long form committal and of the possible advantages to be gained from cross-examining prosecution witnesses fully, will be considered in **Chapter 16**. In an appropriate case, however, this is an important factor in favour of trial on indictment.

5.5.1.5 Marginal factors

The one certain feature about trial on indictment is that it will take a good deal longer to happen. Accordingly, in some cases there may be some use to which the delay can be put. The best example would be where some considerable time was necessary perhaps to trace witnesses or explore some difficult avenue of evidence. It may also be easier to obtain expert evidence if there is a lengthy delay, especially in the case of psychiatric evidence. A delay could also be useful with matters relevant to mitigation, although in that case one would be anticipating the conviction of the accused. For example, if the accused can put the delay to some use in a way which changes the pattern of his life for the better, such as getting married, settling down, or acquiring a job after a lengthy period of unemployment, those things would be useful at the stage of mitigation.

5.5.2 FACTORS IN FAVOUR OF THE MAGISTRATES' COURT

5.5.2.1 Guilty plea

If the defendant firmly intends to plead guilty then unless he can use the delay inherent in Crown Court trial to provide mitigating factors for himself, the lesser sentencing powers of magistrates would normally be a conclusive factor in their favour.

5.5.2.2 Speed

A magistrates' court trial will come on significantly faster than a Crown Court trial. If the accused is nervous, or in custody, this may be a vital factor in favour of the former.

5.5.2.3 Stress

There can be no doubt that the actual trial itself is a greater ordeal in the Crown Court. Not only is it likely that there will be many more people present in court, but the atmosphere, the greater deference accorded to the Crown Court judge, the wigs and gowns, and the feeling that the accused is being constantly scrutinised by the 12 jurors, the judge and the prosecuting counsel, will all put a greater stress on the accused. This is something that should not be dismissed lightly in the case of an accused who is in any way vulnerable.

5.5.2.4   Publicity

It is difficult to generalise about this. The press will have more representatives at a busy Crown Court centre but all of these may be in the same court where something particularly newsworthy is happening. Whether the press will be present in the smaller courts where individuals are being tried on, say, minor theft charges is doubtful. A local worthy, e.g., a local councillor or clergyman is likely to be regarded as newsworthy and may be lucky to escape the attention of the press wherever he is tried.

It is fair to say that the press take less interest in magistrates' courts; however, much will depend on the locality. If it is a small country town with the magistrates' court only sitting two days a week, the press, if there is a local newspaper, will generally have a representative present throughout every case. It is not unusual, for example, to see in the local press headlines such as 'Barchester Man's Day of Shame' and on reading the report find that it concerns only a motoring offence. In a major conurbation, however, there may well be more chance of escaping any press report at all in the magistrates' court.

5.5.2.5   Sentence

Magistrates have limited sentencing powers. In principle, they can only sentence a person to a maximum of six months' imprisonment for one offence and a maximum of 12 months for any number of offences. Their powers to fine are also limited to £5,000 for each offence, except those for which there is some different statutory maximum. However, it must be noted that if, after trying an either way offence summarily and convicting, they conclude that their sentencing powers are inadequate in view of what they have heard about other offences and the accused's criminal record, they do then have the power to commit the accused for sentence to the Crown Court, which may impose any sentence authorised by law for the offence. Therefore, sentence would only make a difference where the accused concluded that he might receive a sentence which would be longer than six months in prison, but not so much longer that the magistrates would be minded to commit him to the Crown Court. In other words, he is gambling on the magistrates not doing the latter.

It must be said that much will depend on one's knowledge of the bench of magistrates and local Crown Court judges. Certainly any advocate in the Crown Court can tell you of judges who are notoriously 'hard' or 'soft' but there is no controlling which judge will deal with which case and there must be many cases where it would be preferable to be dealt with by a 'soft' judge in the Crown Court, rather than a 'hard' local bench of magistrates. A Crown Court judge dealing with a relatively trivial offence may anyway prove more lenient than magistrates, if only because his usual daily diet involves considerably more serious crime.

5.5.2.6   Cost

Trial in the Crown Court will inevitably be more expensive, perhaps many times so, than summary trial. For a private-paying client this may be a major factor. Even for a legally aided client this is not a negligible matter, bearing in mind his contribution towards the costs of his case and a possible costs order in favour of the prosecution on conviction. Whilst such a costs order rarely amounts to the realistic costs of the prosecution it will naturally be larger in the Crown Court than in the magistrates' court.

5.6   Special Procedure in Criminal Damage Cases

There is a unique procedure in cases of alleged criminal damage. Somewhat anomalously, any charge of theft is triable either way and thus an accused may elect Crown Court trial notwithstanding that only a small amount is involved. The rationale of this is said to be that a charge of theft, carrying as it does an element of dishonesty, is of such crucial importance to a person's reputation that he is entitled to be dealt with by a jury of his peers. Criminal damage, notwithstanding that much larger amounts may be involved, and that the mental attitude of the offender may be no less blameworthy, is treated differently. The legislature apparently believes that wilful vandalism for its own sake of something worth £1,000 in some sense carries less of a stigma than shoplifting a tin of peaches. Accordingly, by s. 22, Magistrates' Courts Act 1980, there is a special provision which is as follows:

(a) Where an accused is charged with criminal damage contrary to s. 1(1), Criminal Damage Act 1971 or attempts to commit such offences, then unless the offence involves damage or attempted damage *by fire*, the magistrates must hear any representations made by the prosecution or the defence about the value of the goods involved in the offence. Documentary evidence, e.g., about repairs, may be produced.

(b) If the value involved is then considered to be £2,000 or less, the magistrates treat the case as if it were triable only summarily and the accused has no right to a trial on indictment.

(c) If the value involved is clearly over £2,000 the case is dealt with like any other either way offence and there is a mode of trial hearing.

(d) If the case is dealt with as purely summary, then the maximum sentence available to the magistrates is three months' imprisonment or a £2,500 fine. The magistrates then have no power to commit for sentence to the Crown Court under s. 38 of the 1980 Act.

(e) If the case, notwithstanding being dealt with as an either way offence, is tried summarily, the maximum sentence is six months' imprisonment and a £5,000 fine and the magistrates may, in those circumstances, commit for sentence under s. 38.

(f) If it is unclear whether the value of the goods involved is more or less than £2,000, the clerk of the court should ask the accused for his consent to summary trial. If he does consent to summary trial and is then convicted, the maximum penalty is £2,500 and three months' imprisonment and he cannot be committed for sentence under s. 38.

SIX

BAIL

6.1   Introduction

Bail is the release of a person subject to a duty to surrender to custody in the future. We have already briefly considered the nature of 'police bail', that is when the police make the decision to release from custody either in the course of their enquiries with a duty to report back to the police station at some subsequent time or after charging. When the question of bail arises in that context, the time for the suspect or accused to surrender to custody is fixed by the police either, in the former case, telling him when to return to the police station, or in the latter, specifying on the charge sheet the date on which the case will first come before the magistrates' court. The provisions of the Bail Act 1976 which we are about to consider in detail do not apply strictly in those situations, although the matters which the police will take into account when deciding whether to release a suspect who has been charged on bail, will largely correspond to the provisions of the 1976 Act.

On occasions when magistrates grant bail, they will specify the date of the next hearing, with the exception of the occasion when they commit an accused for trial in the Crown Court. The date of trial in the Crown Court is not fixed by the magistrates and thus bail is, so to speak, open-ended and the duty to surrender to custody comes about when the accused is notified of the date for the commencement of the Crown Court trial.

The question of bail therefore arises from time to time in the magistrates' court when they adjourn proceedings, either when the case is adjourned to be heard on some later date or when the case is part heard and is adjourned overnight or for a longer period, even, in principle, over the lunch adjournment.

Until the coming into force of the Bail Act 1976, it was common practice to grant an accused bail 'on his own recognisance'. This was a fixed sum of money which the accused did not have to provide at the time of granting bail but which, should he fail subsequently to surrender to custody would be forfeited. This practice has been abolished and in its place s. 6 of the Bail Act 1976 provides that 'a defendant who fails without reasonable cause to surrender to custody is guilty of the offence of absconding'. The burden of proving reasonable cause lies on the defendant. It is easy to imagine things which might give a defendant reasonable cause to fail to appear on the date to which he had been bailed, for instance, sudden serious illness or being involved in an accident on the way to court. Absconding is therefore now a separate offence which may lead to punishment quite separately from any imposed in respect of the charge on which the offender is due to stand trial.

The penalty on summary conviction is three months' imprisonment and/or a fine up to £2,000. In the Crown Court the offence is punishable as a criminal contempt with an unlimited fine and/or up to 12 months' imprisonment. If a defendant fails to surrender to bail the court may (and usually will) issue a warrant for his arrest.

6.2   The Right to Bail under s. 4, Bail Act 1976

Section 4 of the 1976 Act gives an accused person what might be described as a prima facie right to bail. However, it must be remembered that this section does not apply at every stage of the criminal process. It does not apply in particular where:

(a)   the custody officer has to consider the question of granting a person bail at a police station after he has been charged; or

(b)   the magistrates, having convicted a person, commit him to the Crown Court for sentence; or

(c)   a person has been convicted by the magistrates and wishes to appeal to the Crown Court against either conviction or sentence.

Although s. 4 does not apply in any of these situations, the custody officer or court will consider the nature of the situation and whether on the broad common-sense criteria contained in the Act generally, it seems appropriate to grant bail. Thus, if there is in reality little risk of the defendant absconding, offending further, or interfering with the course of justice, and he has a fixed address, there may be little likelihood in any of those situations that the accused would actually be refused bail. The point is, however, that he is not granted the protection of s. 4 and has no prima facie *right* to bail.

In essence the court has the prima facie obligation to grant bail to all accused who do not fall within any of the three excluded categories above. In other words, the court has to consider the question of bail and the prima facie right to it:

(a)   for all defendants at all stages of the criminal process up to conviction;

(b)   even after conviction, where the court adjourns the case for reports or enquiries; or

(c)   in sundry other circumstances, in particular where an accused is brought before a magistrates' court for breach of a probation or community service order.

6.2.1   EXCEPTIONS TO s. 4, BAIL ACT 1976

6.2.1.1   An offence punishable with imprisonment

To the prima facie right contained in s. 4 of the 1976 Act, there are naturally exceptions. The exceptions we shall consider are those contained in part I of sch. 1 to the 1976 Act. This provides that where an accused is charged with an offence which is punishable with imprisonment, he need not be granted bail if any of the following circumstances apply, namely:

(a)   the court is satisfied that there are substantial grounds for believing that if released on bail he would:

(i)   fail to surrender to custody; or

(ii)   commit an offence while on bail; or

(iii)   interfere with witnesses or otherwise obstruct the course of justice, whether in relation to himself or some other person;

(b)   the court is satisfied that he should be kept in custody for his own protection or, if he is a juvenile, for his own welfare;

(c)   he is already serving a custodial sentence for some other reason;

(d)   the court is satisfied that it has not been practicable to obtain sufficient information for the purpose of taking the decisions required by the 1976 Act for want of time since the commencement of proceedings against him;

(e)   having been released on bail in connection with the proceedings for the same offence, he has been arrested for absconding;

(f)   where the case has been adjourned for enquiries or a report, it appears to the court that it would be impracticable to complete the enquiries or make the report without keeping the defendant in custody.

6.2.1.2 An offence not punishable with imprisonment

Those are the exceptions which apply where an accused is charged with an offence *punishable with imprisonment*. Where the offence is one which is *not punishable with imprisonment* (e.g., careless driving) then different conditions apply and these are contained in part II of sch. 1 to the 1976 Act. These provide that a defendant need not be granted bail if:

(a) it appears to the court that having been previously granted bail in criminal proceedings, he has failed to surrender to custody in accordance with his obligations under the grant of bail and the court believes, in view of that failure, that the defendant if released on bail would fail to surrender to custody;

(b) the court is satisfied that he should be kept in custody for his own protection or, if he is a child or young person, for his own welfare;

(c) he is already in custody in pursuance of the sentence of any court;

(d) having been released on bail in connection with proceedings for the present offence, he has been arrested already for absconding.

To take first the latter cases of the refusal to grant bail in the case of a non-imprisonable offence. It is apparent that these are not of great practical importance. They would for example apply in the case of someone charged with careless driving who persistently failed to appear before the court. We shall now consider the matter of an application to the magistrates' court for bail in the case of someone charged with an imprisonable offence.

6.2.1.3 Application for bail in respect of an imprisonable offence

The basic requirement is self-explanatory. The phrase 'substantial grounds for believing that' implies that the court must satisfy itself to a reasonably high standard of proof. Referring back to the grounds listed in **6.2.1.1**:

(a) The three subdivisions of the first ground ((i), (ii) and (iii)) are self-explanatory. They are by far the most important in practice.

(b) The ground of 'custody for his own protection' might apply to the alleged perpetrator of some highly unpopular kind of offence, for example a sexual attack on a young child where the alleged offender would return to live in the same locality as the victim's parents or relatives.

(c) This a matter of common sense. If someone is already in custody in respect of some other offence when the fact of his alleged guilt of the present offence first comes to light so that he is actually charged while still in custody, it would obviously be ridiculous if the prima facie right to bail in the Bail Act 1976 could override the fact that he is already legitimately in custody.

(d) The ground that there has not yet been time to obtain the necessary information is one relied on very frequently by the police. It will be remembered that when the accused is produced before the court, he may well have been in police hands for only a matter of hours. The police will often contend in such circumstances that the kind of information necessary to enable the magistrates to reach an informed conclusion when considering the grant of bail is not as yet available until further enquiries are made.

(e) On ground (e) it is a matter of the defendant being rearrested after already having absconded in the present proceedings in which case naturally there would be no further presumption of bail as such, though it is by no means impossible on some proper explanation being given for the failure to surrender to custody (e.g., sudden illness) for further bail to be granted.

(f) This ground concerns the case where proceedings have been adjourned for enquiries but it may be clear that it will be difficult to complete these enquiries because of the nature of the accused. For example, it might be suggested that one cannot complete a psychiatric report upon the accused because it is unlikely that he will voluntarily attend at a hospital to be psychiatrically examined. He may, therefore, be remanded in custody for the purpose of a medical report being prepared. Remands in custody for reports however, may not be for a period exceeding three weeks.

6.2.1.4   The factors to be considered

In considering whether or not the grounds for refusing bail apply, one must have regard to the following matters which are contained in para. 9 of part I of sch. 1 to the 1976 Act. This provides that in taking decisions (i.e. whether or not to grant bail) under the 1976 Act, the court shall have regard to such of the following considerations as appear relevant:

(a) the nature and seriousness of the offence and the probable method of dealing with the defendant for it;

(b) the character, antecedents, associations and community ties of the defendant;

(c) the defendant's record in respect of the fulfilment of his obligations under previous grants of bail (if any) in criminal proceedings;

(d) except in the case of a defendant whose case is adjourned for enquiries or a report, the strength of the evidence of his having committed the offence;

(e) any other matters which appear to be relevant.

6.3   Procedure for Bail Application

It is now appropriate to consider the procedure by which the bail application is made on the first or any subsequent appearance in the magistrates' court.

Generally, the accused will already be in custody, having been arrested, and will be produced from the police station. He is brought before the court and the court will first need to consider the future course of the proceedings. Local practice varies, but in some courts hardly anything other than the question of bail is dealt with on a first appearance. Sometimes, however, a defendant who is pleading guilty in a straightforward case may be dealt with on first appearance.

Let us assume, however, that the defendant is proposing to plead not guilty. The question of an adjournment inevitably arises since contested trials never proceed on first appearance, if only for the reason that the prosecution will not yet be prepared or have their witnesses available. Where the court adjourns a matter it will *remand* the defendant. 'Remand' merely means 'specify whether the accused is to be on bail or in custody at this stage'.

The question of bail must be considered, therefore, in the light of the 1976 Act. The court is granted an inquisitorial function by the Act so that it ought really to enquire as to whether bail is appropriate in every case. However, if the police themselves do not object to bail, it is highly unlikely that the magistrates will raise objections or require to hear any more about the matter. In that case, only a formal application for bail needs to be made. If there are objections to bail, however, the court will go on to consider them. The course of the proceedings will then be as follows:

(a) The prosecution will put forward their objections. Practice tends to vary from court to court and from case to case. Sometimes the Crown Prosecutor will put forward the nature of the objections to bail; sometimes the officer in charge of the case goes into the witness box and gives evidence concerning the question. The rules of evidence do not apply. Indeed, as the criteria to be considered when assessing the question of bail make clear, the accused's criminal record is highly relevant to the question of the grant of bail and therefore will become known to the magistrates at this stage. Quite apart from that, however, much of the police officer's evidence will amount to hearsay (e.g., 'I was told by the victim that . . .'). Moreover, much of the officer's evidence may be merely speculative. A common objection to bail is that the police are investigating other matters in which they suspect the accused might be involved. Clearly, this is highly prejudicial to the accused's prospect of obtaining bail.

(b) Although the rules of evidence do not apply, some attempt may then be made to cross-examine the officer. It is, naturally, difficult to cross-examine effectively about matters to do with other enquiries because the officer may legitimately refuse to answer (for instance because it may alert the defendant and his associates to the course of those further enquiries).

(c) The accused's advocate then makes his application for bail. This ought to be in the form of a considered response to the precise objections put forward by the prosecution. There is prima facie no need to respond to potential grounds for objection which the prosecution have not relied upon, although it is often as well for the sake of clarity in the minds of the magistrates to just pass through other grounds for objection if only to dismiss them.

6.3.1 CONTENTS OF BAIL APPLICATION

The contents of the bail application will mainly consist of a discussion of the objections in the light of the considerations referred to in para. 9 of part I of sch. 1 to the 1976 Act. It is perhaps now as well to consider these points individually.

6.3.1.1 Nature and seriousness of the offence and the probable method of dealing with the defendant for it

In fact, there is no rule as such that a defendant charged with very serious offences cannot have bail. Bail on a murder charge is far from unknown. However, a new para. 9A was inserted into Part I of sch. 1 to the 1976 Act by the Criminal Justice Act 1988; this requires a court granting bail to an accused charged inter alia with murder, manslaughter or rape, or attempts to commit those crimes, to give reasons for granting bail and cause those reasons to be entered into the record of court proceedings.

The criterion is simply one of common sense. If it is inevitable that the accused, if convicted, is going to receive a custodial sentence, perhaps a very lengthy one, then clearly, as a matter of human nature, the temptation to abscond, or perhaps to commit further crimes whilst at liberty with the object of providing for his dependants during the period of custody, will be stronger than in the case of someone charged with a relatively trivial crime.

The discussion of the probable method of dealing with the defendant may involve the defending advocate speculating (somewhat optimistically on occasion) that, despite an apparently serious criminal record, it is by no means sure that the defendant will receive a custodial sentence even if convicted because of mitigating factors to do with the offender's personal circumstances or the sentencing provisions of the Criminal Justice Act 1991 discussed below at **18.5**.

6.3.1.2 Character, antecedents, associations and community ties

'Character' means in this sense, criminal record. 'Antecedents' means the accused's history and background, e.g., upbringing, education, job record and so on.

'Associations' means the type of person with whom he mixes. It may well be contended by the prosecution, for example, that the accused is a member of a gang of professional criminals and habitually mixes with them. The accused's address may indicate this to magistrates with local knowledge in some cases. The method of meeting this particular objection, with others, will be referred to below.

'Community ties' means matters which tend to cement the accused to his present place in terms of family circumstances and location. It is self-evident that a family man with a mortgage and a regular job is considerably less likely to think it is worthwhile uprooting and going 'on the run' than a casual worker living in a bedsitter. Of course, even this is not conclusive and much will depend upon the intermixing of the various criteria. For example, it may be suspected that even a family man with a mortgage and job may well 'abscond' if the offence with which he is charged is serious enough.

6.3.1.3 The accused's record if previously granted bail

If the accused has not been charged with any offence before, this is something which will be to his credit under other criteria but is of no help on this one. If he has committed a number of previous criminal offences and always received bail and always turned up, this provides a reasonably powerful argument for bail. Again the intermix with other matters must be considered. If he has indeed had bail on previous occasions, then clearly he is likely to have a bad criminal record. This may, in its turn, make it more likely that he receives a substantial custodial sentence this time and thus will weaken his argument on the objection to do with the probable method of dealing with him for the offence.

6.3.1.4 The strength of the evidence

This is naturally extremely hard to assess at such an early stage in the proceedings. The prosecution themselves will say in general terms that they have substantial evidence, but will certainly not be called upon to name their witnesses or give the gist of what the witnesses will say. Any kind of forensic evidence will probably not be available at the stage of a first bail application, e.g., the results of fingerprinting or blood sample tests. All one can do is respond in general terms to whatever evidence is alleged to exist by the prosecution by saying, for example, that the admissibility of an alleged confession is strongly disputed, or that the case turns on weak identification evidence.

6.4 Conditions of Bail

Although a defendant prima facie has a right to bail, and to unconditional bail at that, the court may, where it considers it appropriate, impose conditions. These conditions are of three kinds, namely:

(a) sureties;
(b) security by the accused;
(c) miscellaneous conditions.

By s. 3(6) of the 1976 Act a defendant may be required by a court to comply with such requirements as appear to the court to be necessary to secure that he:

(a) surrenders to custody;
(b) does not commit an offence while on bail;
(c) does not interfere with witnesses or otherwise obstruct the course of justice;
(d) makes himself available for the purpose of enabling enquiries or a report to be made to assist the court in dealing with him for the offence.

In other words, the court may not impose conditions merely because it has some general sense of unease about the grant of bail. It must only impose conditions specifically tailored to coping with the problems it foresees in the grant of what would otherwise be unconditional bail. We shall now consider the nature of conditions.

6.4.1 SURETIES

A surety is a person who enters into a recognisance to ensure that the accused appears at court. Accordingly, if the accused does fail to appear, the surety is liable to have his recognisance *estreated* (i.e. forfeited). In other words, a surety is someone who guarantees the accused's appearance in court in a specified sum of money (which does not have to be provided in advance). If the person does not surrender to custody, then prima facie the amount of money is forfeited to the court. The surety, therefore, has every interest in ensuring first that he does not undertake his duties lightly and secondly that he does what he can to ensure that the person does appear at court.

The court does have a discretion where the accused does not appear as to whether or not to order forfeiture of the sum. The court will generally require to be satisfied that the surety has exercised extreme diligence in the matter before the sum will not be ordered to be forfeited; the surety might escape forfeiture by keeping a very close watch on the accused so as to assist the police by notifying them immediately should there be any hint of the accused absconding.

Strictly speaking a surety should only be asked for in order to meet the risk of absconding. It is improper for a surety to be asked for to ensure that further offences are not committed.

6.4.1.1 Suitability of a surety

In considering the suitability of a surety, the court must have regard to the matters contained in s. 8 of the 1976 Act, namely:

    (a)   the surety's financial resources;
    (b)   the character and previous convictions of the surety; and
    (c)   the proximity (whether in point of kinship, place of residence or otherwise) to the person for whom he is surety.

Let us suppose, therefore, that one has a defendant whom one suspects may not be granted unconditional bail. A surety would seem to help the situation and one has come forward. The first thing the court will do is consider an appropriate amount and whether the proposed surety's resources are sufficient. In fact they will generally accept evidence from the surety that he has resources of that amount, whether in the form of savings or value of goods. If documentary evidence is available, then it is of course as well for the surety to bring it to court (e.g., building society accounts, bank statements).

The matter of suitability extends beyond resources, however, to the question of the surety's own standing. If he has a bad character or criminal record, then (while not necessarily absolutely fatal) it may make him less acceptable. Finally, there is the question of proximity between the surety and the accused. Basically the surety is 'keeping an eye' on the accused to ensure he fulfils his obligations. Obviously, therefore, a close relative or someone who lives very close by will be best for this purpose. However, a spouse is often considered not appropriate as a surety in some courts and, on the authority of a case which is more than a century old, it is also considered improper to accept the solicitor of an accused as surety.

It is not necessary for the surety to be present in court, although this is preferable. It is possible to obtain agreement from the magistrates to the grant of bail, subject to sureties, if the sureties come forward to a police station where their suitability can be investigated by the police; if the police are then satisfied the accused may be released from custody.

6.4.2 SECURITY

The giving of a *surety* does not imply payment of money in advance. However, under s. 3(5) of the 1976 Act, if 'it appears that the accused is unlikely to remain in Great Britain until the time appointed to him to surrender to custody he may be required before release on bail to give *security* for his surrender to custody . . . the security may be given by him or on his behalf'. In this situation, therefore, money must be provided in advance, either by the accused personally or by someone else.

A common example is that of a wealthy foreign person accused of a substantial shoplifting offence (e.g., some very valuable item of clothing) from a West End store. It would not generally be appropriate to keep a first offender in custody but, equally, it is somewhat unlikely that he will wish to return to stand trial, especially if he lives thousands of miles away. In these circumstances, the informal practice is to set an amount of security which would roughly correspond to the potential fine and leave it at that. An alternative might be to require surrender of the defendant's passport but this may not be appropriate, e.g., the wealthy visitor may need to return home before the time fixed for the hearing, or may need to go to Paris to continue shoplifting, or go to Northern Cyprus for an extended holiday.

6.4.3 MISCELLANEOUS CONDITIONS

The court may impose other conditions. Some of the most common are:

(a)   surrender of passport;

(b)   the observing of a curfew, that is being at home after a certain hour at night and until a certain hour in the morning;

(c)   to reside at a particular place, or with a particular person;

(d)   not to go to a particular place, or within a particular area (e.g., the area where the offence occurred). This condition is used very flexibly as a means of, for example, preventing an accused going to public houses or football matches;

(e)   not to contact certain individuals.

6.5   Meeting Objections to Bail

It is now appropriate to consider how to meet objections to bail, assuming that these have been put forward by the officer in the case or the Crown Prosecutor. You must ensure that your argument, which should be soundly based on facts, deals with the specific objections. You must immediately assess the prospects of obtaining unconditional bail. Whilst no doubt it is in a sense a more clear cut 'victory' on the issue to obtain unconditional bail for a client, if there is any substantial risk of it being refused, then it is more prudent to examine what conditions might be offered to meet the objections raised.

For example, if the nature of the objection is that the accused, who is an habitual burglar, will continue to commit further burglary offences if allowed bail, there really is little point in offering that he will surrender his passport. In such a situation, the obvious suggestion is a curfew. If it is contended that he will abscond, the appropriate conditions will be that he should report to the police station daily and that he can provide adequate sureties. If the objection is that he will interfere with witnesses, then a condition that he will not go to certain places where those witnesses live or work, or will not contact them would be adequate to meet the suggested objection. The interplay between the various grounds set out for refusing bail and the criteria by which the existence of those grounds are to be judged is obviously capable of enormous variation in any given case.

It should be noted that the court may vary conditions imposed, on the application of either the prosecution or the defendant subsequent to the granting of bail, and that the police have power to arrest without warrant for breach of conditions under s. 7(3) of the 1976 Act.

When the prosecution and defence have put forward their arguments the magistrates will give their decision. If the accused is granted unconditional bail, he is merely notified of the date upon which he is required to surrender to custody. If he is refused bail, or given bail subject to conditions, then there must be a record made of the decision in the prescribed manner and a copy should be given to the defendant in the appropriate form.

6.6   Refusal of Bail

Where a bail application has been refused by the magistrates they will remand the defendant in custody. A court must give reasons for its decision and a note must be made of the reasons and a copy given to the defendant. Before conviction, or committal for trial, this first remand must be for a period which does not exceed eight clear days. In fact, the custom is usually to remand the defendant in custody for a slightly shorter period than this, often to the same weekday of the following week.

Whereas previously an accused was entitled to insist on appearing in court every eight days, that is no longer the position. An accused who is over 17 can be remanded in custody once a magistrates' court has set a date for the next stage of the proceedings, for a period of 28 clear days or to that date, whichever is the less. This may now be done even where the accused does not consent. This provision does not however apply on the occasion of a first remand in custody though it does apply subsequently. Thus the accused will have been able to make the two successive bail applications referred to below. This is by virtue of s. 128A of the Magistrates' Courts Act 1980 inserted by the Criminal Justice Act

1988. If they are however considering such an extended remand the magistrates must have regard to the total period of time the accused would spend in custody if they were so to remand him. They will thus bear in mind, perhaps after a number of such extended remands where the prosecution are slow in preparing the papers for committal, that the remand in custody hitherto, e.g., for several months, may well come close to the likely eventual penalty for the offence should the accused be convicted. In such a case they may consider releasing him notwithstanding no change of circumstances, a possibility which may encourage the prosecution to greater haste in the preparation of the case for committal.

6.6.1 SUCCESSIVE APPLICATIONS FOR BAIL

We shall now consider what further applications for bail may be made where the initial one has been refused.

Until 1981, it was not uncommon for a full-length bail application to be made for a defendant on each successive appearance before the magistrates. It should not be supposed that on a defendant's second appearance he will be substantively dealt with either by summary trial or committal proceedings. There may be adjournments, sometimes many adjournments (especially a case of some substance), in order to enable the prosecution to collect their evidence and prepare. The repetition of bail applications did have some point to it since the case might be heard each time before a new bench of magistrates, and arguments that did not impress the first bench might sometimes impress a more leniently-minded bench. However, there is now a restriction on the number of times that an application can be made, with the object of avoiding undue repetition and waste of court's time. By virtue of part IIA of the 1976 Act (inserted by the Criminal Justice Act 1988), if a court refuses bail it is under a duty at each subsequent hearing to consider bail providing that:

(a) the defendant is still in custody; and
(b) the right to bail under s. 4 of the 1976 Act still applies.

At the first hearing after that at which the court decided not to grant bail, the defence can put forward any argument (including those advanced previously) to support an application for bail. However, on each subsequent remand the court need not hear arguments as to fact or law which it has heard previously, although the duty to at least consider bail remains.

In essence therefore a defendant is allowed two 'full' oral applications for bail, that is one when he first appears in court and a second on his subsequent appearance after the defence solicitor has had longer to marshall his arguments, find sureties, discuss conditions with the defendant, investigate police objections to bail and so on.

At the end of committal proceedings, however often bail has been refused before, it is often possible to suggest new arguments in the light of the further evidence which will have been revealed by that stage. In particular the relevant criterion which requires consideration of 'the strength of the prosecution evidence' may well be viewed differently. Where an accused is committed in custody for trial at the Crown Court, then, notwithstanding that it may be some months before that trial takes place, the magistrates' jurisdiction ceases. Accordingly, if they commit him in custody he will not in principle be produced to any court before his Crown Court trial and further applications for bail, if any, must be made by him to the Crown Court.

6.7 Applications to Crown Court and High Court

If bail is refused by the magistrates after a full application, there are two separate methods for further applications. These are sometimes described as 'appeals' but they are not in truth appeals as such.

filing with the application a so-called 'full argument certificate' from the magistrates' court which certifies that the magistrates did hear full argument on the bail application. If legal aid has been granted, it will cover one such application to the Crown Court.

The hearing takes place in chambers before a Crown Court judge and solicitors have right of audience. Usually the Crown Court will list the case for hearing before a judge in chambers before he starts the day's criminal work at 9.45 or 10.00 a.m. The Crown Court will usually give a hearing date as soon as the form is taken down to the court and notice of this must be served on the prosecution at least 24 hours before the application is made. In fact, it is not uncommon for a Crown Court to list such applications for the following day and for the prosecution to waive the strict requirement for a full clear day's notice.

The prosecution may either attend, indicate that they have no objection, or send in a written notice of objection. In most cases attendance is usual because the prosecution will naturally have many other cases in court that day and it is an easy matter for them to arrange representation by counsel instructed in some other matter. At the hearing, one may rehearse all the matters that were put before the magistrates, and indeed any new matters which have arisen or further arguments.

One may make this application to the Crown Court either immediately bail has been refused or at any stage up to committal for trial.

6.7.2   HIGH COURT

The second method of application is to apply to a judge of the High Court in chambers. This can either be straight after refusal by the magistrates (in which case no 'full argument certificate' is required) or after previous unsuccessful applications to a Crown Court judge. The application is considered to be within the civil jurisdiction of the High Court and is governed by RSC ord. 79.

Application is made by way of a summons with an affidavit in support. The affidavit will be sworn by the defendant's solicitor and describe the background to the case and why it is suggested that the defendant ought to have bail. The summons will be issued at the nearest direct registry and a hearing date will be obtained by agreement with the listing officer of the nearest High Court. Again, 24 hours' notice must be given to the prosecution, but again it is common practice for this to be waived. The hearing is in chambers and a solicitor will therefore have a right of audience

Legal aid issued for the criminal proceedings will not cover such an application, but a separate application may in principle be made for civil legal aid. The Legal Aid Board suggests that there is no firm policy of automatically refusing such applications, although the success rate of applications is not high. Bearing in mind, however, the criteria for the grant of legal aid in civil proceedings, very few such applications, bail having been refused by magistrates and perhaps by a Crown Court judge already, are likely to be considered meritorious. This application to a High Court judge in chambers is usually only made by private-paying defendants. The costs however are not great, the work involved merely being the swearing of an affidavit and issuing of a summons and attending a relatively short appointment, usually with a fixed hearing time before the start of the day's court business. Thus the costs may not be prohibitive even to defendants of modest means.

6.8   Powers of the Crown Court

We have already considered the Crown Court's powers in respect of applications after refusals by the magistrates. Once a case is committed to the Crown Court for trial (see **16.1**) the Crown Court obviously has other powers of its own. In particular it has jurisdiction to grant bail where:

   (a)   a magistrates' court has committed an accused for trial or sentence in custody;

   (b)   an accused is appealing against conviction or sentence from the magistrates' court;

(c)   a person is appealing from the Crown Court to the Divisional Court or is seeking judicial review of its decision;

(d)   the Crown Court judge has certified that a case is fit for appeal to the Court of Appeal against conviction or sentence.

The powers to grant bail are contained in s. 81(1) of the Supreme Court Act 1981. In addition to those powers the Crown Court has inherent jurisdiction to deal with bail during the course of a trial before it. Thus, if an accused is on bail up to the time of his trial, it is normal practice to renew bail for overnight adjournments (and in principle during the lunch times though only rarely is this mentioned).

If circumstances change during the course of a case, bail may be withdrawn. Thus, for example, if the accused delays his trial by turning up too drunk to participate in it, or where the case is obviously going badly for the accused or additional aggravating factors have appeared, or there is some suggestion of interference with witnesses or jurors, bail may be withdrawn.

Where it is clear from the way in which a case is going that a custodial sentence is likely, bail may be withdrawn once the judge has commenced his summing up and therefore bail may be refused over any lunch adjournment, or even overnight if the summing up is a lengthy one or the jury are taking some time to consider. See in particular *Practice Direction (Crime: Bail During Trial)* [1974] 1 WLR 770.

SEVEN

THE LAW OF EVIDENCE (1)

7.1   Introduction

The law of evidence as we know it today has come from a body of rules formulated by the common law judges of the 18th and 19th centuries, followed by a number of radical but piecemeal statutory reforms, in particular: the Criminal Evidence Act 1898; the Police and Criminal Evidence Act 1984; and the Criminal Justice Act 1988.

The law of evidence has many aspects which today appear inconsistent or even bizarre and which originally came about for two reasons. The first of these was that, unbelievable though it now seems, the accused himself was not usually allowed to give evidence at his own trial until 1898. He would thus be faced with accusations which, in the draconian criminal climate of the 18th century, might lead to the death penalty for relatively minor offences, but he would not be allowed to testify against his accusers. A number of procedural and evidential rules were therefore adopted to protect the accused in that situation.

The second reason for some of the stranger rules is that a criminal trial takes place, as it has for centuries, before a jury of laymen who are the ultimate tribunal of fact. Because of the supposed inability of an inexperienced jury to evaluate certain kinds of evidence, complex rules were adopted which prevented certain kinds of evidence being put before a jury because the superficial attractiveness of such kinds of evidence would be too unreliable or prejudicial to the accused.

The result of this is that even today certain kinds of evidence are excluded although a layman would consider them highly relevant, or even virtually conclusive to showing guilt or innocence. Thus for example, as is well known, in the main, complex rules prevent the prosecution bringing in evidence of an accused's previous record even where the criminal record is for offences which are similar to the present crime. Likewise, hearsay evidence is usually excluded even if it is of a relatively compelling kind, unless some specific exception to the hearsay rule permits it. This latter rule may in fact prejudice an accused rather than help him because in principle the rules of evidence are the same for the accused as they are for the prosecution; thus in general an accused is no more entitled to introduce evidence of hearsay than is the prosecution.

In this chapter we shall be considering the rules of criminal evidence mainly as they relate to a Crown Court trial. The rules in relation to magistrates' courts trial are almost the same, with minor exceptions which will be indicated where they arise.

The law of evidence is at its most vital where the person or body deciding on the *facts* is different to the one ruling on the *law*. It is therefore best seen in the context of a criminal trial in the Crown Court where the judge rules on the law, including the admissibility of evidence, and the jury decide what they make of the evidence which is presented to them, i.e. whom they believe. Consequently almost all modern case law of importance is from the Criminal Division of the Court of Appeal, hearing appeals from the Crown Court against alleged errors in rulings by the trial judge.

7.1.1   JUDICIAL CONTROL OF THE EVIDENCE

The judicial control of the evidence to be presented to the jury can be seen at the following stages.

(a) The judge must apply rules concerning *which* witnesses may testify. Thus there are for example special rules regulating whether children may give evidence, whether the prosecution may insist on the accused's spouse testifying, and so on.

(b) There are rules concerning *how* witnesses must testify, e.g., about taking oaths and affirmations and about what questions may or may not be asked of the witness. The judge's control of a criminal trial at this stage includes not just the application of rules of law but also of discretionary rules and rules of practice which are very hard to formulate precisely. For instance the judge will permit counsel to cross-examine the opposing party's witnesses, often at great length and very fiercely, but the judge must see when aggressive questioning oversteps the permitted limits and becomes abusive or bullying and intervene to put a stop to it.

(c) There are rules preventing certain types of evidence altogether, e.g., the well-known rule against hearsay evidence which has the effect that one witness may not testify to the court in terms such as 'X told me he saw the defendant stab the victim'. In some countries this evidence is permitted but the jury are then warned that hearsay may be unreliable, however in the UK such evidence simply cannot be given at all. Likewise, interesting and apparently relevant though the jury might well find it, no evidence can normally be given of the accused's criminal record, even if it is for similar offences. Because of the law's wariness of untrained jurors' drawing hasty conclusions (e.g., 'he's committed 20 previous burglaries so he's probably done this one') the law simply forbids such evidence.

(d) If documents are to be used in a case then there are rules about whether and how they may be proved. Documents which are just statements, i.e. a written statement by a witness, usually cannot be used at all — the witness must be brought to court to testify in person. Other documents may be used, e.g., a will, business records or public documents, subject to certain procedures which the judge must rule upon.

(e) Finally, and perhaps most importantly, the judge's control of the jury is shown when he sums up at the end of the case. Here he must give them firm rulings on points of law, but must tell them that they are the sole judges of matters of fact. He then reminds them (often at very great length) of salient points in all the evidence that they have heard, and as he goes through each witness's testimony he may, within limits, comment on factors which may make that witness more or less credible (e.g., he may point out that the witness had a motive to lie, or was trapped into inconsistencies in cross-examination, or even that he looked shifty and evasive while testifying). The judge must not go too far here and pre-empt the jury's decision, but judges often do contrive, by tones of voice and facial expressions (i.e. things which do not appear on the shorthand writer's official transcript of the summing-up) to convey a definite view that a given witness is lying.

As the judicial summing up has evolved, various practices have now become settled rules of law so that a serious error in summing up will inevitably lead to a conviction being quashed on appeal. Judges must in some cases direct juries, often in very technical terms, about certain aspects of the rules of evidence. Thus there must be a clear direction on who has the burden of proof and to what standard; where certain kinds of witness have testified for the prosecution (such as accomplices of the accused), the judge must carefully direct the jury about the need for further evidence to corroborate the witness; where the accused has not testified, the judge must carefully direct the jury about this (i.e. warn them that they must not conclude that the accused is guilty because he has chosen not to give his version); and many other matters must also be specifically dealt with in the summing up.

Where there is a significant error in the judge's control of the evidence, whether on rulings of admissibility or in the course of his summing up, a resulting conviction will be quashed unless the Court of Appeal can apply the proviso contained in s. 2(1) of the Criminal Appeal Act 1968, i.e. they conclude that despite the error the accused would have been convicted anyway so that no miscarriage of justice has occurred.

7.2 Purpose of the Law of Evidence

The law of evidence has three purposes:

(a) it lays down rules as to what is admissible matter for the purposes of establishing facts in dispute;

(b) it regulates the ways in which such matters can be put before the court;

(c) it lays down rules as to how a judge may, or must, comment on the evidence.

For example, to establish the *actus reus* of a murder by stabbing:

(a) Direct eye-witness evidence is admissible matter; and

(b) It must (usually) be given to the court on oath by the eye-witness himself.

(c) The judge must in summing up remind the jury of what the eye-witness said and may comment on his evidence.

7.3 Classification of Evidence

To succeed in a case the party who wishes to establish his case (usually, but not invariably, the plaintiff in a civil case or the prosecution in a criminal trial) must prove 'the facts in issue'. In most cases one can determine what the 'facts in issue' are by looking at the substantive law and also at the charge or indictment which defines the issues more closely.

Thus for example if the case is a murder case the prosecution must prove the act and the mental state of the accused; if the case involves the tort of negligence, the plaintiff must prove duty, breach and damage. The types of evidence which may be adduced are usually divided into four categories:

(a) *Testimony.* This is an assertion by a witness in court (which must usually be on oath with some few exceptions) of what he has himself perceived by one or more of his five senses.

(b) *Hearsay.* Hearsay is usually inadmissible. Hearsay is 'a statement other than one made by a person while giving oral evidence in proceedings and tendered as evidence of the truth of the facts stated'. Although because of its inherent unreliability hearsay is usually inadmissible there is a host of exceptions to this rule. Where evidence, although hearsay, falls within one of these exceptions it may be admitted in court.

(c) *Documents.* A document may be put in evidence if reference to its terms is needed. Thus private documents such as a contract, a will or a lease may be used to prove their terms. Also public documents such as marriage certificates or certificates of conviction may be used.

(d) *Real evidence.* Real evidence includes things such as a weapon, clothing, a bloodstain or going out of court to view the scene of the incident, as sometimes happens in road traffic cases.

To give an example of all four kinds of evidence arising in a case: A sees B go into C's room and come out; on going in A sees that C has been badly stabbed and hears C say 'I am dying — B killed me'; later the fact that C's will is in B's favour proves the motive; the bloodstained knife with B's fingerprints on it is found nearby.

Another way of looking at evidence is to consider whether the evidence is *direct* or *circumstantial*.

(a) *Direct evidence* is either the testimony of a witness who perceived a fact (e.g., A saw B stab C) or the production of a document constituting the fact (e.g., if the terms of a lease are disputed, production of the actual lease).

(b) *Circumstantial evidence* is that which does not directly establish a fact but is still admissible in order to enable the court to decide as to a fact. Circumstantial evidence usually assists by enabling one to deduce from generalisations. A somewhat elaborate example is as follows:

Example

A is accused of the murder of B, his elderly relative, by poisoning. It is proved that: A was to inherit under B's will; that B had recently been heard to say he was thinking of changing his will; that A was found in possession of strong weed-killer even though he lives in a flat with no garden; that the weed-killer was found in A's flat hidden under the floorboards rather than on open view; that A was in financial difficulties due to his failing business and thus had desperate need of money.

Taken together, these facts seem inevitably to indicate A's guilt. Our own experience shows that A has ample motive and has recently acquired the means to kill B in suspicious circumstances. Although of course the law requires proof of *intention*, and motive in itself is irrelevant to criminal liability, proof of motive is often the way of helping to establish intention. Clearly a prolonged examination of circumstantial evidence can lead to lengthy side-tracks. Thus it might take the court in the above example a long time to hear evidence about A's financial difficulties, and of course even if all this is proved it is still less than positive direct evidence. After all most people stand to gain financially from the death of some relative but murder remains extremely rare. If, in the above example, the evidence about A's financial difficulties became too lengthy and the position remained unclear after substantial evidence about it, the judge would be likely to control the testimony by stopping questioning about matters which seem too remote from the issue.

Conviction by purely circumstantial evidence is not only possible but very common. In such cases circumstantial evidence has been famously compared to the links in a chain leading from the crime to the accused. A better analogy however is strands in a rope, so that even if one is explained away the others may be sufficient to provide the connection.

7.4 Burden of Proof and Standard of Proof: Introduction

'Burden of proof' has two main meanings:

(a) It is the duty of the prosecution or plaintiff to persuade the court (*by which is meant the person or persons who tries or try the facts*) by the end of the case of the truth of certain propositions. In this sense, therefore, the burden of proof falls on the party who will lose if at the end of the case the trier of fact is evenly balanced between belief and disbelief. This burden is known as the 'legal burden' or the 'persuasive burden'. The obligation to discharge this burden is expressed in the maxim 'he who asserts must prove'.

(b) Burden can also mean 'the evidential burden'. The evidential burden is also sometimes called 'the burden of passing the judge' and that phrase gives a good description of it. The evidential burden means the burden of satisfying the judge that there is sufficient evidence of a certain matter in order for him to direct the jury about it and treat it as a 'live' issue in the case. It is as well to consider separately how the evidential burden may arise for both prosecution and defence.

7.4.1 THE PROSECUTION'S EVIDENTIAL BURDEN

The prosecution have to prove *actus reus* and *mens rea*. They have to satisfy the jury of both to the usual criminal standard of proof. However matters may never get as far as the jury. The prosecution commences by calling its evidence and if by the end of all its own evidence it has failed to prove the crime sufficiently there will usually be a submission by the defence of 'no case to answer'. At that stage the judge sends the jury out of court and listens to the submission by the defence and the response to it by the prosecution. If he agrees that there is 'no case to answer' he will withdraw the case from the jury and direct an acquittal. The principles for consideration of a submission of 'no case to answer' are contained in *Practice Note (Submission of No Case)* [1962] 1 All ER 448. Such a submission should be upheld by the judge where:

(a) there has been no evidence to prove an essential element in the alleged offence; *or*

(b) when the prosecution evidence has been so discredited by cross-examination or is so manifestly unreliable that no reasonable tribunal could safely convict on it.

Where such a submission is successful the jury have never had the opportunity to hear the accused's evidence or that of its witnesses, nor has the accused had to make the often difficult decision about whether to testify at all. In other words the prosecution must rely entirely on the evidence which they themselves intend to bring to get past the middle stage of the case and cannot rely on any anticipated assistance they might get from cross-examining the accused if he should decide to testify.

If the prosecution do get past this stage in the case then they have discharged their evidential burden. The jury are called back into court and the case goes on. The jury are not of course told why they were sent out of the court and the jury do not concern themselves at all with the question of evidential burden which in no way pre-empts or anticipates the eventual verdict of the jury after they have heard all the evidence including any that the defence choose to call.

7.4.2   THE DEFENCE'S EVIDENTIAL BURDEN

In contrast to the evidential burden borne by the prosecution, the defence's evidential burden arises somewhat differently. They do not have to *satisfy* the judge of anything as such. All that the defence have to do is to ensure that there is enough evidence about any defence that is to be raised to enable the judge to direct the jury upon the defence as a live issue. In other words the defence cannot invite the jury merely to speculate that there might have been, for example, provocation, self-defence or accident. There has to be some firm evidence about a defence before the judge will direct the jury in relation to it. This does not in any sense mean that the judge has to *believe* the evidence. There does not need to be very much evidence in support of a defence for a judge to be required to direct the jury on it; if a judge does wrongly withdraw a defence from the jury any resulting conviction is likely to be quashed. All that the judge has to find is that there has been *some* evidence, however flimsy, of a given defence so that he can direct the jury about it. The need to discharge this 'evidential burden' in relation to defence matters does not even mean that the accused must give evidence or call witnesses. Sometimes it is possible to obtain sufficient evidence from cross-examination of prosecution witnesses, e.g., as to the existence of provocation in murder. As we shall subsequently see a defendant must cross-examine prosecution witnesses on any matter in respect of which he disagrees with them and thus he must foreshadow any defence that he is to raise in due course by confronting prosecution witnesses with his version in cross-examination.

Again the jury do not concern themselves with questions of the evidential burden on the defence. Once a judge directs the jury about a defence then it falls within their province and if they find that there is a reasonable doubt as to whether or not the defence is true they should acquit.

7.5   Burden of Proof

The general principle is that the legal burden of proving facts lies on the person who asserts them. This protects the individual accused against the State. He need only answer a charge or claim when a reasonable case has been made out. The general rule therefore is that the prosecution or plaintiff bears the burden since each loses if the trier of fact is evenly balanced at the end of the case.

The leading criminal case is *Woolmington* v *DPP* [1935] AC 462 in which W shot his wife and his defence was accident. The trial judge directed the jury that once they were satisfied that W had pulled the trigger it was for *him* to prove his defence of accident. The Criminal Court of Appeal affirmed the conviction on the basis of this direction. In the House of Lords the conviction was quashed. It was for the prosecution to prove beyond a reasonable doubt both *actus reus* and *mens rea*. The jury did not need to be *satisfied* with the accused's explanation, it was sufficient if they were left in a reasonable doubt as to whether his explanation was true. The accused was entitled to be acquitted if they had such a doubt.

7.5.1 EXCEPTIONS TO THE GENERAL RULE IN CRIMINAL CASES

Normally, as we have seen, the prosecution must adduce sufficient evidence of the accused's guilt by the end of their case; otherwise there will be a submission of 'no case to answer' and the judge will direct an acquittal. The prosecution has to adduce sufficient evidence of *actus reus* and *mens rea* as prescribed by the substantive law, but does not have to negative every conceivable defence in advance nor deal with pure speculation.

For example, in *Hill* v *Baxter* [1958] 1 QB 277 the defendant's motor vehicle was involved in an accident and he was charged with dangerous driving. His defence was that he could remember nothing of what happened and must have had a blackout as a result of sudden illness. The magistrates dismissed the charges. It was held on appeal that there was no evidence at all that he was suffering from a blackout. Such a defence was mere speculation and what he had said was just as consistent with having fallen asleep.

This, then, is merely an example of the accused's general evidential burden; he must adduce *some* evidence to make a particular defence a live issue, but once this is adduced the burden of disproving that defence rests on the Crown. This is true of all the usual general or partial defences such as accident, mistake, duress, alibi, etc.

There are four important situations where an accused bears the *legal* burden of satisfying the jury of the *truth* of his defence (on the *civil* standard of proof — see later). The situations are as follows and are all to do with the mental state of the accused, and in practice relevant only on serious charges:

(a) *Insanity: Sodeman* v *R* [1936] 2 All ER 1138. It was held that where S alleged insanity it was for him to prove his defence on the balance of probabilities.

(b) *Unfitness to plead: R* v *Podola* [1960] 1 QB 325. The accused shot a policeman and contended that he was unfit to plead as he suffered from amnesia realting to all the events surrounding the crime. He was thus unable properly to instruct his lawyers. An issue arose as to whether it was for him to prove unfitness to plead or for the prosecution to prove positively that he was fit to plead. It was held that the case was analogous to insanity and it was for the defence to satisfy the jury that the accused was not fit to stand his trial. (Note the Criminal Procedure (Insanity and Unfitness to Plead) Act 1991 has now been passed. It makes no changes to the substantive law on burden and standard of proof but provides that certain medical evidence is required from doctors who have expertise in the diagnosis or treatment of mental disorders. It also provides that where a defendant claims to be unfit to plead the court may conduct a 'trial of the facts' limited to determining whether the defendant committed the *actus reus*. If the *actus reus* is not proved the jury will acquit the defendant.)

(c) *Insane automatism: Bratty* v *AG for Northern Ireland* [1963] AC 386. B strangled a girl and although he remembered something about it he claimed that 'a sort of blackness' came over him. He raised three separate and independent defences at trial namely insane automatism, insanity and diminished responsibility. On all three it was held that he had the burden of satisfying the jury of his defence.

(d) *Diminished responsibility* and the *Homicide Act 1957, s. 2(2): R* v *Dunbar* [1958] 1 QB 1. The accused was charged with murder. He raised the defence of diminished responsibility. It was held that, on the clear wording of the Homicide Act 1957, it was for the accused to satisfy the jury of the truth of his defence.

The above examples are cases where the *full legal burden* is borne by the accused. On other defences the accused has only an *evidential* burden, as previously explained, for example:

(a) *Duress: R* v *Gill* [1963] 2 All ER 688.
(b) *Self-defence: R* v *Lobell* [1957] 1 QB 547.
(c) *Provocation: Mancini* v *DPP* [1942] AC 1.

(d) *Sane automatism and drunkenness:* These were additional alternative defences in *Bratty* v *AG for Northern Ireland* [1963] AC 386.

(e) *Alibi: R* v *Johnson* [1961] 3 All ER 969. This is a good example of the operation of the burden of proof on ordinary factual defences. The accused was charged with robbery and his defence was an alibi. The trial judge directed the jury that it was for the accused to prove the truth of his defence and alibi to the jury's satisfaction. It was held on appeal (quashing the conviction) that there was no special rule about alibi. There was a fundamental misdirection in the case since it was for the prosecution to *disprove* his defence once evidence of it was put before the jury.

7.5.2 WHERE THE PROSECUTION RAISE AN ISSUE

If an issue as to the accused's mental state is raised by the prosecution, it is for them to prove it beyond reasonable doubt (e.g., in cases of insanity or unfitness to plead).

For example, *R* v *Robertson* [1968] 1 WLR 1767: R was charged with murder. He dismissed his legal adviser and conducted the trial himself. The prosecution raised as a preliminary issue the question of the accused's fitness to plead in that he allegedly suffered from insane delusions. It was held that, where insanity or unfitness to plead was raised by the prosecution, the burden of proof was upon them and the standard was proof beyond reasonable doubt.

7.5.3 STATUTES AFFECTING THE BURDEN OF PROOF

It is not uncommon for criminal statutes to say that certain facts may be deemed to exist until the contrary is proved. There are many such statutes and the following are examples.

7.5.3.1 Prevention of Corruption Act 1916, s. 2

This provides that if on a charge under the Prevention of Corruption Act 1906, or the Public Bodies Corrupt Practices Act 1889, it is proved that a gift is given or money paid by a person holding or seeking a contract from a government department or public body to an employee of the department or body the consideration is deemed to be given corruptly unless the contrary is proved. This is therefore an extreme measure because it requires the accused to prove innocent purpose in giving a gift once the fundamental facts, e.g., that the donor holds or seeks a contract from a government department or public body, have been established by the prosecution.

7.5.3.2 Theft Act 1968, s. 25(3)

This provides that it is an offence for a person to have with him when away from his place of abode any article for use in committing burglary or theft (see the 1968 Act for the full text). The section says that proof that the accused had it with him 'shall be evidence' that it was for that unlawful use.

The meaning of these words is not entirely clear. Clearly they cannot mean 'conclusive proof' or 'irrebuttable proof'. According to some authorities this puts an evidential burden on the accused to advance *some* innocent explanation fit to be left to the jury; according to others the effect is not so strong — it merely discharges the prosecution's own evidential burden on the issue of unlawful purpose — i.e., the case is fit, without more, to go to the jury as discharging the evidential burden on *mens rea*.

7.5.3.3 Magistrates' Courts Act 1980, s. 101

This provision (the section of the Magistrates' Courts Act 1952 which s. 101 replaced) applied only to magistrates' court cases until 1974 when it was held in *R* v *Edwards* [1974] 3 WLR 285 that it was declaratory of the common law and therefore applied in the Crown Court as well.

Section 101 states:

> Where the defendant to an information or complaint relies for his defence on any exception, exemption, proviso, excuse or qualification, whether or not it accompanies the description of the offence or matter of complaint in the enactment creating the offence or on which the complaint is founded, the burden of proving the exception, exemption, proviso, excuse or qualification shall be on him; and this notwithstanding that the information or complaint contains an allegation negativing the exception, exemption, proviso, excuse or qualification.

The effect of this is that where the defendant claims to have a particular licence, permission or qualification to do something which would otherwise be criminal, it is for him to prove it, that is, he bears the *legal burden* not just the evidential burden.

See, for example, *R* v *Edwards* [1974] 3 WLR 285, where accused was charged with selling intoxicating liquor without a licence. He did not give evidence at the trial but made an unsworn statement denying that he was the occupier of the premises concerned. He was convicted and appealed on the grounds that the prosecution should have proved *positively* that he had no licence whereas no evidence had been called about the matter. It was held on appeal that there was an exception to the fundamental rule of criminal law that the prosecution had to prove every element of an offence; the exception was limited to offences arising under enactments which prohibited the doing of an act subject to provisos or exemptions. In such a situation it was for the accused to prove that he was entitled to do the otherwise prohibited act and therefore it was for him to prove that he *did* have a licence not for the prosecution to prove positively that he did not.

7.5.3.4   The Case of *R* v *Hunt*

The House of Lords has recently considered the question of the rule in *Woolmington* v *DPP* (see **7.5**) and the exceptions to it in the important case of *R* v *Hunt* [1987] AC 352.

The House of Lords considered *Woolmington* v *DPP* and *R* v *Edwards* and held that in the case of an offence involving the misuse of hard drugs, because of the seriousness of the allegation, it was right to resolve any ambiguity in the burden of proof in favour of the defendant, and thus it was for the prosecution to prove the nature of the substance involved.

Regulations made under the Misuse of Drugs Act 1971 provided that there should be no prosecution in relation to possession of a certain controlled drug if there was less than 0.2 per cent of it in any given solution. At the end of the prosecution case there was a submission of no case to answer based on the fact that the prosecution had failed to prove that the proportion of morphine contained in the powder found in the accused's possession was in excess of this proportion. The Court of Appeal eventually held that the burden was on the defendant to prove that the preparation of morphine was sufficiently weak to fall within the relevant exception contained in the regulations. As the defendant had been unable to discharge that burden of proof the Court of Appeal upheld his conviction. The House of Lords, whilst considering that *R* v *Edwards* (see **7.5.3.3**) was rightly decided, held that, as under the statute and regulations it was a criminal offence to have morphine in one form but not an offence to have it in another form, it was for the prosecution to prove that it had been in the prohibited form because otherwise no offence was established. Accordingly the circumstances were not covered by *R* v *Edwards*.

It should be remembered that s. 101 of the Magistrates' Court Act 1980 and the corresponding principle in the Crown Court, expressed in *R* v *Edwards* are, in essence rules of statutory interpretation. They provide a principle for examining the terms of other statutes to see whether key words in sections creating criminal offences either *define the offence* (in which case the burden of proving every element remains on the prosecution) or implicitly *provide an excuse or defence*, in which case one has to look carefully to see whether the effect is to switch the burden to the defence. There are many such statutes in the purely regulatory sphere concerned with matters such as food and drugs, health and safety and the like. Thus it will always be necessary to examine phrases in sections which create an offence such as 'without reasonable excuse', 'without lawful authority' and the like to see whether the legal burden of proving the defence is in fact switched to the defence.

7.6 Standard of Proof

One party has to prove the truth of the fact in issue. If he fails to do so he will fail overall; therefore he has to adduce more persuasive evidence than his opponent does. If he only adduces an equivalent amount of evidence to his opponent so that the judge of fact is left undecided, then the party who has the legal burden has not discharged it and will fail. Therefore the standard of proof concerns how much more (or better quality) evidence has to be adduced by one party than his opponent in order to be successful.

Cases from the second half of the 19th century show two standards of proof recognised by law:

(a) Proof on a preponderance of probabilities — the civil standard.
(b) Proof beyond reasonable doubt — the criminal standard.

So the standard of proof required of the prosecution is higher than that of a civil plaintiff and it is vital for the judge to direct the jury fully on the standard.

7.6.1 THE CRIMINAL STANDARD

The words 'beyond reasonable doubt' were at one time only one of a number of ways of explaining the criminal standard of proof to a jury. They were however approved in *Woolmington* v *DPP* and may now be said to represent the usual definition. Difficulties have arisen however where judges have sought to explain more fully to a jury what the words 'beyond reasonable doubt' mean. No particular set of words suffices — it is the summing up as a whole that is important. This must be borne in mind when considering individual words or phrases in decided cases.

One formulation that has often been approved is by Denning J (later Lord Denning) in *Miller* v *Minister of Pensions* [1947] 2 All ER 372 at p. 373H:

> Proof beyond reasonable doubt need not reach certainty but it does carry a high degree of probability. Such proof does not mean proof beyond a shadow of a doubt. The law would fail to protect the community if it admitted fanciful possibilities to deflect the course of justice. If the evidence is so strong against a man as to leave only a remote possibility in his favour which can be dismissed with the sentence 'of course it is possible but not in the least probable' the case is proved beyond a reasonable doubt but nothing short of that will suffice.

and as to the civil standard at p. 374A:

> Proof on the civil standard must carry a reasonable degree of probability but not so high as is required in a criminal case. If the evidence is such that the tribunal can say 'we think it more probable than not' the burden is discharged but if the probabilities are equal it is not.

An alternative formulation of the standard of proof was found acceptable in the case of *Ferguson* v *R* [1979] 1 WLR 94 where the composite formula 'satisfied beyond reasonable doubt so that you feel sure of the defendant's guilt' was approved.

7.6.2 WHAT IS A 'REASONABLE DOUBT'?

Courts have from time to time attempted to find a formula which would explain to the jury what the phrase 'reasonable doubt' might mean. Obviously the lengthy lawyer's formula given by Lord Denning above would not be appropriate. Sometimes judges attempt to define 'reasonable doubt' as being 'a doubt for which you could give a reason'. This has usually been disapproved unless there is further explanation.

In *Walters* v *R* [1969] 2 AC 26 a reference to considering the words 'reasonable doubt' as being 'that quality and kind of doubt which, when you are dealing with matters of importance in your own affairs you allow to influence you one way or the other' was approved. However, in *R* v *Gray* (1973) 58 Cr App R 177 the use of the words 'the sort of doubt which might affect you in the conduct of your everyday affairs' was *disapproved* as not stressing sufficiently the importance of the occasion.

7.6.3 CIRCUMSTANTIAL EVIDENCE AND THE STANDARD OF PROOF

A rule was said to derive from the case of *R* v *Hodge* (1838) 2 Lew CC 227 to the effect that where the evidence was entirely circumstantial there must be a specific direction by the trial judge that the jury must be satisfied that 'not only were the circumstances consistent with the accused committing the act but that they were inconsistent with any rational conclusion other than that the accused was the guilty person'.

This was considered in *McGreevy* v *DPP* [1973] 1 WLR 276, where M was charged with murder of a woman. All the evidence against him was circumstantial and involved a consideration of the evidence of over 30 witnesses. The trial judge failed to give the direction from *R* v *Hodge*. On appeal it was held that it was undesirable to lay it down as a rule which would bind judges that a direction to a jury in cases of circumstantial evidence must be given in some special form. All that was required was that the jury should be directed in suitable terms to make it plain to them that they must not convict unless they are satisfied of guilt beyond all reasonable doubt.

7.6.4 WHEN THE BURDEN IS ON THE ACCUSED

When the *legal burden is on the accused* in a criminal case, whether by common law rule or statute (e.g., insanity or diminished responsibility), the burden is not so heavy as that borne by the Crown on the general issue, i.e. it is on the civil standard. The accused must prove matters to the extent of persuading the jury that they are *more likely than not* true.

For example, see *R* v *Carr-Briant* [1943] 2 All ER 156. The accused was charged with corruption under the Prevention of Corruption Act 1906. It was proved that he had made a gift to a government employee. The trial judge, however, directed the jury that the onus of proving his innocence lay on the appellant beyond reasonable doubt. It was held, quashing the conviction, that although the appellant did have the burden of proof it was only to satisfy the jury of his defence upon the civil standard of balance of probabilities and not beyond reasonable doubt.

Moreover, standard of proof must be carefully explained. See *R* v *Swaysland, The Times*, 15 April 1987 where the burden of proof was on the defendant it was not enough to tell the jury that he had to prove it on 'the balance of probabilities' for this might confuse them into thinking that it was, say, 75 per cent probable. The phrase 'more likely than not' was preferable.

7.7 The Importance of a Correct Direction

It is vital that the judge correctly directs the jury on the burden and standard of proof. In many cases where the point under appeal was the failure to give a proper direction on these vital matters. The cases establish that one must look at the direction as a whole. The unfortunate fact is that many judges give highly repetitive directions in which they repeat the point in several different ways and often at several different times throughout the direction. In principle a direction on matters of evidence should commence with dealing with burden and standard of proof but many judges deal with it briefly there, and then return to it at the end. It follows that there may be inconsistent things said in the course of a lengthy direction and the case law establishes that only rarely will the fact that one phrase, or short passage, misstates the burden or standard of proof matter provided that there is a correct explanation elsewhere in the direction.

There have been numerous recent cases in which misstatements by a trial judge of the principles of burden or standard of proof have led to convictions being quashed. Sometimes an otherwise impeccable direction is spoilt by one or two sloppy phrases. For example, in *R* v *Anderson* [1991] Crim LR 361 the judge unfortunately used the phrase: 'if you think the defendant's evidence and that of his witnesses is true or may be true, then . . . acquit'. This clearly indicated that the jury should only acquit if they are satisfied with the truth of the defence. Likewise in *R* v *Bowditch* [1991] Crim LR 831 the judge included a number of unfortunate phrases, in particular 'if you accept the defence as a true explanation' which might also have led the jury to conclude that the burden was on the defendant. In *R* v *McDonald, The Times,* 27 March 1989, the judge used the phrase 'the defence, if it is established' which also led to the conviction being quashed on appeal.

7.7.1 CAN A JUDGE DIRECT THE JURY TO CONVICT?

An interesting question is whether the judge is ever entitled to direct a *conviction*. He can of course direct an *acquittal* in a suitable case. An example is *R* v *Gent* (1989) 89 Cr App R 247 where the accused was charged with conspiracy to obtain drugs. His defence was that whilst he admitted all participation in the operation he had done so as a police informant on the instructions of a police officer who had now retired and was unfit to attend the trial. The judge directed the jury to convict because of the admissions made by G in the course of giving his evidence. On appeal the conviction was quashed. The appellant's evidence in the witness box was very strong evidence of guilt but he was entitled to the verdict of the jury not the judge. Similarly in *R* v *Gordon* (1991) 92 Cr App R 50 the trial judge concluded that the accused had admitted all the relevant evidence of the offence and appeared to be running a defence which on the law was not open to her. The judge thereupon directed the jury to convict. On appeal the court observed that the judge had gone further than he should notwithstanding the hopeless nature of the defence and that it was wrong to direct a conviction. However the proviso in s. 2, Criminal Appeal Act 1968 was applied.

7.7.2 JOINT ENTERPRISE AND BURDEN OF PROOF

One point which has arisen a number of times in reported cases and which provides an interesting conundrum is where there are two defendants (or more) and the facts are such that one or other of them, or possibly both together, must have committed the crime. The judge must first look to see whether there is any evidence of a joint enterprise. If there is then he can safely direct the jury that they have to be satisfied beyond reasonable doubt that one or other or both together did the crime.

The problem arises however where there is no evidence of joint enterprise and the crime was therefore committed either by A or B but there is little evidence pointing to which. The judge must of course sum up separately in relation to each defendant so he must tell the jury that they must be satisfied beyond reasonable doubt that A did it; he must then give the same direction in relation to B. Accordingly if the prosecution has been unable to show which of the two did it, even though one must have, the jury are perfectly right in acquitting both, considering each separately.

An interesting factual example is *R* v *Hyde, Sussex and Collins* (1991) 92 Cr App R 131. In this case three men combined to beat up another but one of the men went too far and gave him a fatal kick in the head. The defence submitted that the jury could not be sure whose act caused the death of the victim and thus none of them should be convicted as the killer, and convictions in respect of assault only should be brought in. The court held that there was sufficient evidence of joint enterprise to make them all guilty of murder.

A different result occurred in *R* v *Aston and Mason* [1991] Crim LR 701. In this case the victim was M's 16-month-old daughter. She was admitted to hospital showing a number of injuries consistent with having been beaten. A was not the child's father but had treated her as his own. Each testified that the child had been alone with the other for important parts of the day in question. The trial judge rejected the appellants' submission of no case to answer on a count alleging murder. They were eventually convicted of cruelty to a child under the Children and Young Persons Act 1933 and manslaughter. On appeal the convictions for manslaughter were quashed against each of them since there was no evidence at the close of the prosecution case which indicated which one of the appellants was responsible for the fatal injuries and each of them had had the opportunity. Neither was there any evidence that they had acted in concert.

7.7.3 WHAT IF THE TRIER OF FACT CANNOT DECIDE?

Where a jury cannot agree on an accused's guilt either unanimously or to the required majority, the judge will discharge the jury and normally order a retrial. Sometimes the prosecution choose not to proceed with a retrial particularly if there has been a long delay since the offence itself and the trial has been a long one.

If in the magistrates' court a case is being tried before only two magistrates and they disagree, the case should be remitted to a new bench for a fresh hearing: see *R v Redbridge Justices, ex parte Ram* [1992] Crim LR 128. Where however a bench of three magistrates are simply unable to make up their minds, this means that the prosecution have failed to discharge their burden and the result should be an acquittal. See, for example, *R v Bromley Justices ex parte Haymills (Contractors) Ltd* [1984] Crim LR 235. The accused firm were charged with using a vehicle with deficient steering. There was conflicting evidence about the steering. At the end of the case the justices refused to make a decision and decided to send the case for a rehearing by another bench. It was held that the three magistrates were required to proceed to a decision. If they were unhappy about convicting the accused then they should acquit.

7.8 Proof without Evidence

The general rule is that all facts in issue in a case, and all facts relevant to the issue, have to be proved by evidence brought at the right time. There are however three basic exception to this principle. These are:

(a) Facts of which judicial notice is taken.
(b) Facts which are the subject of some presumption so that they are taken as established unless some party proves to the contrary.
(c) Facts which are admitted between the parties.

We shall now consider each of these briefly in turn.

7.8.1 JUDICIAL NOTICE

When a court takes judicial notice it declares that it will find that a fact exists even though no evidence has been called to establish it, e.g., that Christmas Day falls on 25 December.

To be a proper fact for judicial notice to be taken, a fact must be so well established as not to be the subject of dispute amongst reasonable men.

There are two categories of cases of judicial notice:

(a) Facts judicially noticed without enquiry.
(b) Facts judicially noticed after enquiry.

7.8.1.1 Facts judicially noticed without enquiry

These are facts which a judge can be expected to receive and act upon from his own knowledge — facts so notorious that evidence is superfluous, e.g., that human fingerprints are unique. The following further examples illustrate the point:

(a)   14 days is too short a period for human gestation: *R* v *Luffe* (1807) 8 East 193.

(b)   One of the purposes of Oxford University is to further learning: *Re Oxford Poor Rate Case* (1853) E & B 184.

(c)   In *R* v *Simpson* [1983] 1 WLR 1494 the accused was charged with having an offensive weapon outside the home. The relevant law is that certain kinds of articles will always be considered offensive weapons, but that whether others (e.g., a chisel) are offensive weapons must be left to the jury to decide after hearing evidence as to whether in the circumstances the item was an offensive weapon or held for some legitimate purpose (e.g., in the case of a chisel by a working carpenter on his way home). In this case the court took *judicial notice* (that is the judge decided as a matter of fact) that a flick-knife is always an offensive weapon.

7.8.1.2   Facts judicially noticed after enquiry

These are cases where the judge may act upon facts which he has ascertained from sources to which it is proper for him to refer.

(a)   Cases where the court acts on information received from a Secretary of State with regard to matters of state (chiefly foreign policy). See, for example, *Duff Development Co.* v *Government of Kelantan* [1924] AC 797 where an action was brought by the plaintiff against the defendants and an issue arose as to whether the defendants were an independent state. If this were the case then the plaintiffs would not be able to sue the defendants in the English courts. A certificate was obtained from the Secretary of State for the Colonies that Kelantan was an independent country and the court took judicial notice of this.

(b)   It appears that in certain cases customs, especially mercantile customs, will be judicially noticed by the courts without formal proof.

(c)   Professional practice, e.g., the practice of conveyancers — *Re Rosher* (1884) 26 ChD 801, and see *Davey* v *Harrow Corporation* [1958] 1 QB 60 where an issue arose as to the exact boundaries of certain property. The court took judicial notice of the fact that a line in an ordnance survey map in accordance with the practice of ordnance surveys, represent the centre line of an existing hedge.

Finally, it should be noted that in many cases the judge will take tacit judicial notice of many matters of worldly experience without the matter ever being referred to in the judgments, or evidence being called concerning it, e.g., that there are very few lawful uses for masks and jemmies, where these are found in the possession of an accused, or, as in *R* v *Thompson* [1918] AC 221 that a person who has powder puffs and indecent photographs of young boys in his possesion is likely to be a homosexual.

7.8.2   PRESUMPTIONS

The subject of presumptions is chiefly relevant in civil evidence. However, it may be of limited importance in criminal evidence, and for that purpose a brief account of it will be given.

A presumption is 'a conclusion which may or must be drawn until the contrary is proved, once certain primary facts are established'. In other words, once the primary fact is proved the court is entitled to (or in some cases must) draw the presumptive conclusion even though no further evidence is called to establish it. There are usually said to be three main categories, namely: presumptions of fact, irrebuttable presumptions of law, and rebuttable presumptions of law.

7.8.2.1   Presumptions of fact

This phrase is really an expression of the usual processes of reasoning and 'is, in reality no more than a slightly grandiose term for the ordinary processes of judicial reasoning about facts'. It describes the process whereby if stolen goods are found in the home of the accused the factual inference may be drawn (or presumption made) that he stole them. This 'presumption' is of course easily rebutted by other factual evidence (e.g., that they were stored there by someone else without his knowledge) but if no such evidence is given the jury *may* (not *must*) draw the inference and presume the theft.

To use the word 'presumption' to describe this kind of common-sense connection between primary facts (the goods being there, and he being the one who stole them) is probably confusing and unhelpful. The high point of judicial woolliness in this area is supplied by *DPP* v *Smith* [1961] AC 290. S was being questioned whilst sitting in his van by a policeman who suspected that he had stolen certain property. S panicked and tried to drive away and the policeman jumped on the side of the van. Shortly after, he was thrown off by the motion of the vehicle and fell under another vehicle, being killed. S was charged with capital murder. In the House of Lords Viscount Kilmuir held that there is a presumption that a man intends the natural and probable consequences of his acts. Once the accused's knowledge of the circumstances and the nature of his acts has been ascertained the only thing that could rebut this presumption would be proof of incapacity to form an intent, insanity or diminished responsibility.

This elevates the fairly obvious proposition that a man usually intends the natural consequences of his acts into a presumption — moreover Viscount Kilmuir said that it did not matter whether one called it a presumption of law or fact. Now by s. 8 of the Criminal Justice Act 1967:

A court or jury, in determining whether a person has committed an offence, —
(a)   shall not be bound in law to infer that he intended or foresaw a result of his actions by reason only of its being a natural and probable consequence of these actions; but
(b)   shall decide whether he did intend or foresee that result by reference to all the evidence, drawing such inference from the evidence as appears proper in the circumstances.

In other words, the existence of any such 'presumption' whether of law or fact is now denied, and the matter is entirely one of fact for the jury in which they may, when they consider whether the accused did intend what occurred to happen, draw whatever inferences common sense dictates.

7.8.2.2   Irrebuttable presumptions of law

These are where conclusive inferences *must* be drawn from a given premises and no evidence in rebuttal is allowed. This is in truth substantive law — it defines the rights of the parties. For example: a child aged under ten cannot be guilty of crime.

7.8.2.3   Rebuttable presumptions of law

The following rebuttable presumptions of law are of some minimal importance in criminal evidence:

(a)   *The presumption of legitimacy.*   This is of a minimal importance in criminal litigation. The presumption, which is that a child born during the currency of the marriage is the child of the husband, can anyway be easily rebutted due to the existence of DNA genetic fingerprinting tests.
(b)   *The presumption of death.*   This provides that given certain conditions, in particular absence and inability to trace for seven years, a person may be presumed dead for certain purposes, chiefly the distribution of estates. Its only direct relevance in criminal evidence is that there is a statutory defence under s. 57 of the Offences Against the Persons Act 1865 whereby on a charge of bigamy there is a defence if the jury are satisfied (the burden being on the accused) that at the time of the second 'marriage' the accused's first spouse had been 'continually absent for the space of seven years last past and shall not have been known (to the accused) to have been living in that time'.
(c)   *The presumption of marriage.*   In brief this presumption is that where the parties went through an apparently valid ceremony the marriage is deemed to be valid and the burden of proving otherwise is on the person who wishes to challenge it.
(d)   *The presumption of regularity, expressed in the latin maxim* omnia preasumuntur rite esse acta. This entitles the court to presume without formal proof (but subject to evidence in rebuttal where appropriate) that official matters are in order and were properly done so that proper procedures have been carried out, persons holding appointments were properly appointed to them and the like.

7.8.3   MATTER WHICH IS ADMITTED

In a criminal trial, just as in a civil one, by virtue of s. 10 of the Criminal Justice Act 1967 matter may be formally admitted. This is often arranged between the parties to cut down the scope of a criminal trial to the true events in issue. Admissions must be made in writing unless made orally before the court itself and must be made by counsel or solicitor for the accused; admissions made under s. 10 may, with the leave of the court, be withdrawn.

The effect of s. 10 is that purely formal matters, such as the execution of documents, may be admitted between the parties at or before the trial. Alternatively, quite substantial admissions may be made which have the effect of limiting the scope of either the prosecution's case or of what the defence is seeking to contend. A defence lawyer will always need carefully to consider whether something is properly admitted where the proving of it might put the prosecution in such difficulties, albeit of a technical nature, that their case would be seriously in jeopardy. It is a recognised tactic in cases of considerable complexity (such as commercial fraud cases) to admit little or nothing so that the issues in front of the jury may be sufficiently voluminous to ensure the maximum of confusion. Sometimes however it may be to the advantage of an accused's defence that he should admit a substantial part of the facts. So, for example, where a householder is burgled and it is the essence of the accused's case that he was not the one responsible, he would gain little in the jury's eyes by failing to admit the formal facts that a burglary occurred. Similarly, on a rape charge, if the substantive defence is mistaken identity, it probably does the accused little good to make the complainant formally prove the fact of intercourse and absence of consent. For a particular discussion of the difficulties of this see *R v Chance* [1988] QB 932 at **12.6**.

EIGHT

THE LAW OF EVIDENCE (2): COMPETENCE AND COMPELLABILITY: TESTIMONY

8.1   Introduction

A witness is *competent* if he can lawfully be called to give evidence, and *compellable* if he can be made to testify even if he is unwilling to do so.

The general rule, subject to the exceptions discussed below, is that all persons are competent to give evidence, and all competent persons are compellable.

One can compel a witness to attend court by a subpoena in civil proceedings or a witness summons or witness order in criminal proceedings. Failure to attend court will result in arrest and/or proceedings for contempt being brought against the witness. If, having come to court, the witness refuses to answer questions, this will again be contempt of court leading to imprisonment either under the general law of contempt or under a specific statute (e.g., Magistrates' Courts Act 1980, s. 97, which permits the magistrates to imprison an unco-operative witness for up to seven days). A witness may claim *privilege* not to answer certain questions in certain situations which will be further discussed in **Chapter 14**. Subject to that, however, a witness, once called, must co-operate fully in the proceedings.

8.2   Exceptions to the General Rule

8.2.1   THOSE OF DEFECTIVE INTELLECT

No witness is competent if prevented by 'lunacy', drunkenness, etc., from giving rational testimony. But the witness is only incompetent so long as the defect lasts, and if it is only temporary the trial may be adjourned provided application is made before the jury are sworn.

In any given case it is for the judge to decide whether a person whose capacity is challenged can understand the nature of the oath. If the judge decides he does then it is for the jury to decide what degree of credit should be given to any such evidence. If the capacity of a witness is challenged, the judge should hear any relevant evidence about it in the presence of the jury so that they have the necessary information to assist them to decide how much credit to give to the witness. Note that for persons of low intelligence the same rules apply as used to apply before 1992 in the case of children (see **8.2.2**). In *R* v *Bellamy* (1985) 82 Cr App R 223 the accused was a man of low mental ability convicted of rape of a woman of similar capacity. When the victim gave evidence the trial judge investigated her competence, hearing evidence from her and a social worker. After questioning her as to her belief in and knowledge of God and the understanding of the importance of telling the truth he decided that she should affirm. It was held on appeal that the judge was clearly right to investigate her competence but having concluded that she was competent and did not object to being sworn she should have been sworn.

8.2.2   CHILDREN

In *criminal cases* until 1992 the provision as to the evidence of children was s. 38 of the Children and Young Persons Act 1933. This permitted a child to give unsworn evidence provided the child was possessed of sufficient intelligence and understood the duty of speaking the truth. It used to be for the judge to examine the child and decide whether or not the child had sufficient understanding. That exercise occurred in the presence of the jury so that they could see for themselves how intelligent the child was. Now, however, s. 52 of the Criminal Justice Act 1991 simply provides that all *children* (that is up to the age of 13 inclusive) shall give *unsworn* evidence in criminal proceedings; and persons above that age shall give *sworn* evidence. It must be borne in mind however that there will nonetheless be an initial enquiry as to whether it is appropriate to take evidence in any form from any particular child in view of the child's intelligence, age and state of understanding.

8.2.2.1   Is there a minimum age?

In *R* v *Wallwork* (1958) 42 Cr App R 153 it appears that a five-year-old child was a witness and there is no particular age which has been held to be too young. The propriety of calling a five-year-old child was doubted in that case by the Court of Appeal especially as, in the event, the child proved too terrified to testify at all when in the witness box. It is not possible however to say with certainty what is the minimum age.

The competence of children has been further discussed in other recent cases in one of which (*R* v *B*, *The Times*, 1 March 1990) a question arose as to whether a six-year-old child was too young to testify. The court observed that the policy of the legislature represented by the repeal of the requirement of corroboration in children's evidence (see **12.3.3**) showed that the public in general found the evidence of young children acceptable. It would be wrong to vet the discretion of the trial judge in such cases.

8.2.3   THE ACCUSED

Bizarre though it now seems, until the last century there were rules designed to stop the accused from giving evidence at all. The rationale was the risk of perjury and the fact that the obvious self-interest of the accused made his evidence specially untrustworthy. It has of course been obvious, at least since 1898, when the accused was first generally allowed to testify, that the fact-finding process represented by a criminal trial is substantially hampered, to the prejudice of the accused, by such a rule. Nonetheless there are still some restrictions on the accused's competence and these are described below.

8.2.3.1   As a witness for the Crown

In general, an accused is not a competent witness for the Crown. He cannot therefore be compelled to testify at his own trial. The rule is however much more important where there are several co-accused because the rule prevents the Crown calling any of several co-accused to testify against another. There are, however, several ways in which one of two or more co-accused may cease to be a co-accused and thus may become competent for the Crown:

(a)   The Attorney-General may file a *nolle prosequi*.

(b)   An order may be made for separate trials, but note that in such a case a co-accused from the first trial may be called at the second but not vice versa.

(c)   The accused may be formally acquitted, e.g., if the prosecution offers no evidence.

(d)   The accused may plead guilty, he may then give evidence for the Crown against a co-accused; it is usually considered desirable that he should be sentenced before giving evidence.

For example, in *R* v *Payne* [1950] 1 All ER 102 the accused and two other men were charged with burglary. The accused pleaded guilty and the others not guilty. Sentence was passed on the accused at once and he was then called by the prosecution to testify at the trial of the other two. The court held that where several are charged jointly in an indictment and one pleads guilty and the other not guilty, sentence should not be passed on the one pleading guilty until the end of the case at which time the court will be in possession of all the facts relating to all the accused and will be able properly to assess the respective degrees of guilt among them. However this direction does not necessarily apply in the case where the man pleading guilty is to be called as a prosecution witness. Such a person should generally be sentenced at once so that there can be no suspicion that his evidence is coloured by the fact that he hopes to get a lighter sentence by reason of the evidence he has given. However, it may sometimes be better for a judge to use his discretion in the matter by waiting until the end of the trial to sentence all the participants when he has heard all the evidence and can best judge their relative culpability.

There are dicta on the dangers of not doing so in *R* v *Weekes* (1982) 74 Cr App R 161. One of several accused was to testify for the Crown in a robbery case and was accordingly sentenced before the trial of the others commenced. The sentence was comparatively light. When the full facts of the case became known it was apparent that shotguns had been used and the court took a much more serious view of the nature of the robberies. The other accused consequently received very much heavier sentences. There was an appeal on the basis of the disparity in sentencing and the court observed that it would be better in such cases always to wait before sentencing the accomplice who is to testify for the Crown. This suggestion however, may be too strong. The case was concerned with disparity in sentencing rather than competence and is perhaps best considered as providing a rule of thumb for serious gang crimes.

It is important, before the prosecution call a co-accused, that all criminal proceedings against him in relation to the charges in question should have been determined (except for questions of sentence). For example, in *R* v *Pipe* (1967) Cr App R 17 the accused was charged with burglary. Another man, S, who had also been charged in relation to these offences but who was being tried separately was called by the prosecution as a witness against him. It was held that it was the duty of the prosecution if they wished to call this accomplice as a witness to let it be known that in no event would proceedings against him be continued and as this had not been done the conviction must be quashed.

8.2.3.2 For a co-accused

It will be rare for one co-accused to want to give evidence *for* another co-accused but not for himself, since he will thereby open himself to cross-examination which presumably is what he wanted to avoid by not testifying, although there could be such cases (e.g., on a *voir dire* as to admissibility of a co-accused's confession). A co-accused is *competent* but *not compellable*.

8.2.4 THE SPOUSE OF THE ACCUSED

The general rule until the coming into force of the Police and Criminal Evidence Act 1984 was that a spouse was not competent for the prosecution at the trial of the other spouse.

The law on competence of spouses is now contained in s. 80 of the Police and Criminal Evidence Act 1984 which provides:

(1) In any proceedings the wife or husband of the accused shall be competent to give evidence—
  (a) subject to subsection (4) below, for the prosecution; and
  (b) on behalf of the accused or any person jointly charged with the accused.
(2) In any proceedings the wife or husband of the accused shall, subject to subsection (4) below, be compellable to give evidence on behalf of the accused.
(3) In any proceedings the wife or husband of the accused shall, subject to subsection (4) below, be compellable to give evidence for the prosecution or on behalf of any person jointly charged with the accused if and only if—

(a)   the offence charged involves an assault on, or injury or a threat of injury to, the wife or husband of the accused or a person who was at the material time under the age of sixteen; or

(b)   the offence charged is a sexual offence alleged to have been committed in respect of a person who was at the material time under that age; or

(c)   the offence charged consists of attempting or conspiring to commit, or of aiding, abetting, counselling, procuring or inciting the commission of, an offence falling within paragraph (a) or (b) above.

(4)   Where a husband and wife are jointly charged with an offence neither spouse shall at the trial be competent or compellable by virtue of subsection (1)(a), (2) or (3) above to give evidence in respect of that offence unless the spouse is not, or is no longer, liable to be convicted of that offence at the trial as a result of pleading guilty or for any other reason.

(5)   In any proceedings a person who has been but is no longer married to the accused shall be competent and compellable to give evidence as if that person and the accused had never been married.

(6)   Where in any proceedings the age of any person at any time is material for the purposes of subsection (3) above, his age at the material time shall for the purposes of that provision be deemed to be or to have been that which appears to the court to be or to have been his age at that time.

(7)   In subsection (3)(b) above 'sexual offence' means an offence under the Sexual Offences Act 1956, the Indecency with Children Act 1960, the Sexual Offences Act 1967, section 54 of the Criminal Law Act 1977 or the Protection of Children Act 1978.

(8)   The failure of the wife or husband of the accused to give evidence shall not be made the subject of any comment by the prosecution.

(9)   Section 1(d) of the Criminal Evidence Act 1898 (communications between husband and wife) and section 43(1) of the Matrimonial Causes Act 1965 (evidence as to marital intercourse) shall cease to have effect.

8.2.4.1   Summary

(a)   *For the Crown.*   Unless he/she is also a co-accused the spouse of an accused is always competent for the Crown and is also compellable for the Crown in the limited class of cases referred to in s. 80(3), namely where the offence charged involves an assault on or injury or threat of injury to the spouse or a person who was under 16, or the charge is a sexual offence involving a person under 16, or attempts to commit or aiding and abetting etc. these classes of offence, though *not* compellable in cases apart from those.

(b)   *For the Accused.*   Unless he/she is also a co-accused a spouse is always competent and compellable *for* his/her spouse.

(c)   *For a Co-accused.*   Unless he/she is also a co-accused the spouse of one of two or more co-accused is always competent for a co-accused and is compellable in the limited class of cases in s. 80(3). Where spouses are co-accused one is never compellable for the other.

Note also:

(a)   Section 80(5) provides that if spouses are no longer married at trial it is as if they were never married for the purpose of establishing competence and compellability.

(b)   Section 80(8) expressly repeats what anyway is still in force in s. 1(b) of the Criminal Evidence Act 1898 — that the prosecution may not comment on the failure of an accused's spouse to testify. The importance of this provision is reaffirmed in *R* v *Naudeer* (1984) 80 Cr App R 9 where N was charged with theft. He gave evidence at his own trial but did not call his wife as a witness although it would seem that she had something she could have said relevant to the facts. Prosecution counsel commented to the jury adversely on the failure of the wife to give evidence. It was held that on appeal this had been quite wrong and the conviction would be quashed.

(c)   When a spouse is competent but not compellable, regard should be had to the case of *R* v *Pitt* [1982] 3 All ER 63. It held that it is desirable for a judge in such a case to explain to a spouse before she took the oath that she was not obliged to testify but that once she did commence to testify she could not pick and choose which questions to answer but was in the position of any other witness and to refuse to answer a proper question would be contempt. This should be explained to her in the absence of the jury.

(d) A 'spouse' to a polygamous marriage is to be treated as if not married to the accused and is thus competent and compellable in every case: *R* v *Khan* (1987) 84 Cr App R 44.

8.3 Testimony

8.3.1 OATHS

The general rule is that all evidence must be given on oath. The Oaths Act 1838 permits an oath to be administered in such a form and with such ceremonies as the person taking it may declare to be binding on him. A solemn affirmation may be administered instead if the witness is not a believer or taking an oath is contrary to his religion; also if it is impracticable to administer the oath in a manner appropriate to the witness's religion. So in *R* v *Kemble* [1990] Crim LR 719 a Moslem took the oath using the New Testament. K was convicted and appealed on the basis of material irregularity. At the appeal evidence was given by an expert in the Moslem faith. The appeal was dismissed. In the case of a person who is neither Christian nor Jew the oath may be administered in any lawful manner and in the present case the Moslem witness had given evidence that he considered the oath binding on him notwithstanding that it was sworn on the wrong book.

8.3.2 UNSWORN EVIDENCE

Unsworn evidence is only admitted in principle in the following situations:

(a) The unsworn evidence of a child under the age of 14 whose intelligence is sufficient to justify the reception of its evidence.

(b) Where the written statements of persons who are not present before the court are admitted under one of the exceptions to the hearsay rule (e.g., s. 23, Criminal Justice Act 1988) that statement is not on oath but it is nonetheless acceptable as testimony. (See **9.10**.)

8.3.3 EVIDENCE THROUGH TELEVISION LINK AND VIDEO

It is inherent in the usual rules of evidence that the witness giving evidence must be present in court. There are however two exceptional situations provided for in recent statutes.

By s. 32 of the Criminal Justice Act 1988, evidence by live television link at a trial on indictment (and on appeal) may be given where either:

(a) the witness is outside the Untied Kingdom, or

(b) the witness is under 14 and the offence charged is one to which s. 32(2) applies — in general, these sections have to do with sexual offences and in any event the leave of the court is required.

The use of s. 32 is highly exceptional. Section 32 reads:

(1) A person other than the accused may give evidence through a live television link on a trial on indictment or an appeal to the criminal division of the Court of Appeal or the hearing of a reference under section 17 of the Criminal Appeal Act 1968 if—
(a) the witness is outside the United Kingdom; or
(b) the witness is under the age of 14 and the offence charged is one to which subsection (2) below applies,
but evidence may not be so given without the leave of the court.
(2) This subsection applies—
(a) to an offence which involves an assault on, or injury or a threat of injury to, a person;
(b) to an offence under section 1 of the Children and Young Persons Act 1933 (cruelty to persons under 16);

(c)   to an offence under the Sexual Offences Act 1956, the Indecency with Children Act 1960, the Sexual Offences Act 1967, section 54 of the Criminal Law Act 1977 or the Protection of Children Act 1978; and

(d)   to an offence which consists of attempting or conspiring to commit, or of aiding, abetting, counselling, procuring or inciting the commission of, an offence failing within paragraph (a), (b) or (c) above.

(3)   A statement made on oath by a witness outside the United Kingdom and given in evidence through a link by virtue of this section shall be treated for the purposes of section 1 of the Perjury Act 1911 as having been made in the proceedings in which it is given in evidence.

(4)   Without prejudice to the generality of any enactment conferring power to make rules to which this subsection applies, such rules may make such provision as appears to the authority making them to be necessary or expedient for the purposes of this section.

(5)   The rules to which subsection (4) above applies are—

(a)   Crown Court Rules; and
(b)   Criminal Appeal Rules.

The second statutory exception to the requirement that the witness must be present in court is s. 54 of the Criminal Justice Act 1991, which has the effect of inserting a new s. 32A in the Criminal Justice Act 1988. This provides for a video tape of an interview with a child witness by 'any adult' to be put in evidence and to constitute the examination-in-chief of the child. It is suggested that often this video tape will be very damning to the accused. Leave to put it in evidence is required and the leave will not be given if the child is not made available for cross-examination. There are substantial problems with the provision as yet unexplored in case law, in particular the likelihood that, in the course of the video-taped interview with the sympathetic adult, inadmissible material, for example hearsay, will be included which it will then be up to the court to insist should be edited under the authority of s. 32A(3). The section is concerned with interviews with a child witness, probably the victim, in relation to sexual offences of the kind referred to in s. 32 of the 1988 Act.

8.4   Stages of Testimony

A witness is subject to three sets of questions: examination-in-chief (**8.5**), cross-examination (**8.6**) and re-examination (**8.7**). Each of these will be considered in turn.

8.5   Examination-in-Chief

The purpose of this is to obtain evidence to support the case of the person who calls the witness. The general rule is that *leading questions* cannot be asked. A leading question is one which:

(a)   assumes the existence of disputed facts as to which the witness is to testify, or
(b)   suggests the required answer.

The reasons why leading questions are prohibited are that a question in form (a) is improper because constant reiteration of facts which are in dispute may influence the jury to regard them as established, and a question in form (b) is improper because it 'coaches' the witness.

Leading questions may be permitted for purely formal or introductory matter or where there is no dispute.

Three separate topics need to be considered in the context of evidence-in-chief (i.e. what evidence a party may obtain from his own witness). These topics are: refreshing the memory; previous consistent statements by the witness; and unfavourable and hostile witnesses.

8.5.1 REFRESHING THE MEMORY

8.5.1.1 Out of court

A witness may refresh his memory of the matters in issue by referring *out of court* (usually just before going into court) to any statement he has previously made, e.g., to the police. It is perfectly proper for the police to give a witness his statement to read through before the case, although it is desirable to inform the defence where this has been done: see *Worley* v *Bentley* [1976] 2 All ER 449.

It is said that, if this were not possible, testifying would become 'more a matter of memory than of truthfulness'. Any relevant statement may be used for this purpose, whenever written by the witness. An advocate has the right to call for and cross-examine on notes or statements used to refresh memory out of court even though they are not brought into court. See *Owen* v *Edwards* [1983] Crim LR 800.

8.5.1.2 In court

A witness may 'refresh his memory' by referring to documentary records of the facts in issue but before he can do this four conditions must be satisfied:

(a) *The document must have been made at substantially the same time as the occurrence of the events about which the witness is testifying.* This is a question of fact in each case — three months was too long in *R* v *Woodcock* [1963] Crim LR 273.

See also *R* v *Simmonds* (1967) 51 Cr App R 316. In a complex case involving conspiracy to evade purchase tax, customs officers conducted numerous interviews with several accused. They did not make any notes of what was said at the time but made up their notes from their recollections, assisted in some cases by written questionnaires, as soon as they returned to their offices. It was held that as they were written up at the first convenient opportunity the officers were entitled to refresh their memories from their notes. Contemporaneity is a matter of fact and degree for the judge.

For the very common practice of police officers writing up their notes together see *R* v *Bass* [1953] 1 All ER 1064. The police officers giving evidence were allowed to refresh their memories from their notebooks. When the notebooks were examined it was observed that the notes were almost identical. The officers contended that they were not made up at the same time, and that one officer made his notes after the appellant had been charged and the other an hour or so later. The officers denied collaborating in preparation of the notes. The court observed that police officers nearly always deny collaboration in the making of notes and that there was no need for them to do so. Nothing could be more natural or proper where two persons had been present at an interview than that they should afterwards make sure that they had a correct version of what was said. Collaboration is a better explanation of almost identical notes than possesion of a super-human memory.

(b) *The document was either supervised by, or read over to, the witness at the time.* It is not essential that the witness made it himself. See *Burrough* v *Martin* [1809] 2 Camp 112 where a captain who had inspected a ship's log throughout the voyage was allowed to refresh his memory from it although the entries had been made by the mate.

(c) *The document must be handed to the opposing advocate so that he may inspect it and cross-examine on it.* The jury may also see it. Note however that the document is not *in itself* evidence unless there is an allegation that it has been fabricated (see below as to 'recent fabrication'), or the advocate cross-examines on those parts of the document not used to refresh the memory. See *R* v *Britton*, *The Times*, 11 March 1987 where the accused on release from custody, typed out a note of his recollection of the events of the night. He was allowed to refresh his memory from this during examination-in-chief. Prosecuting counsel cross-examined him at large on these notes and went beyond those matters on which he had refreshed his memory. Accordingly defence counsel then applied to put in evidence the whole of the notes and make them an exhibit. The judge refused to permit this. It was held that there was a long-standing practice which justified the appellant's application in this case. Accordingly where the opposing counsel cross-examined on an *aide-mémoire* and went beyond the matters on which memory had been refreshed, it was open to the person using the *aide-mémoire* to apply to put it in evidence and have the whole shown to the jury. In the present case the jury might have been confused and wondered why they were being denied the sight of the document in question. There was a lurking doubt as to the conviction and the appeal was allowed.

(d) *The document should be the original.* With the decline of the 'best evidence' rule this may be less important but there seem to be no modern cases on the point.

The whole question of 'refreshing the memory' has been usefully reconsidered and principles reiterated in *R v Sekhon* (1986) 85 Cr App R 19. The accused was charged with drug offences. Observations had been kept by a team of officers who had kept a log. When the officers gave evidence they refreshed their memories from the log and were cross-examined as to the contents of the log. The jury asked to see the log and it was then made an exhibit and the jury retired with it. There was an appeal on the basis that this was improper. It was held that there was no difference between the log and notes used to refresh memory. The following points were established:

(a) The document could be referred to to refresh the witnesses' memory without necessarily being put before the jury.

(b) Such documents must be available for inspection by other parties who can cross-examine. Cross-examination will not make the record evidence and it will not be necessary for a jury to inspect it nor will it be appropriate for it to become an exhibit.

(c) Where the nature of the cross-examination involves a suggestion of fabrication the record may be admissible to rebut this suggestion, and if the nature of the record assists in showing whether or not it is genuine from its appearance.

(d) If the record is inconsistent with the witness's evidence it can be admitted as evidence of inconsistency.

(e) If it is difficult for the jury to follow the cross-examination of a witness who has refreshed his memory it may be appropriate for the record to be put before the jury.

(f) If the record goes before the jury it is not evidence as to the truth of the contents of the record and will not amount to corroboration. Its limited purpose is that of being a tool to assist in the evaluation of the truth of the witness's evidence.

(g) It would be wrong to conduct the case in such a way as to leave the jury to conclude that the document is evidence in itself.

(h) The document may become evidence of the truth of its contents in cases where it provides, because of its nature, material by which its authenticity can be judged in respect of that material and only for the purpose of assessing its authenticity. In that limited context it amounts to evidence in the case.

An unusual recent case in which refreshing the memory was permitted even after a witness had begun to testify is *R v Da Silva* [1990] 1 All ER 29. The accused was charged with robbery. The evidence against him included a confession which he had made to a fellow prisoner, C, in the cells on remand. The alleged confession took place in November 1986 and C made a statement to that effect about a month later. The case came up for trial in October 1987. When testifying, C who was still in custody and who had not seen his witness statement outside court said that he could not remember it and was allowed to withdraw from the witness box to the cells to read the statement. The accused was convicted and appealed that this procedure was irregular. It was held that the judge has discretion to permit a witness who has begun to give evidence to refresh his memory from a statement even though that statement was not made contemporaneously with the events, provided it was made near to the time in question and that the judge is satisfied that:

(a) the witness can no longer recall details of the events because of lapse of time;

(b) the statement was made much nearer the time of the events and represented the witness's recollection at the time it was made;

(c) the witness had not read the statement before going into the witness box; and

(d) the witness wishes to read the statement before continuing his evidence.

In such circumstances a witness may properly withdraw from the witness box to read the statement but there must be no communication with him while he reads it. Alternatively, he may read the statement in the witness box but the statement must be taken from him before he resumes his evidence.

It seems apparent from recent cases that the formerly very strict rules about refreshing the memory are becoming progressively less important. This was so in *R v Sutton* [1991] Crim LR 836 where a prosecution witness was asked in evidence-in-chief about certain matters but the prosecuting counsel forgot to put a number of other matters to him during re-examination. The prosecuting counsel applied for leave for the witness to refresh his memory from a record of an interview with a policeman. On appeal it was argued that this should not be permitted since the witness's memory seemed to be adequate about most matters. The appeal was dismissed. The Court of Appeal held that the essential point was that the court should not deprive itself of the best chance of hearing the truth and provided the proper basis was laid a witness could be asked to refresh his memory either in evidence-in-chief or re-examination.

8.5.2 PREVIOUS CONSISTENT STATEMENTS

The general rule is that a witness cannot be asked in evidence-in-chief whether he made a prior statement, oral or written, consistent with his present testimony — nor can another witness be called to prove such prior consistent statement.

In *R v Roberts* [1942] 1 All ER 187 the accused shot his girlfriend in the course of an argument. His defence was that the gun went off accidentally. He wished to call evidence that, a few hours after being taken into custody, he had been visited in the cell by his father and that he had told his father that it was an accident. The trial judge refused to allow this evidence on the basis that it was of no probative value being merely a prior consistent statement. On appeal it was held that this ruling was correct.

The reason for the rule is that such a statement is self-serving and therefore valueless because so easily manufactured. There are, however, a number of important exceptions in criminal cases where a prior consistent statement is admissible because it has some special value in the circumstances.

8.5.2.1 Complaints in sexual cases

Where absence of consent is among the facts in issue (e.g., rape) it was considered relevant to consider whether a complaint was made by the victim to raise a 'hue and cry' thus showing lack of consent. In more modern times the practice arose of limiting evidence of such complaint to *the fact* that it was made and not the words actually used.

Now, if two conditions are satisfied, evidence of the actual terms of complaint may be admitted; and this rule now applies even in sexual cases where the question of consent is not relevant, e.g., indecent assault on a (willing) child. This is established in *R v Osborne* [1905] 1 KB 551. The accused was charged with indecent assault on a young girl. Two girls were in his shop and he sent one on an errand for him and assaulted the other. The victim then ran away and met the other girl in the street. The other girl asked the victim why she hadn't waited in the shop. The victim then made a complaint that the accused had sexually assaulted her. It was held that evidence of the complaint was admissible provided it was made at the first reasonable opportunity after the offence and that it was not elicited by questions of a leading and inducing or intimidating nature.

The conditions of admissibility of the terms of a sexual complaint are therefore:

   (a) that it should not be elicited by questions of a 'leading and inducing and intimidating character' and

   (b) that it should have been made 'at the first opportunity that reasonably offers itself'.

So questions such as 'Why are you crying' would be in order but 'Did X assault you?' would not be.

One must take all the relationships and surrounding circumstances into account in applying these conditions. A delay of one week in complaining was not fatal on the facts of *R* v *Hedges* (1909) 3 Cr App R 262. The accused raped his own daughter, aged 15. At the time her mother was away from home. The girl did not complain until some eight days later when the mother returned. It was held that in all the circumstances evidence of the complaint was admissible.

The fact that the complaint has been made to others before being made to the witness who narrates it in court is not fatal: see *R* v *Wilbourne* (1917) 12 Cr App R 280. The accused was a doctor at a hospital. The victim alleged that whilst treating her he had raped her. After the rape she had gone home with her sister who had questioned her about the incident and a complaint was made to the sister. When they arrived home a further complaint was made to the mother and it was held that the mother was entitled to narrate the terms of the complaint to the court. The fact that another person had been told in the interim was not material.

This rule was extended to the case of sexual offences against males in *R* v *Camelleri* [1922] 2 KB 122.

It is vital that the judge should direct the jury that a complaint is not evidence of the facts nor is it corroboration. It is merely evidence of consistency of testimony and thus goes to the credibility of the complainant, for example, if consent to sexual intercourse is in issue, as to the absence of consent.

In *R* v *Wallwork* (1958) 42 Cr App R 153 the accused was charged with incest with his five-year-old daughter. The child victim was brought into the witness box but was then too frightened to say anything. The child's grandmother was permitted to give evidence that the child had made a complaint to her shortly after the incident in which she had accused her father of the attack. On appeal it was held that this was improper. The point of admitting evidence of a complaint is that it went to show the consistency of the complainant's evidence. Accordingly, where the complainant herself has not given evidence, another witness may not be called to narrate the terms of the complaint. In the event, however, the proviso now in s. 2 of the Criminal Appeal Act 1968 was applied.

Evidence of recent complaint is admissible only in sexual cases and may not be used in respect of other cases even where there is some analogy, e.g., in robbery (see *R* v *Jarvis & Jarvis* [1991] Crim LR 374).

8.5.2.2 Previous consistent statement admitted to rebut an allegation of recent fabrication by the witness

If it is alleged by the cross-examiner that the accused's story has been recently concocted, a previous statement concerning the nature of his defence becomes admissible. So too if it is suggested that a witness of the accused has made the story up after collaboration with the accused. To bring in this rule it is not enough merely to attack the whole of the witness's evidence — there must be a question in the nature of 'when did you invent this'.

See, for example, *R* v *Oyesiku* (1971) 56 Cr App R 240 in which the accused was charged with assault on a police officer. After the accused had been arrested and before she had been allowed to speak to him in custody, his wife went to see the family solicitor and made a statement about what had occurred which was to the effect that it was the police who had assaulted the accused. At the trial the wife was cross-examined to the effect that she had collaborated with her husband to make up her version. The judge refused to allow the defence solicitor to give evidence that the wife had been to see him and told him a version entirely consistent with what she had said in the witness box before she had had the opportunity of speaking to her husband about the case whilst he was still in custody. On appeal the conviction was quashed. It was held that this was an excellent example of a case where the prior statement should have been admitted to rebut the allegation of fabrication.

This rule does not however permit every defendant who is cross-examined as to the falsity of his version to produce his proof of evidence — *the time when he first made his statement* is what is material: *R* v *Okai* [1987] Crim LR 259.

Where a previous statement is admitted to rebut allegations of recent fabrication the status of the statement is the same as that in the case of evidence of complaint in sexual cases. In other words it is evidence only of the consistency of the witness and not of the facts. It is a distinction which will be lost on most juries.

8.5.2.3 Statements by accused when taxed with incriminating facts

We are not here concerned with admissions of facts relevant to guilt to which the special rules relating to confessions apply. We are now considering things that the accused says on being taxed with incriminating facts where what he says is consistent with what he later says, denying guilt. These statements are not *evidence of the facts stated* but they are *evidence of reaction* and, if the accused later gives or calls evidence to the same effect, they can be relied on by him as *showing consistency* (i.e. it would then be proper for the defence counsel or judge to comment favourably on this aspect).

The leading case is *R* v *Storey* (1968) 52 Cr App R 249. The police broke into the accused's flat and found a large quantity of a controlled drug. In a statement then made to them she explained that the drug belonged to a man who had just brought it into her flat against her will. Her explanation was that the man had telephoned to ask if she wished to 'do business'. She was a prostitute and agreed. When he arrived, however, he tipped out a considerable quantity of the drug on the bed and it appeared that he had other 'business' on his mind. Just then the police burst in. A question that arose was the evidential value of the accused's statement to the police at the very time when they broke into the flat and accused her of the drug offence. It was held that her statement to the police was not evidence of the truth of the facts in it but only of her reaction, consequently, when she did not testify at her trial it was wrong to attach any weight to the statement whose only use would have been to prove consistency.

The rule therefore is, where the accused does not testify, that, as the only use of the statement is to show consistency, there is no testimony for it to be consistent with, and therefore it is of no evidential value.

8.5.2.4 Statements made on recovery of incriminating articles

On the same principles as in the foregoing section, what an accused says when incriminating articles are found in his possession is admissible. He can rely on such statement to show reaction and consistency if he later tells the same story in court. This would apply where, for example, stolen goods the tools of crime or drugs are found.

8.5.2.5 Statements forming part of the identification of the accused

If a person is asked in court to identify a person he believes committed the offence, he will usually be asked if he has identified the person on some previous occasion. If he says 'yes' this is proof of a prior consistent statement. This may occasionally be part of the circumstances of the crime but usually is long after the crime, e.g., at an identification parade.

For example, see *R* v *Christie* [1914] AC 545. The accused was charged with indecent assault upon a little boy. At the trial, evidence was given that shortly after the offence the child and his mother and a police man went up to the accused and the little boy said 'that is the man'. The accused replied 'I am innocent'. It was held that these words were all admissible as forming part of the identification.

The above exceptions have been grouped for convenience under the general heading of consistent statements in evidence-in-chief although sometimes the prior consistent statement will need to be proved at some different time, e.g., when rebutting an allegation of recent fabrications the prior statement will usually be adduced in re-examination after the cross-examiner has made the allegation.

8.5.3   UNFAVOURABLE AND HOSTILE WITNESSES

Parties prepare their cases by having their solicitors take a statement from each witness. This is written down and (if the solicitor is prudent) signed by the witness. This statement is called a 'proof of evidence'. A witness whose evidence in court is on the general lines of his statement is said to be 'coming up to proof'. The following sections deal with the situation where the witness fails to do so.

The rule at common law was that a *party may not impeach his own witness*, i.e. he cannot call evidence from another source to show that his own witness is mistaken, forgetful, or lying, although he can continue calling other (hopefully more favourable) witnesses to the same facts whose evidence may be better. Nor can one cross-examine one's own witness or attack one's own witness's character. The rules are now contained in the Criminal Procedure Act 1865, s. 3 which is declaratory of the common law and now governs the position.

There are two kinds of witness:

(a) An *unfavourable* witness is one who is not 'coming up to proof' and fails to prove some fact in issue or proves an opposite fact. Unfavourable witnesses cannot be attacked as to credit or have their previous inconsistent written statements put to them to show their lack of credibility. Unfavourable witnesses may be so because they are forgetful, mistaken or foolish.

(b) *A hostile witness* is one 'not desirous of telling the truth at the instance of the party calling him'. Where an advocate is examining in chief one of his own witnesses who appears hostile he should first ask the judge to rule that he may treat the witness as hostile. This application should be made in the absence of the jury. Whether or not the witness is hostile may be detected by the judge from his demeanour although his previous written statement is also shown to the judge so that he may see the extent of the inconsistency. If the judge allows the witness to be treated as hostile he may permit cross-examination of a party's own witness, e.g., by leading questions to test his memory and perception and by putting his previous inconsistent statements to him.

In *R v Fraser and Warren* (1956) 40 Cr App R 160 the accused were charged with a serious wounding on C. The victim had given a comprehensive statement in which he named both accused who were known to him and correctly described the weapons which they had. At the trial C gave evidence that he was now unable to identify his attackers and indeed that he was certain that the accused were not the men concerned. Prosecution counsel did nothing about this but the trial judge who knew that C had made a previous statement called for the statement and cross-examined C upon it. It was held that in such a case that it is the duty of counsel for the prosecution to show such a statement to the judge and ask the judge's leave to cross-examine the witness as hostile.

The position therefore is that:

(a) an *unfavourable* witness can be contradicted by other witnesses — (otherwise the order of calling them would be all that matters!) but *cannot be cross-examined* or have previous statements put to him or have his character impeached.

(b) in the *case of hostile witnesses*, the judge has a discretion to allow them to be cross-examined and have previous inconsistent statements put to them. However, one still cannot attack one's own witness's character by putting in his previous criminal record, and thus such a witness is not entirely in the same position as an opposition witness to whom such matters may always be put.

8.5.3.1   What is the effect of the inconsistent statement?

The case of *R v White* (1924) 17 Cr App R 60 provides an example of the effect of a previous inconsistent statement. The accused was charged with riot. A witness G who had previously given sworn and unsworn statements to the effect that W was involved, testified at the trial that W was not involved. The Crown alleged that the witness had been terrorised and was allowed to treat G as a hostile witness. The judge appeared to direct the jury that thereafter they could choose between which of the witness's two versions they preferred to believe. It was held that it was one thing to say that in view of an earlier statement to the contrary a witness is not to be trusted but it is another thing to say that a witness's present testimony may be disbelieved and his earlier statement which he now repudiates be substituted for it. In the circumstances the correct direction was that the witness's evidence could be cancelled out to the extent of the inconsistency and the jury should not have been invited to choose between them.

So the net effect is that in a criminal case the judge must not leave it to the jury to say which of the witness's two versions they prefer — he must direct them that *the whole* of the witness's evidence on the inconsistent matter may be *totally disregarded*.

Despite this clear rule there have been recent cases, albeit on unusual facts, which appear to have slightly modified the principle. So, for example, *R* v *Pestano* [1981] Crim LR 397 involved a witness where the inconsistent part of his testimony was clearly separable from the rest. The witness incriminated two of four defendants but resiled from his deposition in relation to two others. It appears that the prosecution were thereafter allowed to rely on the hostile witness's evidence insofar as it advanced their case in relation to the first two witnesses. On appeal it was held that there was no inflexible rule that a jury should be directed that all evidence contained in statements which were contradicted by previous statements should be regarded as unreliable. That principle was approved in the more recent case of *R* v *Nelson* [1992] Crim LR 653.

8.5.3.2 Hostile witnesses and s. 23, Criminal Justice Act 1988

One interesting problem in the case of hostile witnesses which will be commented on more fully in the section on criminal hearsay is the question of the status of previous statements given to the prosecution. As indicated above, in general the previous statement made by a witness who eventually proves hostile in criminal proceedings can only be used to discredit the witness and is not in itself evidence of the facts stated. Section 23 of the Criminal Justice Act 1988 makes certain kinds of statement admissible in cases where *inter alia* a witness does not give evidence 'through fear'. If therefore the reason for a witness becoming hostile is fear of the consequences of testifying, it may be possible not only to put in his previous statement under the procedures described here but that the status of that statement might be different from the status of statements admitted under s. 3 of the Criminal Procedure Act 1865. Such statements under the 1988 Act might actually be *evidence of the facts* stated in them.

8.6 Cross-examination

Almost all witnesses are liable to be cross-examined. All parties have a right to cross-examine any witness not called by them. Therefore one accused's witness can be cross-examined by the prosecution and by counsel for any co-accused. There are two objectives in such cross-examination:

(a) To elicit information about the facts in issue favourable to the party cross-examining.
(b) To test the truthfulness of, and where necessary cast doubt upon, the evidence given in evidence-in-chief by the witness.

When conducting cross-examination it is an advocate's duty to:

(a) Challenge every part of a witness's evidence which is in conflict with his own case.
(b) Put his own case to the witness insofar as the witness is able to say anything relevant about it.
(c) Put to a witness any allegation against the witness which it is proper to put.

If one fails to challenge the evidence-in-chief on any point one *may* be held to have accepted it and not later be able to call witnesses to contradict it or to comment upon it in closing.

Cross-examination is that part of the advocate's craft which tends most to impress the layman and mystify the novice advocate. It should be clearly remembered that every question must be asked with the specific intention of advancing one or other of the objectives mentioned above. Thorough preparation of cross-examination is absolutely vital to ensure a logical and constructive sequence of questioning and to avoid speculative rambling which takes the case no further.

A defence advocate usually has the advantage of previous disclosure of prosecution evidence and therefore a structured and well planned cross-examination is possible, subject to unforeseen matters arising. In the early days of advocacy when all advocates fear 'drying up', a list of potential questions, in an appropriate order, may form a useful long-stop, though the use of such lists in the heat of the moment can sometimes create difficulties. One must develop the self-confidence to know when a question is not worth asking and it is even more important to be able to identify those questions which genuinely take your client's interests further, whether by being relevant to the very issues in the case or by undermining the credibility of the opposing witness. It is thus vital in the course of preparation to be thoroughly on top of all relevant facts and in addition to have a thorough grasp of the rules of evidence. Few things are more deflating than to be told by the clerk to the magistrates that your question is improper in some respect. In particular the usual exclusionary rules of evidence apply to evidence sought to be obtained by cross-examination as much as to evidence-in-chief. So, for example, the rule against hearsay applies and a question to a witness, the answer to which would inevitably be hearsay, would be disallowed: see *R* v *Thomson* [1912] 3 KB 19.

You must also bear in mind at all times the risk of 'losing the shield' of a client who has a criminal record by inadvertent attacks on the integrity of prosecution witnesses. For a fuller discussion of this see **13.3**.

In cross-examination, leading questions may be asked, indeed they are often essential, much of the cross-examiner's time being taken up with attempting to establish the version of facts which he contends is true. The judge or clerk will control cross-examination and disallow questions he considers improper, abusive, vexatious or oppressive. Having said that, in cases where the liberty of the subject may depend upon the outcome, a good deal of latitude is usually allowed to the defence advocate even if the matter to be put to prosecution witnesses is highly offensive to them.

The two most important topics within the law relating to cross-examination concern previous inconsistent statements and cross-examination on collateral issues.

8.6.1   PREVIOUS INCONSISTENT STATEMENTS

We have considered prior inconsistent statements by one's own witness, and the effect of s. 3 of the Criminal Procedure Act 1865. We will now consider the situation where one knows that one's opponent's witness has made a previous statement inconsistent with his evidence-in-chief. Can one adduce evidence of his former statement?

The relevant sections are ss. 4 and 5 of the 1865 Act:

4.   If a witness, upon cross-examination as to a former statement made by him relative to the subject matter of the indictment or proceeding, and inconsistent with his present testimony, does not distinctly admit that he has made such statement, proof may be given that he did in fact make it; but before such proof can be given the circumstances of the supposed statement, sufficient to designate the particular occasion, must be mentioned to the witness, and he must be asked whether or not he has made such statement.

5.   A witness may be cross-examined as to previous statements made by him in writing, or reduce into writing, relative to the subject matter of the indictment or proceeding, without such writing being shown to him; but if it is intended to contradict such witness by the writing, his attention must, before such contradictory proof can be given, be called to those parts of the writing which are to be used for the purpose of so contradicting him: Provided always, that it shall be competent for

the judge, at any time during the trial, to require the production of the writing for his inspection, and he may thereupon make such use of it for the purposes of the trial as he may think fit.

8.6.1.1   Section 4

Section 4 applies to *oral statements*. If a witness is asked during cross-examination about a former statement made by him which is inconsistent with his present testimony, then if he does not admit that he made such a statement proof may be given that he did in fact make it. However, two things must be done before such proof can be given:

(a)   the circumstances in which the alleged statement were made must be put to the witness, and
(b)   he must then be asked whether he made such a statement.

If he then admits the statement or it is proved under the section, the effect is precisely the same as in the case of a hostile witness's previous statement, i.e. *they cancel each other out* — the former statement is not itself evidence of the facts stated (see *R* v *White* above). (N.B. If the witness is the accused there are special rules as to the effect of a previous admission which is now denied — see below on confessions.)

8.6.1.2   Section 5

Section 5 applies where the previous statement is in writing. A witness can be cross-examined about such a statement without the statement actually being shown to the witness. However, if the cross-examiner actually intends to contradict the witness by using the written statement he must draw the witness's attention to those parts he intends to so use.

A cross-examiner *is not obliged* to put the statement in evidence (remember that to do so makes the *whole* statement available to the jury and there may be matter in it that the cross-examiner would prefer them not to see), and this is so even if he shows it to the witness — this is not 'putting it in evidence'. However, the cross-examiner must do so if he wishes to use the document as a contradictory statement made by the witness, and the witness must of course be given a chance to explain the contradiction.

In such a case, the usual procedure is that counsel asks the witness to read the statement to himself and asks him if he wishes to adhere to what he said in chief. If the witness says 'no', counsel has achieved his object — he has shown the jury that the witness is unreliable. If he says 'yes', then it is necessary for counsel to decide whether or not to use the statement to contradict the witness, and if he does so the whole statement becomes evidence in the case. It is only a witness's *own statement* which should be handed to him — this rule cannot be used as a way of making a witness look at other people's statements and comment on inconsistencies so that those other statements become evidence in the case. See *R* v *Gillespie & Simpson* (1967) 51 Cr App R 172.

There is the important provision in the concluding words of s. 5 that the judge has the overriding discretion at any time to require the document to be produced for his inspection. Although the wide words 'he may thereupon make such use of it . . . as he may think fit' might appear to give him an unfettered discretion it is clear that he is *not entitled* himself to show the statement to the jury and make it evidence in the case. This is up to counsel who is using it, and him only: see *R* v *Birch* (1924) 18 Cr App R 26.

8.6.2   CROSS-EXAMINATION ON COLLATERAL ISSUES

Cross-examination is directed either to the *issues in the case* or *collateral issues*. When it is directed to the issues in the case, what is asked is up to counsel (subject to the judges' control of improper questions), and there is an opportunity for counsel to call evidence in contradiction or rebuttal of what a witness says.

However, there are special rules relating to cross-examination on collateral issues, which are designed to stop a multiplicity of side-tracks being pursued in the interests of saving time.

8.6.2.1 Cross-examination as to credit

The chief collateral issue is credit of the witness, i.e. the extent to which his evidence is trustworthy. The general rule is that a witness's answers in relation to the *issues* in the case can be contradicted by further evidence but that answers relevant only to *credit* are final. As is explained in *Cross on Evidence*:

> As relevance is a matter of degree, it is impossible to devise an exhaustive means of determining when a question is collateral for the purpose of the rule under consideration; Pollock, C.B. said in the leading case of *A-G* v *Hitchcock* (1847)
>
>> The test whether a matter is collateral or not is this: if the answer of a witness is a matter which you would be allowed on your own part to prove in evidence — if it has such a connection with the issues, that you would be allowed to give it in evidence — then it is a matter on which you may contradict him.

The test is sometimes difficult to apply and it is not always easy to see where the issues in the case end and credit begins.

An example of this difficulty is the old rule (now modified as discussed later) that in a rape case the complainant could be asked whether she had previously had consensual intercourse with the accused and if she denied it call evidence to rebut her denial. However, if one also asked her whether she had had intercourse with various other men and she denied it, no evidence in rebuttal could be called. The reasoning was that the first case went to the *issue* (i.e. the likelihood of consent) and the second just to *credit* (loose reputation) but the dividing line is obviously artificial.

An excellent general example is the old case of *R* v *Burke* (1858) 8 Cox CC 44. The accused was charged with rape. A witness was called on behalf of the accused and when being sworn the witness who was Irish professed that he could not speak English. Accordingly he was sworn in Irish and gave his evidence in that language through an interpreter. Later it came to the prosecuting counsel's notice that there were two other witnesses who knew the present witness; they told prosecuting counsel that the witness could speak English perfectly well, had often spoken to them in English, and had even sung a song to them in English. The witness was cross-examined on this matter and he denied again that he could speak English or ever had done so. The prosecution applied to call the two girls to contradict his evidence and thus to prove that he was an untruthful person. The judge refused leave to call the two witnesses. It was held that whether or not this witness could or could not speak English was an entirely collateral matter and nothing to do with guilt or innocence of the prisoner. Although this would have tended to totally discredit the witness it was not allowed; however if the very issue in the case had been his knowledge of English, e.g., his authorship of some relevant document, it would have been permitted.

There are several exceptions to the general rule that answers as to credit are final; in the following cases evidence in rebuttal is allowed:

(a) *At common law* after a witness has given evidence the other side can call evidence to swear that the first witness has *a general reputation as a liar* and that his evidence should not be believed: see *R* v *Richardson and Longman* (1969) 52 Cr App R 317. This is a very old exception rarely used today. Indeed in the case of *Richardson* v *Longman* the judge indicated that he had never heard of the rule before authority was produced to him. Evidence as to the reputation for untruthfulness of a complainant in a sexual case was admitted under this principle in *R* v *Bogie* [1992] Crim LR 301.

(b) *Evidence of the physical or mental condition* of a witness such as to show he is unreliable may be admitted. In *Toohey* v *Metropolitan Police Commissioner* [1965] AC 595 the House of Lords held that it was proper to call a medical witness to give evidence that the alleged victim of a crime had a hysterical personality, and when under the influence of alcohol (as was the case on the facts) might well misunderstand situations (e.g., as on the facts where he had accused two men who were helping him up from where he had fallen with attempting to rob him). The primary importance of *Toohey* is that it sanctions the calling of an expert witness to impugn the reliability of an opponents' witness on medical grounds. The point was made that, where appropriate, a medical witness might be called to swear to the fact that a previous witness had, for example, impaired vision or hearing and the situation in *Toohey* was said to be analogous.

(c) *Previous convictions*. By s. 6 of the Criminal Procedure Act 1865 (applicable to civil proceedings as well) a witness 'may be asked whether he has been convicted of any . . . [crime], and if he denies it the cross-examiner may prove it'. This is so *however little relevant* it is to the issue of the witness's credibility, e.g., whether the conviction was for careless driving or perjury. This does not, of course, apply to the accused who usually cannot be asked this kind of question (see below on the character of accused).

Previous convictions may be proved by certificate from the court of conviction under s. 75, Police and Criminal Evidence Act 1984. Note that s. 4(1) of the Rehabilitation of Offenders Act 1974 prohibits questions about spent convictions in civil proceedings. Section 7(2) of the Act permits such questions in criminal proceedings, but see *Practice Direction (Crime: Spent Convictions)* [1975] 1 WLR 1065 to the effect that questions about such conviction should only be asked where necessary in the interests of justice and with the leave of the trial judge. The judge has a wide discretion in this matter. In *R v Evans* [1992] Crim LR 125 the accused was charged with wounding and his defence was self-defence. His counsel wished to put to the victim a number of previous convictions for dishonesty and violence all of which were spent under the 1974 Act. The judge refused to allow the question. On appeal the court held, ordering a retrial, that where there was a head-on collision between the accused and the alleged victim the judge should have allowed defence counsel to put in the witness's criminal record and he had been wrong in the exercise of his discretion to refuse leave.

(d) *Bias*. Bias generally means taking bribes from a party or having very close relations with one party. It can however also mean the opposite, that is bias *against* a party, e.g., because of a grudge. If such an allegation is put in cross-examination and denied, evidence in rebuttal may be called. For example, in *R v Mendy* (1976) 64 Cr App R 4 the accused was charged with assault. As is usual all the witnesses were kept out of court before they gave evidence. Whilst a police witness was given evidence a constable in court noticed a man in the public gallery taking notes. This man was then seen to leave court and apparently discuss the case with the accused's husband. The husband then gave evidence. On cross-examination he denied that he had spoken to a man who had been taking notes in the public gallery. The prosecution were permitted, rightly it was held, to call evidence of the note-taking and discussion to rebut the husband's evidence on the basis of its bias.

In *R v Shaw* [1888] 16 Cox CC 503 the accused was charged with forgery. The main witness against him was one P who stated that he had laid in wait and seen the accused forging the documents in question. He was asked, in cross-examination, whether he did not have an ancient grudge against the accused arising out of an incident some two years before. He denied this. The defence were then allowed to call a witness to whom P had sworn to get even with the accused because of the grudge.

(e) *Previous inconsistent statements*. The whole question of previous inconsistent statements could be seen as an exemption to the rule on finality of answers on collateral issues. The proof of the making of the inconsistent statement in a criminal trial goes of course to credit — a collateral issue.

(f) *Victims of rape offences*. As indicated above, questions to the complainant as to whether she had previously had consensual intercourse with the accused are relevant to the issue of consent and therefore evidence may be called by *the accused* to rebut a denial. Questions about sexual experience with *other men* were formerly treated as relevant to credit only and the answers were therefore final. If the allegation went beyond mere intercourse with other men and suggested that the alleged victim was actually a prostitute, evidence of her behaviour with other men might be admitted because the victim's profession as a prostitute was central to the issue of consent. See *R v Bashir & Mansur* [1969] 3 All ER

692; and *R v Krausz* (1973) 57 Cr App R 466. Now, however, s. 2(1) of the Sexual Offences (Amendment) Act 1976 provides that at a trial for a 'rape offence' (as defined) the complainant may only be *cross-examined* about her experience with men other than the accused with leave of the judge, such leave only to be given where the judge is satisfied it would be unfair to the accused to refuse it. The same applies where the accused wishes to *call evidence* of the complainant's sexual experience with other men. The leave of the judge will be required on the same basis. An alleged victim of rape may however be cross-examined freely about her sexual relations with the accused himself.

For an early application of the basic rule see *R v Mills* (1978) Cr App R 327. The accused was charged with rape and he wished to call evidence of the victim's sexual experience with other men. The judge formed the view that this was nothing to do with the issue in the case and was entirely designed to blacken the character of the complainant. It was held that in all circumstances it was perfectly proper to disallow the cross-examination.

An interesting case showing a good example of when a court thought leave to call such evidence would have been appropriate is *R v Viola* [1982] 3 All ER 73. The accused was charged with rape. He knew the complainant slightly and whilst in her flat on another matter had intercourse with her. She alleged that the intercourse occurred only after a violent assault. There were a number of suspicious features in the case, *inter alia* that the complainant did not report the rape for some three days. The accused wished to cross-examine the alleged victim on three separate matters, namely:

    (i)   An allegation that very shortly before the rape occurred the victim had made sexual advances to two men who came to her flat.
    (ii) Shortly after the rape the complainant had sexual intercourse with her boyfriend.
    (iii) On the day following the rape a neighbour saw a man in the complainant's flat lying on the sofa wearing nothing except a pair of slippers. The trial judge refused to permit cross-examination on these matters.

It was held on appeal that, although these matters were very much ones of fact and degree, in all the circumstances and taken with the other suspicious elements it would have been proper to allow cross-examination of the complainant on these matters, and in the circumstances the conviction was quashed.

Other cases where the court has held it proper to allow cross-examination about other sexual behaviour include: *R v Cox* (1987) 84 Cr App R 132, where it appeared that the alleged victim had made a false complaint of rape against another man; *R v Ellis* [1990] Crim LR 717, where the alleged victim had substantiated her evidence about her feeling of being violated by having claimed that she had to have a bath immediately — evidence should have been permitted to show that she regularly had baths after consensual sex; and *R v Riley* [1991] Crim LR 460, where the alleged victim had contended that she would never have consented to intercourse with the accused because her young child was sleeping in the room — on appeal it was held that the judge should have allowed the accused to call evidence from a previous boyfriend of the alleged victim that he had regularly had intercourse with her in the bedroom with the child present.

See also *R v Bogie* [1992] Crim LR 301 where it appears that the complainant's past promiscuity was so extreme that it could hardly fail to be relevant on the findings of the case. See also however *R v Brown* (1989) 89 Cr App R 97 where the accused wished to put to the victim details of her promiscuity with other men in that she was alleged to suffer from venereal disease; had had a child by another man six months previous to the rape; and had admitted that she had started what she herself described as a 'casual sex relationship' with another man only 10 days before the alleged rape. The court considered that whilst everything was a matter of degree there was not such evidence of sexual promiscuity of sufficient contemporaneity to the alleged rape as to cross the border between mere credit and an issue in the case.

This concludes the section on collateral issues. It should finally be noted that where it is the *accused* who is being cross-examined, there may be other specific principles to be considered where his credit is being impugned in certain ways, e.g., by adducing evidence of previous convictions in those cases where this is permitted. (See below on the character of the accused.)

8.7   Re-examination

In re-examination of one's own witnesses leading questions may not be asked. Questions must be confined to matters which arise out of cross-examination. A new matter may only be introduced with the leave of the judge and leave will not easily be given.

Re-examination is usually an attempt to salvage evidence which has been shaken in cross-examination. It involves counsel asking his witness, obviously in a more sympathetic manner than that shown by the cross-examiner, to explain any ambiguities or confusion in his evidence. It is an attempt to allow the witness to clarify matters and to re-establish his credit generally. Because re-examination is within the discretion of the judge there is very little case law on it.

8.8   Evidence in Rebuttal

All the evidence which the plaintiff or prosecutor intends to call should be before the court before the end of his case. New evidence can only be called after the defence case with leave of the judge and he will only give leave if the evidence relates to a matter which could not reasonably have been foreseen.

A good example is the old case of *R* v *Day* [1940] 1 All ER 402. The accused was charged with forging a cheque. The prosecution called evidence and then the defence gave evidence denying the forgery. Thereafter counsel for the prosecution applied for leave to call the evidence of a handwriting expert. The judge permitted this. On appeal the conviction was quashed. It was held that the evidence was wrongly admitted as it was not evidence arising on a matter which arose *ex improviso* nor evidence the necessity for which no human ingenuity could have foreseen. It should have been obvious to the prosecution that they would need a handwriting expert from the outset. There had accordingly been a material irregularity.

The judgment is not really as harsh as it may appear. There is some possibility that the accused in such cases might be prejudiced if he did not then have a chance of finding and bringing to court an expert witness of his own to rebut the prosecution's expert witness; there would thus be delay, adjournments and inconvenience.

This rule has been applied with some firmness until relatively recently. However, there are now signs that the court is relaxing it. So in *R* v *Francis*, *The Times*, 31 January 1990 prosecuting counsel in error failed to call a police inspector to prove the circumstances of an identification parade. Later the prosecution were allowed to call the police inspector to rectify his omission. The Court of Appeal agreed that there was 'a further flexible discretion to admit evidence in proper circumstances'.

Similarly, in *R* v *Bowles* [1992] Crim LR 726, whilst the defendant was testifying a juror asked a question as a result of which it seemed appropriate for prosecuting counsel to adduce more evidence. The judge permitted this. The appeal was dismissed. The court conceded that the matter had not really arisen *ex improviso* but should perhaps have occurred to prosecuting counsel before; nor could it be said that the new evidence was a mere formality. Although these were the two recognised exceptions there was no need to confine the possibility of further evidence to them. In all the circumstances of the case no injustice had been caused since the evidence adduced late was non-controversial.

A further illustration of the increasing willingness of the court to be flexible is shown in *R* v *Patel* [1992] Crim LR 739 wherein new evidence was admitted even after counsel's closing speeches. The court actually said that it was probably not helpful to use the *ex improviso* test in such cases. It was always a matter for the judge's discretion and, although the later in the trial an application was made to call such evidence the less likely it would be for a judge to agree, in the present case there was no injustice, especially as the judge had given counsel every opportunity to seek an adjournment or take further instructions or even to apply for the discharge of the jury.

This concludes the notes on testimony, but it is appropriate to consider one further matter before leaving the subject.

8.9 The Judge's Right to Call Witnesses

It is an essential part of the adversarial process that the parties themselves decide which witnesses they wish to call and what questions to ask. In a criminal trial, the competitive nature of the adversarial process has some refinements to mitigate it. First, the prosecution do not have a duty to press ruthlessly for a conviction at any price, they should present evidence aimed at securing conviction but must also, for example, tell the accused of matters helpful to him (e.g., if an identification witness has given a description of the suspect that does not fit the accused). The prosecutor ought to act as a 'minister of justice'.

Likewise in a criminal trial the judge has an overriding duty to see that justice is done and has the power to call a witness whom neither side has called (provided he is competent and compellable of course). This should happen very rarely: see *R* v *Harris* [1927] 2 KB 587, where several accused were charged with dishonesty. A number of the accused pleaded guilty at the outset and thereafter remained in the dock during the trial of the others. At the conclusion of the prosecution and defence cases the judge asked one of the accused who had previously pleaded guilty whether he was prepared to give evidence. The man said that he was, and the judge then called him to give evidence and his evidence strengthened the case against H. The resulting conviction was quashed on appeal. It was held that in order that injustice must not be done to an accused the judge should not call a witness in a criminal trial after the case for the defence is closed except in a case where the matter arises in such a way that no human ingenuity could foresee it. See also *R* v *Cleghorn* [1967] 2 QB 584.

The Court of Appeal has several times recently reaffirmed that a judge's right to call a witness should only be exercised very sparingly. It should only be exercised where the judge concludes that a certain witness should testify in the interests of justice and both parties are declining to call him. This may often occur where the defence would like the witness to be called for the purpose of cross-examination but, if the defence call the witness, they would be unable to cross-examine him since he is their own witness. In such a case the judge should consider an application to call the witness if he thinks the evidence will assist. A judge must be cautious however where neither party wishes to call a witness. So, for example, in *R* v *McDowell* [1984] Crim LR 486 a judge called a witness whom neither side wished to call in order to satisfy a query by a jury member after the jury had retired. The court held that as it was unable to assess the effect of this material irregularity the conviction had to be quashed.

In the rare case where the judge does call a witness he can be cross-examined by both sides but only with the leave of the trial judge. Leave will be given if the evidence is adverse to either party, and thus unless the witness in effect says nothing relevant to the case, leave will usually be given. Cross-examination may be restricted to the areas about which he has testified: see *Coulson* v *Disborough* [1894] 2 QB 316.

NINE

THE LAW OF EVIDENCE (3): THE RULE AGAINST HEARSAY

9.1 Introduction

The rule against hearsay used to be described as the great rule underlying the whole of the law of evidence. It is still of considerable importance but there are now very numerous exceptions to the basic rule forbidding hearsay which are applicable in criminal cases. *Cross on Evidence* gives a definition of the rule as 'A statement other than one made by a person while giving oral evidence in the proceedings is inadmissible as evidence of any fact stated.'

This rule applies to both oral and written statements and it applies even to what the person now giving evidence said out of court. When the rule applies to prevent a witness saying in court what *he himself* said on some other occasion it is usually called 'the rule against narrative' or 'the rule against self-corroboration'. It is important to remember that those occasions discussed in the earlier section on testimony, where a witness *may* repeat what he said on some previous occasion, e.g., sexual complaints, previous consistent statements used to rebut an allegation of recent fabrication, etc., do *not* infringe the hearsay rule because the previous statement is *not evidence of the facts stated* but of the maker's consistency.

There are many justifications of the rule against hearsay. As hearsay statements emanate from a person who is not under oath and is not before the court, that person's lack of truthfulness, defective memory or poor powers of observation cannot be called into question by cross-examination. In addition there is a danger of inaccuracy through repetition, especially of oral statements, and the problem that juries may attach too much weight to hearsay without realising its weaknesses.

There is no doubt that the strict application of the rule in criminal cases may lead to injustice. It means that a case will be decided without hearing all the available evidence, imperfect though some of it may be. It should also not be forgotten that the operation of the rule is not always for the protection of the accused — it may operate to prejudice him — see the facts of *Sparks* v *R* below.

9.1.1 ILLUSTRATIONS OF THE RULE

9.1.1.1 *R* v *Gibson* (1887) 18 QBD 537

A man was struck by a heavy stone and testified that, immediately after, a woman who could not be identified and who was not called at the trial said, pointing to Gibson's house, 'the person who threw the stone went in there'. It was held that the conviction of Gibson would be quashed on the grounds that this hearsay evidence should not have been admitted.

9.1.1.2   *Sparks* v *R* [1964] AC 964

The accused, a white man, was charged with indecent assault on a four-year-old child. He wished to bring evidence that the child had said to her mother after the assault that 'It was a coloured boy who did it.' It was held that there is no rule that permits hearsay evidence merely because it relates to identity or because it favours the accused.

9.1.1.3   *Patel* v *Controller of Customs* [1966] AC 356

It was held that the words 'produce of Morocco' stamped upon bags of coriander were inadmissible to prove the country of origin of the coriander. The words were stamped on the bag with the express intention of asserting a fact and were thus hearsay.

9.1.1.4   *R* v *Muir* [1984] Crim LR 101

The accused was charged with theft of a hired video. He contended that two unknown men whom he had assumed to be from the hire company had collected it from his house. The district manager of the company said that repossession of the equipment could be carried out by the local showroom or by the head office only. He said it had not been repossessed by the local office and that he had contacted head office and been told that no one from there had called on the appellant. It was held on appeal that the question was whether, as a matter of fact the video had been repossessed. As the district manager was the best person to give evidence of this his evidence was reliable. The court appears to have ducked the hearsay problem.

It is suggested with all due deference to the apparent common sense of the outcome that the evidence in question *was* hearsay. There are clearly very great difficulties about proving this kind of negative.

9.1.1.5   *Myers* v *DPP* [1965] AC 1001

The accused were charged with frauds involving dealing in stolen cars with false documents which actually related to scrapped vehicles. It was vital for the prosecution case to identify the actual cars involved which it was possible to do by reference to the number cast into the cylinder block. It was accordingly essential to prove the motor manufacturers' records to show the numbers which corresponded to the stolen cars. These records were microfilmed copies of record cards which had passed along the production line with the vehicle and on to which relevant numbers were enterd by workmen. It was held that these records amounted to hearsay and came within no recognised exception to the rule. The creation of new hearsay exceptions was for the legislature and accordingly the evidence was not admissible. In the circumstances however, the proviso was applied and the convictions affirmed.

The actual effect of this final recognition of the truth that business records were all hearsay, and therefore inadmissible, was reversed by the almost immediate passing of the Criminal Evidence Act 1965.

9.2   Unnoticed Hearsay

It is apparent when reading reports of decided cases that courts do not always appreciate the existence of a hearsay problem. As Cross says this may sometimes be because the court regarded the applicability of some exception as too obvious to mention but there are also instances of the very existence of any problem at all being overlooked.

A clear case of this is *R* v *Cooper* [1969] 1 QB 267 where it is apparent that a considerable volume of hearsay which was not within any of the exceptions to the exclusionary rule, and therefore quite inadmissible, was allowed. Moreover, neither at first instance nor on appeal is there even any reference to the problem existing — the case as reported turning on quite a different point. The accused was charged with assault and whilst on remand in custody he was visited by two friends D and B. D gave evidence that one day whilst walking away from the prison B had confessed to him that he, B, and not Cooper had committed the assault. The trial court seems not to have appreciated that there was any hearsay problem with this evidence. Indeed the trial court subsequently permitted a photograph of B to be produced to prove the close similarity between the defendant and B.

9.3   Is It Hearsay At All?

When one is confronted by a statement made by someone out of court, whether oral or in writing, naturally one needs to consider the possibility that it is hearsay. It is by no means always the case that words said outside court and repeated in it will amount to hearsay. What matters is whether the statement from the speaker outside court is *tendered to prove the truth of its contents*.

The most important case clearly demonstrating this is *Subramaniam* v *Public Prosecutor for Malaya* [1956] 1 WLR 965. The accused was found in possession of ammunition contrary to an emergency regulation. He put forward the defence that he had been captured by terrorists and that at all material times he was acting under duress. He wished to give evidence of the threats made to him by the terrorists but the trial judge ruled that evidence of the conversation with the terrorists was inadmissible hearsay. The accused was convicted and on appeal the Privy Council held that evidence of words spoken is not hearsay and is admissible where it is proposed to establish by the evidence not the *truth* of the statement but the *fact that it was made* as being relevant to an event in issue namely the state of mind of the accused. The conviction was quashed.

9.4   Nature of Hearsay

It is suggested by Cross that you must ask two questions to find out if something is hearsay:

(a)   For what purpose is the statement put in evidence?
(b)   What fact is the statement tendered to prove?

If the statement expressly or impliedly *asserts a fact* the hearsay rule applies, and the *statement must be excluded as inadmissible* unless it comes within one of the exceptions.

9.4.1   EXPRESS ASSERTIONS

Express assertions occur where the witness who is not before the court has stated that a certain state of affairs is the case, e.g., as in the cases of *Gibson* and *Sparks* shown above. With express assertions there must be an intention to communicate, thus non-verbal behaviour such as nods, gestures, pointing or signs may well amount to an express assertion when what the person making the sign did is recounted to the court by another witness. As there must however, be some intention to communicate nobody has ever suggested that, say, a footprint or yawning is subject to the hearsay rule.

9.4.2   IMPLIED ASSERTIONS

The reason why express assertions are excluded by the hearsay rule is obvious. They suffer from all the potential defects referred to above. The position may however be different with *implied* assertions. This is where the maker of the statement did not intend to assert any particular fact. An example is if the prosecution need to establish that X was present at a given place and time but no eye-witness has been found who can positively say he was there. However one person who was there heard someone shout out 'Hallo X'. Since shouting 'Hallo' is not an assertion of anything, would this fall foul of the hearsay rule?

The reason why it has often been suggested that these kind of statements ought to be admissible as exceptions to the hearsay rule is that there is a smaller risk of untruthfulness with implied assertions. It has been suggested for example that if in *R* v *Gibson* (1887) 18 QBD 537 the woman bystander had been heard to shout 'Hallo Mr Gibson where are you going?'. This would have been admissible because the woman was not intending to assert anything to a third party. The authorities in England are not entirely conclusive. Consider the following cases.

9.4.2.1   *R v Teper* [1952] AC 480

The accused was charged with arson of his own shop in order to obtain insurance. Evidence was given by a policeman that some 26 minutes after the fire started and over 200 yards away from the fire he heard a woman's voice shouting 'your place burning and you going away from the fire' and thereupon a black car containing a man who resembled the accused went past. The woman could not be traced at the time of the trial. It was held that the words spoken by the woman were inadmissible hearsay. They asserted a fact, namely the presence of the accused at the time of the crime. The conviction was quashed.

9.4.2.2   *R v Lydon* (1986) 85 Cr App R 221

The case of *Patel* v *Controller of Customs* [1966] AC 356 has been referred to in **9.1.1.3**. A case often contrasted with that is *R v Lydon* (1986) 85 Cr App R 221 where the accused, Sean Lydon, was charged with a robbery at a post office in Oxfordshire. He lived in Neasden, North London. There was identification evidence from a taxi driver who identified him as a man he had taken on a journey from Oxfordshire to Neasden on the day in question. The car used in the robbery was abandoned near where the taxi driver had picked Lydon up and that car had been stolen from the Neasden area. A mile from the post office on the road between it and the place where the car was found abandoned, a gun was found on the grass verge similar to the gun used in the robbery. Near the gun were two pieces of rolled paper on which was written the name 'Sean'. Ink of similar appearance to that ink was found on the gun barrel. It was argued that allowing the pieces of paper to go forward was to permit hearsay evidence. The Court of Appeal held that it was not hearsay evidence but simply a piece of circumstantial evidence refuting the defendant's claimed alibi.

With all respect it seems that this case is dubious authority. Clearly the name written on the pieces of paper does not assert anything very much. But what surely matters is what the *prosecution* intend to assert by the use of the paper. Clearly they wish to 'assert' that Sean was the owner of the gun and was present at the time. Thus the evidence was tendered with a view to inviting the jury to draw conclusions which are of a hearsay nature.

9.4.2.3   *R v Korniak* (1983) 76 Cr App R 145

This is another difficult case. The accused was seen carrying a bag by police officers. It was found to contain valuable jewellery. At first the accused denied the bag was his and told lies but eventually admitted that he had bought the bag from a man who had at first asked £2,000 for it but eventually sold it for only £100. The accused then told the police they would have to 'do' him for receiving stolen property. He was charged with handling. He did not give evidence and at the time of trial there was no evidence to prove that the jewellery was stolen. The direction by the judge was that the jury could infer from the evidence that the jewellery was stolen. On appeal the grounds were that there was no evidence from which the jury could safely infer that the goods were stolen. It was held, rejecting the appeal, that there was ample evidence. Although the accused's own *belief* that it was stolen was relevant only to *mens rea* and not the fact there was sufficient circumstantial evidence of the fact of theft.

This case can be compared with *R v Marshall* [1977] Crim LR 106 where Marshall was charged with handling stolen goods and the only proof that they were stolen was that Marshall admitted that he had bought the goods from a man who had told him they were stolen. It was argued for the accused that such an admission was no more than hearsay and thus the status of the goods as stolen could not be proved. That submission was upheld. This case was not however cited in *Korniak*.

The difficulties of this problem seem to overwhelm the Court of Appeal whenever it has to consider similar cases. Thus in two other cases *R v Horne* [1992] Crim LR 304 and *R v McIntosh* [1992] Crim

LR 651, both concerned with allegations of drug dealing, pieces of paper were found in the premises of each accused which contained figures and computations which apparently could have meant nothing other than matters to do with drugs. In neither case does the court properly analyse the status of those documents although in *McIntosh* the court seems to have thought that the pieces of paper were somewhat like those in *Lydon*.

9.4.2.4   *R v Kearley* [1992] 2 WLR 656

All these cases must be read in the light of this new leading case. It follows on from and in part resolves difficulties caused in two conflicting earlier authorities. The first of these is *Woodhouse v Hall* (1980) 72 Cr App R 39. In this case the Divisional Court held that evidence of conversation between police officers and women working in a massage parlour in which details of availability and cost of sexual services were discussed was admissible as non-hearsay and circumstantial evidence that the premises were operated as a brothel.

Subsequently, however, in *R v Harry* (1986) 86 Cr App R 105 the question was the admissibility of evidence of telephone calls made to certain premises by a person who apparently wished to buy drugs from those premises. In the case of *Harry* one of two co-defendants wished to adduce evidence that the callers had always asked for his co-defendant P in order to suggest that P and not Harry was the dealer. The Court of Appeal held that the proposed evidence was hearsay because it was being offered to prove the truth of facts asserted by the callers.

In *Kearley's* case the Court of Appeal followed *Woodhouse v Hall* rather than *Harry* and held that evidence of the contents of telephone calls received at premises to the effect that the persons calling it expected to be able to buy drugs from the premises was admissible and was not hearsay. In the House of Lords however by a majority of three to two the House held that the evidence of the caller's words were either *irrelevant* to prove that K was supplying drugs because it merely tended to show that the callers believed that he was supplying drugs; or in the alternative that evidence of the calls *was* hearsay because the usefulness of the evidence depended on the trier of fact believing in the implied truth of matters asserted in the calls, namely that the persons telephoning expected to be able to buy drugs from the person at the other end of the telephone. Many find that the reasoning of the House of Lords is less than convincing and the point is clearly nicely balanced since the Court of Appeal reached a different conclusion and the House of Lords only reached its conclusion by a majority of three to two.

We have so far considered the problem of ascertaining whether a given statement made out of court is, or is not, hearsay at all. If it is not hearsay then it is admissible unless it offends some other separate exclusionary rule. If it is hearsay then in principle it is excluded unless it fits one or other of the numerous following exceptions.

9.5   Exceptions to the Rule in Criminal Cases

A number of exceptions have grown up, under common law or statute, some of them dating back some centuries. They are:

(a) Admissions and confessions (**9.6** and **10.1**)
(b) Statements made by deceased persons (**9.7**)
(c) Statements in public documents (**9.8**)
(d) Statements in former proceedings (**9.9**)
(e) Statutory exceptions (**9.10**)
(f) Statements admitted as part of the *res gestae* (**9.11**)

We shall now consider these exceptions in turn.

9.6   Admissions and Confessions

This topic is one of the most vital in practice. Because it is so important and lengthy it will be dealt with separately in **Chapter 10** together with the linked topics of questioning of suspects, the right of silence, and the Codes of Practice issued under the Police and Criminal Evidence Act 1984.

9.7   Statements made by Deceased Persons

Odd though it seems, the fact that the maker of an out-of-court statement has since died is not in itself a ground for the statement to be admitted in evidence. Thus it may well be, for example, that the evidence of the only truly independent eye-witness of a crime is lost because of the rule against hearsay. A number of common law exceptions exist which do permit the evidence of persons who have died before the trial to be put in at the trial. These were developed by the common law judges and there is a different rationale applicable to each of the several exceptions. It must be borne in mind that under ss. 23 and 24 of the Criminal Justice Act 1988, see **9.12.3**, statements *in writing* by deceased persons are now generally admissible. The exceptions which we are about to consider therefore will be chiefly relevant in the case of *oral* statements made by persons who have died before the trial.

9.7.1   DECLARATIONS AGAINST INTEREST

In criminal cases the oral or written statement by a person since deceased of a fact which he knew to be against his *pecuniary or proprietary interest* at the time he made it is admissible as evidence of the facts mentioned in it provided he had personal knowledge of such facts. This rule is now applicable only to criminal proceedings because by virtue of the Civil Evidence Act 1968 all statements of deceased persons are admissible in civil proceedings whether or not they comply with the limitations of being 'against interest' and the other conditions hereafter mentioned.

9.7.1.1   Statements against pecuniary interest

In *Higham* v *Ridgway* (1808) 10 East 109, an entry in the books of a male midwife who had died before the trial was permitted to prove the exact date of birth of a child because the entry also contained an acknowledgment that the midwife's fee had been paid. It was therefore 'against interest' because it would have stopped any further action by him in respect of his fee.

9.7.1.2   Statements against proprietary interest

As possession is prima facie evidence of ownership, a statement by a person in possession of something to the effect that he was *not* the owner is a declaration against interest.

Before this kind of statement as declarations against pecuniary or proprietary interest can be received in evidence four requirements must be satisfied:

(a)   Death of the maker of the statement.

(b)   The statement must have been against the declarant's interest when he made it, i.e. if he makes a statement which may or may not turn out at some subsequent time to be against his interest this statement is not within the rule and is inadmissible.

(c)   The maker must have *known* that the statement was against his pecuniary or proprietary interest. In *Tucker* v *Oldbury UDC* [1912] 2 KB 317, a workman was alleged to have injured his thumb in an accident at work and he later died from the injury. When an action was brought by his dependants the defendants sought to prove some statements made about the cause of the injury by the deceased. It was held that these were not admissible under this heading because at the time he made them the deceased was not aware that he had any right to make a claim and hence did not know that these statements were against his interest.

(d)   The maker must have had personal knowledge of the facts stated.

9.7.2 DECLARATIONS MADE IN THE COURSE OF DUTY

An oral or written statement of a person since deceased made in pursuance of a duty to record or report his acts is admissible as evidence of the truth of the contents of the statement provided that the record or report was made roughly contemporaneously with the doing of the act and provided there was no motive to misrepresent the facts.

In *Mellor* v *Walmesley* [1905] 2 Ch 164, a surveyor was employed to draw a plan of part of a seashore. Some time later it was necessary to prove certain boundaries on the seashore and the plan and field book entries made by the surveyor were produced under this exception to the rule since they were made in the discharge of his professional duty.

There are five conditions which must be met before this kind of evidence is received.

(a) Death of the maker.

(b) The maker must have had a duty to act and to record or report.

(c) The act must have been performed, not merely planned. For example, in *Rowlands* v *De Vecchi* (1882) 1 Cab & El 10, a clerk kept records of letters which he was about to take out to the post box. It was held that this record was inadmissible to prove that a certain letter had been posted because he wrote up the book before he went to the post. Had he written up the book when he had returned from the post the entries would have been admissible.

(d) The record must be made contemporaneously. In *Price* v *Earl of Torrington* (1703) 1 Salk 285, evidence of entries made in books each evening of acts done in the daytime was admitted but in *The Henry Coxon* (1878) 3 PD 156 entries made in a ship's log two days after a collision at sea, by a ship's mate, later deceased, were rejected. The requirement of contemporaneity therefore seems strict.

(e) There must be no motive to misrepresent. This was a further reason for the rejection in *The Henry Coxon* case where the mate had every motive to misrepresent the facts.

This old exception to the hearsay rule is still of use in modern times. For an interesting example see *R* v *McGuire* [1985] Crim LR 663. The accused was convicted of arson by setting fire to his own hotel to obtain insurance monies. Evidence was provided by a Home Office scientific officer who had inspected the hotel soon after the fire. He had recorded certain facts and also given his opinion that the fire was likely to have started in a certain room. This was helpful to the accused's own explanation and at the trial he sought to admit the report both as to the facts and as to the opinion, the scientific officer having died since making this statement. It was held that the report would be admitted as to the *facts* only but not as to the opinion part which was excluded (now the whole of the evidence would be admissible under ss. 24 and 30 of the Criminal Justice Act 1988 — see **14.2.6**).

9.7.3 DYING DECLARATIONS

Oral or written statements of a deceased person are admissible evidence of the cause of his death at a trial for his murder or manslaughter *provided* he was under a settled, hopeless expectation of death when the statement was made *and provided* he would have been a competent witness if called to give evidence at that time.

There are five conditions which must be satisfied before this kind of evidence may be received:

(a) Death of declarant.

(b) Trial for murder or manslaughter — it is not applicable to other crimes such as the offence of causing death by dangerous driving.

(c) The statement *must relate to the cause* of the declarant's death, that is it must identify the assailant or describe the act that was done.

(d) The declarant must have a *settled, hopeless expectation* of death.

So long as the expectation of death is firm it does not matter if the deceased takes some time to die, see *R* v *Bernadotti* (1869) 11 Cox CC 316 in which the victim made a dying declaration believing that he was about to die. He did not in fact die for nearly three weeks. It was held that there was no objection to the admission of the dying declaration. If a man believes himself dying it is equal to the solemnity of taking an oath.

But the expectations of death must be 'settled', see *R* v *Jenkins* (1869) LR 1 CCR 187 in which the victim's statement was taken down by a magistrates' clerk who added at the end the words 'made with no hope of my recovery'. The victim altered the words to read 'made with no *present* hope of my recovery' and it was held that the change of wording showed that the victim did entertain a faint hope and therefore the declaration was excluded.

Note that it is immaterial that the deceased entertained hopes of recovery *after* the statement was made provided that he or she had abandoned all hope of life when the statement was made: see *R* v *Hubbard* (1881) 14 Cox CC 565 in which the accused was charged with the murder of his wife. A dying declaration was made by the wife at a time when she believed that her death was impending. It was however shown that some time later she took a more cheerful view of her condition and thought she would recover. It was held that what matters is the state of mind at the time of making the declaration and the later more optimistic view did not affect the position.

Proof of this settled, hopeless expectation is best provided by the express statement of the deceased, but inferences may be drawn from other things, e.g., the deceased showing interest in funeral arrangements. It is however for the prosecution to prove this expectation positively not for the jury to speculate. See *R* v *Turnbull* (1984) 80 Cr App R 104, where even though the deceased was dying from multiple stab wounds the prosecution could not rely on this exception to prove his dying words because it was not positively shown that he knew he was dying.

In all the above cases the words spoken by the dying person indicated who the attacker was. However, note also *R* v *Scaife* (1836) 2 Lew CC 150 where the evidence admitted was favourable to the accused, the deceased's dying words being an expression of regret that he had provoked Scaife.

(e) The declarant must have been a competent witness had he survived, so in *R* v *Pike* (1829) 3 C & P 598 the declaration of a four-year-old child victim was rejected.

Note finally that there is no requirement that a jury should be warned that a dying declaration should be corroborated even if it is the only evidence against the accused. See *Nembhard* v *R* (1982) 74 Cr App R 144. The words of the declaration must however be clear and unambiguous.

9.8 Statements in Public Documents

In criminal and civil cases such statements are usually admissible evidence of the truth of their contents at common law and by virtue of many statutes. Thus a birth certificate is evidence as to date of birth, name, identity of parents, etc. The rationale of the exception is said to be the fact that such documents are unlikely to be inaccurate as public officials are under a duty to compile them; and the rule in favour of admissibility saves calling public officials to prove the documents. In many cases of course such evidence will be the best evidence available (e.g., a marriage certificate as proof that a marriage occurred after the deaths of the parties, witnesses, and registrar).

Such evidence is not necessarily irrefutable; the kind of evidence needed to refute the evidence in the public document will depend upon the nature of the document, the purpose of production, the kind of case, and the general law of burden and standard of proof.

The conditions of admissibility are:

(a) A public *duty to inquire and record*. This was a recognition of the fact that public officers would have personal knowledge of that which they record. However in the modern world this is not always practicable and the law must move with the times: see *R* v *Halpin* [1975] QB 907 where the accused were charged with conspiracy to defraud a local authority. It was vital to prove that the accused and his wife were the sole shareholders of a certain company which had a contract with the local authority. To prove this the prosecution wished to adduce the file from the Companies Registry containing the annual returns of the company. It was argued on appeal that the returns could not be admitted under this exception because the file was not made by a person having a duty to enquire into and satisfy himself of the truth of the facts recorded in that the Registrar of Companies merely received the returns submitted to him by the company. There was in fact no answer to this argument but the Court of Appeal decided that the common law must 'move with the times' and modified the condition judicially to suit modern conditions in that in the modern, highly complex world public officials could not always have personal knowledge of the records they made.

(b) The matter must be 'public' although it need not concern the entire community.

(c) The document must be *intended to be a permanent record*.

(d) It is said that the document must be *open to public inspection*: see *Lilley* v *Pettit* [1946] KB 401 where the accused was charged with making a false declaration relating to the birth of a child. It was shown that her husband was called up in 1939 and went abroad in 1941. He was subsequently made a prisoner of war by the Japanese and not released until 1945. On 15 May 1944 the accused registered the birth of the child as having been born on 1 May 1944 stating her husband was the father. The prosecution, in order to prove the husband's absence abroad at the material time, wished to adduce the regimental records. It was objected that these were not admissible under this exception because the public did not have access to these records. On appeal it was held that this was right and they were not public documents within the meaning of the rule.

This category, viewed as a separate exception to the hearsay rule, ought now to be virtually obsolete due to the almost complete overlap with s. 24, Criminal Justice Act 1988 (see **9.12.3.2**).

9.9 Statements in Former Proceedings

A number of statutes provide for the reception of evidence of what was said in depositions and testimony at subsequent stages of criminal proceedings. There are also statutes which provide that subject to certain procedural safeguards, certain kinds of witnesses may have their statement taken on oath by a magistrate out of court and that such a statement may be used at a subsequent trial on indictment. The variety of common law and statutory rules relating to this have been largely superseded by s. 24 of the Criminal Justice Act 1988 which covers statements put in evidence in former proceedings which are contained in a record (i.e. the transcript of that evidence). It is worth noting a couple of examples however, because the courts have developed a discretion to exclude such evidence, even though it may fulfil the strict criteria for admissibility and the exercise of that discretion is a good illustration of the way in which the court's other discretions under the Criminal Justice Act 1988 may well be used (see **9.12.3.3**).

In *R* v *Hall* [1973] QB 496, X gave evidence for the prosecution at the trial of the accused and the jury disagreed. Before the retrial X died. At the trial the defence wished to put in evidence the transcript of X's evidence at the first trial because X had shown himself to be a shifty and cantankerous witness and the prosecution case in part depended on X's evidence. The judge refused to permit this, holding that the evidence was inadmissible under the hearsay rule. It was held on appeal that the conviction would be quashed in that the deposition of the witness who had died before trial was admissible in evidence subject to the judge's discretion and the judge had wrongly exercised his discretion in the present case.

Note that in this case the accused's counsel argued also that this was not hearsay at all but fell within the principle in *Subramaniam* v *Public Prosecutor* (see **9.3**), i.e. it was being adduced not to show that it was *true* but to show that it was *said at all* and how it was said.

The admissibility of statements in other proceedings was also considered in *R* v *Binham* [1991] Crim LR 774. In this case the accused was charged with robbery. A shoe worn by him when arrested matched a shoe impression found at the scene. In evidence B claimed that he had bought the shoes after the date of offence at an Oxfam market stall and that he had bought them for the purpose of a job training scheme. The jury disagreed and there was a retrial. By the time of the retrial the Crown had found evidence to show that the story about the shoe was untrue because there was no Oxfam market stall nor had B applied for a job training scheme. The judge admitted evidence of the transcript of B's evidence at the first trial to demonstrate that he had lied. B tried to explain away the discrepancies. He was convicted and appealed contending that it had been wrong to admit the transcript of the earlier evidence. The appeal was dismissed. The previous statements were not hearsay because they were introduced to establish the fact of the accused having told lies rather than to establish the truth of the statement.

From these cases it is possible to see a test as to what sort of evidence from former proceedings is admissible in later criminal proceedings:

> (a) The evidence should have been for or against the accused in relation to substantially the same facts.
> (b) The judge has a wide discretion to exclude it if it would be unfair to the accused to admit it.

9.10 Statutory Exceptions

There are numerous statutes which provide exceptions to the hearsay rule. These can be conveniently divided into three groups, the first of which follows on naturally from the last exception: depositions taken before magistrates (**9.11**); major statutory exceptions (**9.12**); and minor exceptions (**9.13**).

9.11 Statutory Exceptions: Depositions taken before Magistrates and used in Later Proceedings

9.11.1 MAGISTRATES' COURTS ACT 1980, s. 105

This provides that a deposition of a witness who is very ill may be taken out of court by a magistrate provided the defendant is given an opportunity to attend and cross-examine. The deposition must then be served on him and can then be admitted at the trial.

9.11.2 CRIMINAL JUSTICE ACT 1925, s. 13(3)

The deposition of a witness who at the committal proceedings was conditionally ordered to appear at the trial may be read at the trial if he is proved to be dead, insane, too ill to travel, or kept away by the accused. The missing witness must be proved by the evidence given on oath of a credible witness to be within one of these categories and the court must consider the possibility of prejudice to the accused.

An interesting case is *R* v *Blithing* (1983) Cr App R 86. The evidence of a vital witness given at committal proceedings was used at trial after the witness had died. The judge ruled that he should only exclude the evidence if it was 'grossly' unfair to the accused. On appeal it was held that that was too weak a test. The correct test was one of simple unfairness and the judge should have excluded the statement.

The section has also been considered in *R* v *O'Loughlin and McLaughlin* [1988] 3 All ER 431 in which the two accused were charged with conspiracy to cause explosions. Two vital witnesses who gave evidence at committal proceedings had returned to the Irish Republic and told the police they were too frightened to come to trial. The court held that the fact of their fear had not been satisfactorily proved by a policeman simply saying that he believed it to be the case that they were afraid. Neither could it be proved that they were 'kept out of the way . . . by the accused'. Thus the evidence could not be given.

9.12 Major Statutory Exceptions to the Hearsay Rule

9.12.1 CRIMINAL JUSTICE ACT 1967, s. 9; MAGISTRATES' COURTS ACT 1980, s. 102

These are the most important sections in practice. They are in daily use in thousands of criminal cases throughout the country. The sections provide that statements in writing are admissible in criminal proceedings at committal or trial provided the statements are signed and contain a declaration in specified words by the maker that they are true and that the maker knows he is liable to prosecution if he states anything untruthfully.

Before such a statement is admissible in evidence it must be served on the opposing party. That party (whether prosecution or defence) may then object to the statement and if he does object the statement is inadmissible. The objection may be made on any ground at all, or indeed without giving any ground. If a party objects to his opponent using the statement the court has no power to overrule the objection and to allow the statement to be put in. Accordingly these sections are only used for uncontroversial statements.

A case which took prosecutors by surprise and showed that s. 9 should not be used for proving important matters is *Lister* v *Quaife* [1983] 2 All ER 29. In this case the accused was stopped leaving a branch of a chain store carrying a dress bearing a sale sticker. She could not prove that she had bought it but on being charged made a statement saying she had bought it at another branch of the chain store and had brought it back to change it. Before her trial the prosecution notified her that they would be tendering under s. 9 of the 1967 Act two written statements to the effect that no such dress would have been on sale at any of the store's branches at the sale price for three weeks after the date on which she claimed to have originally bought the dress and moreover that the branch at which she claimed to have bought it had no stocks of that particular dress. No objection to the s. 9 notice was served requiring the makers to attend. At trial their statements were read out. The defendant however persisted with her version that the officials of the chain store must be mistaken. The prosecution submitted that once statements were not objected to under s. 9 the defendant could not give evidence contradicting them. The defendant however was acquitted. On appeal by the prosecutor it was held that the statement under s. 9 was not deemed to be conclusive evidence of the matter stated in it but was treated in the same way as any other evidence. It would be better in a case where the evidence in question was crucial to the issue for s. 9 not to be used but the witness to be called in person.

The procedural requirements of s. 9 must be strictly complied with. Thus in *Paterson* v *DPP* [1990] Crim LR 651 the accused was convicted of driving with excess alcohol and as part of the case against him a seven-page statement by a policeman was tendered under s. 9 of the 1967 Act. The statutory declaration required by the Act was at page 7 and referred to '6 pages signed' by the officer. Also, the officer had not signed one of the pages. The prosecution argued that these errors were immaterial, but the court excluded the evidence, holding that the 1967 Act must be strictly complied with.

9.12.2 THE BANKER'S BOOKS EVIDENCE ACT 1879, ss. 3 and 4

Section 3 provides that:

> . . . a copy of any entry in a banker's book shall in all legal proceedings be received as prima facie evidence of such entry, and of the matters, transactions and accounts therein recorded.

Section 4 adds the qualification that the book in question must have been one of the ordinary books in the bank and the entries must have been made in the ordinary course of business. Most of the case law has involved definition of what is a 'bank' and what is meant by a 'banker's book'. This is a useful provision which may in any event be superseded in cases of difficulty by evidence which would be admissible under s. 24 of the Criminal Justice Act 1988 (see **9.12.3.2**).

9.12.3   DOCUMENTARY EVIDENCE UNDER CRIMINAL JUSTICE ACT 1988, ss. 23–28; POLICE AND CRIMINAL EVIDENCE ACT 1984, s. 69

The facts of *Myers* v *DPP* [1965] AC 1001 are set out at **9.1.1.5**. The case was immediately followed by the passing of the Criminal Evidence Act 1965. This was a one-section Act which had the effect of creating a new exception to the hearsay rule whereby, in short, the records of a trade or business were admissible in evidence if the person supplying the information in the record was unavailable to testify for one of certain specified reasons, namely death, absence abroad, illness, he could not be traced or identified or even if found would have no recollection of the matters contained in the records. These last two reasons were the most important in practice and covered the common situation (as in *Myers* v *DPP* itself) where an employee made some kind of record at work and the record became relevant to a criminal trial, often some considerable time after its compilation. The employee (who may, as in *Myers* v *DPP*, be one of many engaged in the activity concerned) cannot then be identified, or if he can be identified would not be able to say that he had any genuine recollection of the circumstances of what he recorded, e.g., because he has made many such written records every day over a long period and has no reason to remember the one with which the criminal trial is concerned.

The 1965 Act worked reasonably well although the restriction of its scope to 'trade or business records' proved inconvenient. In a number of cases this prevented the records of certain bodies being used in evidence because they were not 'trades or businesses'. Thus the records of an NHS hospital, and even the Home Office, were excluded in decided cases even though their records would obviously be just as accurate as, say, the ledger accounts of a corner shop whose records would in fact have been admissible under the 1965 Act.

The Civil Evidence Act 1968 (relevant of course only to civil proceedings) contained a section, s. 4, which was rather similar in principle to the 1965 Act except that this provision permitted in evidence *any* record, not just that of a trade or business, provided that the record concerned was compiled by a person acting under a duty from information supplied by a person who had first-hand knowledge of the matter in question. Thus, whereas the 1965 Act had provided a new category of admissibility of evidence whose reliability was supposed to be guaranteed by the fact that they were trade or business records, the emphasis in the 1968 Act switched to the question of the record being compiled by someone acting under a *duty*.

The Police and Criminal Evidence Act 1984 repealed and replaced the 1965 Act. Section 69 of the 1984 Act deals with computer records and is unaffected by the coming into force of the Criminal Justice Act 1988 (see **9.12.3.6**). Section 68 of the 1984 Act was intended to replace the 'documentary evidence' provisions of the 1965 Act. In place of the comparatively brief formula in the 1965 Act, s. 68 was a lengthy section, itself supplemented by a further lengthy schedule. The working of the section gave rise to a number of difficult cases and it was widely considered unsatisfactory, particularly in the context of evidence contained in police records.

Section 68 was repealed and replaced by the Criminal Justice Act 1988 which now contains the law on documentary evidence. There are two sections which deal with evidence in documents. Section 23 has to do with first-hand hearsay contained in such a document and that document may be of almost any kind. Section 24 has to do with second-hand hearsay made in a document in some kind of business or official context. When deciding upon what additional conditions would need to be satisfied before second-hand hearsay should be admitted, the legislature decided on a test fairly similar to that contained in s. 4 of the Civil Evidence Act, that is to say that evidence provided in a business context is likely to be inherently more reliable than documentary evidence which comes about more casually. In the following parts of this text we shall consider three different aspects of ss. 23 and 24 where there are crucially different provisions which apply, namely:

(a)   First-hand documentary evidence under s. 23.

(b)   Second-hand documentary evidence under s. 24 in an ordinary business context.

(c)   Second-hand documentary evidence under s. 24 which has been prepared expressly for the purpose of a criminal trial or investigation.

These provisions deal with evidence contained in a document. 'Document' is comprehensively defined to include maps, photographs, discs, tapes, videos and films as well as writing on paper. The sections read:

23.   First-hand hearsay

(1)   Subject—

(a)   to subsection (4) below;

(b)   to paragraph 1A of Schedule 2 to the Criminal Appeal Act 1968 (evidence given orally at original trial to be given orally at retrial); and

(c)   to section 69 of the Police and Criminal Evidence Act 1984 (evidence from computer records),

a statement made by a person in a document shall be admissible in criminal proceedings as evidence of any fact of which direct oral evidence by him would be admissible if—

(i)   the requirements of one of the paragraphs of subsection (2) below are satisfied; or

(ii)   the requirements of subsection (3) below are satisfied.

(2)   The requirements mentioned in subsection (1)(i) above are—

(a)   that the person who made the statement is dead or by reason of his bodily or mental condition unfit to attend as a witness;

(b)   that—

(i)   the person who made the statement is outside the United Kingdom; and

(ii)   it is not reasonably practicable to secure his attendance; or

(c)   that all reasonable steps have been taken to find the person who made the statement, but that he cannot be found.

(3)   The requirements mentioned in subsection (1)(ii) above are—

(a)   that the statement was made to a police officer or some other person charged with the duty of investigating offences or charging offenders; and

(b)   that the person who made it does not give oral evidence through fear or because he is kept out of the way.

(4)   Subsection (1) above does not render admissible a confession made by an accused person that would not be admissible under section 76 of the Police and Criminal Evidence Act 1984.

24.   Business etc., documents

(1)   Subject—

(a)   to subsections (3) and (4) below;

(b)   to paragraph 1A of Schedule 2 to the Criminal Appeal Act 1968; and

(c)   to section 69 of the Police and Criminal Evidence Act 1984,

a statement in a document shall be admissible in criminal proceedings as evidence of any fact of which direct oral evidence would be admissible, if the following conditions are satisfied—

(i)   the document was created or received by a person in the course of a trade, business, profession or other occupation, or as the holder of a paid or unpaid office; and

(ii)   the information contained in the document was supplied by a person (whether or not the maker of the statement) who had, or may reasonably be supposed to have had, personal knowledge of the matters dealt with.

(2)   Subsection (1) above applies whether the information contained in the document was supplied directly or indirectly but if it was supplied indirectly, only if each person through whom it was supplied received it—

(a)   in the course of a trade, business, profession or other occupation; or

(b)   as the holder of a paid or unpaid office.

(3)   Subsection (1) above does not render admissible a confession made by an accused person that would not be admissible under section 76 of the Police and Criminal Evidence Act 1984.

(4)   A statement prepared otherwise than in accordance with section 29 below or an order under paragraph 6 of Schedule 13 to this Act or under section 30 or 31 below for the purposes—

(a)   of pending or contemplated criminal proceedings; or

(b)   of a criminal investigation,

shall not be admissible by virtue of subsection (1) above unless—

(i) the requirements of one of the paragraphs of subsection (2) of section 23 above are satisfied; or

(ii) the requirements of subsection (3) of that section are satisfied; or

(iii) the person who made the statement cannot reasonably be expected (having regard to the time which has elapsed since he made the statement and to all the circumstances) to have any recollection of the matters dealt with in the statement.

9.12.3.1   First-hand documentary evidence under s. 23

Section 23 permits a statement made by a person in a document to be admissible as evidence of any fact of which direct oral evidence by him would have been admissible if one of the following reasons is proved:

(a) The person who made the statement is dead or by reason of bodily or mental condition is unfit to attend as a witness.

(b) The person who made the statement is outside the UK and it is not reasonably practicable to secure his attendance.

(c) All reasonable steps have been taken to find the person who made the statement but he cannot be found.

These reasons therefore would allow the putting in evidence of a witness statement of any kind made by a person.

Example: W is on the way to the airport on holiday when he sees a robbery. He has no time to stop and carries on to the airport but whilst on holiday writes a letter to his mother describing the incident he saw. He comes back from his holiday but later dies in an accident. The prosecution appeal for witnesses to the robbery and his mother provides a copy of the letter he wrote to her describing the incident. This would be prima facie admissible

(d) There is in addition a further provision, s. 23(3), for allowing the putting in evidence of a statement made to a police officer or some other person charged with the duty of investigating offences or charging offenders (such as a store detective or a Customs and Excise officer). In the case of such statements the additional ground is that the statement will be admissible if the person who made it does not give oral evidence through fear or because he is kept out of the way.

This provision allows the putting in evidence of first-hand hearsay in written form. However its scope is severely limited by the application of two later sections, ss. 25 and 26 which we shall consider in due course. Before we do so it is now appropriate to consider s. 24.

9.12.3.2   Second-hand hearsay contained in a document, s. 24

A statement in a document may be admissible by s. 24 as evidence of any fact of which direct oral evidence would be admissible, even though it is second-hand hearsay, provided that the following conditions are satisfied:

(a) the document must have been created or received by a person in the course of a trade or business profession or other occupation or as the holder of a paid or unpaid office; and

(b) the information contained in the document must have been supplied by a person (whether or not the maker of the statement) who had or may reasonably be supposed to have had personal knowledge of the matters dealt with.

This provision therefore supposes that there will be either one or two people involved in the 'document-creating process'. If there is any other person or persons so that there is a chain of information ending up with the document then there is further provision that each intermediary between the person who supplies the information and the person who compiles it in a document must have received it either in the course of a trade, business, profession or other occupation or as the holder of a paid or unpaid office.

We shall first deal with documents which arise in an ordinary business context as indicated above.

(a) Business documents

Example 1: A, a delivery driver for a computer firm, delivers 20 computers to the premises of a retail company X Ltd. On his return to his own firm he tells his delivery manager Z that he completed the delivery and the delivery manager makes a note of this in his records. Sometime later, at the premises of the retail company two computers are believed to be missing from stock and an employee is charged with their theft. In order to prove the number of computers that were in fact delivered on this occasion the deliveries record of the computer manufacturers would prima facie be admissible under this provision.

Example 2: S is the unpaid social secretary of a rugby club. Part of his duties include the management and supervision of the bar of the club and the keeping of the accounts for it. The bar is managed by a part-time paid barman. S's job includes receiving deliveries and checking stock. It is suspected that the barman is pilfering from stock and he is eventually charged with theft of some spirits found in his car. At his trial the records of deliveries and accounts kept by S would prima facie be admissible under this provision to establish the pilfering.

Where a document is compiled in what might be described as the course of everyday life, without any regard being had at the time of its making to its usefulness in criminal proceedings, then there is no necessary requirement that the person who made the document or gained the information should be unavailable for any particular reason. A court would thus be able to admit in evidence any such document even though apparently the people involved in its creation were available to testify. However there is a general discretion under s. 25 of the 1988 Act to which we shall come shortly to disallow the giving in evidence of such documents on various criteria which we shall consider.

(b) Criminal investigation documents

In addition to this, where the document was prepared for the purposes of pending or contemplated *criminal proceedings or a criminal investigation*, there is an express provision that the document shall *not* be admissible in criminal proceedings unless either the witness is unavailable for one of the reasons given above in the context of s. 23 for the absence of the original maker of the statement, or an additional reason provided by s. 24(4) namely that 'the person who made the statement cannot reasonably be expected (having regard to the time which has elapsed since he made the statement and to all the circumstances) to have any recollection of the matters dealt with in the statement'. In other words there is a presumption against admissibility of documents which amount to second-hand hearsay and which are prepared expressly for the purpose of criminal proceedings unless one of these particular reasons is shown for not calling as a witness the person who is the possessor of the original information which should be communicated to the court. This applies to both prosecution and defence, although of course in practice the section is much more likely to be relied upon by the prosecution. Quite apart from the need to demonstrate one of these reasons for unavailability the application to put in the evidence is still subject to the court's discretion which we shall shortly consider.

9.12.3.3   The court's discretion to exclude admissible evidence, ss. 25 and 26

A person who wishes to put in documentary evidence under ss. 23 and 24 has first to jump the hurdle of strict admissibility based on the matters we have discussed. Even where that hurdle is cleared, however, that does not mean that the evidence will be admissible. There is a further independent provision which needs to be considered. This is that the court has a set of discretions, contained in ss. 25 and 26 of the 1988 Act, which may lead it to exclude evidence which would be strictly admissible, in the interests of giving the accused a fair trial. The discretions in s. 25 of the Act govern ordinary statements admitted under s. 23 and business documents admitted under s. 24. The discretions in s. 26 govern documents prepared for a criminal investigation or trial.

The discretions

By s. 25 of the 1988 Act, it is provided that where the court is of the opinion that in the interests of justice a statement which is admissible by virtue of s. 23 or s. 24 nevertheless ought not to be admitted, the court may direct that the statement shall not be admitted.

The section goes on to provide that without prejudice to the generality of that, the court has the duty to have regard to the following matters:

(a)   to the nature and source of the document containing the statement and to whether or not having regard to its nature and source and not any other circumstances that appear to the court to be relevant it is likely that the document is authentic;

(b)   to the extent to which the statement appears to supply evidence which would otherwise not be readily available;

(c)   to the relevance of the evidence that it appears to supply to any issue which is likely to have to be determined in the proceedings;

(d)   to any risk, having regard in particular to whether it is likely to be possible to controvert the statement if the person making it does not attend to give oral evidence in the proceedings, that its admission or exclusion will result in unfairness to the accused or, if there is more than one accused, to any of them.

The court then has a broad discretion to exclude evidence which would otherwise be admissible in the interests of justice. This discretion no doubt will most commonly be exercised in the interests of the accused by means of excluding prosecution evidence.

The discretion in relation to criminal investigation documents

Section 26 of the 1988 Act goes on to provide that where a statement which is prima facie admissible under s. 23 or s. 24 appears to the court to have been prepared for the purposes of pending or contemplated criminal proceedings or of a criminal investigation then the statement shall *not* be given in evidence without the leave of the court and there is a *presumption against* admissibility unless the court is of the opinion that the statement should be admitted in the interests of justice. In considering 'the interests of justice' the court has the duty to have regard to the following matters:

(a)   to the contents of the statement;

(b)   to any risk, having regard in particular to whether it is likely to be possible to controvert the statement if the person making it does not attend to give oral evidence in the proceedings, that its admission or exclusion will result in unfairness to the accused or, if there is more than one accused, to any of them; and

(c)   to any other circumstances that appear to the court to be relevant.

This provides therefore a series of further tests. The drafting of the statute is somewhat odd in that parts of the discretion under s. 26 appear to repeat the discretions under s. 25, although without specific reference to other matters which might have been thought relevant, such as the criterion under s. 25 that the court should have regard to 'to the extent to which the statement appears to supply evidence which would otherwise not be readily available'.

9.12.3.4   Miscellaneous matters

Proof of the reason for absence

Applying previous case law it would appear that it will be for the party who wishes to put in some document under s. 23 or s. 24 to show by satisfactory evidence that one of the reasons is made out. Thus, for example, if it is suggested that the statement should be admissible because the witness is absent through fear, then by virtue of a case such as *R* v *O'Loughlin and McLaughlin* [1988] 3 All ER 431 it would seem that the fact that the witness is afraid must be proved by admissible evidence and not by further hearsay. Similarly, as in *R* v *Bray* (1988) 88 Cr App R 354, the practicability of securing the attendance of a witness outside the UK will have to be proved by reasonable evidence (e.g., by evidence of attempts to trace and persuade the witness to return). A further example is *R* v *Case* [1991]

Crim LR 192. This demonstrates that the court will give scrupulous attention to the preliminary proof of the acceptable reason for not calling a witness before allowing the statement. In this case there was a theft from Portuguese tourists and the Crown's case was based on the evidence of the arresting officers who sought leave to admit the tourists' statements under s. 23 of the Criminal Justice Act 1988. The accused's appeal was allowed on the basis that the judge's decision to admit the statements was materially irregular. There was no evidence in proper form as to when the tourists would have returned to Portugal or how long they might be in England, save for comments within the text of the statements themselves giving the tourists' address as that of a London hotel, but indicating that their stay was temporary. The court doubted whether it was proper to look at the statements themselves to see whether any reasons were supplied. The court went on to say that the word 'reasonably practicable' in the subsection implied that financial implications might be considered but there had been no proper prosecution evidence as to practicability. If the matter had been approached properly there might possibly have been such evidence but looking at the overall picture there was a material irregularity.

Production of the document
If a statement in a document is admissible under these provisions it may be proved either by production of the original document or by production of a copy authenticated in such matter as the court may approve. This marks a further weakening of the so-called 'best evidence' rule so that if it is for any reason inconvenient to produce the true document at court (e.g., a business ledger in daily use) a photocopy will be acceptable. 'Document' includes films, tapes and videos.

Confessions
The 1988 Act cannot be used as a way of getting round the much stricter rules with regard to the admissibility of confessions. There are specific provisions excluding the application of these sections to confessions which would otherwise have been inadmissible under s. 76 of the Police and Criminal Evidence Act.

Using documents to discredit witnesses
By sch. 2 to the 1988 Act there is a specific provision that documents may be used not merely as to the issues in the case but to discredit witnesses who are not before the court. If, for example, the prosecution manage to put in evidence a document under s. 23 of the Act and the defendant has other evidence which would have discredited the absent witness whether by proving a prior inconsistent statement or otherwise he may use that evidence.

Documentary evidence and corroboration
There is a specific provision (which merely states the obvious) that a statement given in evidence under the 1988 Act cannot corroborate evidence given orally by the person making it.

The weight to be attached to documentary statements
By sch. 2, para. 3 to the 1988 Act 'in estimating the weight, if any, to be attached to such statement regard shall be had to all the circumstances from which any inference can reasonably be drawn as to its accuracy or otherwise'.

Rules of court
There is a specific provision that rules of court may be made for the purposes of the 1988 Act. Thus rules may well be brought into force prescribing precisely how certain matters are to be proved. The coming into force of the Act however is not dependent on such rules being made and until any such specific rules are made the court will be able to admit documentary evidence under its usual procedures.

Other discretions
Quite apart from the discretions to exclude evidence provided by the 1988 Act there is a specific provision in s. 28 that any other discretions which a court might have to exclude evidence are preserved. Thus discretions under s. 78 or s. 82(3) of the Police and Criminal Evidence Act 1984 will still apply. Of course all these discretions are likely to overlap in any event; so that since a court has a

more or less unfettered discretion to exclude statements which would prima facie be admissible under s. 23 or s. 24 under the provisions of s. 25 or s. 26 of the 1988 Act that power would suffice anyway.

Expert evidence

There is a further provision under s. 30 of the 1988 Act whereby expert reports may be admitted in criminal cases whether or not the author attends to give oral evidence. If the expert does not attend, leave of the court is required to admit the report. Section 30(3) gives various factors which would be taken into account when deciding whether to give leave to admit the report without calling the expert. This will be considered further in the context of opinion evidence at **14.2.6**.

9.12.3.5 Recent developments

A number of cases on documentary evidence came through the courts in 1990 and thereafter. These had to do with documentary evidence admitted under a variety of provisions, either in the last days of s. 68 of the Police and Criminal Evidence Act 1984, s. 13(3) of the Criminal Justice Act 1925 or others. All these cases stress that, as a vital preliminary stage in considering whether evidence which is strictly speaking admissible ought to be allowed to be given at trial, the court must examine the *quality* of the evidence. So in *R* v *Neshet*, *The Times*, 4 March 1990 the evidence in written form from two very elderly ladies who were too frail to come to court was excluded because the very age and physical condition of the witnesses would show their unreliability. A similar result occurred in *Scott* v *R* [1989] 2 WLR 924 when the Privy Council had to consider identification evidence in relation to a Jamaican statute. These cases will certainly be relevant as demonstrating that the court will always want to consider the quality of evidence sought to be admitted under ss. 23 and 24.

9.12.3.6 Cases on ss. 23 and 24 of the Criminal Justice Act 1988

An early case was *R* v *Cole* [1992] All ER 109. The facts of that case could hardly have been more straightforward. It involved an assault witnessed by a number of people. One prosecution witness died before trial and the prosecution wished to put in his evidence under s. 24. The decision is extremely verbose and ultimately concluded that it was in order for the statement to be put in because the defence had witnesses who were going to controvert the dead witness's statement so there was no improper pressure placed on the defendant by allowing it in.

A similarly straightforward case was *R* v *Kennedy* [1992] Crim LR 37. An independent witness to a fight, M, had died before the case came to trial and his statement was read out pursuant to s. 23 of the Criminal Justice Act 1988. The statement had been prepared for the purpose of the investigation and leave was required under s. 26. The judge decided to admit the statement and described to the jury the problems of statements from absent witnesses and the lack of cross-examination. On appeal it was held that the judge had used his discretion correctly. The evidence of the only impartial witness was crucial to enable the jury to decide in a case where two men had been fighting with knives, each alleging the other was the aggressor and he was the innocent victim. The summing up had been conspicuously fair.

There have been two interesting cases on the tests to be applied where it is alleged that the witness does not give evidence 'through fear or because he is being kept out of the way' in s. 23(3)(b). In the most striking case, *R* v *Acton Justices ex parte McMullen* (1990) 92 Cr App R 98, the key witness, a boy of 16, was brought to court by the police but refused to enter court or give evidence because he was terrified of being identified by the accused. The Divisional Court held that the requirements of s. 23(3)(b) were fulfilled. In the case of committal proceedings the discretions in s. 26 of the 1988 Act have to be applied as to whether the statement should be admitted. Although in the instant case the magistrate had not fully appreciated the nature of his discretion, he had supplied an affidavit to say that the outcome would have been no different had he applied the proper discretions under the Act and the court refused to quash the decision to admit the statements in the committal proceedings. Watkins LJ ruled that the matters of 'fear' and 'being kept out of the way' are disjunctive. He indicated that the test which a court should employ in determining whether there was fear sufficient to fall within the terms of s. 23 was that such fear would be found if on the evidence the court was 'sure that the witness was in fear as a consequence of the commission of the material offence or of something said or done subsequently in relation to that offence and the possibility of the witness testifying as to it'. In deciding whether this was made out the court would apply the criminal standard of proof. Watkins LJ went on to say:

> Whatever else may be seen to present difficulties for the court in these provisions, there is no doubt in my mind that the dual tests — admissibility and whether to admit — which have to be applied before a statement is admitted and read to the court will in many circumstances call for the most careful and scrupulous exercise of judgment and discretion.

See also *R* v *Ashford Magistrates Court ex parte Hilden* [1992] Crim LR 879 where the witness who was the victim of an alleged assault took the oath and gave evidence saying that she had no comment upon the alleged injuries. The accused's grandmother was in court and was said to have accompanied the victim to court. The prosecutor thereupon asked for leave to put in her written statement under s. 23(3)(b). The court found that the witness was in fear and admitted the statement. On application for judicial review it was held that for the subsection to apply it was not necessary for a witness to have failed to testify at all; and that it was open to the court to be satisfied that she was in fear by observing her demeanour.

9.12.3.7 Computer records

Section 69 of the Police and Criminal Evidence Act 1984 provided for the admissibility in evidence of computer records. Now, since s. 68 of the 1984 Act is repealed, such computer records will have to fall within s. 23 or s. 24 of the 1988 Act to be admissible. A brief discussion of evidence by computer records is therefore appropriate.

We have already referred to s. 4 of the Civil Evidence Act 1968 which for civil proceedings, although based on the 1965 Act, introduced two new features (applicability to *any* records and requirement that the compiler should have a *duty* to make the record). A further addition for civil proceedings (although so far little used — at least there is apparently no case law on it 20 years after its coming into force) was s. 5 of the 1968 Act which made provision for the admissibility of computer records in civil proceedings.

Section 69 of the 1984 Act provided for computer records to be admissible in criminal cases. The word computer is not defined in the 1984 Act. In the 1968 Act the word 'computer' is defined and this definition is incorporated into the 1988 Act expressly by sch. 2, para. 5. The word computer means 'any device for processing or storing information'. As has been pointed out this somewhat woolly phrase could include a filing cabinet, a typewriter or even a cardboard file. Clearly it includes word processors, calculators, adding machines, etc., as well as computers.

The requirements of s. 69 are negative in form so that the person wishing to put in evidence a computer record must show absence of irregularity in the use of the computer, that is that there are no reasonable grounds for believing the computer records to be inaccurate because of improper use and that the computer was operating properly. Proof of this is to be subject to rules of court and may be given by a certificate purporting to be signed by a 'person occupying a responsible position in relation to the operation of the computer'. In addition the court may require oral evidence about the working of the computer to be given.

Now s. 23 or s. 24 of the 1988 Act must be satisfied as well as s. 69. So there ought usually to be first-hand information available by the person who fed the details into the computer.

This is likely to be a growth area for case law and therefore it may help to summarise the position. Some of the difficulties are faced in the case of *R* v *Harper and Minors* [1989] Crim LR 360. The facts of this case are not material and indeed it turns on s. 68 of the 1984 Act, which has now been repealed. Section 69, however, as we have seen, survives. It is not a self-contained code of admissibility because it lays down additional requirements for the admissibility of a computer record which has already passed the hurdle of what is now in s. 24 of the 1988 Act. The foundation requirements of s. 24 must be proved by oral evidence, in the absence of formal agreement between the parties. If there is a disputed issue as to the admissibility of the computer evidence the issue should be decided on a trial within a trial at which the judge's function will be to decide whether the prosecution (or more rarely the defence) has established the foundation requirements of s. 24 and then of s. 69. It will be appropriate for the judge to give the jury a specific direction that the weight to be attached to documentary evidence produced by computer is entirely a matter for them to assess.

There are the following alternatives with regard to evidence produced by a computer printout:

(a) If the printout is tendered as evidence of any facts stated by any person, both s. 23 or s. 24 of the Criminal Justice Act 1988 and then s. 69 of the 1984 Act must be satisfied.

(b) If the printout is *the very fact* which is to be proved and the computer or machine has not 'added to its own knowledge' (such as a radar meter printout or an intoximeter printout) then the printout is *real evidence* and not hearsay and neither s. 69 nor any other section needs to be satisfied.

(c) If the printout is tendered as evidence of any fact actually observed by the computer itself or by a machine with which it is linked then everything will depend upon the nature of the additional information. For example, if the computer performs complicated calculations which depend on hearsay statements put into it and the computer then draws conclusions, the court will have to examine the nature of the information eventually supplied by the computer.

It is important to consider the case of *R* v *Spiby* [1990] Crim LR 199; (1990) 90 Cr App R 186. Here a computer installed in a hotel recorded, by mechanical means and without the intervention of human mind, information about telephone calls made by hotel guests. The case concerned conspiracy to import drugs and in the course of it the prosecution proved a number of telephone calls made by one of the accused from the hotel. It was proved that calls were made to others of the accused by production of a record showing printout sheets from a computer which metered guests' telephone calls, recorded them and worked out the charges. The manager of the hotel gave evidence that he was familiar with the function of the machine and that though he was not a computer engineer the machine had been working satisfactorily and no one in the relevant period had complained about the resulting bills. It was submitted that the evidence was subject to s. 69 of the 1984 Act and that the manager could not discharge the burden under s. 69 of showing that the computer was working properly. The trial judge held that the documents were real evidence and not hearsay. It was held on appeal that where information is recorded by mechanical means without the intervention of a human mind the record made by the machine is admissible in evidence provided it is accepted that the machine is reliable.

A computer differs from a thermometer or a camera only in that it can perform a variety of functions instead of only one. The records did not depend for their content on anything that had passed through a human mind. The record was entirely mechanical and fell within the class of real evidence. It would have been quite different if a telephone operator in the hotel had gathered the information and typed it into a computer bank and the printout was from that computer. In that case the sections would have applied. The court considered that it was entitled to apply the proposition from *Cross on Evidence* that, if the instruments were of a kind as to which it was common knowledge that they were more often than not in working order, then, in the absence of evidence to the contrary, the court would presume that they were in working order at the appropriate time.

There is an excellent commentary on the case in the *Criminal Law Review*. As Professor Smith points out, the court on the face of it is completely wrong in proceeding from the, no doubt correct, decision that the computer print out in *Spiby* was real evidence (if that phrase has any meaning) to the view that s. 69 has no application. Section 69 provides: 'In any proceedings a statement contained in a document produced by a computer shall not be admissible as evidence of any facts stated therein unless it is shown . . .'. Clearly, whether you call it real evidence or not, the printout from this computer was tendered to prove some facts stated on it, namely the origin and destination of the telephone calls and the printout stated those facts. That does not mean that the printout is necessarily hearsay, but s. 69 clearly applies nonetheless and the court ought to have been satisfied by admissible evidence as to the proper working of the computer before the evidence could be put in. The point is further underlined by para. 12 of sch. 3 to the Police and Criminal Evidence Act 1984 which provides: 'For the purposes of paragraph 11 above, information shall be taken to be supplied to a computer whether it is supplied directly or *with or without human intervention* by means of any appropriate equipment' (emphasis added). The point of s. 69 is to provide for the court to be satisfied by admissible evidence about proper operation of the computer and whether the evidence is hearsay or not is irrelevant.

The court should have considered this also in *R* v *Neville* [1991] Crim LR 288. In this case the Crown sought to adduce a computer printout showing calls made on a mobile telephone. The precise method of proving the calls was somewhat complex because the mobile telephone was hired from one company and a different company carried out the telephone operations. What was material was a computer recorded bill showing the dates, times and duration of each call. The Court of Appeal concluded again that the printout was real evidence and that that excluded any need to consider s. 69. The commentary, again by Professor Smith, seriously questions the correctness of this.

Proving the operation of the computer
It had been widely considered that there would be strict requirements for proof of the proper operation of the computer at the relevant time pursuant to s. 69(1). The requirement seems to have been weakened by the House of Lords in *R* v *Shepherd* [1993] 1 All ER 225 where it was ruled that those certification provisions 'could be satisfied by the oral evidence of a person familiar with the operation of the computer who could give evidence of its reliability and such a person need not be a computer expert'.

Whilst the computer operation in that case was extremely simple (the court had allowed a store detective who had conducted an examination of till rolls to certify that the computer-linked tills were working properly on the day in question), many commentators have doubted whether the House of Lords was right to believe that a non-expert such as a store detective could properly certify the reliability of such equipment.

The Court of Appeal in *R* v *Cochrane* [1993] Crim LR 49, a case decided before the judgments in *Shepherd* were known, ruled that the Crown needed to produce expert evidence as to each stage of the mode of operation of the computers involved in linked transactions in a case having to do with withdrawals from computer-linked 'hole in the wall' building society cash points. The cash point machines were linked to a branch computer which had back-up facilities in memory form before the information was transmitted to a central mainframe computer. None of the witnesses called for the Crown to testify about the operation could in fact say in which town the mainframe computer was located and the Court of Appeal quashed the conviction. None of the witnesses had testified adequately about the operation of the relevant machines.

9.13 Minor Statutory Exceptions

We have now considered the two main classes of statutory exceptions to the hearsay rule. Apart from these there are numerous sections in a variety of statutes which make individual provisons for the reception of hearsay evidence in specific cases. These are of only minor importance. One example will suffice and the one most commonly given is s. 27(4) of the Theft Act 1968.

This provides for the sender or recipient of goods stolen 'in transmission' to give evidence of their sending by statutory declaration. A statutory declaration is a sworn statement. The accused may object and require the maker of the declaration to be called. There is thus a clear parallel with s. 9 of the Criminal Justice Act 1967 and s. 27(4) would seem to be redundant since the procedural requirements of s. 9 are less onerous in that the statement need not be on oath.

9.14 Statements Admitted as Part of the *Res Gestae*

The final group of exceptions falls within the so-called doctrine of '*res gestae*'. *Res gestae* means 'happening', 'series of events', or 'transaction'. Under this doctrine any statement relevant to an incident (usually the commission of a crime itself) may be admissible as an exception to the hearsay rule provided that the evidence arose spontaneously and contemporaneously with the incident. Cross divides the cases into four groups. There is some logic in this although many of the cases are old, the reports are very brief and it is far from clear what principles the court thought it was applying. Often there is little reasoning shown, particularly in the several reports from Cox's Criminal Cases. The four groups are:

(a) Statements accompanying and explaining an act.
(b) Spontaneous statements relating to an event in issue.
(c) Statements concerning the maker's state of mind and emotion.
(d) Statements of contemporaneous physical sensations.

9.14.1 STATEMENTS ACCOMPANYING AND EXPLAINING AN ACT

Before such statements can be admitted there are three conditions

(a) The statement *must relate to the act* it accompanies. For example, in *R* v *Bliss* (1837) 7 A & E 550, on an issue of whether a road was public or private it was sought to adduce evidence that a person who was planting a tree was heard to state that he was doing so on the very boundary of his property. It was held that there was no connection between the act and the statement and therefore this did not come within the exception.

(b) *Contemporaneity*. The whole rationale of the doctrine of *res gestae* is that because the statement is made at the very time of an important event there is no opportunity to fabricate evidence. Contemporaneity is a matter of fact and degree in each case.

(c) The statement must have been *made by the actor*. So in *Howe* v *Malkin* (1878) 40 LT 196 a statement by the plaintiff's father concerning the boundary of his land made whilst certain work was being done on the land by builders was held inadmissible — the statement and the act were by different people. In the *Aylesford Peerage Case* (1885) 11 App Cas 1, a wife's statement of her reasons for leaving her husband were received as they were contemporaneous with her departure. (Note that in such cases the statements may be evidence of intention or state of mind but not of any fact stated.)

This particular subdivision of *res gestae* is not very important because it overlaps and merges into the next subdivision which is of more general scope.

9.14.2 SPONTANEOUS STATEMENTS RELATING TO AN EVENT IN ISSUE

These may be made by the criminal, victims, or observers. What a person says at the time of an event is admissible if it is spontaneous. There must not have been time to devise or contrive anything which may be to the advantage of the person making the statement.

In *Tustin* v *Arnold and Sons* [1915] LJKB 2214, the written statement made by the driver of a vehicle immediately after being involved in a collision was held inadmissible. It lacked the spontaneity necessary to fall within *res gestae*.

In *The Schwalbe* (1861) 4 LT 160, contradictory instructions given by a pilot to a helmsman immediately before a collision were held admissible.

The leading case was *Ratten* v *R* [1972] AC 378. The accused was charged with murder by shooting his wife. His defence was that the gun had gone off accidentally whilst he was cleaning it. The facts were that at about 1.15 p.m. a call was made from the accused's house to the local telephone exchange by a female speaking in a hysterical voice who sobbed and said 'Get me the police please'. The caller gave her address but then rang off. The police were thereupon informed of this by the telephone operator who telephoned the house and spoke to the accused who then asked them to come. The accused objected that the telephone operator's evidence was hearsay. On appeal, eventually to the Privy Council, it was held:

(a)   That the jury properly directed might find that the telephone call was made by the deceased woman.

(b)   That the evidence of the telephone operator was not hearsay and was admissible as evidence of fact relevant to an issue, i.e. that a call had been made by a woman in a hysterical state thus rebutting the suggestion of accident.

(c)   That even if there was an element of hearsay the words were safely admitted under the *res gestae* principle being words spoken spontaneously under the overwhelming pressure of a contemporaneous event.

With all respect to their Lordships, it seems difficult to agree that there is no hearsay element in the words sought to be admitted. Their Lordships impliedly concede their doubts by going on to give a separate ground of admissibility — and this is the modern rule for admissibility. It is submitted that Mrs Ratten did assert a fact by implication in asking for the police, and certainly that the prosecution's wish in tendering the evidence was to assert that fact, i.e., her belief that police assistance was required in view obviously of some act or threat made by her husband.

This consideration of the problems of implied assertion foreshadows the decision in *R v Kearley* referred to above.

The modern English authorities are the cases of *R v Turnbull* (1984) 80 Cr App R 104 and *R v Andrews* [1987] AC 281.

In *R v Turnbull* a man N and two brothers named Turnbull had been out drinking heavily one lunch time. They resumed drinking at 8.00 p.m. that same evening and about half an hour later N staggered into a public house fatally stabbed. When being asked who stabbed him he replied 'Ronnie Tommo'. This was the nickname of one of the Turnbull brothers. It was held at trial that these words were admissible as part of the *res gestae* under the test in *Ratten v R* as being spoken spontaneously after the happening of the crime.

In *R v Andrews* the House of Lords held that hearsay evidence of a statement made by a fatally stabbed man soon after he was attacked and naming his two attackers was properly admitted as evidence of the truth of the facts he had asserted under the *res gestae* principle. *Ratten v R* and *R v Turnbull* were expressly approved. The position was as follows:

(a)   The primary question which the judge had to ask himself in such a case was: can the possibility of concoction or distortion be disregarded?

(b)   To answer that question the judge first had to consider the circumstances in which the particular statement was made in order to satisfy himself that the event was so unusual or dramatic as to dominate the thoughts of the victim so that his utterance was an instinctive reaction to that event thus giving no real opportunity for reasoned reflection.

(c)   In order for the statement to be sufficiently spontaneous it had to be so closely associated with the event which had excited the statement that it could fairly be said that the mind of the declarant was still in control of the event.

(d)   Quite apart from the time factor there might be special features in a case which related to the possibility of distortion.

(e)   As to the possibility of error in the facts narrated in such a statement: if only the ordinary fallibility of human recollection was relied upon that went to the weight to be attached and not to the admissibility of the statement and was therefore a matter for the jury.

There are relatively few cases on *res gestae* and the courts somehow always seem surprised when a point of this kind comes up. Clear examples are *R v Glover* [1991] Crim LR 48 where words said at the time of the attack were overheard by a bystander and were held to be admissible under the principle in *Andrews* and, more questionably, the case of *Edwards and Osakwe v DPP* [1992] Crim LR 576, where the alleged victim of a mugging, who had been very drunk at the time, said, 'They are the ones . . . those two mugged me of my wallet'. The victim however did not attend the hearing and the court permitted his statement to be put in under the principle in *R v Andrews*. This seems a somewhat questionable authority given the surrounding circumstances, the absence of the witness, and the effect of drunkenness (see principle (e) under *Andrews*).

9.14.3 STATEMENTS CONCERNING THE MAKER'S STATE OF MIND AND EMOTION

Such statements are only admissible to prove what the maker's mental or emotional state was, and *not* to prove the *existence of any fact* he said he knew or believed. A clear example is *Thomas v Connell* (1838) 4 M and W 267 — a bankrupt's statement that he knew he was insolvent was admissible to prove his knowledge of the fact at the time when he made a certain payment, but was *not* evidence as such of his insolvency.

In *R v Gandfield* (1846) 2 Cox CC 43, a witness was asked to explain why he had not reported a certain crime to the police for three days. He wished to show that he had not done so because he was afraid of the vengeance of the accused. It was held that it was proper to ask the witness's wife what had been said to her to explain his conduct in failing to report the matter to the police.

A difficult modern case is *R v Blastland* [1985] 3 WLR 345. The accused was charged with buggery and murder of a 12-year-old boy. His version was that he had paid the boy to indulge in some homosexual activity with him but not buggery. During this he had seen a man called 'Mark' nearby and was afraid that he had been observed committing a serious offence. He had therefore run off leaving the boy unharmed. His version was that Mark was the likely murderer. Mark had been interviewed by the police and had at one time made admissions (which he had retracted) to the police. Mark had also told another witness that a young boy had been murdered before this was generally known. It was proved that Mark was a known homosexual. The evidence of what Mark had said was ruled inadmissible as hearsay by the trial judge. On appeal, eventually to the House of Lords, it was held that statements made to a witness by a third party were not excluded by the hearsay rule when they were put in evidence solely to prove the state of mind of the maker of the statement or of the person to whom it was made but that this applied only where the state of mind was directly in issue at the trial or of direct and immediate relevance to the trial. Here Mark's knowledge that the boy had been murdered was not in issue at the trial. The question of how he had come by that knowledge was a matter of pure speculation. In so far as *R v Moghal* (see below) appeared to state anything else it was not accurate.

9.14.3.1 Declarations of intention and *res gestae*

One important area within this head of *res gestae* is the question of an *expression of intention* to perform some act. It seems that a declaration of intention can be received as evidence of a maker's intention at the time and that such a statement raises a presumption of fact that the intention continued for some time afterwards (and it seems sometimes the inference that the intention was carried out).

So, if A is heard to declare on 1 January his intention to murder B, then if B is murdered on 2 January this will be relevant and admissible. If B is murdered on 1 February the declaration of intention may still be admissible — not as direct evidence but as a vital circumstantial fact. If the murder is not until July, however, it may be so remote that there can be no presumption of continuance of an intention.

There is a dearth of clear authority on this difficult area: see the following cases.

R v Buckley (1873) 13 Cox CC 293

The accused was charged with the murder of a policeman. It seems that the accused had been convicted of theft mainly on the testimony of the deceased policeman. On the night of the murder the policeman had told his superior officer that he proposed to go and watch the movements of the accused. The policeman was found two days later and some distance away, having been stabbed to death. It was held that the policeman's expression of intention to go and keep a watch on the prisoner was admissible apparently as part of the *res gestae*. This case may be compared with *R v Wainwright*.

R v Wainwright (1875) 13 Cox CC 171

The accused were charged with murder of a woman. The Crown wished to adduce evidence that when the woman was leaving her lodgings on the afternoon of the murder she had said to a friend that she was on her way to the house of the accused. It was held that this was not admissible as being part of the *res gestae* for it was 'no part of the act of leaving but only an incidental remark. It was a statement of intention which might or might not have been carried out'. See *R v Pook* (noted at 13 Cox CC 171). On the same facts as *R v Wainwright* the Lord Chief Justice refused to permit a similar question about the words spoken by a woman as to where she was going just before her murder.

R v Moghal (1977) 65 Cr App R 56

The accused, M, and his mistress, S, were jointly charged with the murder of the mistress's former lover R. The circumstances were such that only M or S or both could have killed him. The mistress applied to the judge for separate trials and this was granted. She was tried first and acquitted, her defence being that M alone had killed R and she had stood by as a terrified spectator. At M's trial his defence was the converse, that the mistress alone had murdered R and he had stood by a terrified spectator. In order to demonstrate the ferocious character of S he wished to put in evidence a tape recording of a solemn family conference in the Indian community at which, despite the presence of her older relatives, S had made violent threats against the life of R and predicted his early death. The trial judge refused to permit the tape recording to be given in evidence but on appeal it was held, whilst upholding the conviction, that evidence of S's state of mind and feeling before and at the time of the killing of R such as the tape recording were admissible as relevant to M's defence.

It is suggested in *R v Blastland* [1985] 3 WLR 345 that this decision is *obiter* or, if not, that it is incorrect and depends upon the Crown's admission that it was S who carried out the murder.

9.14.4 STATEMENTS OF CONTEMPORANEOUS PHYSICAL SENSATIONS

A person's statement of his contemporaneous physical sensation is admissible as evidence, *but not* what he says as to the possible cause. For example, if the victim of an assault says 'I have a pain in my head', this is admissible, but a further statement as to who struck the victim would not be. For example:

(a)   *R v Gloster* (1888) 16 Cox CC 471. The accused was charged with murder of a woman by performing an abortion on her from which she died. It was held that it was proper to repeat what the deceased had said as to her bodily symptoms but that it was improper to admit what she said as to who had caused them.

(b)   *R v Conde* (1867) 10 Cox CC 547. On a charge of neglect of a child by depriving it of food the child's complaints of feeling hungry were held to be admissible.

(c)   *R v Black* (1922) 16 Cr App R 118. The accused was charged with murder of his wife and neighbours were permitted to give evidence that the wife had complained to them that she suffered from vomiting and great pain after taking medicine which the accused had given her.

Res gestae has aptly been described as 'a lot of rag-tag-and-bobtail material', 'the dustbin of the law of evidence', 'an empty phrase encouraging looseness of thinking and uncertainty of decision'. It has often been, cynically but understandably, urged on young advocates that if they cannot justify to the court why a given piece of evidence, which is clearly hearsay is admissible 'say it is part of the *res gestae*'.

TEN

THE LAW OF EVIDENCE (4): CONFESSIONS, EVIDENCE OF REACTION, AND THE RIGHT OF SILENCE

10.1 Confessions

The law on confessions is now contained in ss. 76 and 77 of the Police and Criminal Evidence Act 1984. These are to be read with the definition of 'confession' in s. 82 and reference must also be made to the Codes of Practice on the Detention, Treatment and Questioning of Persons and the Code of Practice on Tape Recording of Police Interviews issued under ss. 60 and 66 of the 1984 Act.

Before considering the statutory provisions and the case law under them we shall consider four preliminary matters, namely:

    (a)   The procedure by which admissibility of a confession is determined.
    (b)   Editing of confessions.
    (c)   Confessions implicating others.
    (d)   Confessions which also contain self-serving material.

10.1.1 THE PROCEDURE TO DETERMINE ADMISSIBILITY

10.1.1.1 The Crown Court

In opening its case to the jury the prosecution must refrain from referring to any item of evidence the admissibility of which will be challenged by the defence. The defence are of course aware of the nature of the prosecution's case because of the committal proceedings, at which stage the prosecution must reveal their evidence. If the opening speech is unintelligible without reference to the confession (i.e. if it is the only real evidence in the case) the admissibility issue may be taken as a preliminary matter before the opening speech. Otherwise after the opening speech the case proceeds with witnesses being called, examined and cross-examined until the item of disputed evidence is reached. In the case of a confession this will probably be quite early, the investigating officer usually being the second prosecution witness after the victim, although there is no real rule as to this. As soon as the question of the disputed confession is reached, the defence formally object and the jury are sent out of court (without of course knowing why) whilst the issue of admissibility is tried by the judge alone. This hearing is known as the '*voire dire*' or 'trial within a trial'.

Witnesses may be called and are cross-examined in the usual way, legal argument is presented by both sides, and the judge then decides on the admissibility of the confession. This will usually involve him deciding a dispute of fact (e.g., whose version as to what happened at the police station to believe) and then deciding admissibility as a question of law dependent on the facts as found.

If the judge rules that the confession is inadmissible under the above principles, either as being unreliable or under his discretion to exclude it as unfair to the accused, the jury when recalled to the court are never told of the existence of the 'confession' and the trial proceeds. If the confession is ruled *admissible* then the confession is put before the jury. It is still open to the defence to challenge it in any way, e.g., by trying to show the jury that it is untrue or unreliable because of the circumstances in which it was obtained. This may often involve them challenging the police evidence (e.g., as to intimidation of the accused at the police station) in exactly the same terms in which they have just challenged it before the judge on the *voire dire*. Indeed, often hours of cross-examination are repeated virtually word for word as the defence seek to show the jury that the confession is of no weight, the weight to be attached to it being, of course, entirely a question of fact for them.

The use of evidence given at the voire dire

The judge's function, of course, is to decide *admissibility* of the confession. It is for the jury to decide whether it is *true*. It might be thought that an accused who alleges that he only gave a confession because of police violence (or some other impropriety) would be hardly likely to admit that, although the confession was thus not admissible, its contents were true. There are however cases where this has happened.

In *Wong Kam-ming* v *R* [1980] AC 247, several men were charged with murder and the only evidence against this accused was his confession. At the start of the trial the admissibility of the confession was challenged on the grounds that the police had offered inducements to him to make it and that he had been forced to copy out and sign the confession. During the *voire dire* the accused did admit that he had been involved in the attack. The judge subsequently found that the confession was inadmissible. The trial continued and prosecution counsel then called two shorthand writers who had been present at the *voire dire* to testify as to the admission made at that stage by the accused. The judge ruled this was admissible. The defendant appealed successfully to the Privy Council.

This case therefore decided:

(a) It is improper at the *voire dire* to ask an accused if the contents of his confession are true.

(b) Where the confession is ruled inadmissible the prosecution is not allowed at the trial proper to cross-examine the accused as to incriminating testimony given by him at the *voire dire*.

(c) If the confession is ruled inadmissible, the prosecution may not cross-examine the accused as to any prior inconsistent statement made by him at the *voire dire* (a ruling apparently quite contrary to the clear words of s. 4 of the Criminal Procedure Act 1865, which permits such cross-examination as to prior inconsistent statements).

Wong Kam-ming was approved by the House of Lords in *R* v *Brophy* [1981] 2 All ER 705. In *Brophy* the accused, during a *voire dire*, admitted being a member of the IRA, which was one of the charges on which he was being tried. The *voire dire* excluded evidence of his confessions to numerous other charges of murder and causing explosions but the court took notice of what had been said about IRA membership during the *voire dire*. The conviction was quashed by the House of Lords holding that *Wong Kam-ming* v *R* was correctly decided and thus once a confession was ruled inadmissible no reference to it or to the procedure at the *voire dire* could be made at the trial proper.

10.1.1.2 The magistrates' court

In magistrates' courts before the 1984 Act came into force, it used to be considered pointless to hold a formal *voire dire* since the same magistrates decide admissibility as decide on the facts. Such a *voire dire* was held to be inappropriate following the case of *F* v *Chief Constable of Kent* [1982] Crim LR 682.

The terms of s. 76 of the 1984 Act however appear to require that a *voire dire* must always be held to determine admissibility:

(a) where the defence 'represents' that the confession is inadmissible (s. 76(2)), or

(b) where the court of its own motion requires proof of admissibility (s. 76(3)).

Following a certain amount of uncertainty it was held in *R* v *Liverpool Juvenile Court ex parte R* (1987) 86 Cr App R 1 that this literal construction should be adopted and therefore that in procedure by summary trial before magistrates the same thing should happen as in trial by jury, namely that there should be a separate and preliminary investigation into the admissibility of a confession. The difference however is that since the same magistrates will be present in court throughout there is no need to repeat the evidence after that stage if they rule the confession admissible. It has been held that this procedure is not necessarily appropriate at other stages of the criminal process such as committal proceedings. See *R* v *Oxford City Magistrates ex parte Berry* [1987] Crim LR 396.

The facts of these two cases are not material, in each case the Divisional Court ruled that the terms of s. 76 require a *voire dire* even in the magistrates' court where the admissibility of the confession was challenged under s. 76 of the 1984 Act. If the admissibility is challenged however only on some other basis (e.g., unfairness under s. 78 of the Act, see **10.1.7.3**), there is no necessity to hold a *voire dire*. Recent case law in the Divisional Court has held however that magistrates do have a discretion about this and that there may be instances where it is appropriate for a magistrates' court to consider whether to exclude evidence under s. 78 even where they are sitting as committing magistrates rather than in a trial.

10.1.1.3 What if the accused denies he confessed?

It should be noted that there only needs to be a *voire dire* if it is represented that the confession was obtained by oppression or is unreliable. If the accused denies that he ever made a confession, e.g., he says that the police forged his signature on a statement they themselves wrote or that he did not say any of the words attributed to him, this is a straightforward factual matter for the jury and there should not be a *voire dire*. See, for example, *R* v *Flemming* (1988) 86 Cr App R 32.

There was an argument in *Flemming* as to whether the accused's signature was forged on certain notes of interviews with the police. The Court of Appeal confirmed that where it was alleged that signatures and initials were forged and there was expert handwriting evidence on that issue that it was simple matter of fact for the jury and there need not be a *voire dire*. The trial in this case happened at a time when the Police and Criminal Evidence Act 1984 was not in force but the same would apply under the Act.

10.1.2 EDITING OF CONFESSIONS

Suppose that the words of a confession refer to a previous offence or some other inadmissible matter? The rule is that where a confession is to be placed before the jury and it contains inadmissible matter (quite independently of any question of reliability) the confession may be 'edited' to omit the offending part.

In *R* v *Knight and Thompson* (1946) 31 Cr App R 52 the accused were charged with various offences and in the course of their confessions referred to other offences they had committed. The judge ruled that the confessions should be put *in toto* before the jury. It was held that this was wrong and the confessions should have been edited to exclude the references to other offences. Accordingly the defendants' convictions would be quashed.

If the editing is so substantial that the confession is unintelligible after it, the whole may need to be excluded. If the actual document is to be shown to the jury it should be retyped without blanks or erasures which might lead the jury to speculate on the reasons for them. *Practice Direction (Crime: Evidence by Written Statements)* [1986] 1 WLR 805 explains the technical procedures to be followed.

For a recent case showing editing in practice see *R* v *Silcott and others* [1987] Crim LR 765, where inadmissible references to co-accused were deleted and the names substituted by letters of the alphabet.

10.1.3   CONFESSIONS IMPLICATING OTHERS

It should not be forgotten that a confession is an exception to the hearsay rule and is therefore evidence against *the maker* only. This leads to considerable practical difficulties in the case of trial of more than one accused. If A and B were charged with the same offence and A alone had made a confession that he and B carried out the crime, then if they are tried separately there will be no problem. The confession would be quite inadmissible at B's trial as hearsay, and of course at A's trial it would be evidence against A in the usual way. But the more normal procedure with co-accused is to try them together. What about A's confession which is clearly inadmissible as against B? The prejudicial effect as against B will *not* normally be a ground for ordering separate trials, see *R* v *Lake* (1976) 64 Cr App R 172 where the accused and two other men were charged with conspiracy to burgle. The accused applied for a separate trial on the grounds that confessions had been made by the other two accused which implicated him and that these would be inadmissible as against him. It was held that, although the confessions were inadmissible as against him and a strong warning from the trial judge would be necessary, the question of severance was primarily for the trial judge and there was no general rule that in such a case separate trials should be ordered.

It may be that reference to B can be edited out of A's confession without making it unintelligible and if so this should be done. If the reference to B is so prejudicial that it would affect B's chance of a fair trial then the judge may exclude the whole confession (to A's advantage also) as in *R* v *Rogers and Tarran* [1971] Crim LR 413. The accused were charged with corruption and the prosecution wished to adduce a statement made by R which amounted to a confession. Counsel for T argued that the admission of such evidence would be adversely prejudicial to T. It was held that, since R's admission was not evidence against T and would be manifestly prejudicial to him, the defect could not be cured on the facts of the present case by a strong direction to the jury and accordingly the prejudice caused would outweigh the probative value and thus the confession would be excluded.

If the judge rules that the confession can go before the jury he must give a strong direction to them to treat the confession as evidence only against A and not B. They are often assisted in this exercise in mental gymnastics by the judge explaining that it is clearly unfair to hold a statement made by A in B's absence against B who had no chance to reply, when A may have his own reasons for implicating B. Failure to give this direction is fatal to B's conviction.

It must be remembered that this is a rule relating to A implicating B *in his confession*. If A *goes into the witness box* and *gives evidence* implicating B then this is admissible evidence in the normal way. Remember that in such a case a corroboration warning is not essential because A is not a *prosecution* witness — he is a witness in his own behalf — but that where any person may have a purpose of his own to serve such a warning may be desirable (*R* v *Prater* [1960] 2 QB 464). See **12.3.1.1.**

10.1.4   CONFESSIONS WHICH ALSO CONTAIN SELF-SERVING MATERIAL

The difficulty here is that there is a general rule that where a statement is tendered to the jury, the whole statement must be tendered. There may thus be self-serving passages within confessions, especially if these are the record of interrogations rather than the accused's own written statement. The problem consists in the fact that the *confession part is evidence* against the maker, whereas the *self-serving parts are not evidence* of the facts which they state.

By s. 82 of the 1984 Act: 'Confession includes any statement wholly or partly adverse to the person who made it . . . and whether made in words or otherwise.' It must therefore be remembered that the term 'confession' covers things said by a suspect which are far weaker than an outright admission of involvement in the crime. It will encompass anything said by an accused which in any way assists the prosecution to establish their case, and thus quite minor partial admissions count in law as a 'confession' and thus require the prosecution to prove them strictly under s. 76 of the 1984 Act. For example, if, on being questioned about a murder, a suspect, whilst maintaining a complete denial, nonetheless conceded that he hated the victim, even that minor admission would need to be proved by the prosecution strictly under s. 76 if the circumstances in which it was obtained were called into question, because the suspect has admitted something (i.e. motive) which assists the prosecution to demonstrate his guilt. It often happens therefore that the court has to consider 'mixed' statements.

The jury must be told to consider the *whole* statement once the judge has decided that it could in law constitute a confession and is admissible, and to decide as a matter of fact whether they think it is a confession, i.e. whether the self-serving parts nullify any 'confessing' parts.

The correct direction to the jury in such a case seems to be as follows:

(a) The whole statement must be considered in assessing whether it is a confession.
(b) If so, adverse parts are evidence against the accused of facts stated in them.
(c) Favourable parts are not evidence of facts stated in them but may be part of 'the general picture'.

A somewhat briefer and simpler direction, although one that arguably 'fudges' the real difficulty, was suggested more recently in *R* v *Duncan* (1981) 73 Cr App R 359 and this has been approved by the House of Lords in *R* v *Sharp* (1988) 86 Cr App R 274. In *R* v *Duncan* Lord Lane CJ said:

where a mixed statement is under consideration . . . the simplest . . . method . . . is for the jury to be told that the whole statement, both the incriminating parts and the excuses or explanations, must be considered by them in deciding where the truth lies. . . . Equally, where appropriate, the judge may and should point out that the incriminating parts are likely to be true (otherwise why say them?), whereas the excuses do not have the same weight.

10.1.5   THE POLICE AND CRIMINAL EVIDENCE ACT 1984

It is important to consider the full text of ss. 76, 77, 78 and 82 of the Police and Criminal Evidence Act 1984. We have already considered s. 82; s. 78 will be dealt with in due course. It is important to consider the precise wording of ss. 76 and 77:

76.   Confessions

(1) In any proceedings a confession made by an accused person may be given in evidence against him in so far as it is relevant to any matter in issue in the proceedings and is not excluded by the court in pursuance of this section.

(2) If, in any proceedings where the prosecution proposes to give in evidence a confession made by an accused person, it is represented to the court that the confession was or may have been obtained—

(a) by oppression of the person who made it; or

(b) in consequence of anything said or done which was likely, in the circumstances existing at the time, to render unreliable any confession which might be made by him in consequence thereof, the court shall not allow the confession to be given in evidence against him except in so far as the prosecution proves to the court beyond reasonable doubt that the confession (notwithstanding that it may be true) was not obtained as aforesaid.

(3) In any proceedings where the prosecution proposes to give in evidence a confession made by an accused person, the court may of its own motion require the prosecution, as a condition of allowing it to do so, to prove that the confession was not obtained as mentioned in subsection (2) above.

(4) The fact that a confession is wholly or partly excluded in pursuance of this section shall not affect the admissibility in evidence—

(a) of any facts discovered as a result of the confession; or

(b) where the confession is relevant as showing that the accused speaks, writes or expresses himself in a particular way, of so much of the confession as is necessary to show that he does so.

(5)   Evidence that a fact to which this subsection applies was discovered as a result of a statement made by an accused person shall not be admissible unless evidence of how it was discovered is given by him or on his behalf.

(6)   Subsection (5) above applies—

(a)   to any fact discovered as a result of a confession which is wholly excluded in pursuance of this section; and

(b)   to any fact discovered as a result of a confession which is partly so excluded, if the fact is discovered as a result of the excluded part of the confession.

(7)   Nothing in Part VII of this Act shall prejudice the admissibility of a confession made by an accused person.

(8)   In this section 'oppression' includes torture, inhuman or degrading treatment, and the use or threat of violence (whether or not amounting to torture).

77.   Confessions by mentally handicapped persons

(1)   Without prejudice to the general duty of the court at a trial on indictment to direct the jury on any matter on which it appears to the court appropriate to do so, where at such a trial—

(a)   the case against the accused depends wholly or substantially on a confession by him; and

(b)   the court is satisfied—

(i)   that he is mentally handicapped; and

(ii)   that the confession was not made in the presence of an independent person,

the court shall warn the jury that there is special need for caution before convicting the accused in reliance on the confession, and shall explain that the need arises because of the circumstances mentioned in paragraphs (a) and (b) above.

(2)   In any case where at the summary trial of a person for an offence it appears to the court that a warning under subsection (1) above would be required if the trial were on indictment, the court shall treat the case as one in which there is a special need for caution before convicting the accused on his confession.

(3)   In this section—

'independent person' does not include a police officer or a person employed for, or engaged on, police purposes;

'mentally handicapped', in relation to a person, means that he is in a state of arrested or incomplete development of mind which includes significant impairment of intelligence and social functioning; and

'police purposes' has the meaning assigned to it by section 64 of the Police Act 1964.

The prosecution must thus prove beyond reasonable doubt that a confession which is either impugned by the accused or where the court itself raises the issue was not obtained:

(a)   by *oppression* of the person who made it; or

(b)   in consequence of anything said or done which was likely, in the circumstances existing at the time, to render *unreliable* any confession which might be made by him in consequence thereof.

10.1.5.1   Oppression

This is defined by s. 76(8). It 'includes torture, inhuman or degrading treatment, and the use or threat of violence (whether or not amounting to torture)'.

The use of the word 'includes' causes difficulty. It presumably means that the matters referred to are not exhaustive as definitions of oppression, and that lesser conduct may qualify. The obvious problem is that whilst 'oppression' in previous case law usually meant relatively mild conduct which saps the free will (e.g., lengthy questioning etc.) the term now seems essentially to mean the most serious forms of conduct. The reference to 'torture and inhuman or degrading treatment' is borrowed from art. 3 of the European Convention on Human Rights and Fundamental Freedoms and a great deal of case law under that Convention has demonstrated that quite a high level of maltreatment is required to amount to torture etc. Indeed the UK has itself been found to have breached the Convention in its treatment of terrorist suspects in Northern Ireland.

A quite remarkable early case, which manages to discuss 'oppression' without once referring to the statutory definition, is *R v Fulling* [1987] QB 426. The accused was in custody and being interviewed concerning suspected dishonesty in a false insurance claim. After questioning had been unsuccessful a policeman told her that the man with whom she had been living, and with whom she was infatuated, had been having an affair for some years with a woman called Christine who was also in custody in connection with other matters and was in the adjoining cell to the defendant. Thereupon the defendant became very emotional and confessed because, to give her own explanation, she felt she wanted to say anything to get out of the police station. At her trial she applied for the confession to be excluded as having been obtained by oppression. The judge ruled the evidence admissible. Even accepting the accused's version of the interview with the police and the remark about her lover's unfaithfulness he held that this did not amount to oppression. On appeal the Court of Appeal discussed the meaning of the word oppression.

Most remarkably they made no reference at all to the definition of the term contained in the 1984 Act but instead referred to the dictionary definition of oppression which is 'the exercise of authority or power in a burdensome, harsh or wrongful manner; unjust or cruel treatment of subjects, inferiors etc., the imposition of unreasonable or unjust burdens'. The court also embarked on a discussion of the meaning of the term 'oppression' under the old law, though holding that the term under the 1984 Act did not necessarily mean the same thing. The court also observed that whilst a confession could be rendered *unreliable* without there necessarily being any impropriety on the part of the interrogator, it would be hard to imagine a case of oppression without some impropriety.

Assuming therefore that conduct by the person to whom the confession is given is not so extreme as to amount to 'oppression' we turn to the second test.

10.1.5.2 Unreliability

The use of the words 'circumstances', 'reliable', and 'anything said or done' appear to give the court a broad mandate to inquire thoroughly into the circumstances in which the confession was made. There is no requirement that anyone should have behaved *improperly* in any way for a confession to be held unreliable. The words in the section clearly imply a subjective test, i.e. in all the circumstances was anything said or done which was likely to render *this* confession by *this* defendant unreliable. Thus police conduct which would have had no effect on a man of experience, especially one with a criminal record, may well be deemed to render a confession by a more vulnerable suspect unreliable.

The limitation of the circumstances to 'those existing at the time' seems to mean that, as before, the effect of conduct may lapse and cease to be an operative factor, as in the old case of *R v Smith* [1959] 2 QB 35 where the accused made an inadmissible confession but later made a valid one (although it could be argued that 'the circumstances existing at the time' would include Smith's belief that, having 'confessed' once, his second confession would be immaterial and he might have hoped for more favourable treatment by giving it).

10.1.5.3 Miscellaneous points on s. 76

(a) Section 76(4) preserves the existing law. Thus if, say, a suspect gives an inadmissible confession but while confessing says where stolen goods are to be found, and these are found where he said, and are, for example, covered in his fingerprints, the finding of the goods and the fingerprints can be referred to in evidence although no mention of the confession can be made unless the accused himself refers to it (s. 76(5)).

(b) If there is something relevant in the confession to show that the accused *speaks, writes, or expresses himself* in a particular way then even though the confession is ruled inadmissible the part of it which shows that the accused does speak, write, etc. in that way may be admissible for that purpose. An example would be, say, a kidnapping case where the ransom note contains a strikingly mistaken spelling and the confession has the same mistake thus showing that the accused is likely to be the kidnapper.

(c)   There is a special provision in s. 77 of the 1984 Act whereby, in addition to the matters arising under s. 76, in the case of a confession made by a mentally handicapped person (as defined), if the confession was not made in the presence of an 'independent person' (i.e. a person other than a police officer or police employee), the judge must warn the jury of the special need for caution before convicting the accused on any confession made by the mentally handicapped person.

(d)   Case law under the 1984 Act as a whole had led to a largely unexpected development. Before the 1984 Act the law on confessions was reasonably clear and was separate from a different body of law which relates to the exclusion of other evidence (that is apart from confessions) which had been obtained in some way unfairly, e.g., where police trick a suspect into revealing the whereabouts of stolen goods, or act as agents provocateurs by pretending to be members of a criminal gang and thus actually procure the commission of the crime. The separate body of case law on that kind of situation will be considered separately at **11.1** in the section on improperly obtained evidence.

There is a particular provision in the 1984 Act which was widely thought to make no difference at all to the common law. This was s. 78(1) which confers a discretion on the court and provides:

> In any proceedings the court may refuse to allow evidence on which the prosecution proposes to rely to be given if it appears to the court that, having regard to all the circumstances, including the circumstances in which the evidence was obtained, the admission of the evidence would have such an adverse effect on the fairness of the proceedings that the court ought not to admit it.

It was usually thought that this provision would be considered quite separately from the law on confessions but, to the great surprise of many, from the earliest cases the courts have been prepared to apply both s. 76 and s. 78 together. Some cases on this will be considered in the context of the law on the questioning of suspects below but on the obtaining of the confession pure and simple it is important to consider the case of *R* v *Mason* [1988] 1 WLR 139. In this case the accused had been tricked by the police who had falsely pretended that his fingerprint had been found at the scene of the crime. The police had maintained this pretence not only to the accused but to his solicitor. At the end of the prosecution case counsel for the accused objected unsuccessfully to the confession subsequently made. On appeal the conviction was quashed because of the deceit practiced by the police both on the appellant and his solicitor. It seems that the reason why the police conduct was considered particularly bad on this occasion was because of the further lie told to the solicitor. If the lie had only been told to the accused then it is perhaps more questionable whether the confession would have been disallowed.

It is actually a relatively common police interrogation technique to pretend that they have more evidence in their possession than they actually do have, even if it is not usually a claim to such a damning piece of evidence as in this case. It is somewhat difficult to see whether this is a correct application of s. 78 given that it requires the unfairness in the case to be 'in the proceedings'. It is suggested that, however laudable the outcome of this case, the court has in fact applied its mind to general considerations of unfairness in the whole criminal process rather than to the trial itself which arguably is a misinterpretation of s. 78. The court was, perhaps rather disingenuously, anxious to stress that it was not attempting to discipline the police by excluding the evidence. Whilst it did describe the police conduct as 'absolutely reprehensible' the court stressed that s. 78 did no more than restate the common law and that it was no function of the court to use the law of evidence as a way of disciplining the police.

We shall now go on to consider the related topic of the questioning of suspects and then deal with a number of cases under the 1984 Act to examine the general principles.

10.1.6   THE QUESTIONING OF SUSPECTS

Few confessions come about by the guilty person walking into a police station and handing over a previously prepared written statement confessing guilt. In the normal case, confessions come about in response to police questioning. However much additional evidence the police have against a person, they still generally prefer to see if a confession is forthcoming, believing, perhaps correctly, that it will be more difficult for a person to plead not guilty in the face of his own confession than if he had not made one.

So confessions usually come about in the course of interrogation, usually at a police station. Interrogation may end in a full written confession signed by the suspect, or there may merely be statements made admitting some fact relevant to guilt in the course of answering questions without a subsequent written statement. These 'confessions' are usually called 'verbals' and much of a trial used to be taken up with establishing whether or not the words amounting to a confession were ever said, in the common instance where the accused alleged fabrication or misunderstanding by the police who recorded his alleged answers to questions. These problems are now obviated to a large extent as tape recording of interviews is now universal, although even here there will be occasions when 'verbals' are alleged to have occurred at some stage before tape recording can start, e.g., in the police car taking the suspect to the police station or, as we shall see in one recent case, where the suspect made an alleged confession only after the tape recorder was switched off. We shall now deal with the questioning of suspects, and the effect of failure to observe proper procedures on the admissibility of confessions subsequently obtained.

10.1.6.1 Codes of Practice

There are two Codes of Practice issued under ss. 60 and 66 of the 1984 Act which are of importance in the context of confessions. These are the Code of Practice for the Detention, Treatment and Questioning of Persons by Police Officers; and the Code of Practice on the Tape Recording of Police Interviews. Parts of these Codes are set out at the end of **Chapter 5** (see also **4.5**).

The relevance of the Codes of Practice is dealt with in s. 67(11) of the 1984 Act which states:

> In all criminal and civil proceedings any such Code shall be admissible in evidence, and if any provision of such a Code appears to the court or tribunal conducting the proceedings to be relevant to any question arising in the proceedings it shall be taken into account in determining that question.

Accordingly, breach of the Codes ought only in itself to be relevant to the admissibility of a confession if the breach has some factual bearing on the reliability of the confession. Breach of the Codes is a police disciplinary offence but the court will not in general use the breach as a means of punishing the police by excluding the confession. Everything will depend upon the nature and seriousness of the breach and the directness of its relevance to how the confession came about.

The same ought also to apply to the case of breach of other substantive provisions of the 1984 Act. A number of other sections relate to the conduct of interrogations, in particular s. 41 of the 1984 Act prima facie limits the police to a maximum period of 24 hours for the detention of a suspect without charge; s. 58 guarantees a suspect the right to consult privately with a solicitor (unless there are exceptional circumstances); s. 56 guarantees the right for a person to have details of his whereabouts communicated to a friend or relative. Breach of any of these ought only to matter so far as admissibility is concerned if the breach is causally related to the confession.

Reference to the Codes should be made for their precise terms. They provide for reasonable comfort, rest and refreshment during interrogation. They provide that from the moment of arrival in a police station the suspect is in the norminal custody of the custody officer who is a police officer of at least sergeant rank who has the duty of ensuring that full records are kept relating to the custody of the suspect, such as time, duration of questioning, and so on, and who has the power to control the way in which the suspect is treated by the officers actually involved in investigating the case in question. This is so even though those officers are of higher rank than the custody officer. The custody record kept by the custody officer may be called for and used at the trial and therefore it is very much in his interest to keep this meticulously and to ensure proper treatment for the suspect. See further **4.4** and **4.5**.

The Codes further provide for a suspect to be cautioned by the police in the words: 'you do not have to say anything unless you wish to do so but what you say may be given in evidence'. This caution must be administered, or readministered at various times, in particular:

    (a) when he is first suspected;
    (b) upon arrest;
    (c) when resuming questioning after arrest;
    (d) after any break in questioning;
    (e) upon charging.

Note also:

    (a) After a person has been charged he should not be further questioned except for the purpose of minimising harm or loss or clearing up ambiguities.
    (b) If after a person has been charged a policeman wishes to bring to his notice any written statement made by another person he should hand him a copy of that statement but not invite comment on it save to caution him.

That then is a bare outline of the main provisions of the Codes. The Court of Appeal has shown that it is prepared to scrutinise individual words and phrases within the Codes closely and to treat apparently small breaches as fatal to any confession subsequently obtained. It would be wrong however to say that the Court of Appeal's approach has been consistent throughout the cases, varying results having been obtained in different cases where the facts seem somewhat similar.

10.1.7   THE IMPORTANT CONCEPTS

As we have seen there are three concepts that need to be considered:

    (a) oppression;
    (b) unreliability;
    (c) unfairness.

10.1.7.1   Oppression

As explained above, this is defined in s. 76(8) of the 1984 Act in such terms that very serious police misconduct is contemplated. As we have also noted in **10.2.1**, in the first important case on oppression, *R* v *Fulling* [1987] QB 426, the court decided to invoke the dictionary definition of the word 'oppression' and did not refer itself at all to the definition in the Act. This is a highly questionable methods of statutory interpretation and the law might be thought to have taken a wrong turning from that point. In an emotive passage in the judgment the court said: 'There is not a word in our language that expresses more detestable wickedness than oppression' and 'we find it hard to envisage any circumstances in which such oppression would not entail some impropriety on the part of the interrogator'. Not surprisingly on the facts of the case the court did not find oppression in this or any other sense. The Court of Appeal expressed the view that police conduct was 'unsporting' but not 'oppressive'.

However, see *R* v *Davison* [1988] Crim LR 442 in which D was arrested at 6.25 a.m. at home in connection with handling a stolen ring — the proceeds of an armed robbery. He arrived at the police station half an hour later and signed the custody record stating that he did not require a solicitor. Two hours later he was interviewed for some 70 minutes. By the end of the interview the police had no evidence against him in relation to the ring and the judge found that they should have released him at that point. Thereafter the detention became unlawful. Moreover the custody officer was not informed of the position by the investigating officers. More than two hours after that the custody record showed the entry 'a further detention authorised to allow further interview and charges to be made'. Between the end of the first interview and 3.00 p.m. on the same day other evidence came to light that D had provided information which led to another serious armed robbery. The purpose of detaining D incommunicado was connected with this other robbery.

Eventually, some hours later, after an identification of D by a 'supergrass' there was a further interview at which D had asked for access to a solicitor and been denied it. This interview ended in admissions at 8.00 p.m. It was held that notwithstanding the seriousness of the crime under investigation the wholesale breaches of the Act and Codes amounted to oppression in the sense of exercise of power in a wrongful manner. The court excluded the confessions under s. 76 and did not in the circumstances, apply its mind to s. 78.

In another case, however, conduct which seems in total rather worse than that in *Davison* was considered not to be oppressive. In *R v Hughes* [1988] Crim LR 545 the accused was charged with obtaining by deception and handling. On a winter day he was arrested at home and taken to a police station 100 miles away where the offence was under investigation. He was put into a cold cell for 50 minutes. He was allowed to make a phone call on coming out. He asked about the duty solicitor and due to an honest misunderstanding was told there was no duty solicitor available. He was cautioned and agreed to be interviewed without a solicitor and was interviewed for two hours. He then made very damaging admissions. The court held that the confession was rightly admitted and s. 78 should not have been applied despite the apparent breach of s. 58 of the 1984 Act. The Court of Appeal commended the accused's counsel for not pressing the point of oppression because there was no deliberate misconduct by the police.

These three cases are instructive on the question of oppression although the apparent clarity of the concepts within the statute has been considerably blurred by the looseness of some of the language in which the Court of Appeal has discussed recent cases. There seems to be an overlap between oppression and unfairness which seems unnecessary if the court approaches the sections in a logical sequence as will be suggested below.

10.1.7.2 Unreliability

Cases on unreliability tend to be rather more clear cut. Having said that, there is a number of cases where the court seems to have jumped straight from a finding of breach of the Codes of Practice into considering the confessions subsequently obtained as being of necessity 'unreliable' without much evidence that that was so. It is worth giving a couple of simple factual examples from decided cases though it must be reiterated that each case turns on its own facts.

R v Phillips (1988) 86 Cr App R 18
The accused was charged with a number of offences of dishonesty involving a stolen credit card. It was alleged by him that various inducements had been made to make him confess, including the promise of bail and a suggestion that he would not be charged with every single offence but that a large number of them could be 'taken into consideration' so that the police would be saved the work of investigating them. The trial judge found that he had never been offered bail and in relation to the question of having offences taken into consideration the judge unfortunately misunderstood an answer given by the accused in evidence-in-chief. The judge believed that the accused had said that the inducement did not act on his mind. In the circumstances the convictions were quashed on appeal since the prosecution could not be said to have proved beyond reasonable doubt that the confessions were reliable.

R v Harvey [1988] Crim LR 241
The accused and her lesbian lover were present when the victim, a male, was stabbed to death. No one else was present. Both women had blood on their clothes and were arrested near the scene of the crime. On arrest the accused's lover confessed to the murder in her presence. The defendant was a woman of low intelligence who suffered psychopathic disorder aggravated by alcohol abuse. Shortly after the arrest she also confessed to the murder. The other woman later retracted her own confession and indicated that she would be a prosecution witness against Harvey but died before the trial. The only evidence against the accused was her confession. Two psychiatrists gave evidence to the effect that on

hearing the confession of her lover the defendant might herself confess in a childlike attempt to take the blame and protect the lover. In the circumstances evidence of the confession was excluded and the jury directed to acquit.

10.1.7.3   Unfairness

This is the most difficult area. We have already considered the case of *R* v *Mason* (see **10.1.5.3**), where deliberate hoodwinking of the defendant's solicitor by the police led to the confession being excluded. As we have seen the court expressly said that it was not doing so in order to discipline the police but simply in application of the principle of unfairness.

This case was followed by *R* v *Samuel* [1988] 2 All ER 135. The accused was arrested for armed robbery and taken to a police station where he signed the custody record to the effect that he did not want a solicitor at the time. Later in the evening of the same day he did request a solicitor but this was refused because a serious arrestable offence was involved and there was a likelihood of other suspects being inadvertently warned. That evening he was further interviewed and a fourth interview occurred the next morning at which he continued to deny a robbery but admitted to minor burglaries for which he was then arrested. During that morning his mother got a solicitor who was refused access to him. It was decided to delay charging him so that evidence on the robbery could be obtained. In the evening of that day he was charged with the burglaries but his solicitor was still refused access to him. Later that evening he was again interviewed and confessed to the robbery and was charged with this. It was submitted that evidence of the final interview should not be admitted because refusal of access to a solicitor was unjustified throughout.

The appeal was allowed and the conviction quashed. The initial refusal of a solicitor might have been justified because of the alleged use of a firearm in the cases. However, once the accused had been charged with the burglaries, access to a solicitor could no longer be delayed merely because other offences were under consideration. The right to legal advice in s. 58 of the 1984 Act was fundamental and could only be denied if the officer reasonably believed that access to a solicitor would hinder police inquiries. The fear that a solicitor might advise his client not to answer more questions was not an adequate ground. The trial judge had not considered that the police were unjustified in refusing a solicitor and therefore this had led him not to exercise his mind at all as to the effect of s. 78. It therefore fell on the Court of Appeal to exercise that discretion to exclude the confessions. The court did conclude that it was 'undesirable to give general guidance on s. 78' because circumstances might vary so widely between cases.

However this case may be contrasted with *R* v *Alladice* (1988) Cr App R 380. The accused was denied access to a solicitor for inadequate reasons. The Court of Appeal held that s. 58 had been breached but went on to find the breach did not lead automatically to the exclusion of the confession. Apparently the important factor was that Alladice agreed that he had not required legal advice in order to decide whether to speak or remain silent. He had a substantial criminal record and was well aware of his rights and could cope with the absence of a solicitor. He merely wanted a solicitor to be there as an independent witness to see fair play during the interview. The trial judge was right in concluding there was no causal link between the breach of s. 58 and the confession. There was no bad faith on the part of the police. In this case however the Lord Chief Justice did say that 'if the police have acted in bad faith the court will have little difficulty in excluding the evidence'. This is a somewhat strange remark since the presence or absence of bad faith cannot of itself make any difference to reliability or unreliability and it seems to be an unacknowledged expression of the court's intention to use s. 78 to discipline the police.

In deciding how to use s. 78 in connection with refusal of a solicitor therefore, the court has to decide what effect if any that refusal might have had. Sometimes the court holds quite understandably, that it can never know what effect the refusal may have had and acts in the accused's interest by excluding the confession. On other occasions, as in the case of *Alladice*, the court has sufficient information to enable it to conclude that the refusal of a solicitor makes no difference.

An equally difficult question is to know how the court should respond where there is a failure by the police to keep proper custody records. If an accused is to have the chance of challenging his confession at trial it is important that there should be a custody record available for inspection. Arguably therefore an accused will be prejudiced in every case where there is a failure to keep such proper records.

There has been an enormous number of cases reported, particularly in the *Criminal Law Review*, over the last five years on the question of confessions. Many of the reports demonstrate how a single substantial error in police procedure, or a handful of more minor errors, seem to lead to confessions being excluded almost automatically.

Particular areas of difficulty for the police have included knowing when precisely an 'interview' is taking place rather than preliminary questioning; and of complying with important changes of wording in new Codes of Practice which replaced the original Codes in 1991. Purely as factual illustrations the following brief case notes will assist in seeing the general picture.

R v *Absolam [1988] Crim LR 748*
Failure to explain right to legal advice, caution, and properly record interview — confession excluded.

R v *Saunders [1988] Crim LR 523*
S would only be interviewed if nothing was written down. The police wrote up their notes of the interview later. Confession excluded — the police were wrong to allow an 'off the record' interview. The making of contemporaneous notes and the submission of them to the accused for checking is mandatory.

R v *Delaney [1989] Crim LR 139*
D was of low IQ and charged with indecent assault. He suffered emotional disturbance. The police told him that their main concern was to help him with his problems and they failed to record the interview until the next day. Conviction quashed as confession unreliable.

R v *Rogah [1989] Crim LR 141*
F, aged 16, was suspected of mugging. He was asked questions informally in the street some way from the scene of the crime and confessed. The confession was excluded, an 'appropriate adult' should have been allowed to be present, and the police could not allege that their informal discussion with F was not an 'interview'.

R v *Trussler [1988] Crim LR 446*
The accused was arrested and initially a police doctor agreed he was not fit to be interviewed because of his state (he was a drug addict). The doctor confirmed he would be fit to be interviewed six hours later. Eventually he was interviewed on a number of occasions briefly and these were properly recorded. Some hours later, however, the officer in the case decided to have 'a general chat' with the defendant during which a confession was made. The court held that there was no such thing as 'a general chat'; only formal interviews should take place and these should have been properly recorded. Confession excluded.

R v *Dunford, The Times, 16 March 1990*
The accused was charged with participation in an armed robbery in the course of which an arresting officer had been shot. He was arrested near the scene and taken to a police station where he requested a solicitor. This was refused. He was later interviewed for one hour 30 minutes by two officers. He had a lengthy criminal record and was well aware of his rights. At the end of a *voire dire* the judge concluded that there had been a breach of s. 58 but that he would not exclude the evidence in the exercise of his discretion under s. 78. The accused's awareness of his rights was clearly shown by transcript of the interrogation in which he had answered 'no comment' to a series of important questions. The appeal was dismissed.

R v Lamont [1989] Crim LR 813

The appellant was mentally subnormal with a reading and comprehension ability of a child of eight and an IQ of 73. He was aged 23 and living with a woman 12 years his senior and her three children. He had fathered a child by this woman which suffered from ill-health. Apparently the accused resented the extra attention which his cohabitee had to extend to the child and he was charged with attempted murder of the child. During interview he substantially confessed to attempted murder though there was no other real evidence except the confession. It was sought on his behalf to exclude the interview under ss. 76, 77 and 78 of the 1984 Act and, principally, the Code of Practice. The accused had been kept without being interviewed for 18 hours during which he had refused food and he had cried and been very emotional throughout. There was no other adult present although he had been offered and had refused the presence of a solicitor. The judge rejected the allegations that the confession was inadmissible but did direct the jury that there was a special need for caution under s. 77 of the 1984 Act. His appeal was allowed on the basis that a fair summing up under s. 77 of the 1984 Act required a strong direction as to the need for corroboration unless an independent adult was present.

This case is interesting since there will not be many cases on s. 77 because, where the police have behaved in a way which will bring in s. 77 (failure to have an independent adult when interrogating a mentally handicapped person), there is likely to be a preliminary breach of s. 76 which will render the confession unreliable in any event, or in the alternative a claim that the confession should be excluded under s. 78. The judge should have determined that the appellant was mentally handicapped and given the full corroboration warning.

R v Canale [1990] 2 All ER 187

The accused was charged with conspiracy to rob. He had made a number of damning admissions in interviews with police to the effect that he was a member of a gang of professional robbers who lived in France and visited the UK to carry out robberies to finance their lifestyle. There were very serious breaches of the Codes of Practice, in particular a total lack of a contemporaneous record in the interviewing police officers' notebooks and lack of a subsequent record made on the prescribed form. The appellant testified that he had been tricked and induced to make the confessions. It was held on appeal that the lack of a contemporaneous note of the interviews meant that on the *voire dire* the judge was deprived of the very evidence which would have enabled him to decide whether the evidence of the admissions was admissible and subsequently the jury were also deprived of the evidence necessary for them to decide whether his denial of being implicated was true. The police officers had flagrantly and cynically breached the Codes of Practice. The appeal was allowed and the conviction quashed.

R v Bryce [1992] Crim LR 728

An undercover officer contacted the accused and asked him if he had stolen cars for sale. On being told that he had, an appointment was arranged. The accused and the officer met thereafter so that the officer could inspect a car. The officer asked the accused how long ago it had been stolen and received incriminating answers. He then arrested the accused. The accused was interviewed at the police station on tape but made no comments to any questions. When the tape had been switched off the accused said 'I'll tell you what happened but I don't want it recorded'. There was then a conversation during which he admitted guilt.

At trial a submission was made that evidence of both conversations before arrest and the conversation after the tape recorder was switched off should be excluded as they were in the nature of an interrogation and the Codes of Practice had not been followed. The judge refused to exclude any of them. On appeal the conviction was quashed. The officer, by assuming an undercover pose, was circumventing the Codes and each of the early conversations was clearly an interrogation. The interview after the tape was finished was a fresh interview and a fresh caution was needed. (As to the relevance of this case see also *R v Christou & Wright* [1990] Crim LR 729 which is discussed more fully in the context of improperly obtained evidence: see **11.3**.)

10.1.8   SUMMARY

The law's confusion has really been caused by the eliding and overlapping of the three categories of oppression, unreliability and unfairness. Of these three areas the most surprising problem has been created by the way in which the court has dealt with the question of oppression. Under the pre-Act law, oppression was the cumulative effect of conduct, short of threats or inducements, which sapped the free will of an individual so that he spoke when otherwise he would have wished to maintain silence. Typical examples involved overlong questioning.

As we have seen, the definition in the 1984 Act contemplates extreme conduct mainly of a physical nature. To this definition the court have tacked on the extremely artificial dictionary definition. The use of dictionary definitions to express the semantic content of technical legal concepts is usually considered questionable. From that error can be traced a certain amount of the confusion which has crept into the present position. The courts seem to have been prepared to treat conduct that was relatively similar (although the individual circumstances of every case obviously differ) as in some cases *oppression*, in others conduct which would render the confession *unreliable*, and in others conduct such that makes the proceedings *unfair*. It is suggested that the following should be the correct approach:

(a) It must always be remembered that if anybody suggests that a confession has been obtained by oppression or is unreliable that it is for the prosecution to prove beyond reasonable doubt that this is not so. This is why sometimes apparently technical breaches of the Codes have led to exclusion because it is then difficult for the prosecution to demonstrate (the burden being on them) that the breach has had no effect. From that point, the procedure should be as follows.

(b) Is the conduct complained of 'oppression' in the sense of serious misconduct contemplated by s. 76(8)? Although the definition given there is an *inclusive* definition, on any reasonable interpretation of the section for conduct to amount to oppression it must be equivalent to violence or inhuman treatment as the words of the section indicate.

(c) On the assumption that actual oppression is not found, the court must then examine everything said or done which might tend to make the confession unreliable. This gives the court a wide mandate to enquire into all the circumstances in which the confession was obtained from the moment when the suspect was first in contact with the police, or indeed with anyone else connected with a prosecution (e.g., a store detective). Applying a subjective test and bearing in mind that the burden of proving reliability is on the prosecution, the court ought to examine whether there seems to be any causal link between everything that has happened and the giving of a confession. It ought also to be borne in mind that there need be no police misconduct at all under this provision. Thus, to take a straightforward example, if the suspect were to inquire whether giving a confession and pleading guilty would obtain more lenient treatment from the court it would be perfectly accurate for a policeman to say that generally speaking it would indeed lead to a discount on sentence. Despite the fact that that is a perfectly accurate statement of the law it could still be contended that it had the effect of making the confession unreliable because an innocent suspect who thought that he might nonetheless be wrongly convicted might be tempted to make a false confession in order to obtain more lenient treatment.

(d) Finally, having decided whether or not the confession is unreliable, the court should then apply its mind to any representations made to it about fairness *in the proceedings*. It follows from the previous common law and from the express statements made by the court in *R v Mason* (see **10.1.5.3**) that, in deciding this, fairness is all that matters and the courts will not use s. 78 as a means of disciplining the police. Having said that it seems that, whether or not they recognised what they were doing, the court in *R v Mason* did in fact intend to discipline the police. Had they wished to make it clear that they were not doing so they could equally well have proceeded under s. 76(2) because it could have been suggested (that on being misled as to the state of the evidence against him) Mason, concluding that he was going to be wrongly convicted, might have made an untruthful confession to obtain more lenient treatment and that confession could therefore have been excluded on the grounds of reliability.

Finally, regard should be had to s. 82(3) of the 1984 Act which provides that: 'Nothing in this part of this Act shall prejudice any power of the court to exclude evidence (whether by preventing questions from being put or otherwise) at its discretion'.

This is simply a recital of the common law rule giving a court power to exclude evidence in any particular case without providing any criteria on which the power might be exercised. It might have been assumed that it was redundant in the context of s. 78 but that this is not so has been recently confirmed in *R* v *Ajit Singh Sat-Bhambra* (1989) 88 Cr App R 55. In this case a confession had already been admitted in evidence and there was subsequently fresh evidence which caused the judge to reconsider his decision on admissibility. The court held that ss. 76 and 78 deal with the situation where a confession has not yet gone before the jury. Accordingly, once the confession has gone to the jury if further evidence does come out showing that the confession is inadmissible the judge should either discharge the jury or (as in this case) give an appropriate direction to the jury about the value of the confession.

10.2 Admissions and the Reaction of the Accused to Statements made or Questions Asked in his Presence

One can envisage various situations where the prosecution may wish to prove what the accused said to show his reaction to accusations or the course of questioning, for example where a child victim sees his attacker in the street shortly after an attack and goes up to him with his parent and says 'that's the man'. Or the more common example where the police may wish to prove answers made by the accused to interrogation, perhaps very lengthy interrogation. In neither case will the accused's replies (even if they *were* admissible) be intelligible unless the prosecution were *also* permitted to prove what was said by way of accusation or question. The exception to the hearsay rule which permits this is usually called 'statements made in the presence of the accused' or 'statements taxing the accused with incriminating facts'.

One may thus wish to prove two items of hearsay: an accusation — which may itself contain second-hand hearsay, e.g., 'The man who was robbed said he saw you run away with the bag'; and the response to the accusation — an acceptance, a denial, some ambiguous statement, or silence.

There may clearly be serious dangers in allowing evidence of the accusation to be given before the jury. If an account of a lengthy interrogation is given, often repeated accusations or accounts of circumstantial detail may influence the jury to treat facts as established which are actually in dispute or unproved. This difficult problem has been dealt with by the following rules which are not affected by the 1984 Act.

(a) Whilst an accusation when made is never evidence of the facts stated, it may become so to the extent that the accused makes a reply which shows he *accepted* the truth of the accusation.

Example: The victim of an assault sees the perpetrator in the street some time later and tells a policeman. Together they go up to the criminal and the policeman says 'You are the man who attacked this lady'. The criminal says 'Yes I am'. In such cases it is proper to let the whole evidence go before the jury because the accused's simple reply 'Yes I am' in this example amounts to his 'adopting' the accusation. In this case the full rules as to confessions apply, i.e. the confession must be shown to be *reliable*.

(b) If the accused makes an *ambiguous* reply to the accusation the judge must decide as a preliminary issue whether to let the jury hear the evidence at all. It may be necessary to send the jury out and hear arguments in their absence where it is clear from the depositions which the judge sees in advance of trial that this is the case. Where for some reason the judge does not hold a *voire dire* on the issue there is a concept which is known as 'conditional admissibility' which applies. The judge permits the jury to hear the evidence but directs them that the words of accusation are only admissible to introduce the accused's reaction to them, and that unless they find that his reaction indicates that he accepted the accusation they must ignore the accusation and not treat it as evidence of any fact stated in it.

Examples of ambiguous reactions would be some inconclusive remark, an insult, silence, violence, mere facial expression, etc.

(c) If the accused makes a *denial* then neither the accusation nor the reply should be put before the jury because nothing of any evidential value has occurred. An accusation has been made out of court which has also been made in court — by the charge being put to the accused — and he has said it is untrue, which he has also said in court by his not guilty plea. This principle is clear and the only area of difficulty occurs where a denial is made, but one which might have some evidential value because it is *not very strenuous* — or a denial is made which is in an *inconsistent form* with the defence actually adduced at the trial, e.g., an accused who denies at first ever striking the victim but whose defence at trial is that he did so in self-defence.

The rule is that if a denial does have some evidential value because of ambiguity, lack of certainty, or inconsistency, a judge may allow evidence of both accusation and denial to be put to the jury but again he must direct them that such items are only of value if they draw an inference of guilt.

On the question of silence consider the following examples:

(a) *R* v *Hall* [1971] 1 All ER 322. The accused was charged with drug offences. Whilst being questioned by the police he was told that accusations had been made against him by a woman concerned in the offences. He made no reply. The judge directed that an inference of guilt might be drawn from his failure to give an explanation or disclaimer. On appeal the Privy Council quashed the conviction. Lord Diplock said:

> It is a clear principle of the common law that a person is entitled to refrain from answering a question put to him for the purpose of discovering whether he has committed a criminal offence. *A fortiori* he is under no obligation to comment when informed that someone else has accused him of an offence. . . . A caution merely serves to remind the accused of a right he already possesses at common law. The fact that in a particular case he has not been cautioned is no ground for inferring that his silence was not in exercise of his right but was an acknowledgement of the truth of the accusation.

(b) *R* v *Parkes* [1976] 3 All ER 380. The accused and the deceased lived in a house owned by the deceased's mother who lived nearby. One day the mother found the deceased in her room dying of stab wounds. The mother then saw the accused with a knife in his hand and twice accused him of having stabbed her daughter but he made no reply. Subsequently the accused attempted to stab her with the knife also. It was held that in such a case the judge was entitled to instruct the jury that the accused's reaction to the accusations including his silence were matters which they could take into account since the accused and the mother were speaking on even terms.

The concept 'not speaking on even terms' is an important one. Whereas if someone is questioned by a policeman the parties are not 'on even terms' and thus a reaction of silence is of no consequence, but if the parties are 'on even terms' a reaction of silence may lead to an adverse inference. In *R* v *Chandler* [1976] 3 All ER 105 the accused was questioned by the police in the presence of his solicitor and the Court of Appeal held that the parties were speaking on even terms in that case since the solicitor was present and thus the refusal of the accused to answer certain questions could lead to adverse inferences being drawn. This was reaffirmed more recently in *R* v *Dunn* [1990] Crim LR 572 where the accused was interviewed with his solicitor's clerk present and there were breaches of the Codes of Practice which were condoned in the circumstances because the accused had legal advice. See also **4.7.3**.

In *R* v *Horne* [1990] Crim LR 188 the accused was identified by his victim whom he had struck in the face with a glass. The accused said nothing in answer to this allegation which had been made in the presence of the police. The trial judge invited the jury to infer acceptance of guilt from the silence. The Court of Appeal expressly approved the case of *R* v *Chandler*.

It is suggested that the reasoning in these cases is dubious. It substantially detracts from the right of silence if an accused, having received proper advice from his solicitor to say nothing, should have an adverse inference drawn as a result of taking that advice.

10.2.1 CAN CONDUCT EVER AMOUNT TO AN ADMISSION?

The position is uncertain. In *Preece* v *Parry* [1983] Crim LR 170 the court appeared to treat the behaviour of the several accused on arrest (drunken violence and abusiveness to the police) as in some sense being an admission by the accused of the offences for which they were being arrested, which had to do with causing a disturbance in a public house earlier. In *R* v *Madden* [1986] Crim LR 806 the accused was convicted of importing drugs. A trunk which contained cannabis had been delivered to her home having been intercepted earlier. In the ensuing search, letters were found referring to the use and smuggling of cannabis. These letters apparently were admitted at trial although there is no clear indication of a recognition of the hearsay problem.

10.2.2 OTHER MATTERS

Three remaining matters to note are:

(a) Despite the above rules, where an account of interrogation is tendered to the court it is usual to put the whole interrogation before the court (editing out any matter which is inadmissible under any other rules) and not merely those questions and answers which culminate in an admission/confession as such. This is no doubt to preserve coherence but it is far from clear under precisely which rule such hearsay is admitted.

(b) In the Crown Court, where a deposition makes clear to the judge in advance that the form of the admission incorporates some matter which is inadmissible under some separate principle, as we have seen the judge will require the matter to be 'edited' out of the version eventually placed before the jury. If the trial is in the magistrates' court however, where there may be prior written disclosure of evidence, this is not possible, and the admission will be repeated to the magistrates, who ought no doubt to direct themselves to ignore it although whether this is possible in reality is open to doubt.

(c) Where there is a tape recording of an alleged confession the jury may be allowed to hear the tape; this will normally only happen where it is considered important that they hear the precise words used as they were spoken, for reasons of intonation or to judge such things as threatening demeanour, pace of the questioning, etc., to assist them in deciding on the truthfulness of what is said.

10.3 The Right of Silence

As is well known, the accused cannot be compelled to speak at any stage of the criminal process. Even if he refuses to plead this will be interpreted as a 'not guilty' plea. The accused's silence out of court has already been dealt with (see **10.2**). We are now going to consider silence in court.

An accused has two options:

(a) *He can testify on oath.* If he does so he is open to cross-examination like any other witness, although unlike other witnesses he may *not be cross-examined as to his character* except in certain circumstances (see **13.3.2**).

(b) *The accused need say nothing.* If the accused relies on his historic right to say nothing, clearly for the right to be of much value there must be some restraint on the right of the prosecution to comment adversely on this silence. It would obviously be easy to influence the jury towards taking an extremely suspicious view of such conduct — the layman presumably would respond favourably to comment such as 'surely innocent people are eager to give their side of the story'. As we have seen the prosecution may not comment at all on the refusal of an accused's spouse to testify, and the rule is that they may not comment on the refusal to testify of the accused himself either (s. 1(b), Criminal Evidence Act 1898).

See, for example, *R* v *Mutch* [1973] 1 All ER 178 in which the accused was charged with robbery. No formal identification parade was held because the prosecution alleged that in order to confuse anyone attending such parade the accused had altered his appearance by tinting his hair and changing his moustache. The accused declined to testify but did call two witnesses to prove that he had not altered his appearance as alleged. The trial judge told the jury that they were entitled to draw inferences unfavourable to the accused where he was not called as a witness to establish an innocent explanation of facts proved by the prosecution which without such explanation told for his guilt. The appeal was allowed and the conviction quashed. The judge had seriously misdirected the jury concerning the accused's right of silence.

In this case the form of direction from *R* v *Bathurst* [1968] 1 All ER 1175 at p. 1178 was approved for use in almost every case where the accused does not testify:

> [The accused] is not bound to give evidence, . . . he can sit back and see if the prosecution have proved their case and . . . while the jury have been deprived of the opportunity of hearing his story tested in cross-examination, the one thing that they must not do is to assume that he is guilty because he has not gone into the witness box.

It was however suggested that there is a type of case where the prosecution evidence seems prima facie very strong and where some explanation from an innocent accused might have been expected; in such a case a stronger comment may be permissible. See, for example, *R* v *Bernard* (1908) 1 Cr App R 218 where the accused was charged with assisting the issue of a fraudulent company prospectus. His defence was to the effect that he was merely the secretary of the company, had acted as the paid servant of the other directors and had had nothing personally to do with any fraud. He took no share in the profits and alleged that he did not know of the fraud. He did not however testify at his trial. The Court of Criminal Appeal held that the judge had not been wrong in inviting the jury to draw their own conclusions in the absence of explanation on oath by the prisoner. On all the evidence in the case he must have known of the fraudulent nature of the transaction.

In *R* v *Jackson* (1953) 37 Cr App R 43, Lord Goddard CJ said that an example of this principle would usually occur in cases of handling stolen goods which, on it being proved that they were in fact stolen, might call for rather stronger comment than usual in the absence of any evidence from the accused.

The variety of possible circumstances and words of comment are clearly infinite so decided cases are of only limited value as precedents, but three good examples of excessive comment are:

(a) *Waugh* v *R* [1950] AC 203. The accused was a gamekeeper in charge of a plantation. He shot a poacher, allegedly in self-defence. There were no other witnesses although the poacher did make a sort of dying declaration which was incomplete and confused but appeared to allege that the accused had shot him not in self-defence but because he had a grudge against him. The accused did not testify. The judge gave a very strong direction to the jury including the words 'he had not seen fit to go in the witness box and submit himself to cross-examination and have his story tested. He has not done it, why not? You are entitled to ask yourself that. Two persons were present; one is dead and the other is in the dock and he does not tell you his story'. There were eight other references to the accused's failure to give evidence. The Privy Council quashed the conviction holding the judge's direction far exceeded what was proper.

(b) *R* v *Sparrow* [1973] 2 All ER 129. The accused and X stole a car. X had a loaded gun and subsequently shot a police officer when they were stopped. The accused's defence was that he never contemplated that any shooting was likely to take place. He did not testify. The trial judge summed up: 'If there was any real belief in his mind that he never contemplated that any shooting was going to take place is it not essential that he should go into the witness box and tell you that himself and be subject to cross-examination about it?' The accused was convicted and appealed, contending that the judge had directed the jury too strongly about his silence. It was held that the trial judge in his remarks had indicated to the jury that they could equate his absence from the witness box with guilt. In so doing he had overstepped the limits of justifiable comment. However the proviso was applied.

(c)   *R* v *Matthews* [1990] Crim LR 190. The accused disputed the terms of the confession allegedly made. Her counsel made allegations of concoction and fabrication against the police but thereafter called no evidence and the judge said 'You have alleged against the police perjury, conspiracy and fraud . . . I am amazed you are calling no evidence . . . I may have to get the professional etiquette book out.' The grounds of appeal included an objection to this comment, made in the jury's presence, on the basis that the words suggested the defendant had an obligation to give evidence and that counsel had acted unprofessionally. The Court of Appeal held that the words were highly improper but were cured by a clear and adequate summing up on the effect of the right of silence.

10.3.1   SUMMARY

It is said that before the judge can properly comment on the accused's silence in court and invite them to draw adverse inferences, three basic conditions must be satisfied:

(a)   There must be a case to answer. Even if the prosecution case is not so deficient that the judge should have stopped the trial, but is nonetheless weak, comment is improper — a weak case is not strengthened by failure to answer it.

(b)   The accused must have been capable of answering it, i.e. he must have had some material fact he could contribute.

(c)   There must be no apparent reason for failure to testify such as insanity, amnesia, desire to protect others, fear of disclosing criminal record.

Comment is therefore unlikely if the prosecution case is already damaged by cross-examination or internal inconsistency or the defence case has already been put by other witnesses.

It is more likely if there are facts which are peculiarly within the accused's knowledge, e.g., an innocent explanation of apparently incriminating facts.

Note that counsel for a co-accused is *entitled as of right* to comment on another co-accused's failure to testify since s. 1 of the Criminal Evidence Act 1898 is silent on this. For example, in *R* v *Wickham* (1971) 55 Cr App R 199 it was held that, where there was a conflict in the evidence of two co-defendants, counsel for one defendant has the right to comment on the failure of the co-defendant to give evidence and the judge has no discretion to prevent such comment.

Finally, note that the accused has the right to remain silent *before trial* on all matters including the nature of his defence and the names of his witnesses, with the single *general* exception of an alibi defence in the Crown Court. Section 11 of the Criminal Justice Act 1967 requires the accused to give notice of his alibi and the names and addresses of his supporting witnesses to the prosecution before the end of seven days after the committal proceedings. If he does not do so, evidence of alibi can only be given with leave. Even in the case of an alibi the accused has no need to testify — the alibi may be established by other witnesses.

In addition, if the accused wishes to call expert opinion evidence, he is required, by rules of court, to disclose it in advance of trial (see **14.2.6**).

There is a number of specific statutes which have the effect of requiring a suspect to answer questions in certain restricted circumstances. A good example was s. 6 of the Official Secrets Act 1920 which made it an offence to withhold information from a duly authorised policeman investigating infringements of the Official Secrets Act 1911 (now repealed). Other statutes which require persons questioned to supply information, and thus to give away their right of silence, include the Road Traffic Acts and various statutes relating to taxation, rating and gaming.

ELEVEN

THE LAW OF EVIDENCE (5): IMPROPERLY OBTAINED EVIDENCE IN CRIMINAL CASES

11.1 Introduction

Evidence which has been obtained illegally or improperly by the prosecution provides a difficult problem of jurisprudence. In some jurisdictions, particularly the USA, the courts in the main attach a high regard to procedural propriety on the part of public officers, such as the police, and effectively use the law of evidence to discipline them. So if evidence has been obtained unfairly it will be excluded even if it is conclusive of the accused's guilt. The proposition is that the court itself is tainted if it allows illegally obtained evidence to be given before it and that the higher good of the public standing of the court requires it to use its discretion in this way.

In the main, English law has gone in quite the opposite direction and will not allow the law of evidence to be used as a means of disciplining the police. The statement of Crompton J in *R* v *Leatham* (1861) 8 Cox CC 498 still represents English law: 'It matters not how you get it — if you steal it even it would be admissible in evidence.'

The question of improperly obtained evidence arises in three main situations, namely:

(a) Evidence obtained as a result of a confession which has already been ruled inadmissible. For example a confession is obtained by threats or violence and is thus inadmissible but within the confession the suspect has told the police where they can find other incriminating evidence, for example a body or the stolen goods. The question then is whether the finding of the body or the goods is admissible.

(b) Evidence obtained by unlawful search, entry or seizure.

(c) Evidence obtained by entrapment, e.g., by a plain clothes policeman in effect becoming one of a gang of criminals and pretending to participate in their activities.

In all three cases, English law has decided that the law of evidence is not to be used as a means of disciplining the police, so that if evidence is admissible in itself and relevant, it is not made inadmissible by virtue of having been obtained illegally or unfairly. The leading case is *Kuruma* v *R* [1955] AC 197. In this case, at a time when emergency regulations applied in Kenya, it was a capital offence for natives to possess ammunition. Powers of search were conferred by the regulations on policemen of a certain rank. The accused was unlawfully searched by two policemen of a lower rank than that stipulated in the regulations, and they found ammunition upon him. At his trial, he contended that since the search was illegal it would be improper to permit the Crown to take advantage of its own misconduct. The Privy Council held that the only test is whether evidence in such a case is relevant. If it is relevant, it is admissible.

11.1.1 EVIDENCE OBTAINED IN CONSEQUENCE OF AN INADMISSIBLE CONFESSION

In the first of the cases mentioned above, as we have already seen, s. 76(4) of the Police and Criminal Evidence Act 1984 expressly provides that the finding of a thing in consequence even of an inadmissible confession is admissible, although we must also remember s. 76(5) of the 1984 Act which provides:

> Evidence that a fact to which this subsection applies was discovered as a result of a statement made by an accused person shall not be admissible unless evidence of how it was discovered was given by him or on his behalf.

In other words where a confession is excluded but the accused said in it, for example, where something was to be found, the evidence of finding the thing is admissible but no reference back to the reason why the police looked in that place may be made unless the accused himself gives evidence as to how the thing came to be discovered. Therefore if the discovery of the thing in question cannot otherwise be linked to the accused (e.g., by the fact that it has his fingerprints on it), there may be no point in the prosecution adducing the finding of the evidence.

11.1.2 EVIDENCE OBTAINED BY ILLEGAL SEARCH, SEIZURE AND ENTRY

Before the coming into force of s. 78 of the Police and Criminal Evidence Act 1984, which we shall consider below, it was quite clear that in the two other cases mentioned above, namely evidence obtained by unlawful search, seizure or entry, or by entrapment, the authorities were entirely in favour of admissibility and of the principle in *Kuruma*. *Kuruma* itself is a clear illustration of the law in relation to evidence obtained by illegal search.

11.1.3 EVIDENCE OBTAINED BY ENTRAPMENT

Cases such as *R* v *Birtles* (1969) 53 Cr App R 469 and *R* v *McCann* (1971) 56 Cr App R 359 clearly established that, even where police officers acting in plain clothes and participating in a crime go too far and incite criminals to commit offences which would otherwise not have been committed, the law of evidence will not be used to discipline the police. There is no defence of 'entrapment' known to English law and the law of evidence could not be used to create such a defence by the device of excluding otherwise admissible evidence. Where police had gone too far, the question of their misconduct would be dealt with in police disciplinary proceedings; but in so far as the accused was concerned, entrapment would only be relevant to mitigate the sentence imposed, not to the question of admissibility.

11.2 The Court's Discretion to Exclude

The law was restated in the former leading case of *R* v *Sang* [1980] AC 402, which confirmed that the court was only concerned with the relevance of evidence *not* the means by which it was obtained, except in the case of confessions. *Sang* confirmed nonetheless that there is an overriding discretion to exclude evidence if its prejudicial effect outweighs its probative value so as to make it unfair to the accused to admit it. Sometimes improperly obtained evidence might fall into this category but this is a rule of general application and is not only applicable to evidence allegedly obtained illegally. The question for the court is *how fair the trial* will be and not how fair were the police in obtaining the evidence in the manner which they used. This discretion, which existed at common law, is expressly preserved by the words of s. 82(3) of the Police and Criminal Evidence Act 1984. It is important in this context to consider s. 78(1) of the 1984 Act which we have already looked at in connection with its relevance to confessions. The section provides:

> . . . the court may refuse to allow evidence on which the prosecution proposes to rely to be given if it appears to the court that, having regard to all the circumstances, *including the circumstances in which*

the evidence was obtained, the admission of the evidence would have such an adverse effect on the fairness of the proceedings that the court ought not to admit it.

11.3 Test for Admissibility

The test therefore remains 'will it have an adverse effect on the fairness of the proceedings'? It was at first considered difficult to visualise an example of how the actual method of obtaining the evidence could possibly affect the 'proceedings' (i.e. the trial itself) rather than merely demonstrating 'unfairness' in some more general sense, which would surely be irrelevant on the wording of the section. It was widely considered that the section added nothing to such discretion as there was following *R* v *Sang* and that the section would certainly not be used to discipline the police. However, surprisingly, and with one must say a good deal of rather suspect reasoning, the courts have taken a robust view of the nature of their discretion under s. 78.

The somewhat surprising line of cases which have considered s. 78 as supplementary to s. 76 so that breaches of other sections of the 1984 Act (e.g., s. 56 or s. 58) or the Codes of Practice have led to the exclusion of confessions even where the confession had initially been ruled reliable. The most important of these cases, referred to earlier, is that of *R* v *Mason* [1988] 1 WLR 139 where it will be recalled a confession was obtained from an accused after he and his solicitor were both untruthfully told by the police that the police had damning fingerprint evidence and was excluded under s. 78 notwithstanding that it had initially been held reliable under s. 76. In Mason's case the court expressly stated that:

(a) The evidence *was not* excluded in order to discipline the police.

(b) Section 78 does no more than restate the power which the court had at common law.

(c) It was the deception of the solicitor by the police that was particularly offensive and fatal to the evidence.

The reasoning in *Mason*, laudable though the outcome might be felt to be, is suspect. If an innocent man might have confessed on hearing these untruthful representations by the police in the belief that they had framed him and that he might therefore just as well confess (since he would be disbelieved at trial) in order to obtain more lenient treatment, then it would seem that the confession was rendered *unreliable* by the falsehood. If it was not thought to be unreliable then it is hard to take any other view than that s. 78 was used to discipline the police.

What is relevant to this chapter however is to consider whether the court will use s. 78 to exclude evidence which is obtained by entrapment or by illegal search and seizure. A problem is that, although there is some anecdotal evidence that Crown Court judges may be using s. 78 in that way, since the prosecution have no general right of appeal to a higher court where evidence is excluded which is vital to the prosecution's success, such instances will not be fully reported. An exception is the case of *R* v *H* [1987] Crim LR 47. It appears that in this case an improperly obtained admission in a 'tapped' telephone call from a man who was alleged by his former girlfriend to have raped her was excluded by the trial judge. The report however gives insufficient detail to be worth much as authority.

The use of s. 78 has also been considered in *R* v *Gill and Ranuana* [1989] Crim LR 358, where the Court of Appeal considered the 'defence' of entrapment again. The circumstances were that undercover policemen offered themselves as IRA members willing to undertake contract killings for the accused who were conspiring to kill Rajiv Gandhi. Introductions were made by J, a police informer, and the meetings were observed and recorded. The Court of Appeal held that the evidence should not be excluded under s. 78 because the crime was brought about by an agent provocateur. However, the way in which the judgments are expressed seemed to leave open the possibility that had the police themselves been more directly involved, perhaps by setting up the meetings without the intervention of J, the court might have found the facts so gross as to lead to the exclusion of the evidence. Similarly, in *R* v *Jelen and Katz* (1989) 90 Cr App R 456 admissions obtained in the course of a tapped telephone call procured by a man acting as a police informer were also admitted notwithstanding s. 78, the court holding that, since the evidence had been obtained at an early stage of police enquiries before the accused had even been interviewed and since the incriminating remarks did not amount to an obvious confession, the admission of the evidence was not unfair.

As the above cases show, the court seems eager to avoid needing to rule on the use of s. 78 to exclude evidence obtained by alleged entrapment by making a preliminary finding that there was no entrapment. The same applied in *R* v *Edwards* [1991] Cr LR 45 where undercover officers were taken by an informer to E's address. They indicated that they wished to buy drugs and E discussed price and made appropriate arrangements. On E obtaining drugs for them he was arrested. It was suggested that evidence of the whole conduct of the investigation should be excluded under s. 78 on the grounds of entrapment. On appeal the court held that this was clearly not an isolated incident into which E was enticed and it was plain from the facts that E was a habitual established dealer, thus s. 78 did not arise.

In *R* v *Christou and Wright* [1992] QB 979 undercover police officers set up a jeweller's shop in an attempt to recover stolen property and collect evidence against thieves and handlers. Cameras and tape recorders recorded all transactions. Most conversation involved bartering about the price, but to maintain their cover the police would also engage in banter and ask questions to be expected of shady jewellers, such as in which areas of London it would be unwise to resell the goods they were offered. The information obtained helped trace the true owners and discover the dates of thefts. Fingerprints were usually obtained from the suspects by asking them to give a written receipt.

At trial it was argued that the whole concept of the shop involved a deceit or trick designed to deprive visitors of their privilege against self-incrimination. The evidence should be excluded either under *Sang* or under s. 78. No cautions had been administered and the conversations were caught by the Codes of Practice. In dismissing the appeal, the Court of Appeal held that the judge had been right to consider s. 78 and *Sang* but the criteria of unfairness were the same on whichever basis the discretion was exercised. The court held that no trick was applied to the appellants; they had voluntarily applied themselves to the trick. It could not be the case that every trick which produced evidence against an accused meant there had been unfairness. A victim, for example, might be used to help trap a blackmailer. The case of *Mason* was completely different.

The case of *R* v *Keenan* (1990) 90 Cr App R 1 (a case on confessions) held that it was wrong for police officers to adopt or use an undercover pose or disguise to facilitate the asking of questions about an offence uninhibited by the requirements of the Codes with the object of circumventing them. That proposition was taken further in the case of *R* v *Bryce* [1992] Crim LR 728 which has been considered earlier at length in the context of confessions (see **10.1.7.3**). Undercover officers in that case contacted a man suspected of theft and held conversations with him. The Court of Appeal held that the series of questions by the undercover officers offended against the principle set out in *Christou and Wright*. It was blatantly a case of interrogation with the effect of using an undercover pose to circumvent the Code. In addition, the words used were hotly disputed and there was no contemporary record, unlike the tape and video recording in *Christou*.

11.4   The Importance of s. 78 of the 1984 Act

We have now considered s. 78 in its most important aspects of exclusion of confession evidence and as to whether or not it will be used in the case of illegal searches or evidence obtained by entrapment. Section 78 however is of general application. It can be used in respect of any item of prosecution evidence. It is thus the section used to reinforce the Code of Practice in relation to identification so that breach of the procedures at identity parades may lead to all the identification evidence being excluded (see **12.8.3.3**).

Another specific use of it does not involve any suggestion at all of misconduct by the police. It is used when the court has to consider its general discretion on the principles of unfairness to let in evidence of convictions in other proceedings under s. 74 of the 1984 Act. This section, s. 74, does not refer to *the accused's* own previous record as to which quite other considerations apply. It is a section which permits proof of conviction to establish the facts on which prior convictions of *other people* were based. An important use of it is that, where X has been convicted of theft of certain goods, then his conviction can be used at the trial of Y on a charge of handling the same stolen goods as a way of establishing the important preliminary fact that the goods were stolen. Under the previous law this was not possible and the prosecution would, at the trial of the handler, have had to establish anew that the goods were stolen in the first place.

The use of s. 74 is subject to the court's discretion under s. 78 because in some circumstances great prejudice could be caused to a defendant. A number of cases have examined the interrelationship between ss. 74 and 78.

11.5 Sections 78 and 74 of the 1984 Act — Some Cases

In *R* v *Kempster* (1990) 90 Cr App R 14 the accused was charged with four counts of burglary and was jointly charged on some of the counts with three co-accused, all of whom had pleaded guilty. The prosecution led evidence that Kempster had been seen in the company of the other three co-accused at the time of the offences, and the prosecution wished to adduce in evidence the guilty pleas of the others. The trial judge permitted this but unfortunately never applied his mind to the discretion in s. 78 and appeared not to know that he had any discretion in the matter. The conviction was quashed because the guilty pleas of the co-accused were of limited evidential value.

In *R* v *Mattison* [1990] Crim LR 117 the accused was charged in one count with gross indecency with D; and in another count D was charged with gross indecency with M. D pleaded guilty and at M's trial the judge allowed the prosecution to adduce evidence of D's guilty plea. The conviction was quashed, the Court of Appeal holding that the judge should have used his discretion to exclude under s. 78. On the other hand, in *R* v *Chapman* [1991] Crim LR 55, C, with seven others, including his brother, was charged with counts of conspiracy to obtain by deception. All the accused were related and lived on the same caravan site. The accused had charged elderly people large sums for little or no building work. C's brother pleaded guilty to certain counts. The prosecution were allowed, rightly it was held on appeal, to adduce evidence of C's brother's guilty plea. It helped to establish the wider conspiracy. The court however observed that s. 74 should be used sparingly.

Finally, in *R* v *Boyson* [1991] Crim LR 274, B was charged with being concerned in the importation of drugs. She was charged with four others, three of whom pleaded guilty to the same counts. The fourth person was her co-habitee who had been separately convicted of conspiracy. The Crown applied for leave to adduce the evidence of the guilty pleas and convictions. B was convicted and appealed and the Court of Appeal held that the following were the applicable principles:

(a) That s. 74 should be sparingly used and evidence of other convictions should only be introduced when clearly relevant to an issue in the case and must always be followed by a clear direction as to the issues to which the conviction is or is not relevant.

(b) Although the judge had referred in his summing up to the dangers of guilt by association he did not properly deal with the issue of the co-accused's convictions on different offences.

(c) The introduction of each one of the convictions was irrelevant to any issue in B's case and was prejudicial, nor was there any proper direction.

(d) The judge had not considered his discretion under s. 78 properly. Nonetheless there was ample evidence of B's involvement and the proviso was applied. The court expressly disapproved of the apparently growing practice of allowing evidence to go before a jury which is strictly irrelevant, inadmissible, prejudicial, or unfair simply because it is convenient for the jury to 'have the whole picture'.

This case therefore is an extremely useful authority on the way in which ss. 74 and 78 should be considered together.

11.6   Practical Considerations

Section 78 only applies to evidence to be adduced by the prosecution. If it is a co-defendant who wishes to adduce improperly obtained evidence then the judge has a wide discretion, not fettered by statute, to do justice between the parties.

Save in the most exceptional circumstances, magistrates at committal should not themselves use s. 78 to exclude prosecution evidence. Objections under s. 78 should be reserved for the trial. It must be admitted that this is not an entirely logical rule given that magistrates are meant to give attention to matters of admissibility of evidence so as to know whether there is sufficient evidence on which to commit, but there is clear authority for this proposition (see *R* v *King's Lynn Magistrates Court ex parte Holland* [1992] Crim LR 880 and *R* v *Oxford JJ ex parte Berry* [1988] 1 QB 507).

When a defence advocate is considering the prosecution evidence, whether this comes about under the advance disclosure rules in the case of summary trial, or the depositions obtained prior to a Crown Court trial, it is important to weigh each item of prosecution evidence to test its relevance, admissibility and weight. This is inherent in consideration of any kind of evidence.

Quite apart from any questions of strict admissibility however, it is always relevant to consider whether there is any ground for applying to the court to exclude otherwise admissible evidence within its discretion. This application may be framed under the general common law discretions, the rule in *R* v *Sang*, under s. 82(3) of the 1984 Act, or under s. 78 of the 1984 Act. These overlap in many respects, although on the wording of s. 78 special attention has to be given to the question of *how the evidence was obtained*.

It must be borne in mind that one is not, when relying on s. 78 as a ground for seeking the exclusion of evidence, necessarily relying on deliberate and callous flouting of some rule of practice or procedure. It may be, for example, that the police or Crown Prosecutor have simply confused matters procedurally or even proceeded by honest oversight. There are for example instances of the use of s. 78 to which we shall turn shortly where the section has been used to exclude the whole of evidence obtained at an identification parade because of a bona fide mistake made by the police. It is therefore always as well to have in mind the court's discretions to exclude and in particular to have the Codes of Practice and the authority of *Mason* available, the latter being the highest point of the court's willingness to exclude for procedural impropriety. The effect of *Mason* is clearly at its most pointed with confession evidence but there is no reason why it cannot be prayed in aid in other situations, for example evidence obtained in disregard of powers of search, seizure or entry; misconduct in relation to the accused's legal representative; and even the residual possibility that on some particularly gross facts the court will, in effect, be prepared to recognise that entrapment might be a possible ground for exclusion.

TWELVE

THE LAW OF EVIDENCE (6): CORROBORATION: EVIDENCE OF IDENTITY

12.1 Introduction

Corroborative evidence is that which independently tends to support or confirm other evidence.

The general rule is that evidence does not require the support of corroboration — the court may act on the uncorroborated evidence of one witness alone however serious the charge. The law on corroboration has evolved in a piecemeal and haphazard way and now stands as a body of sometimes highly techncial rules covering various categories of situation where the type of evidence, or type of witness, is deemed inherently 'suspicious' in some way so as to require extra caution from a court before it considers its verdict.

There are two classes of cases which are exceptions to the rule that no corroboration is generally required in English law. These are: where corroboration is required as a *matter of law*; and where corroboration is sought as a *matter of practice*.

12.2 Where Corroboration is Required as a Matter of Law

A number of statutes require more than one witness before a conviction can be obtained. The following are examples:

(a) *Treason Act 1795* concerned with compassing the death of the Queen.
(b) *Representation of the People Act 1983, s. 168* which punishes the offence of personation at elections.
(c) *Places of Religious Worship Act 1812* concerned with disturbing religious meetings.
(d) *Perjury Act 1911, s. 12* which states a person cannot be convicted of perjury solely on the evidence of one witness as to the falsity of a statement made on oath. This section replaced the common law which also required corroboration in cases of perjury and seems to have been the only instance of corroboration being required at common law. *R v Threlfall* (1914) 10 Cr App R 112 makes clear that the corroboration required need not be a second witness: a letter or document may suffice.
(e) *Road Traffic Regulation Act 1984, s. 89.* A person cannot be convicted of speeding solely on the evidence of one witness to the effect that in his *opinion* the driver was exceeding the speed limit. Moreover, if two witnesses give their opinion it must concern the speed observed over the same stretch of road. However a person can be convicted on the evidence of one person where that amounts to something more than an opinion: see *Nicholas v Penny* [1950] 2 KB 466. It was held that a police constable who checked a speeding motorist by reference to his own speedometer was relying on something more than 'opinion' and therefore conviction on the evidence of one person was possible.

12.3 Where Corroboration may be Sought as a Matter of Practice

In a number of cases the courts have evolved rules concerning corroboration even though no statute requires it. It was sometimes said that in these cases 'corroboration is required as a matter of practice' but this is an overstatement. What is *required* is a warning from the judge to the jury of the desirability of corroboration in such cases, explaining also the reasons why they ought to be cautious. He will explain that experience has shown the courts that certain types of evidence should be examined very carefully and that it *may* be unsafe to convict without corroboration although they may do so if they feel really sure, even though there is no corroboration. The way in which this direction is to be given will be considered later. It is important in this connection to consider the case of *Attorney-General of Hong Kong* v *Wong Muk Ping* [1987] AC 501 which will be discussed at **12.7**.

The following categories need to be considered:

(a) Cases where witnesses are of such a type that a corroboration warning *must* be given and if it is not a conviction will normally be quashed. These are:

(i) accomplices;
(ii) victims of sexual offences.

(b) Other cases.

12.3.1 ACCOMPLICES

In *Davies* v *DPP* [1954] AC 378 there was a fight between two gangs of 'teddy boys' on Clapham Common. One person drew a knife and a man was stabbed fatally. Originally six people were charged with his murder but finally the appellant alone was convicted, the other participants being convicted only of assault. One of the persons originally charged was Lawson who at the accused's trial for murder gave evidence for the prosecution as to the use of the knife by the accused. The trial judge gave no direction to the jury on the danger of accepting Lawson's evidence without corroboration. The House of Lords held that as L did not know that Davies had a knife he was not in any sense an accomplice to the crime of murder and that 'accomplices' would, for the purposes of corroboration, consist of the following three categories:

(a) Persons who are participants in the actual crime charged.
(b) Handlers at the trial of the thieves from whom they received the stolen goods.
(c) Where the accused has been charged with a specific offence and evidence is admissible that he has committed crimes of this identical type in the past, the evidence of persons who participated in such crimes (see **13.2.2**).

This case states the modern rule and classifies who may be treated as an 'accomplice' for the purpose of the warning. The classic rationale of the rule is of course that by implicating someone else an accomplice may seek to minimise his own role in the crime. The classes of accomplices now appear perhaps unduly restrictive and not entirely consistent with logic. It is far from clear for example why a handler at the trial of a thief is treated as an accomplice but a thief at the trial of a handler is not.

12.3.1.1 Co-accused and corroboration

However, note that the strict requirement to give a corroboration warning applies *only to prosecution witnesses*. What is the position where one of several co-accused, testifying on his own behalf, inculpates a co-accused? *R* v *Prater* [1960] 2 QB 464 appeared to hold that a warning ought to be given in every case where *any witness* may have some purpose of his own to serve which may lead him to give false evidence against an accused. This has however been modified in some cases which hold that it may be desirable to give the warning but it is within the judge's discretion whether to or not.

In *R* v *Prater* [1960] 2 QB 464 the accused was charged with another man, W, with offences of dishonesty. At the trial W gave evidence on his own behalf. It was contended on appeal that the judge should have warned the jury of the danger of convicting the appellant on the evidence of his co-accused. It was held that, although the authorities by no means pointed in the same direction in the case of evidence of a co-accused as distinguished from a Crown witness (an accomplice), in practice it was desirable that a warning should be given to the jury where a witness might have some purpose of his own to serve.

This may go too far however: see *R* v *Whitaker* (1976) 63 Cr App R 193, where the main prosecution witness at Whitaker's trial, O, was the only other person who could have committed the crime if Whitaker had been innocent. The court held that there was no positive requirement for the judge to give a corroboration warning to the jury and that whether he did so or not was in his discretion. Since in the case it was quite clear to the jury that everything depended on them deciding who was telling the truth as between the accused and O, no corroboration warning was necessary.

The leading case on this more flexible category of 'persons with a purpose of their own to serve', which includes not just co-accused testifying on their own behalf but any instance where a prosecution witness may have something to gain from the accused's conviction, is *R* v *Beck* (1982) 74 Cr App R 221. The accused was charged with conspiracy to defraud a finance company by obtaining payments for work done in connection with double glazing by providing fraudulent satisfaction notes. The directors of the finance company which he had allegedly defrauded testified for the prosecution. They had in their turn claimed large amounts from their insurers in respect of the money they claimed to have lost in the alleged frauds. It was suggested by the accused that the directors of the finance company had actively assisted him in the scheme and had known all along that the notes were not genuine. He alleged that they were testifying against him only in order to protect themselves from a charge of fraud by the insurance company. There was also the suggestion that their activities would have amounted to unlawful trading and drawn them to the attention of the Director of Fair Trading. They were not however accomplices as such because they were not participants in the same crime with which he was charged. On appeal the Court of Appeal held that the supposed rule from *R* v *Prater* was something of an overstatement. In every case where a person was not strictly an accomplice, the form and nature of the warning was within the discretion of the trial judge.

There have been many cases since *R* v *Beck* in all of which the correctness of that decision has been confirmed. Whether or not to give a warning is within the discretion of the judge in any given case to be exercised by him in the light of all the facts. So in *R* v *Mainwaring* (1982) 77 Cr App R 99, for example, where the accused ran 'cut throat defences' totally blaming each other, the Court of Appeal concluded that on those facts the full accomplice warning should be given. In similar cases however, in particular *R* v *Knowlden and Knowlden* (1983) 77 Cr App R 94 and *R* v *Loveridge and Loveridge* (1983) 76 Cr App R 125, where the co-accused each blamed the other and the court upheld the judge's direction, which in each case was considerably weaker than the full corroboration warning.

12.3.1.2 Who decides whether a prosecution witness is an accomplice?

The question of whether or not a witness is an accomplice is often answered by his confession, guilty plea or conviction. Otherwise it is for the judge to rule whether there is sufficient evidence to show that the witness *may be* an accomplice (and of course whether in law he could fall into one of the categories) and then for the jury to decide whether he *is* in fact.

12.3.1.3 Summary

(a) If there is evidence to show that a Crown witness may be an accomplice within the three categories, the judge must direct the jury that they may find the witness to be an accomplice and that if they do so decide that it may be unsafe to convict on his evidence unless they find corroboration for it in other evidence.

(b) If it is clear that a Crown witness is an accomplice, e.g., by his own confession, the judge should direct the jury that this is the case and give the corroboration warning above.

(c) If there is no evidence that the witness is an accomplice (as in *Davies* v *DPP*) the judge need give no direction at all about the matter. In the above cases (a) and (b) the corroboration warning is mandatory and a failure to give it will lead to a conviction being quashed even if there was in fact other corroborative evidence.

(d) If the Crown witness or co-accused or defence witness is not strictly an accomplice but may have some purpose of his own to serve, the judge has a discretion whether to give a corroboration warning and it may often be desirable to do so.

(e) If a Crown witness who may be an accomplice gives evidence which is partially favourable to the accused the judge has a discretion whether to give the warning. See *R* v *Royce-Bentley* [1974] All ER 347 where a prosecution witness gave evidence partly against the defendant but in part supported the defendant's innocence. The judge asked defence counsel whether the corroboration warning should be given to the jury and it was agreed that there should be no such warning because to have given it would have made the jury unduly suspicious of that part of the witness's evidence which had favoured the accused.

12.3.1.4   Corroboration in the case of accomplices

There will be a general discussion of the nature of corroboration at **12.4**, but it is appropriate to mention here some matters specifically applicable to accomplices.

The leading case is *R* v *Baskerville* [1916] 2 KB 658 in which Lord Reading LCJ said:

> We hold that evidence in corroboration must be independent *testimony* which affects the accused by connecting or tending to connect him with the crime. In other words it must be evidence which implicates him, which confirms in some material particular not only the evidence that the crime has been committed but also that the prisoner committed it.

This is a general dictum concerning the nature of corroborative evidence but as applied to accomplices it shows that it is not enough merely to show that part of the evidence is *true* — it must also *implicate the accused*.

Example: A and B are accused of theft. A pleads guilty and says that he and B committed the crime and that they buried the goods in a farmer's field. The goods are found there. However this is *not* corroboration of his evidence against B because although it shows that he is telling the truth about his own involvement it does not directly implicate B. On the other hand if B's fingerprints had been found on the goods in the field that would be an item to corroborate A's evidence.

Despite the clear wording of Lord Reading's dictum, corroboration need not be *testimony* as such and relevant documents, fingerprints, or the finding of stolen goods in the accused's possession etc. would certainly suffice.

One accomplice cannot corroborate another at least where they are both within the first of the categories in *DPP* v *Davies*, i.e. both parties to the crime. This is the result of the old case of *R* v *Gay* (1909) 2 Cr App R 327 a result often confirmed in later cases (e.g., in *R* v *Prater* [1960] 2 QB 464). The position is however different in the case of accomplices within the third category where there is less danger of conspiracy since the persons involved were accomplices of the accused in separate crimes. These *may* therefore corroborate each other in a proper case.

In *DPP* v *Kilbourne* [1973] AC 729 the accused was charged with various offences of homosexual indecency with two different groups of boys, one series of offences in 1970 against one group and the second in 1971 against another group. It was held that the evidence of each group of boys could corroborate that of the other group. Where accomplices are within the third class of Lord Simonds in *Davies* v *DPP* there is only slight danger of collaboration and conspiracy between them. The overriding consideration in this case is that where the 'accomplices' are accomplices *to different crimes* there is clearly little danger of them conspiring to falsely implicate the accused.

12.3.2   SEXUAL OFFENCES

Since a charge of any kind of sexual offence may be easier to make than refute it has long been a *rule of practice* to warn the jury that it is not safe to convict on the uncorroborated evidence of a complainant, but that they may do so if satisfied on her truthfulness. This is now a peremptory requirement following *R* v *Trigg* [1963] 1 All ER 490. The accused was charged with rape. No warning was given to the jury of the danger of acting on the complainant's evidence without corroboration. In the circumstances the conviction was quashed on appeal and it was held that it was not generally proper in such a case to apply the proviso in s. 2, Criminal Appeal Act 1968.

Absence of warning will therefore be fatal to conviction even where there may have been ample corroboration, and as in the case of accomplices, it will not be safe to apply the proviso.

12.3.2.1   The nature of corroboration in sexual cases

Corroboration in sexual cases is of course only rarely to be found in eye-witness evidence of the crime itself. It is usually found in things such as state of clothing or scientific evidence. It must be remembered that 'recent complaint' cannot be corroboration because it is not independent of the victim.

The nature of the corroboration must implicate the accused in a material particular. It is not enough, for example, to show recent intercourse, for this does not negative consent *or* implicate the accused. Thus in *R* v *James* (1971) 55 Cr App R 299 the accused was charged with rape. The complainant gave evidence that a man had raped her in her own bed. There was medical evidence that she had had sexual intercourse at the time and the trial judge directed the jury that this was capable of amounting to corroboration. On appeal, quashing the conviction, it was held that although the evidence did confirm that intercourse occurred it neither implicated the accused nor negatived consent and therefore could not amount to corroboration.

12.3.3   EVIDENCE OF CHILDREN

Until 1988 there were strict requirements in relation to corroboration in the case of the evidence of children. Moreover this was so whether the child was the victim of the offence or merely a bystander. Now however, by virtue of s. 34(2) of the Criminal Justice Act 1988, there is no longer any *strict requirement* to warn a jury to look for corroboration merely because the witness is a child. Of course, if the child falls within some other category (e.g., sex-crime victim) a warning may still be required. It may often be prudent to warn anyway. For the court's new attitude to children as witnesses see **8.2.2** as to competence.

12.3.4   WITNESS FALLING WITHIN TWO CATEGORIES

Note that where a person falls within two categories, each of which require corroboration, e.g., accomplice and sex-crime complainant (both possibilities were present in *DPP* v *Kilbourne*), the judge should mention each ground for the need for corroboration with some brief explanation of each.

12.3.5   OTHER CASES

(a) *Identification evidence*. This topic will be more fully dealt with in the later section on identification. Although corroboration in the strict sense is not required, both supporting evidence and a warning to the jury may in certain circumstances be necessary.

(b) In several other cases the courts have been urged to create new categories where a corroboration warning should be required. However, in no case has the court been prepared to accept that there were any other categories of persons beyond those already mentioned for whom such a warning should be mandatory.

The leading case is now the House of Lords case of *R* v *Spencer & others* [1987] AC 128. The accused were members of the nursing staff of a secure hospital who were charged with ill-treating patients. The prosecution relied solely on the uncorroborated evidence of mental patients in each trial. All the mental patients had criminal convictions and suffered from mental disorder. In both trials the judge directed the jury to approach the evidence of the patients with great caution but did not use the words 'dangerous to convict' in relation to the patients' evidence. The accused were all convicted. The Court of Appeal affirmed the convictions. On further appeal the House of Lords held that where the evidence was that of a witness who was not in one of the accepted categories where a corroboration warning was mandatory, but who by reason of his particular mental condition and criminal past fulfilled analogous criteria, although the trial judge ought to warn the jury that it was dangerous to convict on his uncorroborated evidence the actual use of the words 'danger' or 'dangerous' was not essential to an adequate warning provided the jury were made fully aware of the dangers of convicting on such evidence. In the present case the judge's direction had been entirely adequate.

An explanation is given in this case which helps to explain cases such as *R* v *Beck*. Lord Ackner explains that in the established categories where the 'full warning' is obligatory this is because the inherent unreliability of the witnesses may well not be apparent to the jury. Hence it is usual to explain to the jury precisely why accomplices or the victim of sexual assaults may lie for motives not immediately apparent. In other cases the potential unreliability of a principal witness for the prosecution is obvious for all to see and this was such a case because of the character of the victims who had criminal convictions, were mentally unbalanced and were shown to be anti-authoritarian, prone to lie or exaggerate, and might well have had old scores to settle. The judge's warning in the present case in which he had referred to 'using great caution' was adequate.

(c)   Other cases where the courts have recently been unsuccessfully urged to accept new categories requiring corroboration include *R* v *Simmons* [1987] Crim LR 630 (charge of false imprisonment with sexual motive although no sexual offence occurred) and *R* v *Lovell* [1990] Crim LR 111 (assault between members of gypsy families who had engaged in feuds for many years).

12.4   The Nature of Corroboration

Corroborative evidence, it has been held, must implicate the accused directly and therefore is different from circumstantial evidence where a combination or cumulation of facts each in themselves insufficient to indicate guilt may together be enough. When deciding on whether to convict, the jury must consider the credibility of the witness in respect of whom corroboration is required. They may however, in deciding on his basic credibility, go on to look at the corroborative elements as a preliminary test. See *Attorney-General of Hong Kong* v *Wong Muk Ping* at **12.7**.

In other jurisdictions there is a concept known as 'cumulative corroboration' which has departed from this general principle of the need for a direct link to the accused. There is no clear case in England in which the possibility of cumulative corroboration has been recognised although the borderlines between the kind of evidence which is technically capable of being corroboration and others seem to be in the process of being eroded generally. See in particular *R* v *McInnes* at **12.5**.

12.4.1   SOME PARTICULAR ASPECTS OF CORROBORATION

We are now going to consider some aspects of corroboration. There are interesting factual examples even in very old case law. It is important to note however that the courts have only really given detailed technical consideration to corroboration problems over the past decade or so.

In order to amount to corroboration a piece of evidence must:

(a)   Be extraneous to the person whose testimony requires corroboration.
(b)   Be admissible in itself.
(c)   Implicate the accused in a material particular.

12.4.1.1 Corroboration must be extraneous to the person whose testimony requires corroboration

This is why prior consistent statements cannot corroborate because they only provide evidence of consistency. This consistency may of course be consistency in a lie. Otherwise, as Lord Hewart CJ said in *R* v *Whitehead* [1929] 1 KB 99, one would only need to repeat one's story 25 times to get 25 separate instances of corroboration of it.

In *R* v *Whitehead* the accused was charged with having unlawful carnal knowledge of a girl aged under 16 years. The judge directed the jury in effect that the girl's complaint to her mother could amount to corroboration and further that the accused's failure to reply when the charge was put to him could be corroboration. Both directions were held to be wrong and the conviction was quashed. As the complaint to her mother proceeded from the girl herself the evidence did not have the quality of independence required.

In sexual cases, distressed condition, soiled clothing or minor injuries may of course corroborate that the offence occurred, and the absence of consent, but it will always be a question of fact in any case whether the evidence can be corroborative and in particular whether it implicates the accused.

Thus in the old case of *R* v *Redpath* (1962) 46 Cr App R 319 a little girl who was indecently assaulted on some moorland came off the moor in a state of great distress which was observed by a bystander whose presence she had not noticed. Other evidence connected the accused closely with the place of the crime and it was held that, the crucial feature being that the little girl did not know she was being observed at the time when her distress was witnessed, her distress could corroborate.

There are more difficult cases however where the victim has known that her distress would be perceived. Cases which are arguably wrongly decided where it was accepted that distress could, in such circumstances, amount to corroboration include *R* v *Chauhan* (1981) 73 Cr App R 232 where a female employee who had allegedly been indecently assaulted ran to a crowded part of the building demonstrating distress; and *R* v *Dowley* [1983] Crim LR 169 where an ex-wife, having alleged that her husband had attempted to rape her, showed distress to a householder to whose house she ran.

The problem with these kinds of cases is that since the defence was that in each case the allegation was fabricated, the lack of independence in such evidence was a vital defect. After all, if it is suggested that the complainant in a sexual offence has either never been assaulted at all, or has consented, it is a natural consequence that she is inventing a false story. Someone who is sufficiently malicious to do that is likely to be quite capable of simulating distress and even such things as ripping or dirtying her own clothes. It is this lack of independence which is the crucial defect in such evidence. An even stranger case, if it is correctly reported, is the Scottish case of *Cannon* v *HM Advocate, The Times*, 4 May 1992. In this case the victim was allegedly raped at about 10.00 p.m. one evening but made no complaint to anyone, even though her parents only lived next door, until she began crying in front of a friend some 22 hours later. The Scottish court apparently found that the evidence of distress could be corroborative, a quite remarkable conclusion.

12.4.1.2 Corroboration may often be found in the conduct of the accused

This corroboration may be found either on the accused first being questioned, or by evidence from him at trial, or by conduct on some other occasion. Some particular aspects are:

(a)   Evidence during trial may amount to such an *admission of a relevant matter* as to corroborate. See *R* v *Jarrett* [1985] Crim LR 306 where the accused was convicted of rape having pleaded guilty to buggery of the same woman. Medical evidence of the buggery was held capable of corroborating the victim's complaint of rape as it was consistent with her assertion that she had consented to neither act. On appeal it was held that this was correct; the medical evidence on the buggery was capable of corroborating the complaint of rape whether or not the buggery was proved to be forcible.

(b)   *Failure to testify*. This cannot of itself be corroboration: *Cracknell* v *Smith* [1960] 3 All ER 569.

(c)   *Lies told in or out of court.* The law is now contained in the case of *R* v *Lucas* (1981) 73 Cr App R 159 where the accused was charged with importing drugs. An accomplice gave evidence against her, and the court came to consider the effect of possible lies told by the accused. It was held that such a lie could amount to corroboration provided it fulfilled the following criteria:

(i)   It was deliberate.

(ii)   It related to a material issue.

(iii)   The motive for the lie was realisation of guilt and fear of the truth. The jury must thus be reminded that there may be many other reasons for an accused person to lie whether in interrogation or in court, e.g., panic or shame or the desire to invent a false story because the truth sounds unlikely.

(iv)   The statement must clearly be shown to be a lie by evidence other than that which needs corroboration, i.e. by an admission from the accused or evidence from another independent witness.

(d)   *Silence when charged.* The basic rule is that where an accused is questioned by a policeman, silence cannot amount to corroboration because an accused has a right of silence in such a situation and therefore he must be entitled to exercise it. Some cases however hold that where the defendant is accused by some other lay person with whom he is speaking on even terms, a refusal to reply can amount to corroboration. For example, in *R* v *Cramp* (1880) 14 Cox CC 390 the defendant was accused by the victim's father of having attempted to procure an abortion on her. His failure to reply was held to be capable of being corroboration.

(e)   Refusal to consent to the taking of an intimate sample. Under s. 65 of the Police and Criminal Evidence Act 1984, refusal by an accused to consent to the taking of an intimate sample (e.g., a blood sample) without good cause may amount to corroboration of other evidence.

(f)   *Conduct of the accused on other occasions.* It is a general principle of the law of evidence that conduct of an accused person on other occasions is not admissible to prove the crime with which he is at present charged. Exceptionally, however, it may be admitted under the 'similar fact' principle which we shall discuss later at **13.2.2.** Where the conduct of the accused on previous occasions shows marked similarity to some factual aspects of the present charge, so as to provide real probative value, evidence of that conduct on previous occasions is admissible. If the case is one where corroboration is required, the previous conduct may thus corroborate. This is particularly important in the case of sexual offences where commonly some issue of corroboration will arise and the accused's conduct on other occasions is admissible to corroborate. This may arise either in respect of convictions for crimes previously committed by the accused, or in cases where the accused is charged with two or more offences in the present proceedings where one offence may corroborate another.

12.5   Cumulative Corroboration

An important question which was not dealt with in the English cases until very recently is whether, where there are several pieces of evidence which individually cannot be corroboration (because for example they are not extraneous to the witness concerned, or do not individually inculpate the accused), they may together be capable of constituting corroboration because of their cumulative effect. In the Canadian case of *Vetrovec* v *R* (1982) 136 DLR (3d) 89, cumulative corroboration was accepted. The first important English case where the principle was also acknowledged seems to be *R* v *Hills* (1987) 86 Cr App R 26. However, the Court of Appeal in that case stressed that whilst cumulative corroboration might be possible, it is vital that a correct direction be given to the jury about the status of each and every piece of evidence.

The Court held that a combination of pieces of individually innocuous circumstantial evidence not infrequently provided corroboration of an accomplice's evidence but when consideration was given to the question of whether they did so it was always important to consider the real issues in the case and what was in fact proved by the evidence put forward as corroboration. The accused was charged with participation in drug smuggling and gave an innocent explanation of his conduct to the effect that he had believed that he was smuggling only snake skins. The Court of Appeal held that it was always important to consider:

(a)   what the real issues in the case were;
(b)   what the evidence being put forward as corroboration did in fact prove;
(c)   whether that evidence came from a source or sources independent of the accomplice and went some significant part of the way towards showing that the offence was committed and that the accused committed it.

In the present case the judge had purported to identify items of corroboration without reminding himself of what was the real issue in the case, namely whether the accused was knowingly involved in attempting to import heroin. The judge had listed 13 points which were capable of amounting to corroboration and said that none was capable individually of corroborating the accomplice witness but the question was whether they collectively did so because of the light which they threw upon one another. Unfortunately many of the 13 points were not capable of amounting to corroboration because they were themselves dependent upon the accomplice's evidence. In all the circumstances it was unsafe to apply the proviso and the conviction was quashed.

A factually fascinating case in which the question of cumulative corroboration arose was *R* v *McInnes* (1990) 90 Cr App R 99). A girl of seven years fell off her bicycle and was assisted by a passer-by who gave her a lift home. He stopped, pulled her into some bushes and assaulted her. Two days later the appellant was arrested and charged with kidnapping and rape. The girl gave evidence unsworn. She had remarkable powers of observation. She gave a detailed description of her assailant as being slim with ginger hair and a ginger moustache wearing blue jeans and a plain T-shirt; she described the car in detail including the upholstery, a tartan holdall on the back seat, a tear in the plastic material at the base of the gear leaver and the fact that the gear leaver was slightly off-centre. In addition she said the interior was littered with Fox's Glacier mint sweet wrappers. She illustrated this by a series of drawings.

The police arranged a 'video identification parade' wherein the appellant was filmed walking along a stretch of corridor in the police station. Seven other people were filmed in the same way. The girl identified the appellant. There was also a video identification parade of 16 cars in a car park. The girl identified the appellant's car. The police found jeans and a T-shirt answering the description at the appellant's home, and these had been recently washed; the car's interior corresponded in all respects to the girl's description. The girl's evidence was supported by the sworn evidence of a boy who had seen the girl being picked up and who also identified the accused's car.

The outcome of the case does not matter because it mainly hinges on the fact that at the time the girl's evidence required corroboration because she was a child, quite apart from the question of her being the victim of a sexual offence, and there being a difficult question of identification. The court treated the combination of pieces of circumstantial evidence as being potentially corroborative. It is questionable whether this was in fact correct. Although on the facts of the case there seems no possibility that the child was wrong, one must always consider the possibility of a malicious fabrication by a complainant about someone to whom she has taken a dislike. Is it beyond the bounds of possibility that such a complainant might not have seen the car in question parked in the street and taken note of the many matters of detail which seem so forcefully corroborative? It is suggested that the child's knowledge of the inside of the appellant's car is not a fact which is *independent* of her evidence even though it is proved to be truthful by police witnesses. The usefulness of their evidence entirely depends on the primary truthfulness of the child and it is suggested that such evidence in fact lacks independence.

12.6   Corroboration and Identification Together

The special rules and difficulties applicable to identification cases will be considered in **12.8**. Such cases pose considerable difficulties which have led to the courts formulating a very precise direction which has to be given to the jury in all cases which turn on identification. This is known as the *Turnbull direction* from the leading case *R* v *Turnbull* [1976] 3 All ER 549.

The leading case on questions of sexual offences where identification is also in issue is *R* v *Chance* [1988] QB 932. The accused was convicted of rape. The victim had been raped and assaulted in her home and some weeks later the accused was arrested as he tried to force his way into her flat again. He was then identified as the rapist. There was some forensic evidence to connect him with the complainant. It was not denied that the complainant had been raped. The judge gave only a *Turnbull* warning and not the full corroboration warning. The appeal was dismissed. Generally in sexual cases juries should be given the warning that it is dangerous to convict on the uncorroborated evidence of the complainant. The corroboration should be of the fact of commission of the offence and that the defendant was the man who committed it, however there are exceptions:

(a) If identification is not in issue then there is no need for a *Turnbull* warning, but the corroboration warning is required.

(b) If the fact that the offence was committed is not in issue then usually there is no need for a corroboration warning. Even if there has been no formal admission by the defence that the offence has occurred there is no particular danger against which the jury needs to be warned. It would be absurd and offensive to the complainant to insist on a warning in such a case.

(c) If identity is in issue then the *Turnbull* warning is required but no corroboration warning unless the case is a rare one where the sexual nature of the case may have affected the identification evidence or where the judge considers it advisable. In such a case the *Turnbull* direction should be amplified to include a formal corroboration direction tailored to the particular circumstances of the case.

(d) If the offence itself is in issue the usual warning must always be given, that is to say a corroboration warning and the *Turnbull* warning.

It must be remembered that there will usually be no difficulty in such cases. If the accused says that he was not the person who perpetrated the rape then he will be doing himself no good tactically in the jury's eyes (and certainly not at the sentencing stage) by insisting that he requires the complainant to prove that there ever was a rape. This will attract great sympathy to the complainant. In most such cases therefore, unless the facts are very unusual, the accused will concede that there has been a rape but simply say that he is not the offender, and the case will turn entirely on identification.

12.7 The Functions of Judge and Jury

It is for the judge to direct the jury carefully in relation to corroboration. He must remind them of the evidence requiring corroboration, he must explain in general terms why such a witness ought to be corroborated, and he must explain that the jury should judge the credibility of the witness who required corroboration not on his evidence alone but on all the evidence in the case. In other words, the jury must examine the evidence of the witness concerned to see if it is satisfactory and credible and then review the position in the light of the fact that he falls into an especially suspicious category. They may then look for corroboration and arrive at an overall view of whether the witness is truthful. These principles were established by the Privy Council in the important case of *Attorney-General of Hong Kong* v *Wong Muk Ping* [1987] AC 501. The accused was convicted of conspiracy to traffic in dangerous drugs and much of the evidence against him was that of two accomplices. There was a conviction and the defendant appealed. The Court of Appeal of Hong Kong allowed the appeal on the ground that the judge had erred in failing to direct the jury that the accomplice evidence must be credible before any question of corroboration could arise. The Privy Council reinstated the conviction. It was suggested that there had been a misreading of an important passage in the case of *DPP* v *Hester* [1973] AC 296 at p. 315. This passage had been interpreted as meaning that a jury must first consider whether a witness is credible because, so it was said, the purpose of corroboration was not to give validity to evidence which is deficient or suspect but only to confirm and support that which as evidence is sufficient and satisfactory and credible. This dictum had been misunderstood. All that was needed was for the jury to consider in the light of the whole of the evidence whether they found the witness credible. The judge would have directed the jury's mind to the possibilities of fabrication caused by the witnesses being in an especially suspicious category and the direction as given in the case was quite sufficient. The judge is to decide whether the evidence of the accomplice even when corroborated in a material particular would be insufficient, unsatisfactory and incredible. If he did so decide he would direct the jury, in the absence of other evidence, to acquit. But if the suspect evidence was capable, whether corroborated or not, of being sufficient, satisfactory and credible then he must leave it to the jury and it is for the jury to decide on the accused's guilt looking at the evidence as a whole.

As well as directing the jury on the reasons for corroboration and the nature of corroboration, the judge must go through all the evidence in the case and identify individual items which are *capable* of being corroboration. It is then up to the jury to decide whether the individual items which the judge has identified are believable and are found to be corroborative by them. There are many cases of convictions being quashed because the judge wrongly identified some item of evidence as being capable of corroboration when it lacked that technical quality, for example because it was not sufficiently independent of the accomplice or sex-crime victim. See, for example: *R* v *Webber* [1987] Crim LR 413; *R* v *Watson* [1992] Crim LR 434 (which makes it clear that if there is more than one charge the judge must deal carefully with what may or may not be corroboration in relation to each of them); and particularly *R* v *Virgo* (1978) 67 Cr App R 323 where the judge wrongly identified an accomplice's diary as being capable of being corroboration whereas it manifestly was not given that it was not independent of the accomplice who had written it.

With regard to the words used in the warning, where corroboration in the strict sense is required, the judge must use the word 'corroboration' and stress the 'dangers' (or closely equivalent word) of convicting without it. References to 'being careful', 'acting with caution', 'viewing with great care' are too weak and will not do. See *R* v *Vincent & Taylor* [1983] Crim LR 173 and *R* v *Stewart* [1986] Crim LR 805.

In cases where corroboration is involved there is now a very common practice of the judge sending the jury out whilst he discusses informally with both counsel, particularly defence counsel, what form of warning seems appropriate. There is a duty on defence counsel to raise any difficulties with the judge at this stage in an effort to get an appropriate form of warning given and defence counsel should not, if the judge appears to be likely to make some vital error, simply sit back and wait for the inevitably successful appeal. Increased co-operation between counsel and judge is a marked feature of the modern criminal trial, and this is one of its most important aspects.

12.8 Advocacy for the Defence and Corroboration

It is an advocate's duty when acting for a defendant to take any proper point that he can take in his client's interest. In the Crown Court, as we have seen, it is for the judge to give the jury warnings in one of certain forms depending on the nature of the evidence in respect of which corroboration is or may be required. Increasingly in the Crown Court discussion between defence and prosecution counsel and the judge about the nature of the warning is normal. If the judge completely overlooks some important point then it is now the proper practice for defence counsel to remind him of it so that he may correct his summing up rather than, as was formerly the case, for defence counsel to sit tight and wait for a successful appeal. In the magistrates' court it is of course a legal fiction to talk of 'warning'. As there is no separation of function on matters of admissibility and weight in the magistrates' court it is the duty of the defence advocate to make the corroboration points as strongly as he can in his closing speech. He will then hope that, if the magistrates ask for advice from their legally-qualified clerk, the clerk will endorse what the defence advocate has said and help them in identifying items in the case which are capable of being corroboration. Unfortunately one never knows of course whether or not this has happened since the magistrates are not required to give reasons for any of their decisions nor do they rule on preliminary points. A defence advocate may indeed wish to take a corroboration point by way of a submission of no case to answer, as for example where the whole of the prosecution evidence depends on, say, an accomplice and his evidence is partially discredited and there appears to be no item in the case capable of constituting corroboration. A submission based on the absence of corroboration would thus be in order at the half-way stage in such a case.

A defence advocate should be particularly alert on the matter of corroboration when considering the form of commital in a case involving an accomplice. If the accomplice is mixed up in the same crime and the present case is going to the Crown Court, then the accomplice will not be able to testify or have his evidence taken into account at the committal because he will not yet have pleaded, the plea in such cases not being taken before the start of the trial in the Crown Court. Thus he cannot be called by the prosecution because he is still a co-accused at the time of the committal. This may well put the prosecution in difficulty if much of their case depended on the evidence of the accomplice, he having intimated that he intended to plead guilty and assist them. Insisting therefore on a full committal under s. 6(1) of the Magistrates' Courts Act 1980 may be a tactically advantageous decision in such cases.

When preparing one's closing speech for magistrates therefore one should always in corroboration cases be alert to the need to remind them firmly of the corroboration requirements and to assist them in identifying items in the case which can, and cannot, amount to corroboration.

12.9   Evidence of Identity

Evidence of identification has always presented special problems. If the perpetrator of a crime is known to the victim or witness, or apprehended at the scene of the crime, evidence of identification is less hazardous (although not free of problems even here) but in the case of a crime committed swiftly and observed fleetingly by a bystander a number of well-publicised cases have shown the dangers of convicting on identification evidence alone.

The topic is best considered by examining:

(a) Problems of admissibility connected with identification.
(b) Problems of weight in identification evidence.
(c) Procedure at identity parades and the use of photographs and videos.

12.9.1   PROBLEMS OF ADMISSIBILITY

Obviously there is no theoretical objection to a witness testifying that the accused is the man he saw commit the crime. This is direct evidence by a first-hand observer. As will be seen in 12.8.2 however, where this happens (i.e. where the witness sees the accused at the trial for the first time after the offence) it is known as a 'dock identification' and is frowned on except in exceptional circumstances.

But what if there has been, as there now usually will be, some identification procedure between crime and trial at which the witness has picked out the accused to assist the police? If the witness confirms at the trial that he has previously picked out the accused, is he not, in effect, testifying as to a prior consistent statement? Moreover the hearsay implications are compounded if some other person is called to confirm that the witness picked out the accused at the identity parade. The point is inadequately analysed and it is far from clear as to whether the courts have acknowledged the hearsay problem at all. See, for example, *R v Osbourne and Virtue* [1973] 1 QB 678 where the witnesses in court could not remember whom they had picked out at an identity parade. A police inspector who had been present was allowed to testify about what had happened at the parade without the court acknowledging the hearsay point.

Something similar happened in the more recent case of *R v McCay* [1990] 1 WLR 645 where at the trial the witness could not remember the position at which the accused had stood in the line, although he had picked out the accused correctly. The evidence of a police inspector who was present at the parade was permitted, apparently on the basis that ss. 66 and 67 of the Police and Criminal Evidence Act 1984 were statutory authority for such hearsay in criminal proceedings. This decision is highly questionable. These sections authorise the issuing of Codes of Practice for the conduct of identification parades (see 12.9.3.3), but that does not in itself justify hearsay in the circumstances which occurred in *McCay*. The court suggested, in addition, the old case of *Howe v Malkin* (1878) 40 LT 196 (a case on *res gestae*, see **9.14.1**) authorised hearsay in such situations. It has to be said that both these cases have been subject to a great deal of criticism and it has been suggested that the authorities are dubious but it seems likely that they would be upheld if the point were taken again.

12.9.2 PROBLEMS OF WEIGHT IN IDENTIFICATION EVIDENCE

An old practice, now disapproved, is the so-called 'dock identification' (referred to above) where a witness is asked if the man seen at the scene of the crime is present in court. There will clearly be a tendency to look at the man in the dock and pick him just because he is there in that position. In a parliamentary statement on 27 May 1976 the Attorney-General said counsel should not seek a dock identification from a witness who had not previously made a successful identification unless the reasons were exceptional. There is a practice in some courts, where a dock identification is unavoidable, of letting the accused sit anywhere in court before the identifying witness is brought in.

The present law is governed by the case of *R* v *Turnbull* [1976] 3 All ER 549 decided by a Court of Appeal of five judges. This case followed shortly after the report of the Devlin Committee on Evidence of Identification in Criminal Cases which itself was a response to some well-publicised cases which turned on identification evidence and where it was demonstrated that serious miscarriages of justice had occurred. Although the guidelines in *R* v *Turnbull* were said to involve only changes of practice and not of law, the court emphasised that failure to follow them would lead to the conviction being quashed where the failure makes the verdict unsafe. The guidelines are as follows:

(a)   The judge should warn the jury of the special need for caution before convicting the accused in reliance upon the correctness of identification evidence drawing their attention to possibilities of error (p. 551j) and to the fact that a witness may be honest but mistaken.

(b)   The judge should invite the jury to closely examine the circumstances in which the identification was made, including conditions, length of time of observation, how soon afterwards the witness gave a description to the police, and whether the witness knew the defendant (p. 552b).

(c)   The judge should specifically remind the jury of any weaknesses which have appeared in the identification evidence (p. 552c).

(d)   If the prosecution have reason to believe that there is a material discrepancy between the description of the defendant given at first to the police and his actual appearance, they should supply the defence with particulars (p. 552c).

(e)   Where the quality of the identification evidence is good the jury may safely be left to assess it; where it is poor the judge should withdraw the case from the jury and direct an acquittal unless there is other evidence which supports the correctness of the identification. This need not be corroborative in the technical sense, i.e. it need not come from a source independent of the witness. The judge must direct the jury in specific terms about the supporting evidence.

(f)   In particular he must direct them that the fact that the accused elects not to give evidence cannot of itself support it, and also where the accused puts forward an alibi they need not treat any proven falsity of this as supporting evidence if, for example, it was put forward out of stupidity or panic, but they may treat it as supporting evidence if they conclude that it was put forward for the sake of deceiving them (p. 553h).

The main problem with an identification witness is that there is not (usually) any suggestion that the witness is lying. The problem is one of an honest but mistaken witness who is convinced that he has got the right man.

The need for a clear warning following *Turnbull* has been repeatedly stressed. Briefer forms of warning which paraphrase or elide the various parts of the *Turnbull* warning have been criticised on appeal and convictions quashed in such circumstances. It is vitally important in any case based on 'fleeting glimpse' identification that the full warning is given. See in particular *R* v *Tyson* [1985] Crim LR 48.

It must be borne in mind however that the *Turnbull* guidelines only provide a primary test. They do not apply by any means to every case of visual identification. So the warning will not be required for example in cases where there has been a lengthy deliberate observation carried out by police who already know the suspect, and have had a tip-off about his involvement in a crime; or if the real issue is not whether the victim can identify the suspect but whether the victim is telling the truth at all. See, for example, *R* v *Courtnell* [1990] Crim LR 115 where the defence was that the identification witness was totally fabricating his evidence to conceal his own involvement in the crime.

12.9.3 PROCEDURE AT IDENTITY PARADES AND THE USE OF PHOTOGRAPHS

We shall now go on to consider the use of photographs, videos and photofits together with procedure at identity parades. The guidelines are now in the Identification Code issued under s. 66 of the Police Criminal Evidence Act 1984. Part of the Code is set out for reference at **4.9**.

12.9.3.1 Photographs

If the police already have a particular suspect in mind, or indeed have arrested anyone, there is no need for the use of photographs. Photographs should be used to enable the police to get some idea as to who might be a suspect where they have no immediate candidates. If there is a suspect then the police should go straight to the stage of identification parade because obviously there is less evidential value in such a parade where a witness has already recently identified a photograph.

In a case where photographs have been used the defence are placed in a great dilemma. The defence would normally wish to cross-examine a witness searchingly about all matters relevant to his recollection and the circumstances of identification. The danger of course is that if they do this some reference to photographs will come out and the more alert members of the jury will inevitably infer that since the police had a photograph of the accused, the accused must have a criminal record.

Some of the practical problems appear in the case of *R* v *Lamb* (1980) 71 Cr App R 198. The accused was charged with wounding. It was alleged that he and two other men had followed three students out of a restaurant, behaved abusively towards them and that the accused had then attacked one of the students. The accused who had a record of violence was picked out from among 900 photographs by two witnesses of the attack. He then attended an identification parade where the victim and another witness picked him out with varying degrees of confidence. The case against the accused depended entirely on visual identification made over a period of 20 minutes in good lighting conditions but without any other independent evidence. After the jury retired they returned and on request were allowed to see a 'mug' shot of the accused and permitted to have the page on which it appeared with 11 other photographs. These items had already been put in evidence by the Crown. The accused was convicted. On appeal the conviction was quashed and it was held that to put in photographs as part of the prosecution case was a serious irregularity which should not have occurred for it was the equivalent of telling the jury that the accused had a criminal record. In such a case the defence should be informed that photographs were used and it is then up to defence counsel to decide how to conduct his case and whether he wishes to bring out the matter.

None of this should be confused with the situation where police are trying to trace a *known* wanted person's whereabouts, e.g., by showing a photograph door-to-door or on television.

12.9.3.2 Photofits

As an alternative to the use of photographs, a method of attempting to obtain details of the appearance of a suspect, which when first introduced was expected to be more useful than it has proved, is so-called 'photofit' evidence. In this case a detailed description of the facial features of a criminal is obtained from close eye-witnesses. It was widely assumed that such photofit pictures were merely for incidental use in establishing a suspect who could then be put on an identity parade. A very strange result however occurred in the case of *R* v *Cooke* (1987) Cr App R 369.

In *Cooke* the accused was convicted on the basis of a photofit prepared by the victim. After the photofit had been prepared the police arrested the suspect and put him in an identity parade. The victim identified him. In the course of the trial the photofit was put in evidence, the judge having ruled it admissible as 'part of the circumstances of the identification'. This was upheld on appeal. It was considered that neither the hearsay rule not the rule against admission of a previous consistent statement applied to this situation because in preparing the photofit the officer was merely doing what a camera would have done. This result has been much criticised and it is suggested that it is wrong. A photofit is nothing like a camera because there is the interposition of human intelligence. It is suggested that a photofit is hearsay, just as a verbal description of the accused would have been and should have been ruled inadmissible. The decision however, has been upheld in another case, *R* v *Constantinou* [1989] Crim LR 571, on somewhat similar facts.

12.9.3.3 Identity parades

Reference should be made to the full text of the Code of Practice (and see **4.5**) but we will summarise the most important points:

(a)   A parade must contain at least eight persons similar in appearance to the suspect.

(b)   The suspect may choose his own position in the line and change it after each witness has gone down the line.

(c)   The suspect may have a solicitor or friend present.

(d)   The parade must be organised by a uniformed officer of at least the rank of inspector who must not be involved in the case (so as to ensure his impartiality).

(e)   The suspect must be given written information about his rights.

(f)   A full record of everything that happens on the parade must be kept.

(g)   Each witness who walks along the line must be warned that the person he saw may or may not be in the line (so that he should not feel obliged to identify somebody if in any doubt).

(h)   Witnesses must be kept away from each other before and after the holding of the identification parade.

(i)   An accused cannot be compelled to attend the parade. However if he declines to attend this fact may be given in evidence and the prosecution may make alternative arrangements which do not require the accused's consent and which are likely to be less favourable to him.

In addition:

(a)   A parade *must* be held if the suspect asks for one.

(b)   A group identification can be held if the suspect refuses to appear on a parade or fails to turn up to one or if it is impracticable to hold a parade.

(c)   A confrontation which does not require the suspect's consent may take place only when neither a parade nor a group identification is practicable.

(d)   Photographs or other pictorial aids such as photofits should not be shown to a witness where a suspect is already available to be paraded or to participate in a group identification.

It is a time-consuming business to organise a parade with persons sufficiently similar in appearance to the suspect, and all the more so if there are several suspects and witnesses. Procedure in organising parades varies greatly around the country. Some police forces appear unwilling to go to a great deal of trouble to organise the necessary number of relatively similar-looking suspects for parades; much depends on the number of suspects and the degree of difficulty which is anticipated. Increasingly, use is being made of informal methods of confrontation, e.g., street confrontations where the suspect is released into a crowd and invited to walk past the identifying witness.

Particular problems have been experienced in cases involving black suspects or, specifically, dreadlock-wearing suspects where the police have had difficulty in finding sufficient members of the public willing to stand on a parade. It is clearly established that the police must be amenable to reasonable requests, e.g., a request to delay the parade so that the suspect's solicitor can attempt to find members of the public willing to stand in the parade with them (*R* v *Britton and Richards* [1989] Crim LR 144). In general a suspect has a right to a parade if he wants one and reasonable efforts must be made therefore to set up a workable parade (*R* v *Gaynor* [1988] Crim LR 242). Even if the number of suspects make identification parades impossible, there should be group identifications rather than jumping straight to confrontation (*R* v *Ladlow and others* [1989] Crim LR 219, where there were 21 suspects involved).

The police must use some ingenuity in ensuring the parade is fair. Thus, for example, in *R* v *Gall* (1990) 90 Cr App R 64 the suspect had a large scar on his face. Other participants in the parade were made to wear sticking plaster in the position where the scar was. Clearly there will be cases where the police will find it impossible to arrange (e.g., where the suspect has a major deformity.).

It has become apparent recently that the problems of identification have become almost as technical and fraught with appealable points as confession evidence. The possibilities for the police to get what seems a fairly simple procedure (but which is often not) wrong have been demonstrated to be endless on the facts of recent cases. In some of these, relatively minor technicalities have been considered to be sufficient to make the whole process unfair. In others, the police have been excused infringements and the identification procedure upheld. It is difficult to see a consistent policy emerging from the courts. So in the case of *R* v *Gall* mentioned above an investigating officer came into the parade having brought one of the witnesses to it. The witness then identified the accused. It was held that the judge should have excluded all the identification evidence because of the considerable suspicion that could be felt if the investigating officer came into the parade room and spoke to a witness. Similarly in *R* v *Nagah* (1991) 92 Cr App R 344 where the police wrongly refused a suspect the right to a parade, and instead arranged an informal identification by the complainant sitting in a police car, the conviction was quashed. Likewise in *R* v *Finley* [1993] Crim LR 50 the suspect was a slim blonde skinhead and everyone else in the parade was larger and dark. The conviction was quashed for this and other irregularities. On the other hand, in *R* v *Ryan* [1992] Crim LR 187 a key witness was driven to the parade by one investigating officer. Although criticising the officer's conduct the Court of Appeal declined to quash the resulting conviction notwithstanding the substantial breach of the Code.

A situation sometimes encountered by the police and which causes difficulty is where there has been some incident, particularly a robbery or sexual attack, and they come to the scene quickly. If the victim is able to tour the area in a police car there is a chance of finding a suspect. If a suspect is then seen by the victim, is there any point in holding a subsequent parade since she will obviously clearly recognise the person she has just identified? The answer appears to be that a subsequent parade is otiose in those circumstances according to the authorities of *R* v *Brown* [1991] Crim LR 368 and *R* v *Oscar* [1991] Crim LR 778.

12.9.3.4 Challenging identification evidence

When identification evidence is challenged, a variety of possible situations which may occur. Instead of there being simple legal argument as to admissibility in the absence of the jury it may well be appropriate for the judge to receive factual evidence on how the identification was conducted and thus to himself perform a factfinding function. It has sometimes been urged by defence counsel that there should therefore be a *voire dire* in the absence of the jury along the lines of that pertaining to confessions. In two recent cases which tend to the same result, namely *R* v *Beveridge* [1987] Crim LR 401 and *R* v *Flemming* (1988) 86 Cr App R 32, objection was taken to various aspects of the identification process. It seems that the judge was asked to hold a trial within a trial on the issue. In both cases on appeal it was held that whilst this was always an option open to a judge in an appropriate case, basically a judge was able to make up his own mind about the factual issues by reading the depositions and listening to submissions by counsel. It was not necessary in every case for him to go on to hear evidence about the identification even though he might be asked to apply s. 78 of the 1984 Act.

If the whole of the prosecution case depends on identification evidence however, and there are serious objections to the procedures adopted in respect of which the court will need to undertake some factfinding exercise (e.g., as to what really happened during the identification parade) then one should not hesitate to ask for a trial within a trial on that specific point. If one succeeds in establishing one's case then the court is likely to exclude all the identification evidence because non-compliance with identification procedures means that the accused loses a crucial protection since the prosecution are then left with the straight 'jump' from identification at the scene to identification in the dock which, for the reasons previously discussed, is frowned upon.

12.9.3.5 Videos

An interesting development in recent times concerns the showing in court of video films. This has been held possible at least since *Kajala* v *Noble* (1982) 75 Cr App R 149 where a BBC news video was shown in court to allow a witness to identify an accused at a public disturbance. In the USA, filmed reconstructions of torts and crimes are often shown to assist the court in visualising how things have occurred.

This will not be permitted in the UK according to *R* v *Quinn and Bloom* [1962] 2 QB 245. The accused were charged with keeping a disorderly house by permitting indecent striptease acts to perform there. The defence had prepared a film depicting the acts as a deliberate reconstruction of what had happened on the premises. The evidence was excluded as not being the 'best evidence' in that it would be impossible to accurately recreate every movement in the court of the original striptease, especially as a snake was used.

For an incursion into this prohibition however, see the strange recent Hong Kong case on confessions of *Li Shu-Ling* v *R* (1989) 88 Cr App R 82 where a suspect was actually prevailed upon to re-enact a strangling.

Quite a different situation would be the showing of a film depicting something directly relevant to the issue, e.g., in a personal injuries action where the plaintiff is alleged to be totally disabled but is suspected of malingering, a film taken by private detectives showing him jogging. These are quite routinely admitted in evidence. Or as in cases where the actual commission of crimes has been filmed, such as drug-dealing.

Videos which show actual crimes (whether or not supplemented by identifying witnesses) have been admitted in many cases. In such cases the jury are in effect turned into the identification witnesses themselves. Sometimes this has to do with recognising whether the people on the security video are the accused; it may even extend to the jury having to decide whether any offence occurred at all (as where security cameras in a department store appear to show shoplifting but are unclear). So in the early case of *R* v *Dodson & Williams* (1984) 79 Cr App R 220 the jury were invited to say whether the suspects were the men shown on a security camera which filmed a building society robbery; in *R* v *Fowden & White* [1982] Crim LR 588 the suspects were traced having been filmed on a security camera by a store detective who knew the two accused personally. In this case it was also left to the jury to say whether on the film the accused were committing theft at all.

12.9.4 CORROBORATION AND IDENTIFICATION

Where there are issues of both corroboration generally (e.g., a sex crime) and identification, regard should be had to the important decision in the case of *R* v *Chance* [1988] QB 932 referred to earlier (see 12.6).

One should always be aware as a defence advocate of the provisions of the Codes and carefully examine the factual situations surrounding any identification evidence. The fallibility of the police in numerous cases in organising parades has already been mentioned. If it is possible to get crucial identification evidence excluded because of breach of the relevant Code of Practice, it may well be that the whole prosecution case collapses. Accordingly, if one has succeeded in having identification evidence excluded, a submission of no case to answer may often be appropriate in such instances.

THIRTEEN

THE LAW OF EVIDENCE (7): EVIDENCE OF DISPOSITION AND CHARACTER

13.1 Introduction

The word 'disposition' is used to denote a tendency to act think or feel in a particular way. The word 'character' may include disposition, or sometimes mean 'general reputation' or merely the question of whether or not the accused has a criminal record.

13.2 Evidence of Disposition

Evidence of disposition is in general inadmissible for the prosecution both because it is not necessarily logically relevant to the issue of the accused's guilt of the offence with which he is now charged and also because it is clearly highly prejudicial to the accused for the jury to be told of his previous disposition. The risk is that the average jury will lose sight of everything else in the case apart from the striking revelation of the accused's bad character. This is exacerbated in the case of an accused who has convictions for crimes in the past which are notoriously unpopular with the public, such as rape, child abuse, or even house burglary. There is thought to be a tendency in laymen to wish to punish the accused again for his former crimes whatever his guilt of the present offence.

13.2.1 THE GENERAL RULE

The general rule therefore is that evidence of the misconduct of the accused on another occasion *may not be given if its only relevance* is to show a general disposition towards wrongdoing or even a general disposition to commit the type of crime of which he is now accused. Usually in this context 'disposition' will mean the commission of crimes in the past but this need not be so. For example, evidence of regular drinking or a quarrelsome nature might appear to be relevant to some issue. It would be inadmissible under the rule notwithstanding that drinking and quarrelling are not *per se* crimes.

13.2.2 SIMILAR FACT EVIDENCE

The exception to the general rule is the case of so-called 'similar fact' evidence. In this case the law will permit the prosecution to adduce evidence of previous conduct where its nature, *modus operandi* or some other circumstance, shows an unmistakable similarity to the offence charged. This must be strong enough to go beyond any question of coincidence so as to lead the jury to conclude 'this is the work of the same man'.

It should be noted that many cases turn not only on whether evidence of past crime A is relevant at the trial for crime B but on whether the accused who is now charged with two or more offences has the right to have each tried separately before a different jury, so that the jury trying crime A do not hear of crime B and vice versa. Clearly this application to try each charge separately (or 'sever the indictment') may be crucial — a jury trying a man accused of ten different cases of a fairly distinctive type of crime are much less likely to accept that the police have been mistaken ten times. If the accused succeeded in his application to have ten separate trials with each jury kept in ignorance of the other nine cases, he would obviously stand a better chance in each of the ten trials. Even if the accused is tried on all ten charges together because the judge thinks at the outset that the 'similar fact' principle might apply, when the evidence comes out during the trial it is possible for the judge to change his mind. At that stage a very clear direction to the jury must be given that they must approach each crime entirely separately and not treat the fact that the accused is charged with crime A as any evidence relevant to crime B, C, etc. For the exact procedure see *R* v *Scarrott* (**13.2.3**).

It must be remembered that, under the indictment rules and the authorities stemming from them, there are complex rules about which charges may be tried with which other charges and in respect of which offenders (see **17.3.2**). It is *not* only when the similar fact principle applies that two charges can be heard by the same jury. Examples of the difficulty are cases such as *R* v *Dixon* (1991) 92 Cr App R 43 where the accused was charged together with four offences of rape, six of robbery and one of indecent assault. Some of the offences of robbery and the sexual offences concerned the same victim. Issues arose as to the propriety of trying these various charges together in respect of some of which the 'similar fact' principle could be said to apply. The case unfortunately is vague as an authority, the court concluding that most of the charges were correctly tried together whilst quashing some convictions.

A more dramatic case is *R* v *Cannan* (1991) 92 Cr App R 16 where the accused was charged with abduction and sexual offences in respect of victim 1; attempted abduction of victim 2; and abduction and murder of victim 3. The incidents were given wide publicity and the circumstances of the last incident where the victim had been kidnapped and later found murdered were regarded as particularly horrifying. None of the incidents properly fell within the similar fact principle and the accused contended that in the absence of that principle he should have been entitled to separate trials in respect of each victim. The court reviewed the question of whether, in the absence of the similar fact principle, it was right in every case to order severance of the indictment. It was argued strongly on behalf of the defendant that because of the appalling nature of the crimes alleged, the jury would inevitably be prejudiced against him. The Court of Appeal concluded, having reviewed some of the similar fact principles and other cases involving severance and in particular the earlier case of *Dixon*, that it was legitimate for a series of offences to be joined notwithstanding that the similar fact rule did not apply. The judge had given a careful, full and clear warning to the jury to consider each matter separately and the appeal should be dismissed.

When considering similar fact cases, it is also as well to bear in mind the crucial risk in accepting evidence of disposition. As Lord Hewart CJ said in *R* v *Bailey* [1924] KB 300:

> The risk, the danger, the logical fallacy is indeed quite manifest . . . It is so easy to derive from a series of unsatisfactory accusations, if there are enough of them, an accusation which at least appears satisfactory. It is so easy to collect from a mass of ingredients, not one of which is sufficient, a totality which will appear to contain what's missing.

13.2.3 ILLUSTRATIONS OF THE RULE

The leading case is *Makin* v *Attorney-General for New South Wales* [1894] AC 57. The accused were charged with murdering two children whose bodies were found buried under their backyard. Both babies had been received from their mothers by the accused together with a small amount of money for their maintenance on the accused having indicated to the mothers that they wished to adopt the children. There was evidence that several other children, all of whom were found buried in the gardens of houses occupied by the accused, had been 'adopted' in similar circumstances. It was held that this evidence was admissible and relevant as tending to negative any possible defence of death from natural causes or accident. Lord Herschell stated:

> It is undoubtedly not competent for the prosecution to adduce evidence tending to show that the accused has been guilty of criminal acts other than those covered by the indictment for the purpose of leading to the conclusion that the accused is a person likely from his criminal conduct or character to have committed the offence for which he is being tried. On the other hand the mere fact that the evidence adduced tends to show the commission of other crimes does not render it inadmissible if it be relevant to an issue before the jury, and it may be so relevant if it bears upon the question whether the acts alleged to constitute the crime charged in the indictment were designed or accidental, or to rebut a defence which would otherwise be open to the accused.

Another example is in *R* v *Smith* (1915) 11 Cr App R 229 where the accused was charged with murder of a woman. It was shown that he went through a ceremony of marriage with her; she made a will in his favour; he obtained counsel's opinion as to the effect of certain trusts of which she was a beneficiary and learned that he could secure some of the money under these trusts by her death. He bought a bath although they had not previously had one and installed it in a room far from a water supply. The bathroom door had no lock. He took her to see a doctor and described her symptoms in such a way as to make the doctor think that she had had an epileptic fit. She was later found drowned in the bath with her legs stuck up in a way which he had apparently hoped would make people conclude she had drowned in the course of an epileptic fit. Evidence was properly admitted that two other women with whom he had gone through a form of marriage had died in the same way in similar circumstances.

In *R* v *Straffen* [1952] 2 QB 911, the accused was charged with the murder by strangling of two little girls in 1951. He was found unfit to plead and committed to Broadmoor. He escaped from Broadmoor in 1952 and was at large for 48 hours. In that time another little girl went missing and was later found strangled. There were said to be the following similarities between the first two murders and this third murder, namely:

(a) each victim was a young girl;
(b) each was strangled;
(c) there was no sexual or other apparent motive;
(d) that there was no evidence of a struggle;
(e) there was no attempt to conceal the body.

It was held that the evidence of his having committed the earlier two murders was admissible at his trial for the third murder. This case is also an illustration of the fact that the previous conduct proved under the rule need not have led to a conviction as such. It also usefully underlines the point, discussed fully in much more recent cases, that the establishing of primary admissibility of the similar fact evidence is only the first step. The judge must then go on to consider whether the *prejudicial nature* of the evidence *outweighs its probative value* before letting the jury hear it.

In *Noor Mohammed* v *R* [1949] 1 All ER 365, the accused was charged with murder of his wife A by poisoning. There was no direct evidence that he had administered the poison. His previous wife G had also died of poisoning. At the trial, evidence was admitted tending to show that he had murdered G in the same manner by giving her something, allegedly to cure her toothache. He had never been charged with the murder of G. He was convicted of the murder of A and appealed. It was held that, as he was lawfully and necessarily in possession of cyanide in connection with his employment as a goldsmith and as there was no direct evidence in either case that the appellant had administered the poison, the similar fact principle was wrongly applied and his conviction would be quashed.

This case is a good illustration of the importance attached to the admissibility of similar fact evidence to rebut certain defences, amongst them the innocent possession of incriminating matter. Had the accused not been in lawful possession of cyanide for his employment this case might have been decided differently.

One of the most important uses of the similar fact principle was in the case of crimes involving homosexuality. Between the early years of the century and the mid-1970s the principle appeared to be that because homosexuality is so unusual it is admissible at the trial of a person for an offence involving homosexuality to put to him that he has a disposition to homosexual behaviour from other incidents or past convictions. The idea that homosexual offences were in a special category was laid authoritatively to rest in *DPP* v *Boardman* [1975] AC 421. The accused was a headmaster of a boarding school for boys. He was charged with homosexual offences in relation to S and H. At the trial the judge ruled that the evidence of S on the count concerning him was admissible as corroborative evidence in relation to the count concerning H and vice versa. The similar fact principle applied in that the accused's method of approaching each boy was similar and the manner in which he wished to perform the homosexual conduct was likewise similar and allegedly very unusual.

The Law Lords made it clear that homosexuality was not so unusual as to require such offences to be in a special category and that it was important for judges to keep abreast of current standards of sexual behaviour. Earlier cases which had given special attention to homosexual conduct were described as 'like a voice from another world'.

The test was therefore twofold:

(a) does the conduct on another occasion have 'striking similarity' to the crime presently charged and, if so,

(b) is the inevitable prejudice to the accused outweighed by the probative force of the evidence. Lord Wilberforce (p. 445) found the case of *Boardman* 'right on the borderline' so far as the 'striking similarity' was concerned, and the actual result in Boardman has been criticised as setting the standard of 'striking similarity' too low.

The great majority of the case law after *Boardman* is concerned with sexual offences. Because of the requirement for 'striking similarity' more mundane offences such as theft, burglary and the like can only rarely be brought properly within the principle. Occasionally there have been such cases, for example *R* v *Rance and Herron* (1975) 62 Cr App R 118 where, on charges of corruption concerning payments made by builders to local councillors, proof that the accused had on previous occasions bribed another councillor by the same method and had similarly sought to conceal the corrupt payment by a false entry in their own company's books was held properly admitted at trial as the evidence was highly probative. On the rare occasions however where the similar fact principle was applied to more run-of-the-mill crimes, e.g., shoplifting as in *R* v *Mustapha* (1976) 65 Cr App R 26 and *R* v *Seaman* (1978) 67 Cr App R 234, it is usually considered that the cases were wrongly decided and the principle misapplied becuse of the quite mundane circumstances of the incidents in each case.

There were many cases concerning homosexual conduct soon after *Boardman* which left the law in a considerable state of confusion. Two early cases on almost identical facts were *R* v *Novac* (1976) 65 Cr App R 107 and *R* v *Johannsen* (1977) 65 Cr App R 101. In both these cases, groups of middle-aged homosexuals met teenage male prostitutes in amusement arcades in the West End of London and took them back to their homes for orgies. In *Novac's* case the Court of Appeal held that the supposed 'similar fact' evidence of other offences did not fall properly within the principle. In *Johannsen's* case the Court of Appeal held, on facts indistinguishable from *Novac*, that the similar fact principle was properly applied.

In two cases shortly after this however, convictions were quashed because, notwithstanding the appalling nature of the crimes, the surrounding circumstances in each case were just too routine. So in *R* v *Inder* (1977) 67 Cr App R 143 an accused was charged with numerous homosexual offences involving several little boys who lived in the place where he lodged. He had a very bad record for similar offences. The trial judge agreed that the way in which the accused had assaulted the small boys brought him within the similar fact principle and allowed all the offences to be tried before the same jury and details of other offences to be given to them. On appeal the convictions were quashed, the Court of Appeal holding that unfortunately the conduct in this case was run-of-the-mill for this type of offender, or, as it put it, the similarities represented 'the stock-in-trade of a seducer of small boys' and thus the *modus operandi* was not in any way unique. Similarly, in *R* v *Clark* (1977) 67 Cr App R 398 the accused was charged with several counts of sexual offences on his stepson of 16 and his stepdaughter aged 8. The Court of Appeal quashed his conviction holding that it was wrong to try all these charges together.

An important case which unfortunately fails adequately to resolve the confusion caused by the application of *DPP* v *Boardman* in *Novac* and *Johannsen* above is *R* v *Scarrott* [1978] 1 QB 1016, in which Scarman LJ authoritatively describes the procedure to be followed and the factors to be weighed when, as is often the case, the problem of 'similar fact' evidence arises in the context of an application to sever the indictment (p. 1027) and further guidance on the meaning of 'striking similarity' at p. 1022.

In *R* v *Scarrott* the accused was charged with 13 counts of homosexuality in relation to eight boys over a period of four and a half years. His counsel applied to sever the indictment and have separate trials in respect of each boy. The judge ruled that the similar fact principle applied and that the evidence of each boy was admissible in relation to the charges in relation to each other boy. This view was upheld on appeal. There was sufficient similarity in method of approach and method of indecency to each of the boys to come within the similar fact principle. Scarman LJ further held:

(a)   That when an application to sever an indictment is made the judge should have regard to his discretion under the Indictment Rules 1971. He should read the depositions and see whether in his view the offences appear to be of a similar character and form a series. He must ask himself whether in his judgment at that stage it would be open to a jury properly directed to treat the evidence on each count as mutually admissible in view of the striking similarity.

(b)   This is not a final decision as to the admissibility of the evidence. If he allows the multi-count indictment to proceed he may still have to rule later that the similar fact principle does not apply once he has heard the evidence. At that stage, if for example he is impressed with the possibility that the evidence is tainted by conspiracy he may decide that the evidence though strikingly similar is so prejudicial that its prejudicial effect outweighs its probative value. He will then have to make it very clear to the jury as to whether they may or may not treat the evidence of any given complainant as corroboration or mutually admissible in relation to the evidence of any other complainant.

(c)   If he continues to hold that the similar fact principle applies he may direct the jury appropriately that each complainant's evidence is admissible in connection with, and corroborative of, the evidence of the other complainants.

Two more recent cases since *Boardman* show interesting elements of the principle. In the first (*R* v *Barrington*) there was a truly unique *modus operandi*; and in the second (*R* v *Lewis*) a very unusual aspect of the accused's disposition.

In *R* v *Barrington* (1981) 72 Cr App R 280 the accused was charged with offences of indecency with three girls. His defence was that they had got together to concoct false evidence. The Crown then applied for leave to call three other girls in respect of whom no offences were alleged but with whom the accused had gone through the preliminary stage of such offences. These three girls did not know the other victims. The Crown were allowed to call this evidence. The judge ruled that six separate features linked the behaviour in relation to all six girls. Namely:

(a)   The girls were brought to the house to babysit.
(b)   The accused boasted to the girls that he was the script writer of *Dr Who* and a 'friend of the stars'.
(c)   The accused's girlfriend who was present throughout was described as a professional photographer.
(d)   The accused told each girl there was a substantial cash prize for indecent photographs of teenage nude girls.
(e)   He showed each girl pornographic pictures.
(f)   He tried to get the girls to undress for indecent photographs.

It was held that this was a correct application of the similar fact principle and that the evidence of the three girls who were not the victims of any offence was admissible in relation to that of the other three girls because the behaviour was inexplicable on the basis of coincidence and was of positive probative value.

An important case which demonstrates the Court of Appeal's approach to sexual conduct and to the particular importance of the similar fact principle in helping to negative defences such as accident is *R v Lewis* (1983) 76 Cr App R 33. This case is also important because it demonstrates that when one, under this principle, wishes to indicate the accused's disposition to the court, one does not necessarily have to rely on that disposition being evidenced by other incidents or past offences. It is possible that the disposition can be demonstrated by his possession of pornography or other matters which are not in themselves criminal offences.

In *R v Lewis* the accused was charged with indecent assault and indecency with the twin ten-year-old daughters of a woman with whom he was living. He denied that one of the incidents occurred and his defence in relation to the others was accident. Evidence was admitted of his interest in and sympathy with paedophilia. It was held that the evidence was correctly admitted. Whilst the evidence could have had an unduly prejudicial effect if its true impact had not been carefully explained to the jury, this had been done in the present case. The judge had explained that evidence might be relevant to help them decide whether the events involving the girls were innocent or accidental.

The accused's interest in paedophilia (demonstrated by his possession of magazines but *not* by previous convictions) was admissible, apparently on the tacit reasoning that his disposition pure and simple made it likely that he did commit the acts (identity was not in issue). The reasoning in *Lewis* is presumably that paedophiles are so rare that merely demonstrating this accused's interest in paedophilia was sufficient to negative any possibility of accident in touching his stepdaughters.

A very interesting case which demonstrates the real difficulty of the principle and which arguably was wrongly decided is *R v Beggs* (1989) 90 Cr App R 430. The accused, a student, met O at a nightclub frequented by homosexuals. They camped out for the night on the Yorkshire Moors in the course of which the accused cut O's throat. His defence was that he had woken in the night to find O indecently assaulting him and that he had lashed out with a razor blade which he always carried in his wallet. On finding O was dead he panicked and tried to dismember the body but eventually left O on the moors and fled the country. Forensic evidence was to the effect that the description of the incident given by the accused was impossible because O's head must have been held back whilst the cuts to the jugular vein were inflicted. Other wounds were also inconsistent with random slashing because they were quite symmetrical. A great deal of O's blood had been found at the accused's home address and it was there that the Crown contended the killing had occurred. The police conducted extensive other enquiries the result of which was a further five charges of unlawful wounding to others each of them inflicted at various times in strange circumstances by the accused with a razor blade. These were as follows:

(a) A fellow student, W, lived in the same house as O, awoke to find his leg bleeding. His bedclothes were soaked with blood and the accused was nearby. He claimed that the wound had been caused by a protruding bed spring.

(b) Later W awoke to find he had sustained another superficial laceration on his leg and a razor blade was lying nearby. The accused denied responsibility and suggested that burglars had been in the room.

(c) R, who lived in the same house, also awoke to find a laceration on his calf and again the appellant claimed a bed spring was the cause.

(d) L, who also lived in the house, awoke to find a large gash on his leg and no explanation was given.

(e) M was wounded at his own home but was not able positively to identify the accused as the assailant.

The defence applied for the murder count to be severed from the five woundings and this was rejected. The accused was convicted of the murder charge and two of the woundings and acquitted of three of the woundings. The judge held that the evidence was all mutually admissible on the similar fact principle.

The appeal was allowed. The judge had been wrong to consider the evidence on the wounding counts to be strikingly similar to that of the murder count. It did not pass the test in *DPP* v *Boardman*. There were indeed striking dissimilarities because of the nature of the violence, the fact that the wounds were not to vulnerable parts of the body whereas O's throat was slashed; that there was no common factor in relation to the victims; the evidence suggested that perhaps the accused had a propensity to inflict minor wounds on helpless persons. A jury on hearing this evidence would easily conclude that the accused might go too far one day and kill somebody. This evidence was not positively probative and was unduly prejudicial. The Crown submitted that the facts were probative in that they went to rebut the appellant's defence that he had struck out in self defence whilst being indecently assaulted by O. The court held that it did not follow that because a person had acted repeatedly on the offence in the past that that fact could be used to rebut what was essentially a defence which was very dependent on the individual circumstances of the case.

It is suggested in the commentary on this case in the *Criminal Law Review* that as a matter of common-sense many people would conclude that the evidence should have been admissible. After all could it not be thought that a person who has the strange tendency to inflict minor slashing wounds with a razor blade might not go too far one day and cause more serious injury and death? When added to the other suspicious circumstances and the apparent incredibility of the accused's version (on the assumption that we are told sufficient facts in the report) one would have thought that is precisely the kind of case where the evidence of conduct on other occsions might have some value. It is doubtful whether this case would be decided differently under the new (?) principle developed in the case of *DPP* v *P* (see **13.2.4**). As we will see, under that principle the term 'striking similarity' is no longer the crucial one and what is necessary is *real probative value*. It is highly arguable that that feature is present in the case of *Beggs*.

As we have seen the requirement for very unusual behaviour usually restricts the proper application of the similar fact principle to sexual offences or other crimes of violence. Prosecuting authorities made several attempts in the late 1980s to stretch it to prosecution of drug dealers. This possibility seems to have been conclusively laid to rest by the case of *R* v *Wells* (1991) 92 Cr App R 24 where there were numerous similarities between certain types of offences with which the accused was charged involving possession and use of drug-dealing materials. The way in which accounts were kept, types of drugs found, the use of the same 'cutting' agent, the possession of scales and the like were identified as common features. The Court of Appeal however quashed the conviction holding that such materials were common to all drug retailers and therefore it was wrong to try to apply the similar fact principle because there was nothing strikingly unusual about the alleged *modus operandi*.

13.2.4   RECENT DEVELOPMENTS AND APPLICATIONS OF THE SIMILAR FACT PRINCIPLE

The criminal cases so far cited established the following principles:

  (a) Evidence of previous criminal conduct, whether leading to conviction or not, is not admissible to show a general propensity towards crime or even towards the particular type of crime charged.
  (b) Exceptionally it may be admissible if:

    (i) It has some feature which so takes it out of the everyday type of crime as to be 'striking', i.e. sufficiently unusual to have a positive probative value in relation to its similarity with the crime charged.
    (ii) Its positive probative value outweighs the inevitable prejudice to the accused which will ensue from the jury coming to hear of the accused's previous conduct.

(c)   It is a matter of degree as to whether there is sufficient nexus between the present offence and past conduct.

(d)   The nature of the defence is not in itself relevant to the preliminary decision on 'striking similarity' but it is a factor which may influence the judge when deciding in any case where the probative value is less than extremely cogent. There is obviously a great risk of prejudice in the case of an outright denial of involvement.

(e)   Homosexual offences are not in a special category. The prosecution should not be allowed to ask the accused whether he is a homosexual nor it is submitted to achieve the same effect by proof of finding articles commonly used by homosexuals at his residence.

(f)   The issue may arise either at the stage of an application to sever the indictment or in the trial proper.

In 1991 however, there were two cases in quick succession which led to a restatement of the similar fact principle by the House of Lords. The first of these cases was very similar to several other older cases (e.g., *Inder, Clarke* and others).

In *R* v *Brooks* (1991) 92 Cr App R 36 the accused was charged with numerous counts of incest and indecency relating to his three daughters. It was alleged that from an early age he had forced each daughter in turn to engage in sexual intercourse and other sexual acts with him and that as each daughter grew to a certain age she replaced her predecessor. The youngest of the daughters refused to give evidence against her father and a formal verdict of not guilty was entered on the charge relating to her. The accused's defence was that the allegations were entirely false and concocted, being actuated by jealousy and spite. It was argued that as an element of collusion might have been present, the trial judge should have ordered separate trials of the charges in respect of each of the daughters. The judge refused to sever the indictment on the grounds that justice required the jury to hear the whole of the case. The jury convicted the accused unanimously on all the remaining counts.

The accused appealed on the basis that, although the allegations were sufficiently similar in themselves to be within the similar fact rule, the judge should have used his discretion to order separate trials because of the inevitable prejudice to the accused. The convictions were quashed. It was not enough for facts to be similar; they must tell the court something useful. The court must enquire what the evidence set out to prove and whether there were any features of the evidence which made it probative of the facts in a permissible way. In the present case the similarity alleged was the 'stock-in-trade' in the case of father-daughter incest and there was a very real risk here that the two girls had colluded so that particular caution was required. The proper course would have been to treat the evidence of each daughter as inadmissible in the case of the other and to have tried the charges separately.

This case demonstrates the vital importance of the similar fact principle in cases of child abuse. There is of course the risk of collusion between different children, especially if there are matrimonial difficulties between the spouses where the children may take sides and in some cases regrettably be coached by their mother to invent false accusations. Corroboration is required in such cases so that, if the prosecution do not succeed in satisfying the court that the similar fact principle applies and that all charges should be heard by the same jury, there is a strong likelihood of the accused being acquitted by the separate juries who hear each charge or group of charges becuse of the lack of corroboration.

Shortly after the case of *Brooks*, the similar fact principle reached the House of Lords for the first time since *Boardman* in 1975. The case is *DPP* v *P* (1991) 93 Cr App R 267.

The accused was charged with the rape of and incest with his two daughters over a long period. It was suggested that he had used force and threatened both girls and that he had paid for abortions for both of them. He applied for the counts relating to each daughter to be tried separately; the trial judge refused and he was convicted of all charges. He appealed to the Court of Appeal which allowed his appeal on the ground that there were no such striking similarities between the girls' accounts of their father's behaviour to permit the evidence of one girl properly to be admitted on the trial of the counts relating to the other; the Crown appealed to the House of Lords. It was held that evidence of an offence against one victim could be admitted at the trial of an allegation in relation to another victim if the essential feature of the evidence was that its probative force in support of the allegations was sufficiently great to make it just to admit the evidence, notwithstanding that it was prejudicial to the accused as tending to show that he was guilty of another crime.

Such probative force could be derived from striking similarities in the evidence about the manner in which the crime had been committed but there was no justification in restricting the circumstances in which similar fact evidence could be admitted to cases where there was 'striking similarity' since what had to be assessed was the probative force of the evidence. In the present case no injustice had been shown to the accused and the conviction should be restored. Cases like *R* v *Inder, R* v *Clark* and *R* v *Brooks* should be overruled.

This then is a quite remarkable case which appears to extend the circumstances in which evidence of conduct on other occasions can be advanced and replaces the former test of 'striking similarity' with the vaguer test of 'real probative value'. Unlike the former leading case, *DPP* v *Boardman*, where there were five speeches, there was only one in the present case by Lord Mackay and it is a very brief one indeed to effect, if it does, a change in the similar fact principle. It must be remembered however that the question certified for the House of Lords was restricted to cases involving sexual offences against children or young persons. To that extent the observations in the case could be restricted to those offences although clearly they would have powerful persuasive force in respect of other kinds of crimes.

The principle from *DPP* v *P* has been applied in *R* v *Laidman & Agnew* [1992] Crim LR 428 where the accused were convicted of conspiracy to rob, evidence being adduced not merely of a common *modus operandi*, but in fact of the use of identical equipment in two robberies down to the type of car, the use of ammonia solution for squirting in the eyes of security guards, the racial composition of the gang (two white, one black) and other circumstantial details. The Court of Appeal held that since the case of *DPP* v *P* it was unnecessary to point to 'striking similarity' or 'uniqueness'. The question involved balancing the probative value and the prejudicial effect. In *R* v *Mullen* [1992] Crim LR 735 (a case decided just before *DPP* v *P*) it was shown that a number of burglaries attributed to the accused were carried out by a *modus operandi* used by only six offenders in the North East of England. This was proved from records at the National Identification Bureau at New Scotland Yard which holds data (*inter alia*) on the *modus operandi* of burglars. It was held that the probative force of proving that the burglaries were carried out by one of such a small number of potential criminals was very strong.

One final recent case shows the interesting possibility of the *defence* managing to use the principle. In *R* v *McGranaghan* [1992] Crim LR 430 the accused was convicted of offences involving aggravated burglary and rape on three women. There were said to be no less than 15 particular identifying features linking the three crimes and establishing conclusively that they must have been committed by the same man. The precise procedural route which the case took is not important but the key point is that it was established on appeal that the accused was innocent of one of the three offences. Although the evidence against him seemed very strong in relation to the other two, since the prosecution conceded that all three offences must have been committed by the same man, it followed that he could not have been that man and his convictions on all offences were quashed.

13.2.5 ADVOCACY AND TACTICS IN SIMILAR FACT CASES

A defence lawyer will not commonly be presented with a case involving similar fact evidence in the magistrates' court, despite the arguable weakening of the requirements by the case of *DPP* v *P*. In magistrates' courts the use of previous character tends to be restricted to where it arises under the Criminal Evidence Act 1898 which we will discuss shortly. In the Crown Court one's first attack on the prosecution case will inevitably be by way of an application to sever the indictment, that is to have each charge, or each group of charges, or the charges relating to each separate victim, tried separately. Because of the weakening of the similar fact principle in *DPP* v *P* and because of the inevitable consequences in terms of court time and costs, which are to be taken into account in deciding on 'the interests of justice', it may increasingly be the case that applications to sever the indictment are refused where the prosecution depositions show some prima facie case that the similar fact principle applies.

Where one is hoping to sever the indictment one must closely analyse each of the factual elements of the *modus operandi* to see whether it can properly be argued that the kind of offence, incident or method used is too mundane to be within the principle so that the prejudicial effect of the evidence outweighs its probative value. It is a useful exercise to attempt to list every element of the *modus operandi* and then to discuss with the prosecution, or to have counsel approach prosecuting counsel, to see whether the principles said to bring the case within the similar fact rule can be isolated, and any key differences identified for an effective submission. Whilst the use of previous authorities, now more than ever, will be of limited value because of the vast range of factual possibilities, it may sometimes be possible to bring the case within the scope of past decided cases.

13.3 Evidence of Character

The general rule was that the character of any party in a civil case, or any witness in any case, is open to attack. The purpose of such attack is of course to show that the party or witness should not be believed. Answers as to credit in cross-examination are final, as has been indicated earlier, to avoid a multiplicity of side issues. Exceptionally, by s. 6 of the Criminal Procedure Act 1865, where the form of the attack on a witness's character is to allege previous convictions, they may be proved if not admitted.

The fundamental rule, as we have seen earlier, is that the prosecution may not for the purpose of proving an accused's guilt adduce evidence of the character of the defendant whether of previous behaviour, previous convictions, or general reputation. The reason is obviously the extreme prejudice to the accused in the eyes of the jury. The main exception to this is the use of the 'similar fact' principle.

The issues to discuss are:

(a) The good character of the accused and the evidential value of this.
(b) The bad character of the accused and the exceptional circumstances where this may be proved.

13.3.1 THE GOOD CHARACTER OF THE ACCUSED

It has been recognised from the eighteenth century that an accused could call witnesses to speak to his good character, or cross-examine prosecution witnesses in an attempt to get them to do so. This was exceptional and was intended as an additional protection for an accused, who could not testify before 1898.

Under this principle, strictly speaking only evidence of general reputation can be given and an accused should not be allowed to recount to the court individual creditable acts. This principle comes from the old case of *R v Rowton* (1865) Le & Ca 520. More recently it was affirmed in *R v Redgrave* (1981) 74 Cr App R 10 where, on charges alleging indecency with men in a public lavatory, the accused attempted to establish that he was heterosexual by producing letters, valentine cards and holiday photographs showing his relationship with a number of women. The trial judge ruled the evidence inadmissible relying on *Rowton*. This case is perhaps a rather specific example and today many judges would certainly allow an accused to introduce evidence of individual creditable action, for example of his public service, work for charity, etc., at least if carried out over a long period, without interruption.

The important point to note however is that *character is indivisible*. One cannot assert a good character for one type of behaviour without the prosecution having the right to cross-examine or call evidence about other aspects of one's character. See, for example, *R v Winfield* [1939] 4 All ER 164 where the accused was charged with indecent assault upon a woman and called evidence as to his previous good behaviour in relation to women. It was held that in the circumstances the prosecution were entitled to prove the accused's convictions for offences of dishonesty. It was not open to an accused to put only half of his character in issue.

The common law rule is therefore that where an accused calls witnesses or testifies himself as to his good character, the prosecution may cross-examine the witnesses or the accused about their own credibility, the accused's character, and their knowledge of it. They may, moreover, call evidence in rebuttal of the defence evidence. This common law right to rebut an assertion of good character has survived the Criminal Evidence Act 1898 and now overlaps with it.

13.3.1.1 The evidential value of good character

There were two possible views:

(a) that a previous good character makes it less likely that the accused committed the offence;

(b) that previous good character is only relevant to the accused's credibility as a witness.

The issue arises in a clear form where the accused elects not to testify, because then if his character were only relevant to his credit it would be of no relevance and the jury should be directed to ignore it. A case which settles the issue in favour of the wider view is *R v Bryant and Oxley* [1979] QB 108. The accused were charged with robbery and decided not to testify. One of the accused had good character and the judge directed the jury to the effect that the evidence of his good character went only to his credibility and hence where he had not testified was of no use. On appeal it was held that although evidence of good character did go primarily to the issue of credibility it was also capable of being evidence relevant to innocence.

There has been a run of cases in the last three years on the use of the judge's discretion to comment on the good character of an accused. So in *R v Cohen, The Times*, 15 March 1990 the Court of Appeal held that the judge had given insufficient weight when directing the jury to the effect of the good character of a man of 60 and that such a direction should have dealt with his character both as bolstering his credibility and in tending to demonstrate that he was less likely to commit a crime for the first time. Similarly, in *R v Anderson* [1990] Crim LR 862, where an allegation of rape was made against a policeman, there was an inadequate direction as to his good character. In *R v Thanki* [1991] Crim LR 202 the court held that, although it was not obligatory in every case to tell a jury that the effect of good character had to do not just with credibility as a witness but with the likelihood of the accused committing the crime, it would have been appropriate to do so in that case. On the other hand, in *R v Briley* [1991] Crim LR 445 the accused did not testify and the judge gave a very brief direction about the effect of her good character. The court held the judge had a discretion whether to stress the point about the likelihood of a person of good character committing a first offence and each case should be looked at individually. A similar result occurred in *R v Bainbridge* [1991] Crim LR 535.

Thus the principle in *Bryant* and *Oxley* has now been substantially developed. The Court of Appeal has now given comprehensive guidelines in the case of *R v Vye & Wise, The Times*, 22 February 1993. In this case the Court of Appeal held:

(a) Where a defendant had not given evidence at trial but relied on exculpatory statements made to the police or others the judge should direct the jury to have regard to the defendant's good character when considering the credibility of those statements though he might draw to their attention that none of them were made on oath. Clearly if a defendant of good character did not give evidence and had made no statements before trial, no issue as to his credibility arose.

(b) With regard to the 'second limb' direction as to good character making it less likely that the accused committed the crime, there was no distinction between cases where the defendant had testified and cases where he had not. A direction as to the relevance of good character should be given in all such cases although how the judge tailors the direction to the particular circumstances might vary.

(c) Where defendant A had a good character he was entitled to have the judge direct the jury as to its relevance in his case even if he was jointly tried with defendant B of bad character. That left the question what, if anything, the judge should say about defendant B. In some cases the judge might think it best to grasp the nettle in his summing up and tell the jury that they had heard no evidence about B's character and should not speculate. In other cases the judge might think it best to say nothing about the absence of evidence or comment on B's character. Nothing in this principle affected the question of the possibility of separate trials and there was certainly no rule in favour of separate trials for defendants of good and bad character.

This last point clarifies a difficult issue which has recently been before the Court of Appeal in *R* v *Gibson* [1991] Crim LR 705 where one accused had a good character and the other had not. Because of his fear of overstressing the good character of one, the judge simply said 'G is a musician who has not been in trouble before'. On appeal the court quashed the conviction holding that this was inadequate because G's own counsel had dealt with character very briefly expecting the judge to deal with it fully.

13.3.2   THE BAD CHARACTER OF THE ACCUSED

Apart from the general rule mentioned above as to rebuttal of evidence of good character at common law, the law on character is now contained in the Criminal Evidence Act 1898.

Subsections 1(e) and (f) of the Act provide:

(e)   A person charged and being a witness in pursuance of this Act may be asked any question in cross-examination notwithstanding that it would tend to criminate him as to the offence charged;

(f)   A person charged and called as a witness in pursuance of this Act shall not be asked, and if asked shall not be required to answer, any question tending to show that he has committed or been convicted of or been charged with any offence other than that wherewith he is then charged, or is of bad character, unless—

(i)   the proof that he has committed or been convicted of such other offence is admissible evidence to show that he is guilty of the offence wherewith he is then charged; or

(ii)   he has personally or by his advocate asked questions of the witness for the prosecution with a view to establish his own good character, or has given evidence of his good character, or the nature or conduct of the defence is such as to involve imputations on the character of the prosecutor or the witnesses for the prosecution; or

(iii)   he has given evidence against any other person charged in the same proceedings.

The statute was enacted to make special provision for the accused when he became a competent witness. Parliament had to decide how far he could be cross-examined as to his character and there were two distinct possibilities:

(a)   The accused could have been given *complete immunity*, which would have meant that he was in a better position than other witnesses as he would have been able to attack the character of all prosecution witnesses without fear of repercussions.

(b)   He could have been treated as an *ordinary witness* so that he would have been liable to cross-examination as to his previous convictions to show lack of credibility. The obvious risk of this is that the jury will make what has been called the 'forbidden connection' and use their knowledge of his bad character as a matter *not relevant* to *credibility* but to *guilt*.

In fact the 1898 Act adopts a compromise of those two possibilities. The accused is provided with a shield from the disclosure of his record until he acts in such a way as to 'throw away his shield'. This can be done in one of three ways:

(a)   By raising his own good character.
(b)   By casting imputations on the character of the prosecution or its witnesses.
(c)   By giving evidence against a co-accused.

Subsections 1(e) and (f) of the 1898 Act have caused great problems of construction and it is important to consider them in detail.

On a first reading subsection 1(e) would seem to justify any questions as to character, but the generally accepted view is that it must be read subject to s. 1(f) so that an accused may not in fact be asked about his character but only about matters directly connected with the offence charged.

Subsection 1(f) in general prohibits four types of questions:

(a) Those tending to show that an accused has been charged with other offences.
(b) Those tending to show that an accused has committed other offences.
(c) Those tending to show that an accused is of bad character.
(d) Those tending to show that an accused has previous convictions.

Under s. 1(f)(ii) and (iii) some action by the accused is necessary before the sections are brought into play but the operation of s. 1(f)(i) is not (unlike (ii) and (iii)), dependent on the way in which the accused conducts his defence.

It is important to note that questions which are prohibited are those 'tending to show' the various matters described in the subsection. The effect of these words 'tending to show' has been analysed in a number of cases. The most recent and clear example is *R* v *Anderson* [1988] Crim LR 297 where the accused was charged with being part of an IRA conspiracy to cause explosions. In her evidence, A admitted IRA membership but said that her role was helping prisoners escape from Ireland to the Continent. Prosecuting counsel was then allowed to cross-examine her to the effect that she was wanted for other offences as her own evidence had already 'tended to show' other crimes by admitting that she was a member of the IRA. This was held proper on appeal.

The words, 'charged with' require a brief discussion. Questions tending to show convictions are separately prohibited so what does the prohibition on questions tending to show that a person has been 'charged with' other offences mean? Surely it must mean that one cannot ask questions 'tending to show' charges that ended in an acquittal? That might appear obvious but the problem is, in the exceptional circumstances where the prosecution *can* cross-examine about character, can they ask about charges which ended in acquittal? The answer generally is that they cannot on the authority of *Maxwell* v *DPP* [1934] AC 309. In this case the House of Lords held that questions of a doctor charged with manslaughter were improper where they revealed that he had previousy been charged with, and acquitted of, another manslaughter in circumstances which were somewhat similar (but not sufficiently similar as to be within the similar fact principle). The words in the subsection 'charged with' are thus virtually redundant unless the facts are very exceptional. It may occasionally be the position that an accused wishes to introduce evidence of an acquittal and if it is sufficiently relevant that may be permitted, e.g., to show that certain prosecution witnesses have been disbelieved by a jury on previous occasions or that he has been forced into false confessions on other occasions.

We shall now consider the three subsections of the Act in turn.

13.3.2.1 Section 1(f)(i)

This subsection covers cases where evidence of previous character would anyway be admissible in itself. It must be remembered that the whole text of s. 1(f) deals only with cross-examination of an accused by prosecuting counsel or counsel for co-defendants. The situation envisaged in s. 1(f)(i) is the case where the prosecution will already have had the right to adduce evidence of other offences as part of their own case; in such cases where the accused gives evidence he may then be cross-examined about the previous offences if necessary. The use of this subsection does not depend upon the way in which the accused conducts his case. It follows on from whatever rights the prosecution may have had to adduce evidence of his previous character in evidence-in-chief. The subsection applies in two instances:

(a) Where the prosecution are entitled to prove other offences under the similar fact principle discussed earlier.

(b) Where evidence of previous crimes is specifically admissible under a particular statute. There are numerous such statutes and they are basically of two kinds:

(i) where the *definition of the offence* is such that it can *only be committed by a previously convicted person*, e.g., s. 21 of the Firearms Act 1968, which makes it an offence for certain convicted persons to possess firearms, or the offence of driving while disqualified where the prosecution must prove the previous disqualification. In these instances, proof of the previous conviction is essential to the offence.

(ii) The second class of statute is where a previous conviction can be used to show *some mental element* in the crime, e.g., s. 27(3) of the Theft Act 1968, which may be summarised as providing that on a charge of handling stolen goods evidence of a conviction for theft or handling within the last five years is admissible to prove that the accused knew or believed that the goods were stolen.

13.3.2.2   Section 1(f)(ii)

This subsection can be conveniently divided into two parts:

(a) Where the accused puts his character in issue.
(b) Where the nature or conduct of the defence is such as to involve imputations on the character of the prosecution or a prosecution witness.

(a) *Where the accused puts his character in issue*
Generally, the accused's own evidence of his character will take the form of some allusion to his innocent or praiseworthy past. Decided cases show that the courts are certainly not reluctant to hold that he has put his character in issue on what might seem relatively innocuous assertions falling far short of a claim to absence of a criminal record. It seems that asserting any fact not directly relevant to guilt whose purpose may lead the jury to infer that one is not the sort of person likely to commit a crime is sufficient to put character in issue, for example in *R* v *Ferguson* (1909) 2 Cr App R 250 where the accused claimed to be 'a regular attender at Mass' it was held that he had put character in issue. The result was the same in *R* v *Coulman* (1927) 20 Cr App R 106 where the accused claimed to be 'a family man in regular work'. In each case the accused, whilst no doubt having the good qualities referred to in his claim, had several convictions for dishonesty and thus it was appropriate for the prosecution to cross-examine on the whole character.

However, to hold that an accused who wore a regimental blazer in the dock was asserting his good character was going too far, according to the rather brief report of *R* v *Hamilton* [1969] Crim LR 489. An interesting recent case demonstrating the judge's discretion on this is *R* v *Bailey* [1989] Crim LR 723. The accused was convicted of assault. He denied touching the victim but admitted that there had been an argument between them and offensive remarks. He wished to present himself to the court as a man of good character. He had four spent convictions, the most recent being 25 years earlier for handling stolen goods. The judge refused to permit him to present himself as a man of good character but did allow him to say that he had no offences of violence against him and no offences of any kind for 25 years. He was convicted and appealed that the judge had been too harsh in forbidding him from presenting himself as a man of good character. It was held that, although most judges would have exercised their discretion in favour of the appellant, there was nothing to suggest that this judge had not exercised her discretion properly. If the judge had totally refused the application for Bailey to mention any aspect of good character the court might well have interfered, however in the present case the court would not.

It will be remembered that the Rehabilitation of Offenders Act 1974, which forbids mention of 'spent' convictions, has no relevance in criminal cases, but *Practice Direction (Crime: Spent Convictions)* [1975] 1 WLR 1065 requires that the leave of the judge should be obtained before using such convictions so that the spirit of the 1974 Act should be honoured. The case of *Bailey* seems to suggest that there will be a different test depending on whether it is the prosecution applying to cross-examine on the spent convictions (in which case in the present instance they would surely not have been allowed to do so) and cases where the accused wishes to rely on the *Practice Direction* positively to assert a good character which he does not, in all truth, have.

In all of these cases the effect of the subsection is to permit the prosecution to cross-examine the accused if he gives evidence. They also have the right at *common law* to *call witnesses* of their own *in rebuttal* of the assertion of good character, and these witnesses may of course give evidence of previous convictions of the accused. One should not lose sight of the fact that the subsection therefore deals with cross-examination of the accused; it has no relevance if the accused declines to testify, though the common law rule would still allow the prosecution to call evidence in rebuttal.

A very important case which demonstrates two important aspects of s. 1(f)(ii) and in which there was considerable confusion in the judge's mind is *R* v *Butterwasser* [1948] KB 4. The accused was charged with wounding and his evidence was that the alleged victim had been the aggressor. The accused did not give evidence. The trial judge held that by virtue of s. 1(f)(ii) of the 1898 Act the police were entitled to read out a record of the accused's previous convictions. The appeal was allowed. The 1898 Act referred only to cross-examination. An accused did not put his own character in issue by attacking the character of the prosecution witnesses through his counsel in cross-examination, nor does the Act have any application unless the accused testifies.

Asserting *good character* does not mean only lack of previous convictions. Clearly it would be foolish for an accused who has previous convictions to do that. It covers reputation and disposition even down to the marginal matters referred to in *R* v *Ferguson* and *R* v *Coulman* above. (Conversely cross-examination as to, or evidence of, *bad character* in a criminal trial is almost entirely limited to previous convictions.)

(b) *Imputations on the character of the prosecutor or his witnesses*

The leading case on this part of s. 1(f)(ii) is now *Selvey* v *DPP* [1970] AC 304. Before this case there was a problem as to whether the accused lost his shield by making imputations on prosecution witnesses which were necessary to *develop his defence*, or whether he only lost it if the imputations were *merely to attack* their credibility. Clearly in some cases the whole defence will hinge upon attacking the character of prosecution witnesses, e.g., any defence of self-defence; or that it was a prosecution witness who actually committed the offence; or that the complainant consented in a rape case; or simply that a prosecution witness is lying on oath. The problem is answered by *Selvey* v *DPP*.

The accused had convictions for homosexual and dishonesty offences. He was charged with buggery. He denied the charge and when testifying alleged, in effect, that the complainant was a male prostitute who had fabricated the complaint. The trial judge then permitted the prosecution to cross-examine the accused concerning his homosexual convictions. In explaining the meaning of s. 1(f)(ii), the House of Lords held:

(a)   The words of the statute must be given their ordinary and natural meaning.

(b)   The subsection permits cross-examination of the accused as to character where he casts imputations on prosecution witnesses either in order to show their unreliablity or where he does so in order to establish his defence.

(c)   In a rape case the accused can allege consent without losing his shield.

(d)   If what is said amounts in reality to no more than a denial of the charge then an accused does not lose his shield.

(e)   There is an unfettered judicial discretion to exclude cross-examination as to character even if strictly permissible but there is no general rule that this discretion should be exercised in favour of the accused even where the nature of his defence necessarily involves his attacking prosecution witnesses.

What is an imputation?

The difficult question which is for the judge to decide is: 'What is an imputation?' The courts have tried, not always with great success, to draw a distinction between what is merely a *denial* of the charge by the accused in forceful language and what amounts to an imputation. This has led to some illogical consequences. It has for example been held that where the accused describes a prosecution witness as 'a liar', that even though this may in effect be an allegation of perjury it should be treated as just a denial of the charge in forceful language. Quite recently in the case of *R* v *Wignall* [1993] Crim LR 63 the court had to consider the dividing line between a firm denial and a positive allegation of fabrication. In this case the alleged victim of theft mentioned something which she had said to the accused. The accused's counsel asked her very forcefully why she had never previously mentioned this and thereupon counsel accused her of concocting the evidence and telling an untruth. The judge held that this amounted to an imputation and granted an application by the Crown to adduce the several previous convictions of Wignall in cross-examination. The appeal was allowed, the Court of Appeal holding that the cross-examination by W's counsel should really have been treated merely as a forceful denial of the charge rather than an accusation of positive fabrication. Counsel had to be allowed a certain latitude. It was always important for the court to consider its duty to produce a fair trial.

Positive allegations that a defence witness is guilty of malicious prosecution or fabrication of evidence, or of course committed the crime himself, are bound to let in evidence of the accused's character. A more difficult situation arose in *R* v *Bishop* [1975] QB 274 where on a charge of burglary the accused tried to explain the presence of his fingerprints in the victim's room by alleging a homosexual relationship between himself and the victim. The court held that this amounted to making an imputation since alleging that a victim was homosexual was an allegation of immorality even though homosexuality was not illegal. It is questionable whether in similar circumstances alleging a heterosexual relationship or even an adulterous one would lead to the same result.

In the 1970s a practice arose of cross-examining police witnesses, carefully alleging that their version of events was 'wrong' or 'mistaken' rather than fabricated and at that time putting an allegation in that way did not generally involve losing the shield. This practice was brought to an abrupt halt by the case of *R* v *Tanner* (1978) 66 Cr App R 56 where the judge asked the accused to say positively whether he was accusing a policeman of complete invention. When the accused agreed that that was the position the trial judge then allowed cross-examination of the accused on his record under s. 1(f)(ii). The case of *Tanner* was approved in the leading case *R* v *Britzman and Hall* [1983] 1 All ER 369 where the Court of Appeal laid down guidelines for consideration of the discretion under s. 1(f)(ii):

(a) Where there is merely a denial, however emphatic or offensively made, of an act or even a short series of acts amounting to one incident or one interview, the judge's discretion should be used in favour of the defendant. The position would be different however if there was a denial of evidence of a long period of detailed observation or of long conversations.

(b) Cross-examination should only be allowed if the judge is sure there is no possibility of mistake, misunderstanding or confusion and the jury will inevitably have to decide whether prosecution witnesses have fabricated evidence. Defendants sometimes make wild allegations when giving evidence and allowance should be made for the strain of being in the witness box and the exaggerated use of language which sometimes results from strain or lack of education or mental instability. Particular care should be taken when a defendant is led into making allegations during cross-examination. A defendant who is driven to explaining away the evidence by saying it was made up or planted on him usually convicts himself without having his previous convictions brought out.

(c) There is no need for the prosecution to rely on s. 1(f)(ii) if the evidence against the defendant is already overwhelming.

'Trapping' an accused
It is wrong for prosecuting counsel however, notwithstanding *R* v *Britzman and Hall*, to lure or trap an accused into making a more forceful imputation than he would otherwise have made or into saying things he was reluctant to say. So in some cases where an accused has been bullied by counsel into making his allegation more forcefully than he meant to, the shield should not be lost. (See guideline (b) above in *R* v *Britzman and Hall*.)

13.3.2.3 The purpose of the cross-examination under s. 1(f)(ii)

The purpose is to undermine the accused's credit as a witness and *not* to show that he committed the crime charged. The judge must direct the jury carefully on this. The difference is of course fairly elusive to most juries. His record is relevant as to whether his imputation is believable and thereafter as to his credibility generally. No specific way of putting matters to the jury so that they will clearly grasp this seems to have been found. Whatever the rationale is supposed to be, it is really a case of 'tit for tat'. Even if the imputation is incontrovertibly true (e.g., that a prosecution witness has, in fact, a conviction for perjury) the shield is lost.

A recent case which clearly illustrates the correct direction is *R* v *Prince* [1990] Crim LR 49. P was tried for robbery. His counsel led evidence that he had previous convictions for numerous other offences but that in this instance his defence was a complete denial. In summing up, the trial judge directed the jury that a previous conviction even for other offences of robbery did not signify guilt as such but that the jury should put that in the balance and give whatever weight it thought to those convictions. Defence counsel asked the judge to reconsider this direction but he refused. The accused was convicted but his appeal was allowed. The omission of the crucial matter of a direction as to the criminal record affecting only P's credibility as a witness was a misdirection. The judge should always direct the jury that offences of previous convictions for dishonesty or other offences are relevant only to credit and not to guilt.

13.3.2.4 Miscellaneous matters

Before leaving s. 1(f)(ii) it is appropriate to consider three miscellaneous matters namely:

(a) Against whom must the imputation be made to bring in s. 1(f)(ii)?
(b) May anything about early offences other than the fact of conviction be proved?
(c) Judicial discretion.

(a) *Against whom must the imputation be made to bring in s. 1(f)(ii)?* According to the section, the imputation must be made on the character of the 'prosecutor or the witnesses for the prosecution'. It is not entirely clear at present who the 'prosecutor' is. At the time of the 1898 Act the prosecutor was the victim and the section would probably now be interpreted so that a gratuitous attack on a victim who was not called as a witness would bring the accused within the section.

Attacks on other persons who are not called as witnesses do not fall foul of the section see, for example, *R* v *Lee* (1975) 62 Cr App R 33 where allegations by the defence that two other men who were not called as witnesses actually committed the crime did not invoke s. 1(f)(ii), or *R* v *Biggin* [1920] KB 213 where allegations that the murder victim had provoked the accused by making improper advances did not invoke s. 1(f)(ii). The deceased was not the 'prosecutor' nor a witness. A more contemporary problem would arise if the accused should choose to make an attack on the character of absent witnesses whose evidence is tendered under one of the exceptions to the hearsay rule, e.g., ss. 23 and 24 of the Criminal Justice Act 1988. There is no clear authority as to whether this would in fact bring in the section.

(b) *May anything about earlier offences other than the fact of conviction be proved?* The authority on this is slightly unclear due to a conflict in the case law, but the better view is established by the case of *R* v *France and France* [1979] Crim LR 48. In this case the three accused went into a jeweller's shop. Two of the accused distracted the shopkeeper's attention whilst another stole items from a window display. The defence case involved making imputations upon the character of police witnesses. Leave was therefore given to the prosecution to cross-examine the accused on their criminal record but the cross-examination went beyond mere details of the offences for which they had been convicted and into questions of how they had committed the previous crime. Their previous *modus operandi* had in fact been identical to the present crime although the case did not really fall within the similar fact principle. It was held on appeal that as cross-examination under s. 1(f)(ii) is admitted as relevant to the credibility of the witness, it was irrelevant to show that the method of the previous crimes was similar to the present one.

A similar mistake, with the same result, happened in the more recent case of *R* v *Khan* [1991] Crim LR 51.

Although an accused may not therefore be questioned about how he committed previous offences under the section, it has long been accepted that, in using s. 1(f)(ii) where the accused has lost his shield, the prosecution may ask the accused not just about his past convictions, but about *how he pleaded* at his former trials. It seems acceptable on the issue of credit to show that an accused has been convicted despite a not guilty plea and thus, presumably, has been disbelieved by a jury.

(c) *Judicial discretion*. Even though an accused may have made sufficient imputations to permit s. 1(f)(ii) to be invoked, the judge has a discretion to disallow cross-examination in a given case where 'it may be fraught with results which immeasurably outweigh the result of the question put by the defence and make a fair trial impossible': see *R v Jenkins* (1945) 31 Cr App R 1 (at p. 15). Thus a judge should take into account the gravity of any imputations made compared with the prejudicial results to the accused of his character being disclosed. For example, if the present charge is relatively trivial and the accused makes some imputation in conducting his defence (e.g., says that a store detective has fabricated evidence of shoplifting) but the accused's record is for very bad previous offences such that a jury would inevitably become prejudiced against him when hearing of them, a judge may well prevent the prosecution relying on s. 1(f)(ii) notwithstanding that technically it is applicable to the case.

No doubt, despite *Selvey v DPP*, a judge will usually wish to bear in mind the issue of how essential to the defence the imputation was and be the more favourably inclined to use his discretion to disallow cross-examination in a case where it was *essential to attack the prosecution witnesses*, rather than one of *gratuitous imputation*.

Case law in the early 1980s carefully considered the extent to which a jury could really perform the mental acrobatics of hearing an accused's criminal record and then treating it as relevant only to the question of his credibility as a witness. A Court of Appeal case, *R v Watts* (1983) 77 Cr App R 126, established, briefly, that the court should always bear in mind the difficulty of the jury performing the 'intellectual acrobatics' involved. That case was however specifically overruled by the leading case of *R v Powell* [1985] 1 WLR 1364. Where the accused was charged with living on the earnings of prostitution. He deliberately attacked the conduct of a prosecution witness to discredit him and moreover put his own character in issue. The trial judge permitted cross-examination as to his previous convictions which were for offences closely resembling the present offences. On appeal against conviction it was held that, although the extent to which previous offences resembled the present one was a matter for the judge to take into consideration in exercising his discretion, he was not necessarily obliged to disallow cross-examination where there was a close resemblance. In *R v Watts* the court did fall into error by interfering too lightly with the exercise of the judge's discretion and by overlooking the 'tit for tat' principle enunciated in *DPP v Selvey*. In the present case the judge had indeed been too diffident in not permitting cross-examination simply on the basis of the imputation made irrespective of the question of the accused putting his own character in issue.

13.3.2.5 Section 1(f)(iii)

This provides that where one or more co-accused has 'given evidence against any other person charged in the same proceedings', the shield may be lost.

The reason for the rule is that where one co-accused gives evidence agaisnt another he has become, *in effect*, a prosecution witness (albeit not competent to be called by them), and nothing should be done to inhibit an accused from discrediting his accusers. It has accordingly been held that a judge has *no discretion* to refuse a co-accused his right to cross-examine under s. 1(f)(iii) although he does of course, as we have seen, have a discretion under s. 1(f)(ii). It is for the judge to decide whether what the co-accused has said amounts to 'giving evidence against'.

What is meant by 'has given evidence against'?
These words involve a consideration *not* of a co-accused's intention and certainly not of any requirement for actual malice against a co-accused. All one needs to consider is the objective tendency of his evidence — *its likely effect on his co-accused's case*.

In *Murdoch v Taylor* [1965] AC 574 the accused M and another man L were charged with receiving stolen cameras. The accused gave evidence to the effect that he had not known what the contents of a certain box were because it was entirely L's responsibility. The judge held that L's counsel was entitled to take advantage of s. 1(f)(iii) and cross-examine M as to his previous convictions. The conviction was upheld on appeal. The accused had given 'evidence against' L. There was no requirement for hostile intent.

In *R* v *Davis* [1975] 1 All ER 233 the accused and X visited a private house to inspect antiques which were for sale. After their visit it was discovered that two valuable items were missing. Only the accused or X or both could have stolen them. They were jointly charged. The accused denied stealing the articles and also expressly denied saying that his co-accused X had done so. Nevertheless the trial judge allowed an application by counsel for X to cross-examine the accused under s. 1(f)(iii). On appeal this was held to be correct. As only the accused or X or both could have stolen the articles the accused's denial that he had done so necessarily undermined the defence of X and therefore he had 'given evidence against' X.

It should be noted that if one co-accused's evidence is inconsistent with another's but would tend to make that other's conviction *less* likely, then that does not amount to 'giving evidence against' a co-accused. So in *R* v *Bruce* [1975] 3 All ER 277 on robbery charges, the defence of some of the co-accused was that there had been a plan to commit a robbery but that they had played no part in it, but B gave evidence that there had never been any plan to rob anyone. It was held on appeal that it had been wrong for the trial judge to allow counsel for other co-accused to cross examine B under s. 1(f)(iii). Notwithstanding that B's evidence was inconsistent with that of the other co-accused it tended to make their acquittal more rather than less likely.

Guidance for a judge called upon to decide whether one accused has 'given evidence against' another is contained in the leading case of *R* v *Varley* [1982] 2 All ER 519. The co-accused A and B were jointly charged with robbery. At trial, A admitted that he and B had participated in the robbery but stated that he had been forced to do so by threats on his life made by B. B gave evidence that he had taken no part in the robbery and that A's evidence was untrue. The trial judge permitted counsel for A to cross-examine B on his previous record under s. 1(f)(iii). On dismissing the appeal, the Court of Appeal laid down the following guidelines:

(a) If it is established that a person jointly charged has given evidence against a co-defendant that defendant has a right to cross-examine the other on his record and the trial judge has no discretion to refuse an application.

(b) Such evidence may be given either in chief or during cross-examination.

(c) It has to be objectively decided whether the evidence either supports the prosecution case in a material respect or undermines the defence of the co-accused. Hostile intent is irrelevant.

(d) If consideration has to be given to the undermining of the other's defence, care must be taken to see that the evidence clearly does have that effect. Inconvenience to or inconsistency with the other's defence is not of itself sufficient.

(e) Mere denial of participation in a joint venture is not of itself sufficient to rank as evidence against a co-accused. Such denial must lead to the conclusion that if the witness did not participate then it must have been the other accused who did.

(f) Where one defendant asserts a view of a joint venture which is directly contradicted by the other, such contradiction may be evidence against the co-accused.

There has been a flurry of recent cases considering the effect of *Varley* in its application to individual facts. The outcome of these cases depends on the facts and in particular on the extent to which defences adduced by co-defendants are mutually inconsistent.

13.3.2.6 Character arising in other circumstances between co-accused

Character can often arise in difficult circumstances without the 1898 Act being necessarily involved. See the difficult case of *R* v *Miller* [1952] 2 All ER 667. A, B and C were charged with conspiracy to evade customs duties. The defence of B was that he was not concerned in the conspiracy but that C had masqueraded as him (B) and used his (B's) office to commit the offences. To further that defence B's counsel asked a prosecution witness whether at a time when there were no illegal importations C had not been in prison throughout the period on other matters. In the circumstances the question was relevant. The application for a new trial was refused.

On a strict interpretation of the section these facts would not amount to 'giving evidence' although the tendency would obviously be the same (*R* v *Miller* itself did not involve s. 1(f)). Clearly if the co-accused *repeats* the suggestion made to the prosecution witness in *his own evidence*, s. 1(f)(iii) would apply. Where the 1898 Act does not apply, as in *R* v *Miller*, a judge has a duty to balance the interests of the co-accused and ought not to permit evidence of character to be introduced unless it is clearly relevant to guilt.

13.3.2.7   The meaning of 'in the same proceedings'

These words were substituted by the Criminal Evidence Act 1979 for the original words 'with the same offence' which had led to obvious problems since it by no means follows that co-accused are always charged with the same offence. It must be remembered that the mere fact that one accused is likely to give evidence against a co-accused is not by itself a ground for ordering separate trials: see *R* v *Hoggins* [1967] 3 All ER 334.

13.3.2.8   'Who may cross-examine under s. 1(f)(iii)'

Where there are two or more co-accused in a criminal trial, it is far from unknown that they may reach relatively complex agreements on procedure and tactics. Suppose, for example, a certain crime must have been committed by one, or other, or both of two men each of whom has a long criminal record and have been colleagues in crime on many occasions. They might agree that each will be separately represented at trial and that each will totally blame the other for the crime. They will thus hope that when the judge directs the jury, as he must, to consider each of them separately if there is insufficient evidence of joint enterprise, and to be sure in each individual case that first A is guilty beyond reasonable doubt and then alternatively that B is guilty beyond reasonable doubt, there is some possibility that the jury, taking careful note of the burden and standard of proof, will have to acquit both because they cannot be sure which of them is guilty. By this tactic each ensures that the jury is left under the impression that the two men both have good character. Had each availed himself of his right to cross-examine under s. 1(f)(iii) then obviously the jury would have been highly likely to draw the conclusion (especially if some of the offences are revealed to have been committed jointly by the men on other occasions), that they both committed the crime and both would have been convicted. The issue is whether in that situation the Crown are permitted to cross-examine under s. 1(f)(iii). There seems to be no reason why not, because nothing in the section stipulates who can make use of the right to cross-examine where it arises. See, for example, *R* v *Seigley* (1911) 6 Cr App R 106 where the accused together with K was charged with theft. The accused gave evidence hostile to K. K's counsel did not cross-examine the accused on his character but the prosecution were permitted to do so under s. 1(f)(iii).

The rule is thus that the prosecution may, subject to the judge's discretion to prohibit it, cross-examine under s. 1(f)(iii) but *only exceptionally*. See *R* v *Lovett* [1973] 1 All ER 744 where L was charged with theft of a television set and G his co-accused with handling it. L cast serious imputations on a prosecution witness and gave evidence against G. G's counsel immediately cross-examined him on his previous convictions. He was convicted and G was acquitted. On L's appeal the Court of Appeal held that cross-examination under s. 1(f)(iii) as it then was worded was improper because the two co-accused were not charged with the same offence (see now Criminal Evidence Act 1979 referred to above). But as counsel for the prosecution had intended to seek leave to cross-examine under s. 1(f)(iii) the Court of Appeal exercised discretion and dismissed the appeal.

Likewise, exceptionally a co-accused may cross-examine under s. 1(f)(ii) where an accused has cast imputations on the prosecution, and the prosecution for any reason neglects to do so. Such cases will now be rare, older authorities usually turning on the problem caused by the words in the 1898 Act which were replaced by the 1979 Act.

13.3.3   INADVERTENT REFERENCES TO CHARACTER

Finally, one should note that if some *inadvertent* reference to an accused's character is made in the case (e.g., as by a witness in *R* v *Smith* (1915) 11 Cr App R 229 who unexpectedly referred to the accused as having been in prison) the judge has three options:

(a)   To stop the trial and discharge the jury. This is a matter within his discretion and he will bear in mind the inconvenience and expense of a new trial, the nature of the reference to character, and the prejudice to any co-accused.

(b)   To ignore the matter if it is likely to be overlooked or forgotten by the jury. One must doubt whether this will often be proper, except perhaps if the reference was very oblique (e.g., if a witness says 'I knew the accused in Barlinnie' — it would perhaps not be obvious that he meant Barlinnie Prison — at least to an English jury).

(c)   To let the trial proceed and give a very clear direction to the jury on the irrelevance of character to guilt.

It is suggested that in order that justice may be seen to be done it will usually be best to discharge the jury, in principle, although considerations of convenience and cost must also play a part, e.g., if the revelation comes near the end of a lengthy multi-defendant trial.

13.3.4   THE ACCUSED'S RECORD: TACTICS TO ADOPT

One must first remain clearly aware of the overall picture. If an accused has a criminal record but also has other creditable aspects of his past, then one must weigh the effect on the jury of the two. If for example there are some trivial thefts committed 20 years ago and the accused has led an admirable lifestyle since, then it may be worth bringing out evidence of character. His total reform, quite independently of any good works he has latterly done, will be an extra feature after a bad start in life and may help to persuade the jury. More normally however one will wish to keep bad character from the jury. The following points should be borne in mind:

(a)   That if one has to strongly attack prosecution witnesses, it may still be possible to do so without the judge or magistrates finding that there has been an 'imputation'. For example, to suggest that identification witnesses are completely wrong and are being stubborn in their persistence in wrongly identifying the accused would probably not fall foul of s. 1(f)(ii).

(b)   Similarly, it may be possible to suggest that police officers have got some aspects of the Codes of Practice wrong and have, say, carried out an identification parade in breach of the Code of Practice, albeit in good faith, without falling foul of the section.

(c)   It may be possible to make very forceful denials of the charge and put it to prosecution witnesses that they are lying in such a way as not to fall foul of the section. Everything will depend upon the latitude given to the accused by the court under the principles in *Britzman and Hall*.

(d)   To go anywhere beyond this however and to make positive allegations of fabrication of evidence, perjury or flouting of the Codes of Practice, or to suggest improper motives in bringing the prosecution such as personal malice or grudges, will inevitably fall foul of the section and the accused's character will be brought out if he testifies.

(e)   It must always be borne in mind that it is a perfectly viable tactical option for the accused to have all the imputations he wishes made on his behalf, but not to testify. If he does that then he cannot be cross-examined about his record nor can the prosecution bring it out by any other means so long as there is no positive assertion of good character.

(f)   Nonetheless it is often seen as a bad tactic to fail to give evidence. Magistrates particularly do not like defendants relying on their right of silence in most cases and although there have been some spectacular examples of acquittals in big cases where defendants have not testified and where the judge has given an impeccable *Bathurst* direction, it is generally thought risky not to do so. Jurors naturally speculate and inevitably feel disappointed that an accused has not given his version. Nonetheless this is a tactic to be carefully considered in an appropriate case.

(g)   Sometimes it will be decided that there is no option but for an accused to testify and that imputations must be made against prosecution witnesses. If the accused's only defence is that evidence was planted on him or that admissions have been totally fabricated by the police, then there is really no alternative but to say these things if one wishes to have any hope of an acquittal. In such a case where the character is bound to come out there are some well recognised techniques for mitigating the damage namely:

(i) If character is inevitably going to come out then it is much better for the accused to appear to volunteer it in his evidence-in-chief. He can do this with the appearance of candour and this takes away the possibility of the prosecution triumphantly rising to cross-examine on his lengthy criminal record.

(ii) Where bad character must inevitably come out, then there is absolutely no harm in trying to make the best of things and to point to things which demonstrate good character as well. It may for example be possible to indicate that although there was a bad run of burglaries in the accused's record ten years ago, all of these were at a time when he was suffering from heroin addiction and were undertaken in a desperate effort to finance this habit. One can then go on to show that remedial treatment has worked and that there have been no convictions in the last ten years, during which time the accused has acquired a wife, home, family and regular employment and thus one can paint a picture for the jury of an accused who is, virtually, a man of good character.

(h) It must always be borne in mind that if one says anything which makes a co-accused's conviction more likely, under the principles in *Varley*, that, unless there is some agreement with the co-accused about the matter, he will be entitled to cross-examine. There are usually few problems with the subtleties of this rule since in most such cases it is a clear case of one co-accused blaming another. If the case becomes more subtle, regard will have to be had to the principles in *Varley* and the corresponding risks.

(i) In the magistrates' court, if character has come out, then powerful stress should be given in the closing speech to the magistrates about the evidential uses of their knowledge of bad character which are entirely for assessing the credibility of the accused. In the Crown Court the judge's direction to the jury on this point should be particularly carefully noted.

(j) If the accused in fact has good character, then this may be stressed in any convenient way and it may be in some kinds of case that a great deal should be made of it by not only asserting absence of criminal record and describing positive creditable acts, but by the calling of witnesses. A particularly effective witness, for example, in alleged dishonesty cases, would be an employer or past employer for whom the accused has worked, especially in a job involving handling money, where there have been no discrepancies or shortages over a long period.

FOURTEEN

THE LAW OF EVIDENCE (8): EVIDENCE OF OPINION: PRIVILEGE

14.1 Introduction

The general rule is that a witness may only testify as to matters *actually observed* by him and he may not give his *opinion* on those matters. The drawing of inference from observed facts is the whole function of the trier of facts, i.e., in a criminal case the jury.

The distinction between fact and opinion is easy enough to see in cases at either end of the spectrum — thus a statement that A was driving on the wrong side of the road is clearly fact; that he was driving negligently is opinion; but statements of how fast someone was driving or as to identity of handwriting are clearly both. Where it is impossible to separate facts from inferences based on them the law usually permits the witness to narrate both.

In *civil* cases this is sanctioned by s. 3(2) of the Civil Evidence Act 1972 which states:

> It is hereby declared that, where a person is called as a witness in any civil proceedings, a statement of opinion by him on any relevant matters on which he is not qualified to give expert evidence, if made as a way of conveying relevant facts personally perceived by him, is admissible as evidence of what he perceived.

It is suggested that this represents the present state of the law for criminal proceedings too so that a witness who is merely compendiously narrating his perceptions may state what appears to be opinion.

Example

A witness wishes to say 'X was drunk'. Whilst this is a matter of opinion the witness would certainly be permitted to say it since, if asked, he could narrate the matters of *fact* on which his opinion was based, e.g., he could say 'X staggered'; 'his breath smelt of drink'; 'his speech was slurred'; 'his eyes were glazed', etc.

14.2 Expert Witnesses

To the general rule prohibiting evidence of opinion there is one exception, namely the case of expert witnesses. Expert opinion evidence is in principle admissible as to matters upon which the judge or jury may legitimately require assistance. The most common modern use of experts is that of a medical witness in personal injury litigation. Other frequent instances are the evidence of consultant engineers, handwriting experts and valuers, evidence of current commercial practices, and so on.

14.2.1   WHO IS AN EXPERT?

It is for the judge to decide whether a witness is an expert, that is whether he has undergone sufficient course of study to be an expert. Such evidence is always introduced by a statement of qualifications etc., although no *formal* qualifications are required unless the nature of the activity about which expert evidence is to be given demands them. Thus, for example, in the old case of *R* v *Silverlock* [1894] 2 QB 766 the expert evidence of a solicitor who had acquired expertise in handwriting identification was admitted even though he was an amateur. It should be noted that, in the modern era, forensic document examination is acknowledged as a proper scientific discipline and the evidence of an enthusiastic amateur would be unlikely to be accepted now. Nonetheless the possession of diplomas and degrees is not a necessary requirement so that, for example, evidence of an experienced car mechanic would undoubtedly be acceptable about some matters to do with motor vehicles notwithstanding absence of formal qualifications.

14.2.2   THE SCOPE OF EXPERT EVIDENCE: THE 'ULTIMATE ISSUE' RULE

There was a rule to the effect that expert evidence was *not admissible* on the *very question* which the jury had to decide. The reason was said to be that this would usurp the function of the jury and that the accused (or parties in a civil case) was entitled to be tried by jury (or judge) and not by experts. Thus, for example, it was held proper to ask a medical expert to comment on the mental state of the accused but not proper to ask the direct question as to whether he was sane. It is now generally considered that, in cases involving, in particular, the mental state of the accused, expert evidence may be admissible even if it is on the 'ultimate issue' so that a consultant psychiatrist may be asked about the sanity of the accused.

14.2.3   THE SCOPE OF EXPERT EVIDENCE: WHEN IS AN EXPERT REQUIRED?

In criminal cases, expert evidence is admissible to furnish a court with a scientific explanation of matters outside the experience and knowledge of the jury. But the fact that an expert has impressive scientific qualifications does not of itself make his opinion on matters of human nature and behaviour any more helpful than that of the jurors themselves.

The rule is thus that expert evidence is inadmissible as being superfluous where the subject matter in the trial does not call for expertise. See, for example, *R* v *Chard* (1971) 56 Cr App R 268 where the accused was charged with murder. Counsel desired to question a medical witness on the supposed inability of the accused to form any intent to kill or do grievous bodily harm. It was held that the question was rightly ruled improper by the trial judge. Where no issue of insanity, diminished responsibility or mental illness has arisen and it is conceded that the accused is entirely normal, it is not permissible to call a medical witness to give his opinion about how the defendant's mind might have operated at the material time.

See also *R* v *Turner* [1975] QB 834 where the accused was charged with murder of his girlfriend by hitting her several times with a hammer. His defence was provocation in that she had just told him of her infidelity with other men and that he was not the father of her expected child. The accused wished to call a psychiatrist to give his opinion based on information from medical records and interviews that the defendant was not suffering from a mental illness and not violent by nature but that his personality was such that he could have been provoked in the circumstances and thus was likely to be telling the truth. The judge ruled the psychiatric evidence inadmissible. It was held on appeal that the question of whether the defendant was suffering from mental illness was not in issue and the psychiatric evidence, although arguably admissible, was irrelevant and had been rightly excluded. The defendant's veracity and the likelihood of his having been provoked were matters within the competence and experience of the jury and the psychiatric evidence was superfluous.

In connection specifically with defences applicable to a murder charge therefore, it could be said that *automatism, insanity and unfitness to plead* will be appropriate for expert evidence but *duress, provocation*, etc. will not. It is not clear how far this is affected by cases such as *DPP* v *Camplin* [1978]

AC 705, which approved a partially subjective test for the reasonableness of reaction to provocation. One would well envisage circumstances where expert evidence might indeed be of help to the jury without arrogating their function.

One difficult modern case which is distinguished from the *R* v *Turner* line of cases is *Lowery* v *R* [1974] AC 85. The accused and K were charged with the sadistic murder of a young girl. They were Hell's Angels and the only explanation put forward was that they wanted to see what it was like to 'kill a chick'. The Crown alleged that they had acted together but each alleged that the other had killed the girl. The accused gave evidence of his good character, stressed the unlikelihood of his behaving in such a manner and said that becuse of his fear of K he had been unable to prevent the murder. K alleged that he had been unable to appreciate what was happening due to being under the influence of drugs and that L had committed the killing. The defence for K was allowed to call the evidence of a psychologist as to their respective personalities and on that evidence the jury were invited to conclude that the appellant was the more likely of the two to have killed the girl. On appeal that this evidence was improperly admitted against the appellant, the Privy Council held that the evidence of the psychologist was relevant in support of K's case to show that his version of the facts was more probable than that put forward by the appellant and the whole substance of the appellant's case placed its admissibility beyond doubt.

This case is generally said to turn upon its own facts and to be distinguishable on the grounds that:

(a)   The accused had put his own character in issue.

(b)   The evidence came from the co-accused rather than the Crown, and different considerations apply (see Lord Morris of Borth-y-Gest at p. 102 approving the Court of Appeal).

(c)   Juries may need special help to decide which of two accused has the more aggressive personality.

One case which is a further illustration of point (c) in *Lowery's* case, i.e. that in unusual situations the jury may need special help from expert evidence, is *DPP* v *A and B C Chewing Gum Ltd* [1968] 1 QB 159. Chewing gum was sold to children and the packets contained 'battle cards' showing horrifying scenes of warfare. The accused were charged under the Obscene Publications Act 1959 and it was suggested that the cards were likely to deprave and corrupt children. Evidence of psychiatrists was held admissible on the question of whether these things would tend to deprave and corrupt children. Had the case concerned adults, such matters would have been within the competence of the jury, but in the case of children 'the jury need all the help they can get'.

A recent case right on the borderline is *R* v *Masih* [1986] Crim LR 395. The accused and two others were charged with rape. The accused had driven the victim and the other accused to a remote part of the countryside where the victim was raped by the two co-accused and finally by the appellant. It was possible that the appellant had been impelled to commit the rape by the others who thought that by persuading him to act as they had done they might silence him as a witness. At his trial his counsel submitted that certain matters relating to his mental capacity should be dealt with by expert psychiatric evidence, namely:

(a)   that he had an IQ of 72 making him borderline subnormal;

(b)   that he was extremely immature with a limited understanding of people and was docile and easily frightened;

(c)   that his low intelligence and immaturity meant he might be confused in interpreting consent or unwillingness in a situation; and

(d)   that his response in police interviews indicated a strong desire to please and conform to the expectation of others.

The judge refused to admit the evidence because the accused did not suffer from any psychiatric illness and was not insane. The resulting appeal was dismissed. Principles on which such evidence might be admitted were governed by *R* v *Turner*. The application of these principles to a particular case presented difficulty. There might well be cases where a jury could not form their own conclusions about the behaviour of people and expert evidence would be required to assist them. However in this case the judge had come to the right conclusion. It might however well be the case that the behaviour of people who were mentally defective or abnormal would be a matter for psychiatric evidence in another case. The court came to the conclusion that where the capacity of an individual whose IQ came below 69 to form any specific intent was involved expert evidence might be appropriate.

An interesting recent case which has considered psychiatric evidence where there was no evidence of abnormality as such is *R* v *Reynolds* [1989] Crim LR 220. The accused worked in a chemist's shop. As the chemist was preparing to lock up the accused decided to steal the takings. Thinking that the chemist had seen him the accused struck her with a hammer killing her. He then took the money and left the shop. He was then aged 17. He said in evidence that he had not intended to hurt the chemist badly nor to kill her but hoped that the first blow would render her unconscious briefly. Neither insanity nor diminished responsibility were issues at the trial. The defence wished to adduce the evidence of two psychiatrists, one of whom said that he did not believe that the thought of physically injuring the chemist had crossed the accused's mind and that his ability to separate reality from fantasy was seriously flawed. The defence argued that the jury should be assisted by expert evidence on these matters. The court held that the judge had been right in excluding this evidence on the basis that it was for the jury to decide from all the facts and circumstances what had been in the mind of the accused. This was not an exceptional case, it was a routine *Turner* situation.

14.2.4   HOW MUCH MUST AN EXPERT KNOW?

An expert need not have personal knowledge of every relevant matter within the field of his expertise. Once someone qualifies as an expert he is entitled to base his testimony on academic or learned articles, professional publications, research data from the experiments of others, etc.: see *R* v *Abadom* [1983] 1 All ER 364. The accused was charged with robbery and much of the Crown's case rested on evidence that fragments of glass found embedded in his shoes had come from a window broken in the course of the robbery. An expert witness for the Crown gave forensic evidence that the glass from the window and the fragments found in the shoes had an identical refractive index which was very rare. The witness gave evidence that he had in fact consulted statistics compiled by the Home Office and had found that this index occurred in only 4 per cent of all glass samples. This clearly implied a very strong probability that the glass had come from this window. The accused appealed against his conviction contending that the expert's evidence was hearsay and inadmissible because it was based on statistics of which he had no personal knowledge. It was held that where an expert witness was asked to express his opinion on a question his opinion must be based on primary facts of which he had personal knowledge. However once such facts were provided the expert witness was then entitled to draw on the work of others in his field of expertise as part of the process of arriving at his conclusion. He must, however, refer to that material in his evidence so that the cogency and probative value of his conclusions could be tested by reference to the material.

In this case expert testimony even though based on what was clearly hearsay (e.g., research experiments carried out by others) was properly admitted. See also *H* v *Schering Chemicals Ltd* [1983] 1 All ER 849.

In a civil action for damages against a drug company it was held that expert witnesses would be able to refer to learned articles and the findings of research in their fields, and the court would regard references to reputable authority within the expert's field of expertise as supporting any interferences which the expert drew in the case in question.

14.2.5   THE RESPONSIBILITIES OF EXPERT WITNESSES

In *National Justice Compania Naviera SA* v *Prudential Assurance Co. Ltd*, *The Times*, 5 March 1993 the court explained the duties of an expert witness in civil cases. In particular:

(a) Expert evidence should be the independent product of the expert uninfluenced as to form or content by the exigencies of litigation.

(b) Independent assistance should be provided by way of objective, unbiased opinion. An expert witness should never assume the role of advocate.

(c) Facts or assumptions upon which the opinion was based should be stated, together with material facts which could detract from the conclusion in the opinion.

(d) An expert witness should make it clear when a question or issue fell outside his expertise.

(e) If the opinion was not properly researched because it was considered that insufficient data was available the expert should say so. If the witness could not assert that the report contained the truth, the whole truth and nothing but the truth, then that qualification should be stated on the report.

(f) If after exchange of reports an expert witness changed his mind on a material matter, that change of view should be communicated to the other side and to the court.

(g) Photographs, plans, survey reports and other documents referred to in the expert evidence had to be provided to the other side at the same time as the exchange of reports.

Although this case is specifically referable to civil proceedings, the principles, being eminently sensible, would seem to be equally applicable in criminal cases.

14.2.6 PROCEDURAL RULES GOVERNING EXPERT EVIDENCE

In civil cases there is now a general requirement for prior disclosure of expert evidence in advance of trial. This requirement is said to assist with efficiency and fairness in that each side is well aware of what the other side's experts will say and each can in turn obtain their own expert witnesses' comments upon the findings of the opposing experts. Thus counsel is fully armed at trial with the material on which to cross-examine opposing expert witnesses.

In criminal cases there was no such requirement of disclosure until s. 81(1) of the Police and Criminal Evidence Act 1984. By that section:

Crown Court rules may make provision for—

(a) requiring any party to proceedings before the court to disclose to the other party or parties any expert evidence which he proposes to adduce in the proceedings; and

(b) prohibiting a party who fails to comply . . . from adducing that evidence without leave of the court.

Rules of court have now been made implementing the section which are broadly similar to those applicable in civil proceedings so that for the first time the defence must disclose their expert evidence to the prosecution.

There is a particular provision relating to expert evidence in s. 30 of the Criminal Justice Act 1988, which provides:

(1) An expert report shall be admissible as evidence in criminal proceedings, whether or not the person making it attends to give oral evidence in those proceedings.

(2) If it is proposed that the person making the report shall not give oral evidence, the report shall only be admissible with the leave of the court.

(3) For the purpose of determining whether to give leave the court shall have regard—

(a) to the contents of the report;

(b) to the reasons why it is proposed that the person making the report shall not give oral evidence;

(c) to any risk, having regard in particular to whether it is likely to be possible to controvert statements in the report if the person making it does not attend to give oral evidence in the proceedings, that its admission or exclusion will result in unfairness to the accused or, if there is more than one, to any of them; and

(d) to any other circumstances that appear to the court to be relevant.

(4) An expert report, when admitted, shall be evidence of any fact or opinion of which the person making it could have given oral evidence.

(5)   In this section 'expert report' means a written report by a person dealing wholly or mainly with matters of which he is (or would if living be) qualified to give expert evidence.

The section thus recites criteria for admission of a report in the absence of the expert witness concerned which are substantially the same as the criteria in s. 25 of the 1988 Act for the adducing of documentary evidence generally. A special section was required to deal with the position of expert evidence because ss. 23 and 24 only deal with witnesses giving evidence of any *fact*. As we have seen, expert evidence is concerned with both facts and *opinion*. The term 'expert report' is defined by s. 30(5).

Despite the fact that expert evidence may be admissible in the absence of the expert, in the normal course of things if it becomes known that the expert evidence is to be contested, then clearly the court will want to be satisfied that there is a good reason why the expert is unavailable to testify and be cross-examined. The court will look particularly to the protection of the accused and thus will presumably be more assiduous in requiring that the prosecution's experts attend than those of the defence.

14.2.7   USING AN EXPERT IN CRIMINAL PROCEEDINGS

Where one wishes to use medical evidence in criminal proceedings, very much the same considerations apply as in civil cases. An appropriate expert with a medico-legal practice should be consulted. Inevitably this is likely to be a psychiatrist in cases where the mental state of the accused is in issue. All necessary instructions should be sent to the expert. Special consideration needs to be given to the question of his fees. In the case of a psychiatrist it may well be that he needs to see the accused on more than one occasion to form any view; and if the accused is remanded in custody these interviews will of necessity take place at the remand centre, and thus one may well be paying for a great deal more of the expert's time than say in the case of an orthopaedic specialist in a personal injury case.

In such cases a detailed conference with counsel before trial with the expert present is also undoubtedly going to be of major assistance. With prior disclosure of expert evidence it may of course be possible to obtain agreement with the prosecution, but if it is not possible then the whole case is likely to turn on the conflict between the experts. It should be borne in mind that this may arise not only on questions of guilt or innocence but on questions of disposal of the accused whether by prison or by some form of treatment. Radically different views between medical men as to the proper method of treatment of persons, even persons accused of the most serious of all crimes, is well known. Care should be taken when choosing an expert to ensure that he will be taken seriously by the judge. Some psychiatrists contend that even the most violent offenders can be treated as out-patients and such evidence is looked on with great scepticism by the judge. As in all cases of expert evidence, counsel should be approached for his suggestions as to which witness to employ in such cases.

With regard to the more esoteric disciplines of forensic science, until very recently there was a huge imbalance in the resources available to defence and prosecution. There are however now a number of independent forensic science laboratories capable of carrying out much the same kind of tests which the prosecution will carry out. Often these are staffed by former Home Office scientific officers who are therefore well versed in the criminal process. A key difficulty is likely to be that the prosecution have a great deal more manpower to bring to bear on the problems, and that they will get in earlier and obtain samples, specimens, etc., and test them in a much fresher state. For this reason consideration needs to be given to expert evidence as soon as one is consulted in an appropriate case.

Again careful attention must be paid to the legal aid or fee situation and the necessary authorities to employ potentially expensive experts obtained. At the time of writing it is suggested that the Home Office's own forensic science laboratories may become open to private work and thus supply evidence for both defence and prosecution. If difficulty is encountered in finding the right kind of expert the Law Society provides a register of experts; and again an approach to the counsel that one intends to use at trial for his recommendation may be worthwhile.

14.3 Privilege

In general, public policy favours the open and frank conduct of legal proceedings. This means that any question ought to be able to be asked at trial, and an answer insisted upon, and that any material document should be made available to all parties, and to the court, for inspection. However this cannot be an absolute rule. There are conflicting interests and in some circumstances facts or documents whose relevance may appear vital to the fair conduct of litigation can be withheld, either in the public interest or in exercise of private privilege, that is a rule which protects certain kinds of private communications from disclosure. It is now appropriate to consider the doctrine of privilege under its two main heads: private privilege and public interest privilege.

14.3.1 PRIVATE PRIVILEGE

14.3.1.1 Self-incrimination

In a criminal case no witness can be compelled to answer any question which would, in the opinion of the judge, have a tendency to expose the witness to any criminal charge. In the case of an *accused*, by s. 1(e) of the Criminal Evidence Act 1898 he may not be asked questions which tend to show that he may be guilty of any other offence than that with which he is presently charged. The effect of s. 1(e) is of course to be read subject to s. 1(f) so that if his 'shield' is lost then such questions can be asked, not merely about previous convictions, but in certain circumstances, about offences for which he has not been tried.

14.3.1.2 Legal professional privilege

In both civil and criminal proceedings, comunications, oral or written, can be withheld from evidence (and inspection before trial) by both the client and the legal adviser with the client's consent if *either* the communication:

(a) was to enable the client to obtain legal advice; or
(b) was with reference to litigation.

(a) *Lawyer-client communications*
The privilege applies whether the communication relates to litigation or not — the important point is said to be that anyone taking legal advice is asking about legal rights which may have to be enforced by litigation, however unlikely it may seem. The communication must be with reference to the lawyer-client relationship in some way, so that casual conversations between friends who also happen to be solicitor and client are not within the privilege. The privilege extends to all forms of communication, written, verbal, telex, etc.

(b) *Communications with third parties for the purpose of actual or pending litigation*
For this privilege to apply there must be a definite prospect of litigation but it is not necessary that the accused should have been charged, or even arrested. The communication must have been made, or the document brought into existence, for the purpose of enabling the legal adviser to act or advise with regard to litigation. So the following are obvious examples of privilege applying: advice from counsel to solicitor on conduct of the action (this is also privileged as a lawyer-client communication); statements taken from witnesses by the solicitor; medical reports or other expert witnesses reports obtained for litigation.

There is now a statutory definition of 'items subject to legal privilege' in s. 10 of the Police and Criminal Evidence Act 1984. This section gives protection to such items against seizure pursuant to a search warrant. Although enacted for that limited purpose it has been said in the House of Lords in *R* v *Central Criminal Court ex parte Francis and Francis* [1988] WLR 989 that it is a statutory enactment of the common law. Section 10 provides:

(1)   Subject to subsection (2) below, in this Act 'items subject to legal privilege means—

(a)   communications between a professional legal adviser and his client or any person representing his client made in connection with the giving of legal advice to the client;

(b)   communications between a professional legal adviser and his client or any person representing his client or between such an adviser or his client or any such representative and any other person made in connection with or in contemplation of legal proceedings and for the purposes of such proceedings; and

(c)   items enclosed with or referred to in such communications and made—

(i)   in connection with the giving of legal advice; or

(ii)   in connection with or in contemplation of legal proceedings and for the purposes of such proceedings,

when they are in the possession of a person who is entitled to possession of them.

(2)   Items held with the intention of furthering a criminal purpose are not items subject to legal privilege.

In the context purely of search warrants, therefore, a client who had material subject to legal professional privilege is placed in something of a quandary because if he refuses physically to hand it over to police executing a search warrant in reliance on his privilege he may be charged with obstruction if his interpretation of what is subject to the privilege is wrong. On the other hand, if he does hand it over, even under protest, he may be held to have waived his privilege. For this reason, full and accurate legal advice to a client faced with a search warrant is often required. Search warrants are rarely executed at solicitor's premises unless the solicitor is himself alleged to be involved in the crimes concerned. We turn now to the exceptions to the rule.

14.3.1.3   Exceptions to the rule

Even though legal professional privilege prima facie applies, the general principle may be affected by the following exceptions:

(a)   *Waiver by the client.* It must be remembered that the privilege belongs to the client not the solicitor and the client may always waive it and direct the solicitor to disclose the relevant material.

(b)   *Communications to facilitate crime or fraud.* In *R* v *Cox and Railton* (1884) 14 QBD 153 a fraudulent doucment was executed and backdated to defeat the effects of a judgment. At the trial of Cox and Railton, the prosecution called a solicitor to say that the accused had consulted him as to how to defeat the judgment and he had told them it could not lawfully be done. It was held that communications to facilitate crime or fraud are not privileged. If the lawyer participates in the fraud he ceases to act as a lawyer; if he is himself innocent of any fraud, as in this case, the privilege is still lost if the clients have a criminal purpose.

(c)   *Information tending to establish the innocence of some other party.* In *R* v *Barton* [1972] 2 All ER 1192 the accused was charged with fraudulent conversion of the assets of an estate. He was a legal executive working for a firm of solicitors. He served a solicitor with a witness order incorporating a notice to produce documents relating to the estate, which he claimed would tend to establish his innocence. It was assumed that the documents were protected by legal professional privilege. Nevertheless the trial judge ordered the solicitor to produce them and concluded:

If there are documents in the possession or control of a solicitor which on production help to further the defence of an accused man, then in my judgment no privilege attaches. I cannot conceive that our law would permit a solicitor or other person to screen from a jury information which, if disclosed to the jury, would perhaps enable a man either to establish his innocence or to resist an allegation made by the Crown.

It has sometimes been doubted whether this case was correctly decided whatever the obvious justice of the outcome. The precise ambit of this exception might well be very difficult to establish. It is perhaps surprising that there has been little case law on it since this single first instance decision.

14.3.1.4   Inadvertent disclosure of privileged documents

One difficult question is: Is the privilege lost if the privileged document falls into the hands of someone else, e.g., one's opponent? The rule is that where this happens in criminal proceedings the privilege is usually lost.

So in *Calcraft* v *Guest* [1989] 1 QB 759 certain documents which would have been privileged fell accidentally into the defendant's hands. It was held that secondary evidence of their contents would be admitted.

In *R* v *Tompkins* (1977) 67 Cr App R 181 the defendant had given certain evidence in examination-in-chief. A note which he had earlier written to his counsel and which had apparently been found on the courtroom floor and given by mistake to prosecuting counsel was put to him in cross-examination. The note in effect contradicted his earlier evidence. The contents of the note were not read out but upon seeing it the defendant admitted that he had not told the truth earlier.

It was held that the prosecution had been entitled to make use of the note although originally privileged. Its actual loss entitled the prosecution to make use of it once it was in their hands.

There is clearly some overlap here with the question of improperly obtained evidence. Thus if, say, vital solicitor client communications were obtained by the police burgling a solicitor's offices, there would be nothing in the law of *privilege* which would exclude the evidence so obtained. The court would then have to consider the ambit of s. 78 of the Police and Criminal Evidence Act 1984 and in particular cases such as *R* v *Mason* which we have discussed earlier, **11.3**.

14.3.1.5   Other professions

There is no professional privilege for other professions, even those such as accountants who may give quasi-legal advice. However, in *British Steel Corporation* v *Granada Television Ltd* [1982] AC 1096 two judges in the Court of Appeal appeared to hold that whilst denying that any special privilege existed, the press and broadcasting companies would not generally be compelled by the courts to disclose their confidential sources of information, on the general grounds of public policy. These views were expressly rejected by all but Lord Salmon in the House of Lords. However, now by s. 10 Contempt of Court Act 1981:

> No court may require a person to disclose, nor is any person guilty of contempt of court for refusing to disclose, the source of information contained in a publication for which he is responsible, unless it be established to the satisfaction of the court that disclosure is necessary in the interests of justice or national security or for the prevention of disorder or crime.

In essence therefore a new type of partial privilege is created by the section. One should note that:

(a)   The words 'interests of justice' in s. 10 refer to the administration of justice, that is legal proceedings in court rather than any abstract concept of the phrase — see *X Ltd* v *Morgan-Grampian (Publishers) Ltd* [1991] 1 AC 1.
(b)   The words 'is necessary for the prevention of disorder or crime' do not have to refer to any particular crime but may refer to crime in general. See: *Re an Inquiry under the Companies Securities (Insider Dealing) Act 1985* [1988] AC 660.

14.3.2   PUBLIC INTEREST PRIVILEGE

Where evidence is excluded because of some public interest in withholding it which outweighs the usual public interest in open litigation, it is usually now called 'public interest privilege', or 'public interest immunity'. In older cases the term 'Crown privilege' appears but this is no longer apposite. Many of the bodies who have been able to claim the privilege have not been in any sense the Crown, indeed in some cases there has been no connection between the body and government at all.

Although most of the important cases have arisen in a civil context, the principles of public interest immunity are exactly the same in criminal proceedings. In civil cases, of course, the principle is likely to be called into question at the stage of discovery of documents rather than the trial itself. As there is no corresponding stage in criminal proceedings the matter arises rather differently. An important case demonstrating the principle is *Burmah Oil Co. Ltd* v *Bank of England* [1980] AC 1090. Discovery was sought of various memoranda of meetings attended by government ministers and other documents which would have revealed the inner workings of high-level government. It was held that it would be going too far to lay down that no document in any particular category should ever in any circumstances be produced, even when they were high-level documents to do with government. The nature of the litigation and the apparent importance to it of the documents in question might in an extreme case demand production even of the most sensitive communications at the highest level. The courts are concerned with the consideration that it is in the public interest that justice should be done and should be publicly recognised as having been done. This might lead, though only in a very limited number of cases, to the inner workings of government being exposed to the public gaze (Lord Keith of Kinkel).

Lord Wilberforce (dissenting) however said:

> with regard to the suggestion that persons preparing minutes, writing memoranda etc. might make them less candid if they thought they might one day be exposed to public gaze, it now seems rather fashionable to decry this (alleged possible loss of candour) but if as a ground it may at one time have been exaggerated it has now in my opinion received an excessive dose of cold water. I am certainly not prepared, against the view of the minister to discount the need in the formation of such very controversial policy as that with which we are here involved, for frank and uninhibited advice from the bank to the government and from and between civil servants and ministers.

The court is essentially engaged in a balancing exercise. It must weigh the conflicting principles of public interest giving due weight to the minister's views and eventually deciding whether confidentiality or candour is the more important in each case. In *Air Canada* v *Secretary of State for Trade (No. 2)* [1983] 2 AC 394 the House of Lords held that even Cabinet documents might in certain circumstances have to be disclosed, e.g., if serious misconduct is alleged against a Cabinet Minister. Conversely, relatively low-level documents may be withheld if they are not of significant relevance to a case. It must also be remembered that in connection with actions involving departments of state that many public bodies are involved in areas with little true 'political content' and much of their activity and the documents it generates are of purely commercial importance. In such cases it would be more difficult to sustain a claim to public interest privilege.

It is difficult closely to categorise the types of public document where exclusion is likely to be ordered. Most confusingly, even cases involving essentially the same type of document have sometimes ended in conflicting decisions. This is most apparent in a series of cases where there has been an inquiry into police conduct under s. 49 of the Police Act 1964. The question has often arisen whether statements given for the purpose of that police investigation should be liable for disclosure in other forms of proceedings, especially civil cases brought for false imprisonment or wrongful arrest. It is difficult to see any coherent thread arising in the case law. The courts have sometimes held that police enquiries would be hampered if persons who made statements knew that they might subsequently be disclosed for other proceedings; and sometimes have held that the overriding public interest, at least where the serious misconduct alleged against the police amounted to criminal offences, required that such things should be disclosed. For cases against disclosure see *Neilson* v *Laugharne* [1981] 1 QB 736; *Makanjuola* v *Commissioner of Police of the Metropolis* (1989) NLJR 468; *Evans* v *Chief Constable of Surrey* [1988] QB 588; and *R* v *Metropolitan Police Commissioner ex parte Hart-Leverton, The Guardian*, 4 February 1989. A case in favour of disclosure is *Peach* v *Commissioner of Police of the Metropolis* [1986] QB 1064.

It should be noted that the matter of public interest is a matter for the court. Accordingly, in some recent cases, the courts have held that they should consider the matter even where the Crown has not raised the issue.

14.3.2.1 Confidentiality and privilege

As we have seen above, only the legal profession has its communications protected by privilege as such. There is however a lesser legal concept, that of 'confidentiality' which may exist in all manner of professional-client relationships. The court will often give weight to this principle and attempt to protect it unless disclosure of the document is truly vital for the doing of justice in the litigation. Thus in civil cases, doctor-patient communications and confidential business communications to which no genuine *privilege* can be said to attach have sometimes been protected.

Such a point arose in a criminal context, albeit not a criminal case, in *W* v *Egdell*, *The Times*, 20 November 1989. A consultant psychiatrist who had become aware of certain matters, in the course of a confidential relationship with a patient whom he was treating for serious mental illness and who had committed multiple killings, was afraid that a decision might be made which might lead to the release of the patient from a secure mental hospital. Accordingly he disclosed to the Home Office certain confidential information which he had obtained from the patient whilst treating him. He was afraid that, unless the responsible authority was able to make an informed judgment that the risk of repetition of murder was small, that there was a risk of the patient being released. The patient on finding that the doctor had passed on a copy of his report to the mental hospital commenced proceedings against the doctor alleging breach of the duty of confidence. It was held that the court must balance the public interest in confidentiality and the greater public interest. In the present case the court held that, since there was no professional privilege involved, the doctor was justified in taking the course he did in the wider public interest.

14.3.2.2 Information given for the purpose of criminal investigation

Finally, one originally separate basis of public privilege which has merged somewhat into the mainstream is the rule that no question may be asked in proceedings which would tend to lead to the identification of any person who has given information leading to the institution of a prosecution. There is said to be an overriding public interest in protecting the anonymity of such informants. The principle has been extended to cover bodies other than the police who need to rely on a supply of confidential information, for example, in *Alfred Crompton Amusement Machines Ltd* v *Commissioners of Customs and Excise (No. 2)* [1974] AC 405. In this case Commissioners of Customs and Excise received information from customers of a company relating to the company's liability to purchase tax. The circumstances were such that the customers' information was obviously intended to be confidential. It was held that although the 'confidentiality' was not in itself absolutely decisive as a ground of privilege in the present case, disclosure would be likely to result not only in a breach of confidence but in information not being given so candidly in future.

A similar case is *Rogers* v *Home Secretary*, *Gaming Board* v *Rogers* [1973] AC 388 the Gaming Board refused an application by Rogers for licences to enable him to operate gaming establishments. The refusal followed a letter to the Board from the Assistant Chief Constable of Sussex concerning Rogers. Rogers obtained a copy of this letter and laid an information against the Assistant Chief Constable alleging criminal libel. The issue arose in the form of an application to set aside certain witness summonses requiring the Chief Constable of Sussex and the Secretary of the Board to attend at the magistrates' court proceedings and to produce documents. The House of Lords held that the witness summonses should be set aside. The documents concerned were necessary to enable the Board adequately to perform its duties. The type of documents which gave information about applicants for gaming licences should be treated with the same kind of confidentiality as communications from police informers.

See also *Buckley* v *Law Society (No. 2)* [1984] 3 All ER 313 where it was held that, where the Society had a duty under the Solicitors Act 1974 to intervene in the practice of a solicitor suspected of dishonesty (which was a power exercised in the public interest), the Society was entitled to refuse to disclose the identity of persons who had supplied information about solicitors suspected of dishonesty.

The main use of the principle however is in respect of police informants. The rule derives from the case of *Marks* v *Beyfus* (1890) 25 QBD 494 which established both the principle, that a policeman was entitled to refuse to answer a question which would have revealed his informant, and the exception, namely that there was also a public policy which might sometimes allow for the need to answer the question about the name of the informant where there was good reason to think it would help establish the innocence of the accused.

The principle was upheld in *R* v *Hallet* [1986] Crim LR 462 where the accused was charged with conspiracy to import cocaine. The police had relied on information given to them by informers. The trial judge refused an application that the informants' identities should be disclosed to the defence. The accused appealed against conviction. It was held, dismissing the appeal, that evidence as to the identity of informants is excluded unless the judge concludes it is necessary to override that rule and admit the evidence in order to prevent a miscarriage of justice and in order to prevent the possibility that a man may, by reason of the exclusion of that evidence, be deprived of the opportunity of casting doubt upon the case against him.

The principle was extended to withholding details of the location of police observation posts in *R* v *Rankine* (1986) 83 Cr App R 18. The accused was charged with drug offences. Police gave evidence of observing him committing the offences. Prosecuting counsel asked that the location of the police observation post should not be identified other than to say that it was some 65 yards away from the accused at the time of the crime and that the officers had used image intensifiers. The accused appealed against the refusal to give further details of the observation post. It was held, dismissing the appeal, that it is in the public interest that nothing should be done to discourage members of the public from providing information to the police and likewise these rules apply with equal force to the identification of the owner or occupier of premises which the police have been allowed to use for surveillance.

This was confirmed more recently in *Blake and Austin* v *DPP* [1993] Crim LR 283 in which the court observed that the guidelines set out in another case, *R* v *Johnson* (1989) 88 Cr App R 131, should be observed. These principles required the policeman in the case to give positive evidence as to the attitude of the occupiers of the house used as an observation post to the disclosure of its location. If those householders objected then their objections should be upheld.

The police have sometimes tried to extend this principle to enable them to refuse to answer all manner of questions about the surrounding circumstances of an investigation. See, for example, *R* v *Daley and Brown* [1988] Crim LR 239 where on charges of theft, police officers who were carrying out a surveillance operation in the East End of London claimed to have seen the two accused committing the crime. The defence was that the police evidence was a total fabrication and that when their surveillance had proved abortive they had made up the evidence. Officers refused to answer questions about the surveillance including a question about the colour, make and model of the police vehicle used on the day in question. The police would not even tell prosecuting counsel about the vehicles. The judge allowed the prosecution to withhold the information on public interest grounds. The accused successfully appealed against conviction. This was not a case like that of *Rankine* where identification of premises should be withheld because that would have tended to identify the owner of those premises. Here what was sought was relatively low-level information in order to enable the appellants to challenge the prosecution case factually. The trial judge was not entitled to fetter counsel for the defence in the way he had done and to exclude the evidence. It was a material irregularity.

Examples of the main exception to the rule are contained in cases such as *R* v *Agar* (1989) 90 Cr App R 318. In this case the defendant alleged that the police had induced an informer to go to a house at which the police had themselves planted drugs and which the accused was to visit. Defence counsel wished to cross-examine with a view to revealing the plot between the informer and the police. The judge prevented this and on appeal the conviction was quashed on the basis that:

(a) It was a well-established rule of public policy to protect disclosure of the identity of informers but an exception had to be made where it was necessary to make such disclosure for the purpose of defence to a criminal charge.

(b) Distinctions would sometimes have to be drawn between professional informers who supply information regularly for reward and a case such as the present where it was alleged that the informer in a single instance had given information to the police to get himself out of difficulties or to get favours from the police in relation to that offence.

A first instance case providing a similar outcome and an example of police practice is *R* v *Williams and Bellinfantie* [1988] Crim LR 113. The accused were charged with conspiracy to rob a wages office and offences relating to possession of a rifle. Police had observed both defendants enter the premises empty-handed. Shortly afterwards the police found them hiding in a cleaner's cupboard with a rifle and a holdall. The police gave evidence that there had been a prior informant and that a third man, who had been employed as a cleaner at the premises, had been arrested but released without charge. The accused wished to ask the police whether their informant had been this man, the cleaner. Their case was that they had agreed to steal from the premises and that the cleaner had recruited them to do so but that they had no idea that force was to be used or that a firearm was to be provided and their case was that the firearm and holdall had been supplied by the cleaner in the cupboard and they had been surprised to find them there. Clearly if this was true the cleaner had a motive to plant the rifle in the cupboard in that this would make it a more serious crime. In addition there was some dispute as to whether the accused W had himself volunteered the name of the cleaner to the police. In all the circumstances the judge directed the police to answer the question 'was X your informant'. This was an exceptional case because of the nature of the defence. In order to maintain the policy of the Metropolitan Police that questions about informants would not be answered the prosecution thereupon agreed to offer no further evidence following the ruling that the question should be answered and the defendants were both acquitted on the direction of the trial judge.

14.4   Practicalities of Privilege in Criminal Proceedings

The case law demonstrates that privilege is of far more importance as a concept in civil cases. In criminal proceedings it is rare that the defence will need to concern themselves with privilege in respect of their own documents but there are two possible situations where this may arise:

(a) Where there has been unlawful search and seizure by the police or prosecuting authorities either at the client's premises or more rarely at the solicitor's offices. Arguments demanding the return of the material based on privilege may then need to be mounted either in the course of proceedings or by civil proceedings for an injunction requiring their return.

(b) It may sometimes be that prosecution authorities suggest to a solicitor that they should be permitted to inspect his files or other documents because the solicitor has unwittingly been used as a dupe in a fraud by the client and thus comes within the principle of *R* v *Cox and Railton* above. This may for example happen where it is alleged that the client has been involved in mortgage fraud by making false applications for mortgage finance, perhaps in different identities using different solicitors, and the police wish to interview the solicitor as a witness and obtain copies of documents. At this time the solicitor will need to give very careful consideration to the legal and professional position. It may in a difficult case be necessary to take advice from the Law Society or from counsel. Prosecuting authorities who habitually meet this situation often supply copies of relevant Practice Rules or case law to demonstrate to anxious solicitors the exception to the usual rules of client privilege. Care must always be taken to ensure that the course of action suggested by the prosecution does indeed fall within such a principle.

14.4.1   Prosecution documents

It may be suggested by the defence that some document in the prosecution's possession should be disclosed. There is of course no formal stage of discovery in criminal cases, but there is a clear principle that, if the prosecution have evidence which favours the defence, they are obliged to give the defence at least that witness's name and address if not his statement (*R* v *Bryant* (1946) 31 Cr App R 146, approved more recently in *R* v *Lawson* (1989) 90 Cr App R 107). That duty of disclosure relates to witnesses of fact and also to expert evidence, see *R* v *Maguire, The Times*, 28 June 1991.

The Attorney-General has issued guidelines about disclosure which in fact go far beyond what is strictly required in the case law. Those guidelines are set out at [1982] 1 All ER 734. The Crown Prosecution Service is in principle obliged to follow those guidelines and to disclose to the defence all 'unused material' including statements from potential witnesses whose evidence the prosecution do not intend to use and which might assist the defence. Depending on the bulk of the material, the defence may either be given copies of it all or be allowed to inspect the originals. It should be noted that this principle does not apply to *every* item of evidence in the case. The prosecution need not disclose the statements of witnesses which in principle help them and do not assist the defence, but where they do not intend to call those witnesses (because they feel they may be unreliable). Likewise unused material which is sensitive and includes details, e.g., of a police informant, need not be disclosed. It forms part of the Bar Code of Conduct that prosecuting counsel must consider whether all witness statements have been properly served in accordance with the guidelines.

If the material is not served then it may either give rise to the possibility of a successful appeal or, if it comes to light considerably later, may lead to a successful application for judicial review as in the case of *R* v *Leyland Justices, ex parte Hawthorn* [1979] QB 283, where the statement of a witness favourable to the defence was not disclosed, or even as in a case like *R* v *Bolton Justices, ex parte Scally* [1991] 1 QB 537, where through an honest mistake a conviction had been obtained on a potentially unsafe basis without any police impropriety.

If some essential part of the defence case will involve an attack on the prosecution for which the identity of a police informant or details of police procedures, e.g., the location of observation posts, are thought essential, the case law will have to be carefully considered to see whether it may be possible to suggest that the information sought by cross-examination falls into the category of low-level facts as in *R* v *Daley and Brown* above (**14.3.2.2**). Or even that, although the prosecution contend that they ought not to be obliged to disclose the identity of their informant, the informant falls into the category of 'one-off' suppliers of information to escape his own difficulties, as in the case of *R* v *Agar* above (**14.3.2.2**), rather than being a professional police informant.

Much more rarely in criminal cases it may be contended, on ministerial certificate, that there is some public interest immunity of a more significant kind, that is that evidence prejudicial to the public interest should be withheld. A certificate signed by the minister must deal with all relevant matters setting out the identity and nature of the documentary evidence with sufficient particularity and the grounds of the objection. It will then be for the court to decide, in accordance with the established case law, on which side of the dividing line the relevant document falls.

FIFTEEN

SUMMARY TRIAL

15.1   Introduction

Where a defendant is charged with an offence which is triable purely summarily, or after a mode of trial hearing, has consented to summary trial of an either way offence, then the trial will take place. As we have seen this is most unlikely to be at the first hearing. If the accused has been in custody then the first hearing will be the day after he is charged; if he has not been in custody, it may be some time later, but even so the practice of most courts is to inform the defendant in advance that if he pleads not guilty the case will not proceed at the first hearing. Indeed, in the case of purely summary offences which have been commenced by the issue of a summons, i.e. so that no question of bail arises, the accused may be told that if he proposes to plead not guilty, he should notify the court in writing and then need not attend court on the first hearing because the prosecution will not have their witnesses present. Even after a mode of trial hearing there may well be two or three further hearings before the actual trial takes place. This will particularly be the case over the summer months when police witnesses and others may be away on holiday, thus rendering a number of hearing dates ineffective. Eventually, however, the trial will take place on one of the dates fixed for it and the accused will be expected to be there. Before we can discuss summary trial, it is important to consider a number of preliminary matters.

15.2   Joint Trials

Two or more accused may be charged in one information with having committed an offence jointly. Where this occurs then almost inevitably they will be tried together.

Where there are two or more informations against one accused, the magistrates may try the informations together if neither of the parties object. However, even if the defendant does object, the court still has power to try two or more informations together, if it is of the opinion that it is in the interests of justice to do so because they form part of a series of offences of the same or similar character.

The interests of justice include a consideration of the convenience of the prosecution, as well as the question of minimising any risk of injustice to the accused. This arises from the case of *Re Clayton* [1983] 2 AC 473. This case overturned the former general rule that an accused had the right to object to being tried by the same court on different informations at the same time. In principle, under the old law, an accused was entitled to insist on separate trials for each of the informations no matter how many there might be. If the accused does successfully represent to the magistrates that a number of informations against him ought to be tried by different benches and the magistrates agree, those magistrates should not then proceed to try any of them because they will of course now know of the

221

other alleged offences. See *R* v *Liverpool Justice ex parte Topping* [1983] 1 WLR 119. They would therefore adjourn the trials so that they could be heard successively by differently constituted benches.

15.3   Amendment of the Information

Section 123 of the Magistrates' Courts Act 1980 provides that a defendant cannot object to an information, summons or warrant on the ground of any defect in it in substance or form or because of any variance between it and the prosecution evidence. However, if the accused has been misled by a variance between the information and the prosecution evidence, he must be granted an adjournment if he requires one.

This section is worded in such a way that in principle it would seem to enable the court to continue with the trial, no matter how defective the information was. However, a restricted meaning has been given to the section by a number of cases. These establish that where the defect is trivial so that there can be no question of the accused being misled by it, the section applies, e.g., the misspelling of names, places or the giving of wrong dates due to typing errors. In such a case, there is probably no need for the court even to consider formally amending the information. If there is a more substantial variation, then the prosecution should apply for leave to amend. If the amendment has been such that the accused is prejudiced (e.g., if he had not collected and called his evidence to meet matters which are relevant to the amendment) he is entitled to an adjournment. An example is the leading case of *Wright* v *Nicholson* [1970] 1 WLR 142 where an information charged that an accused committed a certain offence on 17 August. The evidence of the alleged victim was vague as to when the incident happened and it could have been at any time in the month of August. W had called alibi evidence in respect of 17 August only but was convicted on the basis that he committed the offence some time in August. It was held on appeal that W had been misled and had been severely prejudiced since he had been unable to consider calling alibi evidence for other days in August.

Amendment of the information can remedy almost any defect if there is an adjournment granted to enable the accused to meet it. However, an information laid against completely the wrong person is so fundamental a defect that it cannot be cured by amendment. This is not to say however, that a mere misspelling in the defendant's name will bring the case within that category.

15.4   Absence of the Defendant

If the defendant is absent, then in cases begun by summons, he may be tried in his absence provided service of the summons has been proved to the satisfaction of the court. This is by virtue of s. 11 of the Magistrates' Courts Act 1980. A plea of not guilty will be entered and the prosecution will be required to prove their case strictly.

If the defendant is represented in court by counsel or a solicitor, he is normally deemed to be present unless he is on bail, in which case his personal attendance to surrender to custody is required. Thus, the accused must in principle be present at mode of trial proceedings and generally at committal proceedings. If he has been bailed to appear and does not do so, then the magistrates may issue a warrant for his arrest.

Where the trial proceeds in his absence and he is represented by counsel or solicitor, his representative may conduct the case on his behalf, cross-examine prosecution witnesses, call defence witnesses and make speeches, just as if the accused were present.

15.5   Plea of Guilty by Post

Under s. 12 of the Magistrates' Courts Act 1980 the prosecution may give an accused of 16 or over the opportunity of pleading guilty by post where he is called to appear to answer an information alleging a summary offence for which the maximum penalty does not exceed three months' imprisonment.

In such a case, the prosecution serves on the accused, together with the summons, a notice explaining how he can plead guilty by post and what the course of events will be if he does so. In addition, the prosecution serve a brief statement of the facts as they allege them to be. The form sent to the defendant notifies him that, if he pleads guilty by post, he will only have evidence given against him to the extent of the reading out of the statement of facts in open court and no other evidence will be brought. The prosecution are usually quite happy to put the statement of facts in a fairly neutral form in the hope of persuading the accused to plead guilty and to save the court and the prosecution time.

The accused in such a situation should return the form to the court indicating that he proposes to plead guilty. There is space on the form for him to set out any mitigating circumstances and details of his means. He is informed, however, that he is not bound by his plea of guilty and may appear at court at any time up to the hearing of the summons and withdraw the plea of guilty and be tried on the basis of a not guilty plea. The procedure thereafter is as follows:

(a) The prosecution will read out the charge and the particulars of the offence as stated in the statement of facts, but may give no other information to the court about the crime.

(b) The defendant's form setting out his means and any mitigating circumstances is read out by the clerk of the court.

(c) The court will normally pass sentence straight away. If, however, it does propose to disqualify the offender from driving or imprison him, it must call him before the court and will adjourn the case for that purpose.

If there is something ambiguous in the plea of guilty by post, for example where the accused's statement of mitigating circumstances suggests facts which it seems would actually amount to a defence, rather than to mitigation, then the magistrates may refuse to accept the plea and may adjourn the case for a hearing.

If the prosecution do not offer the accused the opportunity to plead guilty by post, then there is nothing he can do to compel them to adopt this procedure. This is so even in the case of straightforward driving offences. The availability of fixed penalties for offences such as speeding has in some areas largely replaced pleas of guilty by post. The police however are still likely to lay an information rather than apply a fixed penalty in cases where they consider that a fixed penalty (currently £32 for endorsable offences) would be inadequate in the light of the road conditions, or the speed which the vehicle was doing. The prosecution, in the case of most driving offences, will usually opt to offer a plea of guilty by post unless it is obvious from the circumstances that the accused is likely to be disqualified.

15.6 Non-appearance of Prosecution

If the prosecution fails to appear at the time and place fixed for summary trial, the magistrates have discretion either to dismiss the information or adjourn. If the case has already begun and been adjourned as part heard, then the magistrates have the option to proceed in the absence of the prosecution, although this will only happen rarely.

15.7 Outline of Procedure

We shall now consider an outline of the procedure at summary trial of either a summary offence or an either way offence on a not guilty plea.

(a) The charge will be read to the defendant and he will be asked whether he proposes to plead guilty or not guilty. In such a situation his plea must be unequivocal. The court has a discretion to allow a change of plea from guilty to not guilty at any time before sentence. Thus if, for example, as in the case of mistakenly pleading guilty by post, the accused pleads guilty, say, to a charge of theft but in stating his mitigation says something along the lines of 'I never knew I had it' or 'I thought it was mine at the time' the magistrates ought to allow him to withdraw his guilty plea, substitute a not guilty plea and either proceed with the hearing then and there, or, more probably, adjourn it so that he can receive legal advice and/or call evidence.

(b)   The prosecution may make an opening speech stating the facts of the case and indicating which witnesses will be called to prove them. It is important to note that in the magistrates' court the prosecution do not in general have a closing speech and therefore this is the only chance the prosecution have to address the court. However, it must be remembered that magistrates are likely to be considerably more experienced than jurors and thus may need less in the way of introductory matter.

(c)   The prosecution then call evidence which may consist of witnesses or written evidence tendered in the form of statements under s. 9, Criminal Justice Act 1967 (this topic has been dealt with in the section on hearsay evidence, see **9.12.1**). The witnesses will give evidence and are then subject to cross-examination and may be re-examined.

(d)   At the end of the prosecution evidence, the defence may make a submission of no case to answer. This submission should be upheld if:

(i)   there is no evidence to prove an essential element of the offence charged; or

(ii)   the prosecution evidence has been so discredited as a result of cross-examination or is so manifestly unreliable that no reasonable tribunal could safely convict upon it.

In other words, at this stage, the magistrates may simply decide whether on the basis of what they have heard so far, there is any possibility of them finding the case proved beyond reasonable doubt. The prosecution have a right of reply to this submission. If the submission is successful, the case is over. The magistrates discharge the accused and then go on to make any appropriate orders for costs or return of legal aid contribution. If the submission is not upheld the case continues and the defence may then present their case.

15.7.1   THE DEFENCE CASE

The procedure for the defence case is as follows:

(a)   The defence may make an opening speech but in principle are limited to one address only and it is customary for the defence solicitor to make a closing speech rather than an opening one, for obvious reasons. Such a speech gives the advocate the opportunity to comment on all the evidence if made at the end, but if made at this time only gives a chance to comment on the prosecution evidence and to introduce the defence evidence.

(b)   The defence witnesses are then called and the defendant testifies first.

(c)   Exceptionally the court may grant the prosecution leave to call further evidence after the defence case for the purposes of rebutting defence evidence. Rebuttal evidence may only be called on a matter which could not reasonably have been foreseen and which arises suddenly. It will be recalled that the defence have no general obligation to give details of their case in advance of the trial. Accordingly, if, for example, a sudden allegation is made against a policeman and the prosecution are taken by surprise, they will now have the opportunity to call evidence to rebut it. A similar situation might arise in the case of an alibi. It will be recalled that in the magistrates' court there is no obligation to give advance notice of intention to call alibi evidence (whereas there is in the Crown Court as we have seen). Accordingly, the prosecution, if they have time to get the witnesses to court (and they may be allowed an adjournment for this purpose) may call rebutting evidence. If it is perfectly clear from the outset, however, that the trial is one in which evidence of a certain kind would inevitably be necessary, then the prosecution will not be permitted to call evidence in rebuttal. An example taken from a leading case is one which involved a charge of forgery where, at the close of the defence evidence after the defendant had denied the forgery, the prosecution applied for leave to call a handwriting expert to prove that the forged signature was written by the accused. It was held that it should have been obvious from the outset that in a case of alleged forgery handwriting evidence would be required and the prosecution were penalised for their lack of foresight by their application to call rebuttal evidence being refused. See **8.8**.

(d) Finally, there is the defence closing speech, unless the defendant has already made an opening speech. The prosecution may only address the court after this with the leave of the court, but leave will always be granted where a point of law is raised on which the prosecution wish to reply. This is merely one aspect of the right either party has to raise a point of law and argue it at any stage during the proceedings. If exceptionally the prosecution were allowed to address the court on the facts or evidence, then the defence would always have the right to address the court last. The magistrates then reach their decision. They may retire for this purpose. Their verdict is by a majority. If there are only two magistrates and they disagree, they should adjourn the case for rehearing by a different bench. The magistrates may be advised by their clerk on matters of law or evidence, but not on issues of fact. Accordingly, if no matter of law arises in the course of the hearing, it is wrong for the clerk to retire with the magistrates.

If the defendant is acquitted, he will be discharged and may be able to make an application for costs (for the principles see **2.4.2**). If he is convicted, the court will proceed to sentence after dealing with mitigation and other matters. These matters are dealt with at great length hereafter at **18.1** onwards.

If the accused has pleaded guilty at the outset, the prosecution will then read out a statement of how the offence occurred and the court will proceed to hear mitigation, consider the obtaining of reports, and sentence.

15.8   Committal for Sentence: Magistrates' Courts Act 1980, s. 38

The principles of sentencing generally are dealt with at **18.1**. It is important here, for the sake of continuity, to indicate the circumstances in which a magistrates' court, after having dealt summarily with an either way offence where they have convicted an offender, have the power to commit him to the Crown Court for sentence because they feel that their own sentencing powers are inadequate. This may occur under s. 38 of the Magistrates' Courts Act 1980 in the case of an adult offender. There is a similar power under s. 37 in relation to persons aged between 15 and 17 when convicted in the youth court.

Section 38 of the Magistrates' Courts Act 1980 (as substituted by s. 25 of the Criminal Justice Act 1991) now provides:

(1) This section applies where on the summary trial of an offence triable either way . . . a person who is not less than 18 years old is convicted of the offence.
(2) If the court is of the opinion—
     (a) that the offence or the combination of the offence and one or more offences associated with it was so serious that greater punishment should be inflicted for the offence than the court has power to impose; or
     (b) in the case of a violent or sexual offence committed by a person who is not less than 21 years old, that a sentence of imprisonment for a term longer than the court has power to impose is necessary to protect the public from serious harm from him
the court may . . . commit the offender in custody or on bail to the Crown Court for sentence . . .

The effect of these words is to focus upon the seriousness of the present offence and other offences associated with it rather than, as was previously the case, the offender's criminal record. The criteria reflect those in s. 2(2) of the Criminal Justice Act 1991 which is dealt with in more detail in **18.5**. As a result, committals to the Crown Court for sentence by way of s. 38 should be rare. The revelation of the accused's previous convictions ought not in principle to make a great deal of difference and thus committals are likely to be limited to cases where either the accused asks for further offences to be taken into consideration (which naturally may make the magistrates take a different view) or where facts about the offence charged come to light which were not drawn to the magistrates' attention at the time when they accepted jurisdiction. Thus if, for example, what they believed was a relatively trivial assault when accepting jurisdiction proves to have involved some serious or permanent injury to the victim, that might be a relevant factor. Such cases should also be rare since the prosecution, when urging the magistrates in matters of jurisdiction, have the duty to ensure that an outline of the full circumstances of the offence is made known to them.

SIXTEEN

COMMITTAL PROCEEDINGS

16.1 Introduction

As we have seen, criminal offences fall into three categories:

(a) Those triable only summarily in which case trial before the magistrates is inevitable and there is no option.

(b) Those triable only on indictment in which case trial is by the Crown Court before a judge and jury.

(c) Those triable either way where there will be a mode of trial hearing to determine the manner in which the case is to continue.

With very few exceptions, not relevant to this text, all criminal proceedings commence in the magistrates' court. In the case of those triable only summarily or those triable either way where the magistrates opt for, and the accused is happy to accept, summary trial that is precisely what happens. In the case of those triable only on indictment and those triable either way where the magistrates themselves choose to send the case to the Crown Court or where the accused elects trial, there is still a preliminary hearing before the magistrates.

Crown Court trials are expensive and time-consuming. Moreover, there is always a considerable waiting list for trial on indictment which means that an accused remanded in custody may be detained for a substantial period before trial and even if released on bail will possibly be subject to stress and anxiety before the trial.

In order to filter out prosecutions with little prospect of success, almost all trials on indictment are preceded by a preliminary hearing before the magistrates which is known as committal proceedings. These proceedings are not a trial as such. They simply involve the prosecution demonstrating that it has a reasonable or *prima facie* case which it is proper to call upon the accused to answer before a judge and jury in the Crown Court. Magistrates conducting these preliminary hearings are referred to as *examining justices*, and contrary to the usual rule, one examining justice may sit alone for the purpose of committal proceedings.

The onus on the prosecution to show that it has a prima facie case is not a heavy one. The examining justices only have to be satisfied that there is sufficient evidence on which a reasonable jury *could* (not *would*) find the defendant guilty. In practice this means that most preliminary hearings do result in a committal for trial.

Before 1967 all committal proceedings took the form described below which is often referred to as 'full committal proceedings' or 'long form' committal proceedings. However, since 1967 two different types of committal proceedings have been available, those with consideration of the evidence and those without such consideration. The provision for both types of committal proceedings is now found in s. 6 of the Magistrates' Courts Act 1980. We shall now consider both types of committal proceedings. The relevant law is contained in the Magistrates' Courts Act 1980 and the Magistrates' Courts Rules 1981 (SI 1981 No. 552).

16.2 Committals with Consideration of the Evidence

These are provided for by s. 6(1) of the Magistrates' Courts Act 1980. It should be noted that it is open to either the prosecution or the defence to insist on a s. 6(1) committal in any case. If the prosecution choose not to offer the defence the choice of a committal without consideration of the evidence under s. 6(2) of the 1980 Act (see **16.3**) or if the defence having been offered this choice do not accept the option, then a s. 6(1) committal, that is a full committal, will be held. The procedure is as follows.

16.2.1 THE CHARGE IS READ TO THE ACCUSED

At this stage, the accused is not required to state his plea.

16.2.2 THE PROSECUTION OPENS ITS CASE

The Crown Prosecutor makes a speech telling the examining magistrates what the case concerns, the charge or charges on which it is suggested the accused should be committed for trial and the nature of the evidence he intends to call. It must be noted that the prosecution does not have to present all its available evidence at this stage. All that it needs to present is that which it deems sufficient evidence to establish a prima facie case. Thus if there are half-a-dozen eye-witnesses to the same thing the prosecution may be content to call only one or two of them at this stage.

16.2.3 THE PROSECUTION CALLS ITS EVIDENCE

The evidence may be oral and if so the witness is subject to the usual process of examination-in-chief, cross-examination and re-examination. During this process the clerk makes a written note of the evidence and when testimony is complete the clerk reads this to the witness and invites him to sign it. When signed and authenticated by a counter-signature of one of the examining magistrates the document is known as a deposition. Depositions may be used as evidence at the trial in the Crown Court in certain exceptional circumstances (see **9.11**). As well as verbal evidence, the defence may accept at this stage the giving of some of the prosecution evidence in the form of written statements under s. 102 of the Magistrates' Courts Act 1980. This section is in identical terms to s. 9 of the Criminal Justice Act 1967, which is discussed at **9.12.1**. It provides that hearsay evidence (i.e. written statements) may be tendered to the courts in committal proceedings provided that:

(a) each statement is signed by the maker;
(b) it contains a declaration by the maker that it is true to the best of his knowledge and belief and that he makes it knowing that if it is tendered in evidence he could be prosecuted for wilfully stating anything in it that he knew to be false or did not believe to be true;
(c) it is given in advance to each of the other parties to the committal proceedings; and
(d) it was not objected to by any other party.

Accordingly, if there are parts of the prosecution evidence which are at this stage uncontroversial or purely formal they may be put in evidence and read out to the court. The defence will normally only object to the use of a s. 102 statement if it wishes to cross-examine the maker at this stage, e.g., with a view to discrediting the witness.

16.2.4 SUBMISSION OF NO CASE TO ANSWER AND CHANGE OF CHARGE

At the conclusion of the prosecution's evidence at the committal the defence may make a submission of no case to answer. The considerations which apply where such a submission is made are discussed fully at **7.4.1**. For the sake of completeness we will summarise them here. The submission that there is no case to answer may properly be upheld when:

(a) there has been no evidence to prove an essential element in the alleged offence; or
(b) the evidence adduced by the prosecution has been discredited as a result of cross-examination or is so manifestly unreliable that no reasonable tribunal could safely convict on it.

It must be remembered at this stage that it by no means follows that the magistrates will commit the accused for trial on the same charge which the prosecution have brought. For example, the prosecution may have charged the accused with robbery. The magistrates may come to the conclusion that while the circumstances do disclose a prima facie case of theft there has been no evidence to prove the element of force required for robbery and therefore they may decide to commit the accused on a charge of theft alone. This must be borne carefully in mind at this stage. Thus merely showing that the element of force was lacking on a robbery charge would by no means lead to the accused's discharge.

16.2.5 READING OUT THE CHARGE

If no submission of no case to answer is made or if one is made and not upheld by the magistrates then the charge is read over to the defendant who is cautioned in terms similar to the police caution and asked whether he has anything to say in answer to the charge. This is not an invitation to plead.

16.2.6 THE ALIBI WARNING IS GIVEN TO THE ACCUSED

As has been explained in the section on evidence an accused has no general obligation to indicate to the prosecution what his defence will be at trial. There is one main exception to this principle and that is where the accused wishes to raise an alibi defence, that is, to say that he was somewhere other than at the scene of the alleged offence at the relevant time. By s. 11 of the Criminal Justice Act 1967 an accused must give to the prosecution particulars of his alibi either at, or no later than, seven days after the end of committal proceedings. If he fails to do so then he may only give evidence of an alibi defence where the trial judge gives him leave to do so. It is customary to give written notice of alibi to the CPS after the committal proceedings rather than at them. The particulars required are the name and address of any alibi witnesses and details of where the accused says he was at the relevant time.

16.2.7 GIVING EVIDENCE TO THE MAGISTRATES

The next step is for the defendant and, if he wishes, any witnesses to give evidence to the magistrates. Where the defendant or his witnesses do give evidence then it is again taken down in longhand and signed and constitutes a deposition. The giving of defence evidence is rare, most defendants preferring to reserve their position until the Crown Court trial.

16.2.8 INSUFFICIENT EVIDENCE FOR TRIAL

If defence evidence has been given, the defence may make a submission that there is not sufficient evidence taken as a whole on which to commit the accused for trial. The test is again whether there is a prima facie case, but the magistrates must have regard to all the evidence that they have now heard. If they decide that there is no case they discharge the accused. This does not however constitute an acquittal. The prosecution may, so to speak, make a further attempt to 'get their act together' and may recharge the accused for that offence or other offences and start the procedure again.

16.2.9   THE CROWN COURT AND CHARGES

If the magistrates decide to commit the accused to the Crown Court then they have to decide to which Crown Court they will commit him and on which charges. In relation to the first of these matters it is simply a matter of geographical convenience unless there is some special feature, such as that the incidents have provoked some local feelings which may make it better to have the accused tried out of the area.

As to the charges on which they commit the accused, this will usually be the charges which the prosecution brought against him at the outset. Sometimes however the magistrates may decide that there is insufficient evidence of some aspect of those charges and commit him for some other offence disclosed by the evidence, as in the example given above of a charge of robbery being brought; if the magistrates are not satisfied that there was any evidence of force, they may commit only on a charge of theft.

In addition, regard must sometimes be had to the relatively new powers under ss. 40 and 41 of the Criminal Justice Act 1988. Under these sections, magistrates who commit an accused for trial at the Crown Court may be able to commit him also in respect of linked summary offences so that all matters can conveniently be disposed of on the same occasion. The provisions are as follows:

(a) Section 40 of the 1988 Act provides that if the accused has been committed for trial in respect of an indictable offence, and the evidence that was before the committal court also discloses a summary offence, then the *prosecution* may include a count in the indictment for the summary offence. There are however two conditions that must be satisfied:

(i) the summary charge must either be founded on the same facts or evidence as the indictable charge or it must be for a series of offences of the same or a similar character; *and*
(ii) the summary charge must be one of those specified in the section or by subsequent statutory instrument: these at present include the charges of common assault; taking a motor vehicle without the owner's consent; driving while disqualified; and criminal damage.

It must be noted therefore that it is not a case of the *committing court* adding counts to the indictment. It is entirely up to the prosecution to do this at a later stage if the facts at committal disclosed the extra summary offence, and that offence is linked in one of the ways mentioned with the indictable offence for which committal has taken place. Once in the Crown Court the charges will be tried before the same jury. However, on conviction of the summary offence the Crown Court's power of sentence are limited to those which the magistrates would have had.

(b) Under s. 41 of the 1988 Act, magistrates who commit a defendant to the Crown Court for trial of an either way offence, e.g., theft, may also commit for trial in respect of any summary offence which is:

(i) punishable with imprisonment or disqualification (such as careless driving or taking a conveyance); *and*
(ii) arises out of circumstances which are the same as or connected with the either way offence.

This procedure is not strictly speaking 'committing for trial'. What happens in the Crown Court is that the defendant is tried on the indictable offence alone. At the end of that trial, if he is convicted, the summary offence is put to him, and if he pleads guilty to that then the Crown Court can sentence him for it, although its powers are again limited to the maximum sentencing powers of a magistrates' court. If however the defendant pleads not guilty to the summary offence, the summary offence is remitted to the magistrates' court for trial.

This procedure then allows a linked offence of a certain degree of seriousness to be dealt with at the Crown Court but only where there has been a conviction for the either way offence and a plea of guilty to that linked summary offence.

16.2.10   OTHER MATTERS

On the decision to commit for trial, then certain other matters require to be dealt with.

16.2.10.1 Publicity

The next matter to be dealt with is the question of publicity. Committal proceedings, even full comittal proceedings, often involve only the prosecution side of the case as we shall see below. If it were open to the press to report these proceedings then a one-sided view of the case might emerge and, moreover, matters highly prejudicial to an accused might come out. For this reason the press are prevented by s. 8 of the Magistrates' Courts Act 1980 from reporting anything more about committal proceedings than the names, address, ages and occupation of the parties and witnesses and the names of their legal representatives; the charges against the accused; and the outcome of applications for bail and legal aid. The reason for this restriction is that the persons in the area from whom the jurors will be chosen who eventually try the case in the Crown Court should not be prejudiced by reading a one-sided version of events (or preferably any version of events) in advance but should be open-minded when they judge the case on what they hear in the Crown Court at the appropriate time. Full reporting of what happens, that is of the allegations made and the evidence given, is allowed only if reporting restrictions are specifically lifted by the court. It ought to be said that s. 8 also applies to any previous hearings before the court, e.g., the mode of trial hearing or remands.

If the accused actually wants publicity however, for example so that a missing witness might come forward to give evidence on his behalf, then it is open to him to apply to the examining justices to lift reporting restrictions. If he does so they must comply, in which case the press (if it is sufficiently interested) may report more about the case. Where there is more than one accused and one wants reporting restrictions lifted and another or others do not then the magistrates should consider the interests of justice before deciding whether to grant the application. The burden is on the person who wishes the reporting restrictions to be lifted to show that his chance of a fair trial is prejudiced through lack of publicity.

16.2.10.2 Witnesses

At the end of the committal hearing the court will make a witness order for prosecution witnesses to attend the eventual trial at the Crown Court. Such witness orders are made in one of two forms, either *full* witness orders in which case the witness is required to attend to give oral evidence or *conditional* witness orders in which case the witness is only required to attend court if the defence subsequently notify the prosecution that they require the witness's presence there. If the defence accept conditional witness orders and do not later give the prosecution notice that they require the witness to attend Crown Court trial then the prosecution may read out the witness's statement which will be in the form required by s. 9, Criminal Justice Act 1967. In this way the defence can partly control the witnesses which the prosecution must call in the Crown Court.

16.2.10.3 Bail

As we have seen, the mere decision to commit the defendant for trial will not in itself constitute a change of circumstances sufficient to ground the making of a third bail application if two full applications have already been made unsuccessfully. Despite the fact that the accused may after committal be in custody uninterruptedly for some weeks or months, that is not in itself a sufficient new feature. It may well be however, if the prosecution evidence has been thoroughly explored by cross-examination at the committal, that a submission can be made and that the court might take a different view of the strength of the prosecution evidence, which is of course one of the relevant considerations for deciding on a bail application. By virtue of s. 22 of the Prosecution of Offences Act 1985 there are regulations which lay down custody time limits between commital for trial and the start of the trial. The present time limit prescribed is a maximum of 112 days. Where that time limit expires then the accused in principle has an absolute right to bail and the exceptions to that right in the Bail Act 1976 do not apply. However, the prosecution have the power to apply for an extension of the time limit and this is commonly granted in difficult cases where the prosecution can justify the length of time which they are taking to prepare the case for trial.

16.2.10.4 Legal aid

Unless a through order has been made for legal aid to cover the Crown Court trial, it is appropriate to apply to the magistrates for legal aid to be extended. In fact it is in principle a *new* legal aid order that is made but this is the terminology invariably used. If one forgets to do this at the committal proceedings one can in any event apply to the Crown Court directly by completing a straightforward application form. It is usual to tell the magistrates in committal proceedings that the accused's means have not changed since his earlier application for legal aid for the magistrates' court proceedings.

16.2.10.5 Prosecution costs

Under s. 17 of the Prosecution of Offences Act 1985, the Crown Prosecutor (who usually conducts the case before magistrates) need make no application for costs at the end of committal proceedings. There is no point in applying for costs from central funds, as was previously the practice, where the prosecution is anyway publicly funded. If there is a private prosecutor then it may be appropriate to make application for costs out of central funds. It would not of course be appropriate ever at this stage to claim costs from the defendant since his guilt has not been established.

16.2.10.6 Defence costs

If the defendant is discharged then defence costs may be claimed from central funds unless (by virtue of regulations made by the Lord Chancellor) the court concludes that the prosecution's unnecessary or improper conduct has put the defendant to expense, in which case the order may be made direct against the prosecution.

16.3   Committals without Consideration of the Evidence

These are provided for by s. 6(2) of the Magistrates' Courts Act 1980. This section allows the accused to consent to being committed for trial and would be appropriate where:

(a)   the accused intends in any event to plead guilty; or
(b)   where although he intends to plead not guilty he accepts that on the prosecution evidence there is a prima facie case against him.

The section permits the accused to be committed without consideration of the evidence if:

(a)   all the evidence to be tendered consists of written statements made in the proper form in compliance with s. 102 of the 1980 Act;
(b)   and the accused (or where there is more than one, all the accused) is legally represented; and
(c)   none of the accused wishes to make a submission of no case to answer.

In the case of a committal under s. 6(2) of the 1980 Act the accused will have been served (usually at his solicitor's office) with copies of the prosecution's statements in s. 102 form some time in advance of the hearing. It must be noted that, although in the overwhelming majority of cases the prosecution themselves want a short form of committal, in view of saving time and costs and because they will naturally consider that they do have a prima facie case, there is no obligation on them to offer this form of committal to the accused. If they do not want to do so and propose to go ahead with a full committal there is nothing that the defendant can do about it. Having received the s. 102 statements with a view to committal under s. 6(2) it is always open to the defence solicitor to change his mind, in the light perhaps of how weak the prosecution evidence looks, and to insist on a full committal.

The defendant should attend, in principle, although (unless he is on bail) he need not do so provided that his solicitor is present. Thereafter the following is the order of events:

(a)   The charge is read out though again no plea is taken.

(b)   The clerk will ask the defence whether they wish for reporting restrictions to be lifted. The same considerations as before will apply although of course the press will not actually hear the substance of the prosecution evidence. It is open however to the defence solicitor to mention any matter to the court on which press assistance might be required (e.g., the tracing of a missing witness).

(c)   The clerk then asks the prosecution to confirm that all their evidence is in the form of s. 102 statements, that copies have been given to the defendant already and that the defendants are all legally represented. The clerk then asks the defence formally to confirm that they do not object to any statement, wish to testify themselves or call witnesses, or wish to submit that there is no case to answer.

(d)   The s. 102 statements are not read out to the court nor do the magistrates need to consider their contents. It is simply a matter of counting the number of s. 102 statements presented. Thereafter, the magistrates announce the committal for trial to the Crown Court on the charges which the prosecution have brought. Since they do not examine the evidence at all they will naturally not need to consider whether all the elements are proved or whether some lesser charge might be appropriate.

(c)   Thereafter, the procedure to be followed is the same as that in the case of a committal with consideration of the evidence, that is:

(i)   The alibi warning is given and defence notice of alibi is required, either then or within seven days.

(ii)   Witness orders are made, either full or conditional, in respect of each witness whose evidence is contained in the s. 102 statements.

(iii) A bail application is made, if necessary.

(iv) An application for legal aid may be made for the Crown Court.

16.4   Choice of Committal Proceedings

We shall now consider the factors which might make either party choose one rather than the other form of committal proceedings.

The prosecution may decide upon a full committal where they wish to test their own witnesses. This is particularly appropriate where identification is in issue. In cases of disputed identity the Attorney-General issued guidelines in 1976 suggesting to prosecutors that the prosecution should always ask for a committal with consideration of the evidence and call their identification witnesses. Thus if the identification evidence is discredited the case will go no further. In further guidelines issued in 1979 however, the Attorney-General in effect reverted to leaving the matter to the discretion of the opposing parties. These guidelines provide that the prosecution should not usually in identification cases seek a committal under s. 6(2) of the Magistrates' Courts Act 1980 but might do so where both parties and the examining magistrates considered the short form of committal the more appropriate procedure. With the exception of identification cases and miscellaneous cases where the prosecution may wish to see how their own witnesses perform, the prosecution will almost always be willing to have the short form committal. It must be emphasised again that neither at the long nor the short form committal are they required to call or put before the court all the evidence which they will eventually call in the Crown Court.

Accordingly, the tactical decision as to whether or not to insist on the long form of committal is usually that of the defence. There are two basic reasons for the defence to choose a long form committal:

(a)   the hope of having the case disposed of there and then, that is making a successful submission of no case to answer or 'no case on which to commit' as it is sometimes called;

(b)   whether or not this may be successful, in any event to see the prosecution witnesses and assess their performance and to probe the prosecution's case.

We shall now consider the points in favour of and against having a full committal.

16.4.1 Points in favour of a full committal

(a) One can see how prosecution witnesses perform. This may be an invaluable aid in assessing the strength of one's own case. Moreover one may probe their version for details not given in the bare bones of their statements to the police. These will be the s. 102 statements which will probably have been disclosed to the defence anyway. It will be recalled that the Advance Information Rules entitle the defendant to see the prosecution evidence (or a summary of it) in advance of the mode of trial hearing.

(b) The magistrates must of course consider the evidence available on which to commit the accused for trial. This means naturally that the rules of evidence do apply. If it is therefore suggested that a material part of the prosecution case is inadmissible, e.g., is based on hearsay, then it is appropriate to make a submission about this matter at the committal proceedings. The magistrates cannot properly say that there is evidence on which to commit the accused for trial if the evidence in question is not admissible. Thus one can mount any proper objection to evidence and require the magistrates to rule on it. Where the magistrates so rule then by r. 70(5) of the Magistrates' Courts Rules 1981 the words 'treated as inadmissible' should be written against the offending part of the prosecution depositions. Submissions about prosecution evidence should however be confined to matters of *admissibility*. Submissions about the *weight* of evidence, e.g., the poor quality of identification, or the lack of corroboration, are unlikely to succeed given the low standard of proof required in committal proceedings.

Unless the facts are very extreme a magistrates' court should not consider the use of its discretion to exclude otherwise admissible evidence under s. 78 of the Police and Criminal Evidence Act 1984 as this discretion is better left to the Crown Court. The case law does however demonstrate a residual power in the magistrates to consider the use of this discretion.

(c) One may wish to see how prosecution witnesses respond to certain lines of speculative cross-examination. It may be, for example, that one wishes to consider a somewhat dangerous path which may, if unsuccessful, lead to the witness giving evidence in a way which is more harmful to the accused than appears from the basis of his statement. If this does in fact occur at the committal proceedings one can be sure to advise counsel at the Crown Court trial to avoid that approach to that particular witness.

(d) One can attempt to draw prosecution witnesses out into areas beyond the scope of their often brief statement to the police. It is a fact of life that even with intelligent lay witnesses the more one can get them to say the more likely it is that apparent inconsistencies and self-contradictions will arise or can be exploited. Although the depositions are not in themselves evidence to be put in at the trial in the Crown Court, they can be used as a previous inconsistent statement on the basis of which to cross-examine a witness. Suppose therefore that in the course of lengthy cross-examination one can get a witness to say something in the magistrates' court about how a certain event occurred. If in the Crown Court when he is testifying on the same matter there is any difference in the version he gives, even quite a minor change in terminology, one can sometimes seize upon this as the weak point in his evidence on which perhaps to discredit him. Giving evidence in the Crown Court is a considerably more stressful experience than in the magistrates' court. Witnesses may tend to exaggerate under those stresses. Suppose that, in describing an incident which led to a fight, a witness who in the magistrates' court had said that the defendant was 'acting pretty stupidly' in the Crown Court could be persuaded to say that the defendant was 'acting like a maniac'. One can easily see the line of cross-examination about the witness's credibility that would follow. It could be put to the witness that he had changed his evidence since the magistrates' court, and he was now deliberately exaggerating to try to incriminate the accused, and thus forfeited all credibility. Thus the sheer bulk of additional testimony that one can get to flesh out the sometimes skeletal statements which the police will have obtained when they took the witness's statement may be of great tactical assistance.

(e) Even if one has opted for a committal with consideration of the evidence then it does not necessarily follow that one needs at this stage to attack the evidence or cross-examine each of the prosecution witnesses. Moreover, if one has asked for a long form committal with a realistic hope of the magistrates not committing the accused for trial rather than for gaining a tactical advantage in the eventual Crown Court trial, one still has a tactical decision to make. Suppose that one's submission of no case to answer has been rejected after a thorough cross-examination of the prosecution witnesses. There is still the option as to whether or not to call one's own client. The general practice is not to give any of the defence evidence at this stage. This is because firstly one is perfectly entitled to keep one's evidence secret until the trial (with the single exception of an alibi defence) and secondly because putting the defendant or his witnesses in the witness box will give the prosecution that self-same advantage that has just been discussed in relation to prosecution witnesses, namely they will now be able to cross-examine at length on the circumstances of the incident and themselves obtain a detailed version of what the accused and his witnesses will say. One would normally therefore only consider calling the accused and his witnesses where one felt that the prosecution evidence was not strong and that there was some realistic hope that the magistrates, having heard the totality of the evidence, prosecution and defence, would decide there is no case on which to commit. An example might be where the accused had very strong alibi evidence, e.g., not just his own testimony but that of, say, two wholly reputable and disinterested witnesses.

16.4.2 POINTS AGAINST A FULL COMMITTAL

The disadvantages of having a long form committal are obvious as the converse of the advantages. One may rehearse prosecution witnesses in their evidence and give them a taste of how cross-examination feels so that they are more assured the next time. Likewise by the very manner in which one conducts one's cross-examination one may give away to the prosecution the nature of the defence and allow them to call other evidence with which to meet it. The advantages to the prosecution of giving their witnesses a 'dry run' should not be underestimated. Testifying may be a nerve-racking experience for a witness and there is no doubt that it is less of an ordeal where one has had an opportunity to practise.

There is additionally the matter of cost. A full committal may need several hours, or days, to achieve what the short form committal can achieve in minutes. For a privately-paying client this is obviously an important factor, and even for the legal aid client cost may be of some relevance in view of possible contribution orders or orders for payment of prosecution costs if he is eventually convicted.

16.5 Notice of Further Evidence

Finally, one further point should be noted. It has been stressed throughout that the prosecution are under no obligation to call all their evidence whether in person or by statements in s. 102 form at the committal hearing. All they need to call is sufficient evidence to show a prima facie case. This does not however mean that they are entitled to keep secret, and surprise the accused with, the evidence of other witnesses. After committal the prosecution are obliged to give the accused notice of the evidence of all the witnesses whom they propose to call at the trial. This is done by subsequently serving on the accused's solicitor copies of the statements comprising the additional evidence which is to be called at trial in the Crown Court.

16.6 Alternatives to Committal

There are two alternative procedures to committal though both are rarely used.

(a) *Voluntary bills of indictment*. Although this procedure is in principle available in any case, its use is limited by *Practice Direction (Crime: Voluntary Bills)* [1991] WLR 1633. The procedure should only be used where the interests of justice require it and where either committal proceedings have been held but have resulted in the discharge of the accused or the holding of committal proceedings would for some other reason be undesirable. Where the procedure applies, the prosecution apply direct to a High Court judge for a 'voluntary bill' and the case by-passes the committal stage. The application is usually made on written submissions.

(b) *Notice of transfer*. In the case of two exceptional kinds of crime, a 'notice of transfer' can be used to by-pass the committal stage and reduce delays. The two kinds of case are:

    (i)   serious and complex fraud where the circumstances make it appropriate for the management of the case to be taken over by the Crown Court without delay (Criminal Justice Act 1987, s. 4(1)(a)); and

    (ii)   those involving child witnesses who are the victims of sexual offences or offences of cruelty or violence (Criminal Justice Act 1991, s. 53).

In both cases the notice of transfer may be lodged at any time between the accused being charged and the commencement of committal proceedings. It is given to the magistrates' court which would otherwise have conducted the committal. There is a procedure permitting the accused to challenge this notice by applying to the Crown Court to dismiss the transferred charges.

SEVENTEEN

THE CROWN COURT: PREPARATION AND TRIAL

17.1 Introduction

The Crown Court is part of the Supreme Court. Its jurisdiction is to deal with:

(a) Trials on indictment.
(b) Offenders who have been committed for sentence by the magistrates' court under s. 37 or s. 38 of the Magistrates' Courts Act 1980.
(c) Appeals from magistrates' courts against conviction and/or sentence.
(d) Sundry miscellaneous civil matters (e.g., appeals on licensing matters).

17.1.1 THE JUDGES OF THE CROWN COURT

There are four categories of judge who sit in the Crown Court. These are:

(a) High Court judges, almost invariably from the Queen's Bench Division, who spend part of the time sitting in criminal cases.
(b) Circuit judges who divide their time between criminal work in the Crown Court and acting as judge in the county court on civil or matrimonial matters.
(c) Recorders who are part-time practitioners, usually barristers but also some solicitors, who sit for a fixed number of days each year as a judge of the Crown Court.
(d) Assistant recorders who are respectively in all ways equivalent to a circuit judge or a recorder and are likewise appointed from private practitioners at the Bar or solicitors to sit for a number of days per year.

17.1.2 MODES OF ADDRESS

High Court judges, all judges at the Central Criminal Court in London, and the judges who perform the honorary offices of Recorder of Liverpool or Manchester are addressed as 'My Lord' or 'My Lady'. All other judges in the Crown Court are addressed as 'Your Honour'.

17.1.3 DISTRIBUTION OF WORK

17.1.3.1 Geographically

The whole Crown Court in England and Wales is considered to be a single court sitting in different locations. The courts are grouped into six circuits each one with its own separately organised practising Bar. Cases may be committed by the magistrates to any given location, which will not necessarily be the one nearest to the committing court. Considerations will include the length of lists at individual Crown Courts and other special factors, e.g., the fact that a certain offence has aroused a lot of feeling locally may mean that it should be tried in some distant Crown Court, e.g., in London rather than in the Crown Court for the town where the committal took place and the facts occurred.

Locations are classified as first, second or third tier. First-tier locations will always have a High Court judge available because they will also deal with a substantial amount of civil work. These include trial centres in the largest towns such as Manchester and Birmingham. Second-tier locations have no facilities for civil work but may draw on a High Court judge entirely for criminal work at times. Third-tier locations have neither High Court civil work nor High Court judges.

17.1.3.2 Classification by judge

Offences are divided into four classes:

(a) Class one is murder, treason and certain other offences, e.g., offences contrary to the Official Secrets Act.

(b) Class two are other very serious crimes including manslaughter, rape and intercourse with a girl under 13.

Those in class one and two must be tried by a High Court judge unless the presiding judge of the circuit releases a certain case for trial by a circuit judge.

(c) Class three offences consist of those triable only on indictment and not in any other class (there are very few of these), they may be tried by a High Court judge, a circuit judge or recorder in accordance with directions by the presiding judge of each circuit.

(d) Class four offences, which are the largest group by far, includes all offences triable either way plus robbery and wounding/causing grievous bodily harm. These will in general be handled by a circuit judge or recorder in accordance with directions given by the presiding judge.

17.2 Between Committal and Trial

After the committal hearing your client will have been remanded either on bail or in custody for trial at the Crown Court. Depending on local conditions and in particular the length of local lists, clients on bail may usually expect a wait of many months for their trial. Clients in custody will wait a somewhat shorter time, but in cases of any complexity or where a long trial is anticipated a wait of some months is also likely to be involved. It will be recalled that by virtue of s. 22 of the Prosecution of Offences Act 1985 (see **16.2.10.3**) in principle there should only be a maximum delay of 112 days between committal and arraignment where a defendant is in custody but the prosecution may apply for this period to be extended and extension is liberally granted.

There ought therefore, given adequate resources within the office, to be ample time to prepare thoroughly the defence case and moreover, given the delay between first obtaining instructions and the committal, even if the latter was only a 'paper' committal under s. 6(2) of the 1980 Act, one should be relatively well informed at this stage of what the case is about and it may be that the final preparation for the trial only takes some fine tuning of information that is already to hand. We shall now consider some of the procedural and tactical features of the process between committal and trial.

17.3 The Indictment

The indictment is the formal document which contains a list of the charges against the accused to which he is invited to plead at the beginning of his trial. In principle a jury may only try one indictment at a time but the indictment may contain any number of counts. A form of sample indictment charging two counts appears below:

INDICTMENT   NO. 940115

THE CROWN COURT AT MIDDLEMARCH

The Queen v *Stephen Woodward*

STEPHEN WOODWARD is charged as follows

Count 1.   *Statement of Offence*

ATTEMPTED BURGLARY, contrary to s. 1(1) of the Criminal Attempts Act 1981

Particulars of Offence

Stephen Woodward on the 15th day of January 1994 attempted to enter as a trespasser a building known as 3 West Road Middlemarch with intent to steal therein.

Count 2.   *Statement of Offence*

HANDLING STOLEN GOODS, contrary to s. 22(1) of the Theft Act 1968.

Particulars of Offence

Stephen Woodward on a day unknown between the 3rd day of January 1994 and the 17th day of January 1994 dishonestly received certain stolen goods namely a Yakimura model 21 television belonging to Ian Grant knowing or believing the same to be stolen.

5 May 1994

M Jones
An Officer of the Crown Court

As will be observed, the heading is in a standard form describing the Crown Court and the parties and each count then contains a statement of the offence and the particulars of the offence. As will be observed the particulars are in an extremely brief format and give no details whatsoever of *modus operandi* or surrounding circumstances.

The indictment may charge two or more accused in a single count if the prosecution case is that they were acting together to commit the offence. If several persons were involved in some offences but not in all of them and the counts may properly be joined together (see below 17.3.2) then it is still proper for them all to be charged within the same indictment.

Indictments are usually drafted by officers of the Crown Court and only in cases of considerable complexity are the papers automatically sent to prosecuting counsel to draft the indictment. In fact, increasingly, a CPS lawyer after the committal will prepare a so-called 'schedule' which is in essence a draft of the potential indictment and is sent on to the Crown Court with the committal papers for the Crown Court officer to formally prepare the indictment.

It will be recalled that at the end of the committal the examining justices will have indicated the charges on which they are going to commit the accused (and this may involve them indicating that they are refusing to commit him on certain others for which the prosecution had argued). It may come as a surprise to find that the person drafting the indictment is not bound in any way by the magistrates' view as to the offences for which there was a case on which to commit. The Crown Court officer (or CPS lawyer) may include in the indictment counts for *any* indictable offence disclosed by the depositions or which in his opinion is disclosed by the depositions, whether or not the magistrates committed on those charges (Administration of Justice (Miscellaneous Provisions) Act 1933, s. 2(2)).

Thus, for example, if the magistrates, in a case of handbag snatching, committed only on a charge of theft, but the CPS lawyer considers that there was a sufficient element of violence for the charge justifiably to be one of robbery, the indictment may include a count in the alternative for both theft and robbery. Even more commonly, alternative counts for theft and handling are inserted where stolen goods are recovered from an individual but it is unclear as to whether he was the thief or a handler. It makes no difference as indicated above even if the magistrates expressly refuse to commit on the more serious charge. It is suggested however that the power to include a count for an offence which the examining justices have *expressly* refused to commit should be sparingly exercised (*R* v *Kempster* [1989] 1 WLR 1125).

17.3.1 DRAFTING THE INDICTMENT

Although the indictment is a fairly short document there are numerous pitfalls for the unwary. The drafting of indictments is governed by the Indictments Act 1915 and the Indictments Rules 1971. The essential rule is r. 6 which says that 'the particulars must disclose the essential elements of the offence but even failure to disclose an essential element may be disregarded if the accused is not thereby prejudiced or embarrassed in his defence' (r. 6(b) and (c)).

17.3.2 JOINDER OF COUNTS IN AN INDICTMENT

Several counts against an accused may be put in one indictment by virtue of the Indictment Rules, r. 9 which provides:

> Charges for any offences may be joined in the same indictment if those charges are founded on the same fact or form or are part of a series of offences of the same or a similar character.

Thus in the well-known case of *R* v *Mansfield* [1977] 1 WLR 1102 where the accused started different fires in different hotels, in the course of one of which seven people died, the seven charges for murder were rightly put in the same indictment with the relevant charges of arson as they constituted a series of offences albeit that no personal injury was caused to anyone in the later fires.

Under this provision also, quite commonly gangs of professional bank robbers may be charged with a series of offences, even in some cases when committed over a period of some years. All participants may likewise be charged, including those who only drove the getaway car or handled the stolen money as well as the robbers themselves, even though not everyone is involved in each individual offence.

Despite this prima facie provision, the judge, if he is of the opinion that the accused may be 'prejudiced or embarrassed in his defence' through having all the counts against him tried in the same indictment, may make an order to 'sever the indictment' under s. 5(3) of the Indictments Act 1915. This applies where the joinder of counts is technically permitted by r. 9 but if a single jury dealt with the trial of all the counts there would be a risk of prejudice. The judge is under a duty to order separate trials where the evidence relevant to one count might become intermingled with that of other counts or where one or other of the counts is of such a scandalous or offensive nature that it would inevitably prejudice the jury against the accused in relation to the other matters even if proof was lacking on those other matters.

The principle is often applied to sever counts and order separate trials of different sexual offences involving different victims if there is insufficient probative value between them for the 'similar fact' principle to apply. Nonetheless the recent case of *R* v *Cannan* (1991) 92 Cr App R 16 (see also **13.2.2**) indicates that even in sexual cases where the 'similar fact' principle does not strictly apply a judge has a discretion whether to order severance or not and the Court of Appeal will not interfere with that discretion unless the judge has exercised it on improper principles.

17.3.3   SUMMARY

(a)   An individual may be charged with any offence disclosed by the depositions given at the committal.

(b)   An individual may be charged with alternative counts where it is unclear from the facts whether the jury ought to convict of one offence or another, e.g., of theft or handling, so that it is proper to let the jury decide after hearing all the evidence.

(c)   Two or more counts may be joined in any indictment if they form part of the same facts or a series of offences of the same or a similar character; the similarity need not be so close as to be within the similar fact rule.

(d)   Two or more defendants may be charged in a single count with having committed a single offence, and two or more counts in an indictment may charge different individuals with separate offences even though there is no one count against them all collectively.

17.3.4   JOINDER OF ACCUSED

All parties to any individual offence normally will be joined together in a single count. This applies, moreover, not only to the principal offenders but to everyone else involved including those who merely aid, abet, counsel or procure. The judge has a discretion to order separate trials of defendants who are accused of committing an offence jointly but this should be very rarely used. The Court of Appeal indicated in *R* v *Moghal* (1977) 65 Cr App R 56 that separate trials should only be ordered in very exceptional cases, the trial in that case having gone badly wrong because one of two accused had persuaded a judge at an early stage to let her be tried alone, had then alleged duress against the co-accused and been acquitted in circumstances where, had they both been tried together, that would have been an inconceivable outcome especially given that the allegation was of a particularly brutal murder. Had they both been tried together it seemed on the facts likely that she would have been convicted as the main perpetrator.

The judge will bear in mind the interests of justice, which include the costs involved in holding separate trials so that even in quite extreme cases, e.g., where one accused has made a full confession which would be inadmissible against the others but will inevitably be put before the jury in the course of the full trial, the prejudice of that alone may not be a reason for ordering separate trials (*R* v *Lake* (1976) 64 Cr App R 172).

17.3.5   OVERLOADING THE INDICTMENT

A number of recent trials has demonstrated the problem of 'overloading the indictment'. This is a matter of common sense and practice. In the well-known case of *R* v *Thorne* (1978) 66 Cr App R 6 there were 14 different defendants charged on numerous counts of robbery and related offences including conspiracy, handling and attempting to pervert the course of justice. The trial involved more than 20 barristers and ten firms of solicitors and lasted more than four months including a 12-day summing up. The Court of Appeal observed, whilst not allowing the appeal merely because the trial had been too long and complex, that the trial ought to have been split up into shorter trials.

17.3.6   APPLICATIONS IN RELATION TO THE INDICTMENT

The most important applications likely to be made are as follows.

17.3.6.1   An application by the defence to sever the indictment

Such an application is an attempt to persuade the trial judge to order that two or more counts in the indictment should be tried separately in respect of one accused, or that certain defendants should be tried separately from others and often in a particular order. This application is usually made immediately after a plea has been taken. In some cases increasingly where there is complexity, there is a pre-trial review of the case by the judge who is likely to conduct the trial with both counsel present in an attempt to see what agreements can be secured to make the trial shorter and more economical. At present this remains a relatively informal procedure with many local variations.

17.3.6.2 Amendment of the indictment

It is likely to be the prosecution who apply to amend the indictment and this may be permitted even well into the trial, although an adjournment must then be allowed to the defence if the trial is put on a different footing. If the amendment is so vital that it substantially invalidates or makes useless some of the evidence given hitherto, that may be grounds for an appeal or for the jury to be discharged and a retrial ordered.

17.3.6.3 Appeals in relation to defective indictments

If there is an error in the indictment which is not corrected by an amendment during the trial there may be an appeal. Serious defects may lead to a successful appeal. Mistakes in the giving of names or dates are unlikely to be sufficiently material, the key test being whether the error prejudiced or embarrassed the accused. In addition, since many such appeals are based on technicalities, the Court of Appeal is quite likely to 'apply the proviso' under s. 2 of the Criminal Appeal Act 1968. Probably the most likely basis for a sucecssful appeal will be that the judge was wrong in refusing to sever and thus that prejudice has been caused to the accused, particularly in sexual cases.

17.4 The Arraignment

All trials on indictment begin with the 'arraignment' which consists of formally putting the counts in the indictment to the accused and inviting him to plead to each. The jury are not empanelled at this stage and in most courts the procedure is that matters are 'listed to plead' where nothing else is dealt with but the taking of the plea. This is an obvious effort to clarify matters, improve listing and avoid the situation where there is a late change of plea causing wasted time and inconvenience. Exceptionally, if solicitors write to the CPS and the court and indicate that there is categorically to be a not guilty plea, the matter may be listed for trial without this preliminary stage. Otherwise the accused is brought before the court with both counsel present and he is invited to plead to each of the counts in the indictment. If he pleads guilty to all the counts there is no need to involve a jury and the court will then proceed to sentence or adjourn for sentence in order that reports or enquiries can be made. If he pleads not guilty to all offences the matter will be adjourned for jury trial, often some months later, especially if the accused is not in custody. If the accused pleads guilty to some offences but not others, prosecuting counsel will consider whether the overall admissions of guilt are sufficient for the accused to be fairly dealt with in his view. If so, he may, in respect of the counts to which the accused pleads not guilty, invite the judge to 'leave them on the court file'. In such a case the counts remain open but may not be proceeded with without leave of the court or of the Court of Appeal and, although this does not amount to a formal acquittal, only very exceptionally would the court permit these charges to be reopened. If counsel is not satisfied that the accused could be satisfactorily dealt with overall, as for example where he has only pleaded guilty to one minor offence out of several, then the sentencing for that offence is likely to be postponed until the offences for which he has pleaded not guilty are dealt with.

If there are co-accused and one pleads guilty and the other not guilty, the usual but not inevitable practice is for the judge to adjourn the case of the one who has pleaded guilty so that he is sentenced at the end of the trial of the one pleading not guilty after all the facts have come out so that it can more clearly be seen, for example, who is the ringleader and who the mere follower or how responsibility should otherwise be apportioned. However, if the prosecution wished to call the accused who pleaded guilty as a prosecution witness it may be preferable to sentence the accomplice before he testifies so that he is aware that there is no purpose in him changing his evidence to receive a more favourable outcome. In trials of professional criminals however it may be better to leave the sentencing of all to the end, even where one is to testify for the prosecution, so that the judge can assess their relative culpability (see especially *R* v *Weekes* (1982) 74 Cr App R 161 and **8.2.3.1**).

17.5   Plea Bargaining

As indicated earlier, there is a certain amount of scope for negotiating techniques in the criminal process. It may be possible for example to persuade the CPS not to charge at all, to withdraw a charge once made, to charge a lesser offence, or to caution (see **4.7.2**). Once matters have reached the Crown Court however then any 'negotiations' are likely to involve counsel.

The term 'plea bargaining' is used in a number of different senses. It may involve:

(a)   An agreement that if the accused pleads guilty to certain offences his sentence will not exceed some given maximum, or some particular form (typically that he will not receive a custodial sentence).

(b)   It may involve an agreement by the prosecution that if the accused will plead guilty to certain offences they may refrain from putting other or more serious offences to him.

(c)   It may involve the prosecution agreeing with the defence that they will accept a plea of guilty to a lesser offence than the one charged.

(d)   It may refer to the prosecution undertaking not to proceed on certain counts in the indictment if the accused will plead guilty to the remainder.

The position in England and Wales in relation to plea bargaining is that:

(a)   The first of these situations ((a) above) is governed by the case of *R* v *Turner* [1970] 2 QB 321 which clearly establishes that any improper pressure by or in the presence of the judge to plead guilty in the expectation of a certain sentence renders a guilty plea a nullity and thus the conviction is liable to be quashed on appeal.

(b)   The second form of undertaking ((b) above) is improper though in reality it merges somewhat into the third form ((c) above) which *is* proper, as is the fourth ((d) above). Usually it involves a discussion between prosecuting and defence counsel, with or without the solicitors present. It is unclear in the case law whether the judge's approval is strictly required in law. According to *R* v *Coward* (1980) 70 Cr App R 70 the onus is on prosecuting counsel to decide what pleas to accept. In effect it is difficult for a judge to force the prosecution to proceed, but other cases have indicated that a judge may express his disapproval so strongly that prosecuting counsel is likely in effect to be forced to go on. Unlike in civil cases any arrangements must really be struck before the trial has commenced, because once it has commenced and the prosecution evidence has established a case to answer, discontinuance or the acceptance of lesser pleas do require the consent of the judge.

17.6   The Jury

The trial will commence with the jury being empanelled. Jurors may be challenged by the defence 'for cause' so if there is any reason to suspect impropriety or overt bias such challenges may still be made, but the defence now no longer has the power to make 'peremptory challenges' without reason. The prosecution may ask any juror to 'stand by' but in the light of guidelines issued by the Attorney-General, reported at (1989) 88 Cr App R 123, such challenges are rarely made. The judge has a power to remove a juror from the jury and might exercise it, e.g., where it is clear that a juror cannot read or write and much of the trial depends on documentary evidence. There is much case law as to the extent to which, if at all, a judge should seek to intervene to ensure racially or sexually balanced juries.

17.7   The Course of the Trial

The evidential rules relevant to the course of a trial are discussed in **Chapter 8**. Procedurally the following is the order of events:

(a)   After the jury have been informed of the charges to which the accused has pleaded not guilty, prosecuting counsel will open the case. He will summarise the facts and the evidence he proposes to adduce and explain, in factual and reasonably simple language, the way in which he proposes to establish his case and how well his evidence pieces together. He will introduce the witnesses that he proposes to call and say what each is likely to say and will indicate in outline the relevant law and the elements of the offence which he must establish whilst always reminding them that it is the judge who will give them a final direction on matters of law.

In the opening speech counsel must *not* refer to any matters of evidence whose admissibility he knows will be challenged by the defence and he will have received intimation of this by exchange of letters from the solicitors or by discussion with defence counsel immediately before the start.

(b) The prosecution will then call its witnesses one by one and each in turn is subject to examination-in-chief, to cross-examination by or on behalf of each of the defendants, and to re-examination where appropriate. Counsel will also put in evidence any formal admissions which have been agreed under s. 10 of the Criminal Justice Act 1967 and witness statements which are admissible under some principle of evidence, e.g., under s. 9, Criminal Justice Act 1967 or ss. 23 and 24, Criminal Justice Act 1988.

If at any stage the prosecution wishes to introduce evidence the admissibility of which is challenged by the defence there will be a *voire dire*, or trial within a trial, at which the prosecution will need to establish to the judge's satisfaction that the relevant exception to the hearsay rule is made out or that a confession is reliable and thus admissible under s. 76, Police and Criminal Evidence Act 1984; that notwithstanding s. 78 of the 1984 Act it does not make the trial unfair if a given item of evidence is introduced; that one of the reasons for unavailability of a witness under s. 24, Criminal Justice Act 1988 applies; or as the case may be. All these matters are more fully discussed in the chapters on evidence.

(c) At the end of the prosecution case there may be a submission of no case to answer. The nature of this submission and the principles on which it should be allowed are described more fully at **7.4.1**.

(d) If there is a case to answer, the defence present their case. It may be that the defence need adduce no evidence at all and that defence counsel wishes merely to make a closing speech. The defence may make an opening speech if they wish unless only the accused and character witnesses are to be called in which case defence counsel does not have an opening speech (s. 2, Criminal Evidence Act 1898).

The accused may testify but is not compelled to, but if he does he must testify before his witnesses unless the judge otherwise orders (s. 79, Police and Criminal Evidence Act 1984).

The other witnesses of fact and/expert witnesses will be called and each in turn will be subject to examination-in-chief and cross-examination, not only from the prosecution but from the counsel for every other defendant who has not called the witness.

(e) Counsel then have closing speeches. Prosecuting counsel sums up the case to the jury and at this stage, as throughout, he must act as a 'minister of justice' and must not strive at all costs for a conviction. He will remind the jury of the most cogent parts of the prosecution evidence and comment upon inconsistencies or contradictions in the defence evidence. He must not comment upon the failure of the accused to give evidence or to call his spouse. The prosecution do not in fact invariably choose to make a closing speech.

The defence then have their closing speech and may comment in any way appropriate on the whole of the case that is justified by the evidence. It is not appropriate however for counsel to suggest fanciful explanations unsupported by any actual evidence.

(f) The judge then sums up. Explanations of various aspects of what should appear in a judicial summing up appear throughout the chapters on evidence. There should be clear explanations of the respective roles of judge and jury, of the law, of the burden and standard of proof, and of any other relevant point of evidence on which a specific form of direction is required, e.g., corroboration, identification evidence, the need to consider the case against each of two or more accused quite separately, the use of their knowledge of the defendant's bad character if any, or the relevance of the defendant exercising his right of silence.

The judge may comment on the evidence but should not indicate so strongly what is credible and what is not that the jury are likely to adopt the judge's views. The judge may nonetheless comment on manifest implausibilities or contradictions.

Increasingly a judge may invite counsel to assist him on the law and form of a direction especially in matters such as corroboration where there are many technicalities. Defence counsel is under an obligation to assist at this stage rather than as was formerly the practice being entitled to sit tight in the hope of a successful appeal against a manifest misdirection. The point is however not entirely clear and depends in part on the Bar's Code of Conduct. In *R* v *Edwards* (1983) 77 Cr App R 5 it was suggested that in principle defence counsel should not keep silent in those circumstances but should assist the judge to ensure that the present trial is a fair one by intervening if he notices a clear misdirection.

(g)   The jury are then directed to retire and consider their verdict, which must be a unanimous one, and to appoint a foreman. If in the course of their retirement the jury wish to ask any question, both question and answer should be given publicly in open court and not, for example, by private note to the judge. It may be necessary for the judge to completely redirect the jury in the light of some question which may indicate that they have misunderstood some aspect of the case.

After a minimum of two hours and ten minutes (longer in complex cases) the judge may indicate to the jury that he will accept a *majority* verdict by no less than ten to two or if the jury is reduced below 12, a majority of nine to one or better.

If the jury still prove unable to agree then, after what the judge considers to be an appropriate time, he may discharge them. He may not bring improper pressure to bear on them however to return with a verdict more quickly than they are able to. If the jury are discharged there may be a retrial, though the prosecution, depending on all the facts, may decide not to proceed, e.g., in view of the passage of time or the way certain evidence has come out.

If the jury return an unambiguous verdict it must be accepted by the judge. If the verdict on any count is ambiguous the judge should attempt to clarify it by questions (e.g., where the jury purport to find the accused guilty of both murder and manslaughter in respect of the same incident). The more confused that the jury's verdict is, the more likely it is that an appeal will be successful on the basis that they must have misunderstood their duty.

(h)   At the conclusion of the trial, if the verdict on any charge is one of guilty, the judge will proceed to sentence and before doing so will deal with mitigation and other matters such as obtaining of pre-sentence reports (see **Chapter 18**). It may be necessary to remand the accused, on bail or in custody, until further information is available for sentencing. There may indeed be other trials involving the same accused which are being dealt with separately and later, and it may not be appropriate to sentence until the outcome of those trials.

In the event of a guilty verdict it will be necessary to consider the possibility of appeal (see **Chapter 20**).

If the verdict is not guilty the accused will be discharged and counsel for the accused will ask for any other appropriate orders, e.g., for costs from central funds, the remission of legal aid contributions, etc.

17.8   Preparation for Trial

We have thus far dealt with the procedure in getting to the outcome of a Crown Court trial. It is now appropriate to consider preparation for that trial.

Considerations relevant to managing a criminal practice have been discussed earlier in **Chapter 3**. The importance of keeping accurate records, proper file management, and the possibility of having to run substantial cases with teams of people have been dealt with there. Criminal practitioners whose main interest is advocacy may well not be involved any further in cases past the committal stage and, as suggested earlier, many of the most specialist criminal firms have quite separate sections dealing with cases between committal and trial.

The most important immediate procedural aspects include the following:

(a)   Service of appropriate alibi notice under s. 11, Criminal Justice Act 1967 giving the necessary particulars to the police so that the alibi can be investigated. An alibi means:

> That by reason of the presence of the defendant at a particular place or in a particular area or at a particular time he was not, or was unlikely to have been, at the place where the offence is alleged to have been committed at the time of its alleged commission.

It must be borne in mind that there is a requirement to serve this notice even if your client has no idea where he was on the day in question (e.g., where the offence was some long time before) provided that he is certain that he was not at the place where the crime was committed. Naturally the more detail one can give in this notice, and the more witnesses one can call upon, the better it is.

(b)   The possibility of agreeing the tape recorded evidence under *Practice Direction (Crime: Tape Recording of Police Interviews)* [1989] 1 WLR 631. This will involve listening to the tape, and discussing it with the client, and possibly with counsel.

(c)   The indictment should be received in due course and should be checked for technical or procedural difficulties and if necessary counsel should be consulted.

(d)   Custody time limits should be borne in mind. If the client is in custody, no more than 112 days should elapse between committal and arraignment. However, the prosecution may apply, in writing or if necessary orally, for that period to be extended and an extension will very commonly be needed in many Crown Courts in view of listing delays, even in quite routine cases.

17.8.1   FURTHER PREPARATION

17.8.1.1   Costs

If the case is going to the Crown Court clearly there will be substantial expense ahead. It is vital to ensure that an appropriate legal aid order has been obtained at the end of the committal or by a further application to the Crown Court. If the client has been paying privately hitherto it may be that an application to the Crown Court is now required in view of the substantial expense ahead and the depletion of the client's savings hitherto. One must bear in mind that applications for prior authorisation may be advisable in the case of substantial expenditure particularly on expert witnesses. Specific application will need to be made to use a Queen's Counsel at trial. It may be possible to arrange informal payments on account where cases are very substantial and a long delay is likely. It is necessary to write to the Chief Clerk at the taxing office at the Crown Court indicating what work has been done hitherto, what work is involved ahead and what is an appropriate figure for costs and substantial disbursements.

17.8.1.2   The client

After committal it is appropriate, however familiar the client appears to be with the criminal process, to advise him further about the subsequent procedures up to the start of his trial. In the light of committal documents and perhaps the way in which an oral committal went, it may be necessary substantially to improve and update his own proof of evidence. This must be done not only in respect of matters of guilt or innocence but with a view to ultimate mitigation. It will be vital to deal with every single factual aspect of the prosecution depositions in so far as the client is likely to know anything about them or can comment on them. Depositions should be supplied to the client where necessary for him to consider thoroughly, although some discretion should be used in this. It is for example sometimes appropriate to delete witnesses' names and/or addresses from depositions and to delete details from statements in sexual cases which are supplied to a client in custody, where such papers may circulate and be misused.

17.8.1.3   Prosecution evidence

This will have been obtained in the form of depositions whether or not at full committal. As indicated earlier however, the prosecution have no obligation to call all their evidence at committal or even to indicate who their witnesses are. They only need call sufficient evidence to show a prima facie case. That does not mean however that they are entitled to keep their evidence secret until trial in respect of any witness.

The prosecution will after committal need to serve a 'notice of additional evidence' in respect of any witnesses whom they did not use at the committal stage. This should be served on both the defence and the court and is usually served in a signed statement complying with s. 9 of the Criminal Justice Act 1967. One will need to consider carefully any new aspect of the case which this raises and whether the evidence is so uncontroversial that it can be agreed under s. 9 or whether new evidence needs to be found on the client's behalf to meet extra points made in this statement. It may be necessary to consult counsel as to his view of the evidential effect.

17.8.1.4   Additional evidence for the defence

It may be necessary to interview new witnesses or reinterview other witnesses in the light of what comes out at committal and any additional evidence served by the prosecution.

17.8.1.5   Expert evidence

If the case is one where expert evidence seems likely to be required, an appropriate expert should be instructed as soon as possible to provide a report. Typical experts might be, for example, forensic document examiners, forensic scientists of other kinds, psychiatrists and the like. Expert evidence is the only example of evidence, apart from an alibi notice, of which an accused needs to give the prosecution warning before the Crown Court trial by virtue of the Crown Court (Advance Notice of Expert Evidence) Rules 1987. These apply to both defence and prosecution and require the prior disclosure of expert evidence in much the same way as is applicable in civil cases.

17.8.1.6   Plans

If the physical layout of the scene of the alleged crime is relevant (e.g., the interior of a public house) then it may be necessary to visit it, photograph it, or even prepare maps and plans. Where these are done they should be served on the other parties with a statement under s. 9, Criminal Justice Act 1967 if necessary to indicate their authenticity.

17.8.1.7   Writing to the prosecution

It is worth writing to the prosecution, and this may well be done when sending the alibi notice, about any outstanding matters. You should already have obtained your own client's criminal record and it will have been important to have gone through this with him at a far earlier stage to confirm that he accepts any recorded offences. It will be necessary to ask whether they have any unused evidence which they are obliged to disclose under the Attorney-General's guidelines; it will be necessary to ask for the criminal record of any witnesses they propose to call; it may be necessary to correspond with them in an effort to have any particular statements which might otherwise be admissible edited. This also applies to the tape or the transcript of any tape which may be played in court so as, for example, to take out any references made in interview to a client's previous bad character.

247

17.8.1.8 Interviewing prosecution witnesses

Although it is perfectly proper to interview any witness it is often said, though on no particular authority, that it is unwise for a solicitor to interview prosecution witnesses without notifying the prosecution in advance. Some consider it best to have two persons present to provide a corroborated note of what is said to avoid any suggestion of attempting to influence a witness. It is the writer's view that this is somewhat over cautious and that no reputable solicitor would be likely to be accused of attempting to tamper with prosecution evidence merely by interviewing a witness.

17.8.1.9 Use of counsel

The purposes for which counsel may be used have been indicated earlier. No one but counsel may conduct a Crown Court jury trial and therefore an appropriate barrister will have been selected earlier. One will need to consider whether it is necessary to obtain advice on evidence or tactics; advice on plea; or perhaps to have a conference with the counsel of one's choice with or without the client present.

An appropriate brief should be prepared, as late in the day as possible to take account of any new developments but not so late that counsel does not have time thoroughly to digest it.

17.8.1.10 Pre-trial review

It may be appropriate to ask the court to arrange a pre-trial review or directions hearing in conjunction with the listing office. Directions hearings are only provided for automatically in cases of complex fraud trials but increasingly are used, albeit with local variations, for the sake of making the trial process more efficient in relation to all kinds of case, especially those of length or complexity.

17.8.1.11 Ensuring the attendance of witnesses

One must take all relevant steps to ensure the attendance of witnesses including the obtaining and service of necessary witness summonses. These are obtained from the Crown Court (or indeed the High Court) and conduct money ought in practice to be served although there is no strict requirement to do so. This should only amount to travelling expenses to court. The sum is reclaimed from the court with the witness expenses and therefore should be collected from the witness. If a witness on service of the summons seems extremely reluctant, even though he had given a proof of evidence before, one may need to reconsider the desirability of calling him. Relevant dates of, for example, holidays, hospital appointments and the like should be obtained. One should ask one's own witnesses at interview whether or not they have a criminal record and each witness statement should of course be signed in case of problems with the witness later whereupon it may become necessary to treat the witness as hostile. Witnesses should be told about the course that the evidence will take and the role of judge and prosecuting counsel, although this may happen outside court. Witnesses will need to be told that they may only be warned the night before of the date of the trial.

17.8.1.12 Date of trial

When the case comes into the warned list the client should be notified and if he is on bail he should be asked to keep in daily touch unless a fixed date is given. In the Crown Court a fixed date is usually only given for very substantial trials or where there is a good deal of expert evidence.

17.8.1.13 Sentence and mitigation

It is usually appropriate to give some consideration to sentence and mitigation however good the defence case seems. It may be appropriate to obtain references from character witnesses, who can also be used on questions of guilt so long as the accused has no criminal record, and expert evidence from, for example, doctors may be necessary on matters of mitigation also. The client should be advised of the likely range of sentences and of the risk that conducting the case in certain ways may increase those sentences (e.g., by scandalous or improper imputations on prosecution witnesses) although one should not shrink from making any appropriate imputation which is essential for the defence.

17.9   At the Trial

It is important to attend by a responsible representative. The witnesses should be marshalled and any other assistance that counsel requires given. It is vital to take as full note of the evidence and other events as possible especially when counsel is conducting cross-examination and may not be able himself to make full notes, e.g., not merely of what the witnesses say but of the judge's comments or other interventions. One should be in such a position as to be able to take instructions from the client in the dock during the trial. It will be necessary to assist witnesses to claim on expenses forms from the appropriate office of the Crown Court.

If the trial lasts more than one day it is important to see that the client's bail is extended overnight and counsel should be reminded to make this application strongly, though it may be refused once the judge has commenced summing up.

After the trial the client should be advised fully as to what has occurred if he has been acquitted. It may be that in the circumstances disclosed that he may wish to consider some form of civil action, although there is no action available as such for inconvenience or distress caused by a failed prosecution unless it can be brought within the heads of one of the normal torts, e.g., malicious prosecution. If the client has been convicted he should be advised about the effect of any sentence passed on him, e.g., time for payment of a fine, compensation order or other penalties. If the client is in custody he will need to be visited in the cells, usually with counsel, to receive advice about the precise terms of imprisonment which he has received and is likely to have to serve. Advice then and there will need to be given about appeal but it is usually better to say that this needs to be considered when the heat of the moment has passed and perhaps to arrange to see him on some subsequent occasion or to give him written advice (a legal aid order covers initial advice on appeal).

17.9.1   ACTION WITH OTHERS

Where a client has been sentenced to imprisonment it will be well known to the solicitor to which prison he will be taken immediately but after assessment he may quite shortly be transferred to some other prison. Enquiries may be made from the prison to which he has initially been taken or otherwise at the Home Office Prison Index, 11th Floor, Calthorpe House, Birmingham. It may be appropriate if the accused has a family or friends to inform them of the nature of the sentence, the client's whereabouts and the procedure for prison visits. Counsel may be asked to advise in writing on appeal and settle initial grounds (pending receipt of transcript).

17.9.2   COSTS

Once the case is concluded if it is a 'standard fee' case the application form should be completed and lodged by post at the Crown Court and payment should then take place very swiftly. If the case is not a case for standard fees then a proper bill must be prepared for determination by the Crown Court taxing officer and that should be lodged within three months. Full supplementary documentation may need to be supplied just as with a civil bill, e.g., attendance notes, disbursement vouchers and the like.

EIGHTEEN

SENTENCING AND PROCEDURES AFTER CONVICTION

18.1 Introduction

In this chapter we shall be considering sentencing and procedures after conviction. We will consider what will happen initially after a guilty verdict is returned, or a plea of guilty entered. We shall then consider the range of sentences available to the courts in the usual case before turning to the regime imposed by the Criminal Justice Acts 1991 and 1993 which indicates the processes through which a court must go before selecting a certain type of sentence, and in deciding upon its length or severity. We shall conclude with a discussion of the principles underlying the making of a plea in mitigation.

A conviction may follow either a plea of guilty or a plea of not guilty. In neither case need the court proceed to sentence immediately. It may, and in some cases must, adjourn the proceedings and sentence at a future date for a number of reasons. Examples would be:

(a) Where a pre-sentence report (formerly called a social enquiry report) or a psychiatric or medical report needs to be prepared so that the court has more information available.

(b) Where there is insufficient information to enable the court to proceed immediately to sentence.

(c) In cases where the defendant has been convicted in his absence and the court has in mind either to disqualify him from driving or imprison him they must adjourn the case to enable the defendant to be brought before the court.

When the court does propose to adjourn proceedings for sentence for any reason the defendant will be remanded. In other words, the court will have to consider the question of bail or custody pending sentence. It must be remembered that the *prima facie* presumption in favour of bail contained in the Bail Act 1976 does *not* apply at this stage except where the court is adjourning to obtain reports on the offender. Even here the court may well now impose conditions even if bail has previously been unconditional. The initial procedures are likely to include one or all of the following matters:

(a) Outlining the facts of the case.
(b) The defendant's antecedents.
(c) Offences taken into consideration.

18.1.1 THE FACTS OF THE CASE

If the defendant has been convicted after a not guilty plea then the court will have been made aware of all the evidence in the case. In addition to deciding the issue of guilt or innocence they will know which version of the facts they are minded to believe. In other words they may have already heard matters relevant to sentencing. For example, suppose that the accused is charged with an assault arising out of a fight and his defence has been self-defence. It may well be that although the court convicts him, having found that his actions did not amount to self-defence, it will nonetheless be apparent that there was gross provocation and this may clearly be a matter relevant to the sentence which it will impose.

There is more difficulty where the defendant has pleaded guilty. In this case there will be no evidence on oath but the prosecution will summarise the facts of the case. In a straightforward case there is no problem, but what if the defendant, whilst admitting his guilt, wishes to give some entirely different version of how matters occurred? What if there is a substantial difference between how the prosecution says an incident occurred and what the defendant has to say?

At this stage it must be remembered that the prosecution is supposed to be acting as a 'minister of justice'. They should maintain a relatively neutral attitude about matters and in particular never press for any particular sentence nor explain the facts of the crime in an emotive or exaggerated way. If it appears that there is a genuine and material dispute about how an incident occurred, then the advocates for prosecution and defence should each make their submissions about the matter, but thereafter the sentencing court should either:

(a) Accept the defence account, or
(b) Allow prosecution and defence to call evidence about the matter. This is called a 'Newton' hearing from the leading case *R* v *Newton* (1982) 77 Cr App R 13.

In the Crown Court where this happens after a guilty plea there is no jury, the judge himself deciding which version of the facts he prefers to believe. The sentencing court will therefore now be aware so far as possible of the facts of the crime itself.

18.1.2 THE DEFENDANT'S ANTECEDENTS

These are usually presented to the court by the Crown Prosecutor or one of the police officers involved in the case. The 'antecedents' are details of the offender's age, upbringing, education, employment record and domestic circumstances. Also there is some account of his previous criminal record, although this is not in substitution for the actual printout of his criminal record which will also be supplied, but the antecedents officer will give more background information, for example, he will mention the actual date of release from each previous sentence and deal with whether or not the accused had bail and the like.

The rules of evidence do not apply at this stage but the antecedents officer may be cross-examined by the defendant's advocate in an effort to elicit more favourable details about the defendant's past, for example that he co-operated with the police from the outset, that he has now found a job or got married. It must be remembered that the Rehabilitation of Offenders Act 1974 does not apply in criminal proceedings, but pursuant to *Practice Direction (Crime: Spent Convictions)* [1975] 1 WLR 1065, details of 'spent' convictions should not be read out in court unless the court gives leave to do so.

18.1.3 OFFENCES TAKEN INTO CONSIDERATION

In the course of being questioned about the present offence the offender may well have been questioned also about other offences. Where the offender proposes to plead guilty then he may well have admitted other past crimes. There is no need for the prosecution to charge him with each of the crimes which he has admitted. One option available to the prosecution is merely to charge him with a few selected crimes and allow him to have the others 'taken into consideration'. This is a somewhat informal procedure, although sanctioned by long usage, in which the prosecution have the advantage of clearing up unsolved crimes and the defendant has the advantage of having the slate wiped clean in so far as these other offences are concerned so that he could not be prosecuted for them after his trial for the present offences is concluded.

The offences to be taken into consideration should be prepared in a proper schedule with all relevant details by the police. They should be offences of a broadly similar nature or of a less serious nature than the present charge. The sentencing court cannot specifically impose a sentence in respect of offences which are to be taken into consideration (although it may order compensation to the victims of those offences) but such offences will be taken into account in a general way when deciding on sentence.

It may be helpful to give an example. A very common type of crime which is taken into consideration is house burglary. Suppose that the offender has made it his habitual practice to go out to one of the wealthier suburbs of the city in which he lives and break into houses at weekends. He may well have done this over a period of a year or more before he is caught. When he is caught he may admit the most recent crimes in the course of interrogation. As other incidents which have not been solved by the police are put to him he may well be prepared to admit those also.

It is very important to stress when acting for a defendant that the list of offences to be taken into consideration should be gone through very carefully with the defendant to ensure that he is right in admitting those other offences. For example, in the incidents just cited it is most unlikely, if regular weekend burglaries had been carried out over a year, that the defendant will any longer remember the precise locations or addresses of the houses which he has burgled or the exact goods which he took away from each. There may be a tendency on the part of the police to slip in anything conceivably likely, in order to improve their detection statistics. On the assumption however that the defendant admits, let us say, 30 such burglaries, the probable practice of the prosecution would be to charge him only with a selected four or five and to have the others 'taken into consideration'. Whilst it may at first sight appear that to admit a course of conduct of regular burglary involving say 30 houses is a very significantly different scale of crime to admitting only the four or five with which one is actually charged, the sentencing practice of the court is such that very little in the way of an extra sentence will be imposed for the other offences. The maximum penalty for one burglary is 14 years and therefore in relation to the five offences to which the accused specifically pleads guilty the maximum is ample and would far exceed anything the court would realistically be minded to impose. The consideration of the other offences referred to in the example would probably make very little difference.

It ought to be mentioned that 'TICs', as they are called, may also be relevant for a defendant who has been convicted after pleading *not guilty*. In the nature of things however such cases will be rare and the usual case of offences taken into consideration occurs where the offender is prepared to admit the crimes with which he is presently charged in advance of trial and the prosecution will thus have ample opportunity to put the other matters to him.

We shall now go on to consider remaining matters in the following order:

(a) Reports (**18.2**).
(b) Types of sentence (**18.3**).
(c) Other orders including compensation and costs (**18.4**).
(d) The structured approach to sentencing under the Criminal Justice Acts 1991 and 1993 (**18.5**).
(e) The plea in mitigation (**18.7**).

18.2 Reports

There may be some situations where the court, even with the offender's criminal record and a detailed and helpful plea in mitigation made by the defence advocate, feels it is unlikely to have sufficient information about the convicted person to enable it to pass sentence. In such a situation it may obtain reports on the offender from a variety of sources and we shall now consider these.

18.2.1 PRE-SENTENCE REPORTS

Such reports are prepared, in the case of adults, by the probation service. They are not usually prepared in advance of trial unless the defendant has already indicated a guilty plea or is already on probation. The report is prepared after one or several interviews between a probation officer and the offender, sometimes in the offender's home environment. The offence will be discussed with the offender and the report will deal with his background, education, upbringing, circumstances, financial position and any particular personal, medical or social problems which he seems to have. Such a report is needed in almost every case before a custodial sentence or before the majority of forms of community sentence can be considered. Unlike the old 'social enquiry report' which often was obtained with an eye to the welfare of the convicted person, a pre-sentence report is expressly to assist the court in deciding on punishment. It will often conclude with a recommendation for a particular type of sentence and may especially deal with the offender's likely response to probation or community service.

If there is no report prepared before conviction then inevitably there will have to be an adjournment to enable one to be prepared and the usual term of such adjournment is three weeks. It is generally considered more satisfactory to have such a report prepared whilst the offender is at liberty, though it is not conclusively the case that when adjourning for a pre-sentence report the court should never remand in custody. Everything will depend upon the facts of the case, remembering that the prima facie right to bail in the Bail Act 1976 *does* apply at this stage.

When considering the regime imposed by the Criminal Justice Act 1991 we shall consider specifically the occasions when a pre-sentence report is required at **18.5.1.3**.

18.2.2 MEDICAL AND PSYCHIATRIC REPORTS

It may be that the court will consider that the occurrence of the offence is connected with some medical condition, in which case they may require the making of medical reports on the accused. A common example is where there is some suggestion of a drug habit or alcoholism which is relevant to why the offender committed the offence, e.g., to provide money to sustain the habit or whilst under the influence of alcohol or the drug. In such a situation the court has power to remand the offender (in custody or on bail) for the preparation of such reports, bearing in mind again that the prima facie right to bail does apply at this stage. Alternatively, the offender may be remanded to a hospital for a report to be prepared under s. 35 of the Mental Health Act 1983. The court is likely to do this either if the offender appears dangerous or if it seems he will not co-operate with the making of a report voluntarily.

Section 4(1) of the Criminal Justice Act 1991 requires a court sentencing an offender who 'is or appears to be mentally disordered' to obtain and consider a medical report before passing a custodial sentence in almost every case.

Both pre-sentence reports and medical reports are prepared in order to be presented to the court, but will be disclosed on a confidential basis in advance to the offender's legal representative.

18.2.3 REPORTS FOR THE DEFENCE

Although reports in both the instances so far considered are made by order of the court it should not be forgotten that it is always open to the legal representative of an offender himself to commission suitable reports. Such reports would be particularly appropriate where it is already apparent that the prosecution have medical evidence to the effect that the offender should be committed to a secure hospital. It may be that the offender is meanwhile receiving treatment from his own consultant who may be prepared to make a different recommendation, e.g., that the offender could safely be released into the community provided he voluntarily agrees to adopt a certain course of treatment. The possibility of the defence commissioning its own reports should not be overlooked.

One important thing to consider is the stage at which reports might be requested. Suppose that an offender has been convicted and there is no pre-sentence report available (as there will not normally be in the case of an offender pleading not guilty). One can make a lengthy plea in mitigation as part of which one might suggest that the court ought to obtain more information before finally sentencing the offender.

More usually an attempt will be made to save the court's time by asking the court to form a preliminary view as to whether it is likely to require a pre-sentence report. This may be done quite early on. The defendant's advocate may simply say that there appear to be matters to do with the offender's upbringing or home circumstances which have contributed to the problems which led to the offence and in view of the relative scarcity of information, and the likely range of sentences which the court will be minded to impose, that the court should obtain a pre-sentence report. One can then ask the court (whether magistrates or Crown Court judge) for a preliminary indication of whether it is in sympathy with that view. If it is not, then that is a clear indication that a custodial sentence, and most types of community sentence, are not in the court's mind and thus one can address the rest of the plea in mitigation to the other possible outcomes. If a pre-sentence report is then ordered the full plea in mitigation can be made when the report is to hand. It may be that otherwise there will be a great deal of repetition of material which is anyway contained in the eventual report.

18.3   Types of Sentence

We shall now consider the types of sentence which the court has the power to impose. It should not be forgotten that sentencing may have a number of purposes, some of which are mutually contradictory. They are generally considered to be:

(a) *Deterrence*. That by seeing that an accused is caught, convicted and punished in some disagreeable way for a crime, like-minded people may be deterred from committing such offences.

(b) *Retribution*. To express society's dislike for or outrage at the type of conduct for which the offender has been convicted.

(c) *Prevention*. Where the offender is a menace to society then by incarceration he is at least kept out of circulation for the period of that incarceration and society's welfare improved by his being prevented from committing further offences during that time.

(d) *Rehabilitation*. This aims at the reform of the offender, to help him to return to ordinary social living and to mend his ways and become a useful member of the community.

Until 1991, in pursuance of these diverse aims, sentences could be classified into two categories, namely *tariff* sentences, which represent so to speak the 'going rate' for the type of crime involved and which look to the punishment pure and simple of the offender, and *individualised* sentences which look in some way to treat the needs of the offender. The offender's needs will generally be treated by a rehabilitation-type sentence, e.g., community service or probation, although it should not be overlooked that rehabilitation may on occasion be prompted by something that also appears a deterrent to future misconduct. The aims of deterrence and rehabilitation are to some extent merged by the concepts in the Criminal Justice Act 1991 which treats most kinds of community sentences as 'punishment' as well as rehabilitation.

18.3.1   THE COURTS

We shall now consider the sentences available to the particular courts.

18.3.1.1   The Crown Court

The Crown Court may impose any penalty up to the maximum prescribed by law for the offence. Thus in the case of a theft which is punishable under the Theft Act by a penalty of up to seven years' imprisonment the court may impose seven years or less and/or a fine of an unlimited amount or any other penalty prescribed by law which is applicable up to the maximum for that type of penalty, e.g., community service up to the maximum. Moreover, where the Crown Court tries more than one offence in relation to the same offender, it may in principle impose *consecutive* prison sentences each within the maximum prescribed by statute for the offence or it may make those sentences *concurrent* so that they run together.

Example

An offender is charged with theft (maximum seven years) and burglary (maximum 14 years) and is convicted of both. The Crown Court (having a potential maximum of 21 years in total available) may decide to impose a sentence of two years in respect of the theft, and one year in respect of the burglary and make them consecutive. The total term to be served (subject to early release, see **18.3.2.1**) will be three years. If the court makes the terms concurrent the total term to be served will be two years.

18.3.1.2   Magistrates' courts

The magistrates' court has the power to impose a penalty of up to six months' imprisonment and/or a fine of £5,000 for any one offence unless the statutory maximum for the offence is less than that. An example is careless driving under s. 3 of the Road Traffic Act 1988 where the maximum punishment is a £1,000 fine and there is no power to imprison. Where magistrates try more than one offence against the same offender then their total powers are as follows:

(a)   If all the offences are summary offences the aggregate total sentence imposed must not exceed six months.

(b)   If however there are two or more offences both triable either way then the magistrates may impose up to a total aggregate sentence of 12 months.

(c)   If the magistrates convict of one offence triable either way and one purely summary offence the maximum is six months.

18.3.1.3   Which court?

As we have seen a magistrates' court may commit a person to the Crown Court for *trial* in the case of an either way offence or an offence triable only on indictment. In addition however, as we have seen, a magistrates' court, after hearing a case triable either way and convicting the offender, may commit him to the Crown Court for sentence if it is of the opinion that greater punishment should be inflicted than it has power to impose. Where this happens the Crown Court may deal with the defendant as if he had been convicted on indictment and thus impose a sentence on him up to the maximum provided by the statute concerned. By s. 38 of the Magistrates' Courts Act 1980 (inserted in redrafted form by the Criminal Justice Act 1991, s. 25) a magistrates' court may now only commit for sentence if it is of the opinion:

(a)   that the offence or the combination of the offence and one or more offences associated with it was so serious that greater punishment should be inflicted for the offence than the court has power to impose; or

(b)   in the case of a violent or sexual offence committed by a person who is not less than 21 years old, that a sentence of imprisonment for a term longer than the court has power to impose is necessary to protect the public from serious harm from him.

18.3.1.4   The powers of one court to deal with sentences imposed by others

Suspended sentences

It should be noted that the Crown Court may deal with a suspended sentence of imprisonment imposed either by that or any other Crown Court or by any magistrates' court. Thus any Crown Court may decide whether or not to activate a previously imposed suspended sentence on further conviction. A magistrates' court however can only deal with a suspended sentence imposed by itself or by some other magistrates' court.

Probation

The Crown Court can deal with an offender who has reoffended whilst on probation no matter which court imposed the probation order. However, if a probation order was made by a magistrates' court the Crown Court's sentencing powers in respect of the breach of probation and its powers of resentencing in respect of the original offence are limited to those of the magistrates. A magistrates' court can in general only deal with probation orders imposed either by itself or by some other magistrates' court, and in the case of other magistrates' courts the consent of the supervising court must be obtained. This is not generally a difficult matter and consents may be obtained by relatively informal means.

18.3.2 SENTENCING OFFENDERS OVER 21 YEARS OF AGE

18.3.2.1 Imprisonment

A person of 21 years or over may as we have seen be sentenced to imprisonment by the Crown Court up to the maximum length of the term fixed by the statute creating the offence in question, or by a magistrates' court within the limit of six months for any one offence or up to a maximum aggregate of 12 months when dealing with two or more offences triable either way. Time spent in custody before trial and during trial is treated as part of the term of imprisonment. The previous system of 'remission for good conduct' is replaced by a system of unconditional release, and release on licence, whereby prisoners of good behaviour may be released at certain stages during a sentence subject to recall in the case of further offending. In outline the system is:

(a) Offenders sentenced to 12 months or less are released after serving half of their sentence automatically and unconditionally if of good behaviour.

(b) Offenders sentenced to between 12 months and four years are released automatically on licence after having served half their sentence provided they are of good behaviour.

(c) Prisoners of good behaviour sentenced to more than four years are released automatically after serving two-thirds of their sentence but may be considered at the half-way point for release on licence by the Parole Board.

18.3.2.2 Legal aid and custodial sentences

A person who has not previously received a custodial sentence and who is not legally represented at the time of sentence cannot be sent to prison unless he has had the opportunity to apply for legal aid and declines to do so or his application for legal aid has been refused only on the grounds of means (s. 2(1), Powers of Criminal Courts Act 1973).

Some general comment on what one should say in a plea of mitigation appears later. Obviously unless there is some very special consideration in the case (e.g., a foreigner who above all fears a deportation order from the court) an immediately effective term of imprisonment is the worst thing that may happen to an offender. The plea in mitigation will generally be aimed above all else at avoiding this.

18.3.2.3 Suspended sentences under s. 22 of the Powers of Criminal Courts Act 1973

A court which passes a sentence of imprisonment for a term of no more than two years may order that it be suspended for a period of between one and two years. This latter period is called 'the operational period' and if the offender does not commit an imprisonable offence during that time the suspended sentence lapses. If however he does commit an imprisonable offence during that period the sentence is brought into effect unless the sentencing court for the later offence decides that it would be unjust to do this.

This power is available to both magistrates' courts and the Crown Court although naturally in the magistrates' court the period of imprisonment imposed is subject to the maximum powers of the magistrates (see **18.3.1.2**).

A suspended sentence is often seen by the layman or by the popular press as a very easy option since it appears that the criminal has walked out of court a 'free' man whereas other, lesser offenders may have received substantial fines. A suspended sentence however should in principle only be imposed if the court *first* decides to imprison the offender and then carries on separately to consider whether that sentence can be suspended. Suspended sentences should not be used in order to intimidate petty offenders. The court's powers to suspend a sentence are now more restricted than previously because by virtue of s. 22(2)(b) of the Powers of Criminal Courts Act 1973 (as substituted by the Criminal Justice Act 1991) it is provided that a court shall *not* pass a suspended sentence unless it is of the opinion: 'That the exercise of that power can be justified by the exceptional circumstances of the case.' This makes it even clearer that the court will in effect have already chosen a sentence of imprisonment before passing on to consider special circumstances which make its suspension desirable.

Activation of a suspended sentence

In what circumstances should a suspended sentence be activated? Suppose that a person who is convicted of an offence of dishonesty and who has some previous convictions is sentenced to a term of imprisonment for six months suspended for one year. That sentence will be activated if during the year he reoffends unless the court considers it unjust to impose it. Circumstances which might make a court hesitate to activate the original six months' term even after a further offence would be where, for example, the subsequent offence is of a completely different type, say an assault arising out of football hooliganism whereas previous offences have been for dishonesty, or where the second offence happened very late indeed during the operative period, e.g., after 11 months of the year had elapsed. In principle however a suspended sentence represents something of a 'last chance' for an offender and thus ought generally to be activated, in addition of course to any further punishment imposed for the subsequent offence.

Suspended sentence supervision order

The Crown Court has a further power not open to the magistrates' court which is a useful addition to the sentencing options. It has the power to impose a suspended sentence supervision order under which the offender receives a suspended sentence but in addition there is a condition that he should be under the supervision of a probation officer. To all intents and purposes this may be seen as something like a period of probation allied to a suspended sentence. Until 1991 it was not possible to combine probation with a custodial penalty although this is now permitted under the Criminal Justice Act 1991 and therefore this combination is likely largely to replace suspended sentence supervision orders since it will have the same net effect and is available to magistrates' courts as well as the Crown Court.

The magistrates' powers to activate a suspended sentence

It ought finally to be noted that a magistrates' court does not have the power to activate a suspended sentence imposed by the Crown Court although it does have the power to activate a suspended sentence imposed by itself or by any other magistrates' court. Where an offender comes before the magistrates' court whilst still subject to the operational period of a Crown Court suspended sentence, the magistrates must either commit the offender in custody or on bail to the Crown Court in relation to that matter or notify the Crown Court in writing of the action they have taken. It is then up to the Crown Court to take action in relation to the offender, if the judge of the Crown Court so requires. The magistrates may go on to sentence for the new offence which has occurred within the operational period. By not committing the offender to the Crown Court the magistrates are impliedly indicating that they do not consider it appropriate to activate the sentence.

18.3.2.4 Fines

A magistrates' court may impose an overall maximum fine of £5,000 per offence unless the statute creating the offence prescribes a different figure as the maximum. If the offence is also punishable with imprisonment the statute will indicate whether the fine is an alternative to imprisonment or may be imposed with it.

The Crown Court may fine an offender any amount at all unless statute prescribes a maximum. Fines can be imposed as well as or instead of imprisonment and in combination with almost all other penalties.

Fines are obviously an appropriate method of dealing with trivial offences, especially motoring offences (in combination with other penalties). They may also be appropriate for offences of dishonesty or even violence where the offences are not serious and the offender has no substantial criminal record. They do however present obvious problems of fairness. For example, it may seem in principle wrong to fine an individual who is only in receipt of welfare benefits since by definition welfare benefits are generally taken to be at subsistence level and it would be wrong to depress a person below even this. Equally however it is wrong that wealthy persons should in effect be able to 'buy' their way out of a sentence of imprisonment because of their ability to pay a substantial fine.

In the Crown Court this problem has always been left to the judge to decide. In the magistrates' courts however, s. 18 of the Criminal Justice Act 1991 attempted to impose a mathematical basis of fairness by providing so called 'unit fines' whereby a strictly mathematical formula was imposed depending upon the seriousness of the offence and the level of the offender's income. This system in its brief life gave rise to many allegedly ludicrous anomalies whereby, for example, relatively prosperous people were fined many hundreds of pounds for trivial driving offences, whereas impecunious persons were fined nominal amounts for quite serious offences, such as burglary.

The moral and computational difficulties caused by s. 18 of the 1991 Act have already been laid to rest because s. 65 of the Criminal Justice Act 1993 now inserts a new s. 18 into the 1991 Act and the new section reads:

(1) Before fixing the amount of any fine, a court shall enquire into the financial circumstances of the offender.

(2) The amount of any fine fixed by a court shall be such as, in the opinion of the court, reflects the seriousness of the offence.

(3) In fixing the amount of any fine, a court shall take into account the circumstances of the case including among other things, the financial circumstances of the offender so far as they are known, or appear, to the court . . .

This provision is supplemented by sch. 3 of the Act which enables the court to make a 'financial circumstances order' in respect of any offender whereby it will have the power to look carefully into his exact financial status in terms of income, outgoings and dependants.

The new s. 18 therefore allows the magistrates' court to employ a wide and general discretion in making the level of fine fit the seriousness of the offence and the means of the offender without being hamstrung by the complexities of the unit fine system.

Payment of fines is usually permitted by instalments over a period of one year. A fine is enforced by the clerk of the magistrates' court and a defendant may be arrested or summoned before the court and committed to prison for non-payment of fines.

18.3.2.5 Community sentences

A community sentence consists of one or more community orders (Criminal Justice Act 1991, s. 6). These community orders are as follows:

(a) probation order;
(b) community service order;
(c) combination order;
(d) curfew order;
(e) supervision order;
(f) attendance centre order.

Of these, the first four are available in respect of offenders aged 16 or over; a supervision order is available for an offender aged between 10 and 17; and an attendance sentence order is available for an offender aged between 10 and 20.

We shall now discuss the orders which apply to offenders over the age of 21 in turn; those which apply only to persons under that age are dealt with at **18.3.3.2**.

Probation order

All the sentences so far discussed (with the possible exception of a suspended sentence supervision order in the Crown Court) are in the nature of tariff sentences. They look to punishment rather than reform. Probation however may be imposed by either magistrates or the Crown Court. Either court dealing with an offender who is 17 or over may, with his consent, place him on probation for a period of between six months and three years. The nature of probation is that a person must keep in touch with his probation officer and comply with the latter's directions and be of good behaviour. He must in principle visit the probation officer at times to be specified by the latter.

The court may additionally impose conditions in the probation order. Examples of additional conditions might be that the person resides at a fixed address, e.g., with his family or some other relative or at a probation hostel, or that he receives treatment for some medical condition or attends a day centre, i.e. premises where there are facilities and advice to assist in the rehabilitation of offenders. Also negative requirements may be imposed requiring the person on probation to refrain from certain activities during the term of the probation order.

The probation officer allocated to the person on probation will be one who is attached to the magistrates' court area in which the person on probation resides and this may be different from the area of the court imposing the sentence. The magistrates' court for that area then becomes known as the 'supervising court'.

Probation is a sentence in its own right and can now be combined with most other penalties, in particular a suspended sentence, a fine or a community service order.

A probation order, like a suspended sentence, is not meant to be an easy option. It should only be imposed when someone seems to be the kind of person for whom probation would be useful in the sense of assisting his reform or rehabilitation. An offender must consent to a community order such as probation and the consent obtained from the offender must be genuine and must not be extracted, for example, by the judge indicating that the offender either consents or will as an alternative receive a custodial sentence. A probation order is only ever made after a pre-sentence report has recommended that probation would be helpful in the circumstances of an individual's case. It would be most obviously useful for someone who has some discernible social or family problem. It would not for example be imposed upon a mature person who is living in settled family circumstances without any apparent difficulty of adjustment to the community.

If there is a further offence committed during the period of the probation order or some other breach of its terms, then when the offender is brought back before the sentencing court or the supervising court, the individual may be sentenced for the original offence in addition to being sentenced for the new offence. The original probation order may be quashed and another sentence substituted for it, or the probation order may be left in force with a fine being imposed for the breach, or may be extended for a further term if the accused consents.

Community service order

Where the court is dealing with an offender aged 16 or over and the offence is an imprisonable one a comunity service order may be made. This is an order that the person perform without pay work which is deemed to be of value to the community. The order must fix the precise number of hours to be worked and there is a minimum of 40 and a maximum of 240 (120 if the offender is aged only 16). If the offender fails to comply with the order he may be fined up to £1,000 or the order may be revoked and the offender resentenced.

Before such a sentence can be imposed there must be a pre-sentence report from a probation officer indicating that the offender is suitable for the work and that he consents and that appropriate work is available in the locality. The type of work is usually gardening, improving public spaces, decorating old people's homes, etc. It must be performed under the supervision of a probation officer.

Whilst there is no prescribed maximum age this sentence is often thought to be appropriate for young offenders. This is especially the case where the offender has been convicted of offences which are unpleasant but not necessarily extremely serious, for example vandalism of some kind. The work is meant to be both a temporary restriction on his liberty and to give him some sense of usefulness and social purpose.

A community service order may not be combined with most other penalties for the same offence although it may be combined with disqualification from driving, endorsement of driving licence and orders for compensation and costs. It may however, as in the case of probation, be combined with other penalties and imposed in conjunction with penalties for another offence where these have been tried together.

Combination order

A combination order is a mixture of a probation order and a community service order. It is particularly aimed at 'persistent property offenders', e.g., vandals and burglars. The probation element must be for a minimum of 12 months and the community service element between 40 and 120 hours. A pre-sentence report must be obtained which should specifically recommend this form of punishment.

Curfew order

The curfew order has been introduced by s. 12 of the Criminal Justice Act 1991 (although the relevant provisions are not yet in force). It requires the offender to remain at a particular place (which is obviously likely to be at home) for between two and 12 hours on any days over a period which must not exceed six months from the date of sentence. It is specifically aimed, according to the White Paper which preceded the Crimial Justice Act 1991, at preventing some forms of theft of and from cars, pub brawls and other similar disorders. A curfew order may also be used to keep people away from particular places. The order must be preceded by a pre-sentence report which must consider the attitude of any person likely to be affected by the enforced presence of the accused! Electronic monitoring by tagging may be employed. The consent of the offender is required but refusal of consent may well involve an alternative custodial sentence.

18.3.2.6 Absolute and conditional discharge under s. 7 of the Powers of Criminal Courts Act 1973

The court may impose these penalties in relation to relatively trivial offences. A court dealing with an offender which does not wish to punish him at all, for example because his offence was merely technical, may give an absolute discharge. An example would be in the case of a driving offence of strict liablity where there is no real moral blame on the defendant. Take for example a defendant who has just had his vehicle serviced by a reputable garage when the brakes suddenly fail. He would be guilty of the offence of driving a car with defective brakes, for which no *mens rea* is required. However in all the circumstances a court would not consider his offence sufficiently blameworthy to impose any punishment and an absolute discharge would suffice.

A conditional discharge is like a somewhat watered down version of a suspended sentence in that, if the offender does not offend during the period of the discharge, the conditional discharge lapses. Thus an individual who is conditionally discharged for a year and commits no further offence is then free of any punishment in respect of the original offence, but if he does reoffend then in principle he can be dealt with again for the first offence. Discharges are imposed where immediate punishment is deemed to be unnecessary and probation is not required by the circumstances. A conditional discharge may apply for a period of up to three years.

18.3.2.7 Binding over

One final method of dealing with an offender should be mentioned. This is binding over to keep the peace. This ancient power was originally contained in the Justice of the Peace Act 1361 and is now in s. 115 of the Magistrates' Courts Act 1980. The way in which this power is used is subject to a great deal of local variation.

Its proper use is where a person before the court has by his behaviour led the court to believe that a breach of the peace might arise from his future behaviour. In such a case that person may be bound over to keep the peace and be of good behaviour in a given sum of money. If he fails to keep the peace within the period fixed by the court then the sum of money is forfeited. Refusal to enter into the recognisance may involve him being sent to prison for contempt of court. Some magistrates use this power, probably quite wrongly, in respect of almost any kind of offence including shoplifting, but its most appropriate use is in relatively petty disputes involving disturbances or minor violence, in particular quarrels between neighbours. Commonly in such cases the CPS decline to become involved, and the neighbours will issue private prosecutions against each other for minor assaults arising out of some fracas. When they come before the court, it is likely to bind both of them over to keep the peace. A bind over may be ordered in addition to any other penalty for an offence and indeed even where the person concerned has been acquitted. Anyone before the court may be subject to a bind over, even a witness, as is commonly the case in disturbances arising out of industrial disputes or disputes between hunt saboteurs and hunt followers.

18.3.3 SENTENCING OFFENDERS BETWEEN 17 AND 20 YEARS OF AGE

18.3.3.1 Custodial sentences

An offender within these age ranges is sentenced to detention in a young offender's institution. Under s. 1A of the Criminal Justice Act 1982 a convicting court may impose such a sentence in respect of an imprisonable offence if it considers that the defendant qualifies. The maximum term is the maximum available to that court in respect of the offence in question, in other words a magistrates' court may impose detention for up to six months for each offence (up to the overall maximum of 12 months) unless the statute in question prescribes some other maximum, and the Crown Court may impose up to the maximum for the offence in question. The *minimum* term which the court may impose is, however, prescribed and is 21 days.

These orders are broadly subject to the same provisions in respect of release on licence as sentences of imprisonment for persons of 21 or over in adult prisons. In addition it should be noted that the court which imposes a detention order must:

(a) give reasons why the defendant qualifies for an order; and
(b) explain to the defendant in ordinary language why it is imposing such a detention order.

It should also be noted that the courts have no power to *suspend* custodial sentences in respect of persons under 21. Accordingly when one is presenting a plea in mitigation for someone within this age group it is worth stressing in the plea in mitigation that if the offender were 21 or over the option of a suspended sentence would be available to the court and that therefore the court might consider that this offender merits a 'last chance' by virtue of some non-custodial sentence since the courts do not have the option of suspending the sentence which they might otherwise impose.

18.3.3.2 Non-custodial penalties

(a) Such offenders may be fined up to the same maximum as an adult (an attendance centre order may be imposed for non-payment of a fine in addition to any other powers).
(b) A community service order may be made in respect of an offender within this age group with his consent and subject to the same conditions as previously described.
(c) Probation may be imposed with the consent of a person in the 17 to 20 age group.
(d) A supervision order or attendance centre order may be made (see below).
(e) Absolute and conditional discharges may be imposed upon offenders within this age group, in the same circumstances and subject to the same criteria as in the case of offenders aged 21 or more.

Supervision order
These are available only in respect of offenders aged up to 17. The order may apply for up to three years and the supervisor is usually a social worker for the local authority in whose area the offender

lives, although it may sometimes be a probation officer. It is the duty of the supervisor to 'advise, assist and befriend' the offender. In many ways it is similar to a probation order but the range of extra conditions is somewhat wider, for example the offender may be ordered to live away from home for up to 90 days at a time, e.g., on a useful course of training. It will be noted that there is an overlap between the age ranges so that an offender of 17 may be given either supervision or probation as the court sees fit in the light of any recommendations made.

Attendance centre order

The court dealing with an offender under the age of 21 for an imprisonable offence may make an attendance centre order if:

(a) the court has been notified that there is a suitable centre available; and

(b) the offender has not previously received a custodial sentence.

The number of hours attendance must be fixed by the court. It must be at least 12 and not more than 36.

Attendance centres are generally run by police officers in their leisure time. There is a certain amount of discipline and physical exercise and perhaps, depending on availability of staff, handicraft. The aim is partly to deprive the defender of leisure time but also to encourage more sensible use of leisure. Often such centres are held on Saturday afternoons. Although not primarily intended for football hooligans it has occurred to magistrates that by making attendance centre orders for one hour at a time over successive Saturdays they do have the power to prevent an offender attending football matches for virtually an entire season. More commonly, attendance centre orders in two-hour sessions are imposed.

It should also be noted that an attendance centre order may be made for default in paying a fine or breach of a probation or supervision order.

18.3.4 **PENALTIES IN ROAD TRAFFIC CASES**

The Road Traffic Acts 1988 and 1991 and the Road Traffic Offenders Act 1988 provide a code for penalties in the case of criminal offences committed in connection with vehicles. In essence there are two types of offences, namely:

(a) Those punishable by disqualification which may be either mandatory or discretionary.

(b) Those where, in addition to some other penalty imposed (e.g., a fine), the offender's driving licence must be endorsed with a certain number of penalty points as prescribed in the Road Traffic Offenders Act 1988 and the Road Traffic Act 1991. In some cases the offence, however committed, is subject to a prescribed number of penalty points (e.g., using a motor vehicle with defective brakes — three points), in others there is a band of penalty points prescribed and the court may impose any number of points within that band depending on the gravity of the offence. Thus for careless driving, which may vary in circumstances from one isolated act of inattention to something only just short of dangerous driving, a band of between three and nine points is prescribed.

In principle when, within a period of three years the individual has had endorsed on his licence a total of 12 penalty points or more, he must be disqualified for at least six months unless there are certain circumstances which make the court think it appropriate not to disqualify him.

That is an outline of the code and we shall now consider the provisions in somewhat more detail.

18.3.4.1 **Disqualification**

Certain offences carry mandatory disqualifications, e.g.:

(a) causing death by dangerous driving;

(b) dangerous driving;

(c) offences connected with driving with excessive alcohol in the blood or when unfit through drugs.

In general terms, where an offence carries obligatory endorsement, e.g., careless driving, there is a *discretion* in the court to disqualify the defendant for the offences alone. They would normally only do so if the facts of the offence were very gross indeed.

Quite separately from the above, an offender may be disqualified under the points system, still often called the 'totting up' system. Where an offender is convicted and a penalty is imposed which involves the number of points endorsed on the offender's licence within the preceding three years totalling 12 or more, the court must in principle disqualify him for at least six months unless it thinks it fit not to do so.

18.3.4.2 Endorsement of driving licence

A driving licence must be endorsed with the appropriate number of penalty points within the limits set out in sch. 2 to the Road Trafffic Offenders Act 1988 unless there are circumstances permitting the court not to do so (to which we shall come in due course).

If the offender is disqualified for the offence itself (rather than under the totting up provisions) then the licence is not endorsed with further penalty points although particulars of the offence for which the offender is disqualified are recorded on the licence. In other words, a person who is being disqualified for a specific offence does not receive any penalty points.

Example

An offender who has a clean licence is disqualified for a particularly gross case of speeding (say exceeding 100 mph on a motorway) for a period of 6 months. Speeding carries from 3 to 6 penalty points. However, in the present case these would not be endorsed on the offender's licence. Thus at the end of his period of disqualification, the offender still has no penalty points on his licence and so, if when he begins driving again he commits other offences for which the total penalty points are, say, 10 he will not be subject to disqualification for exceeding 12 penalty points as he would otherwise have been.

Some offences for which there are prima facie obligatory disqualification (such as dangerous driving) also carry an alternative number of penalty points (in the case of dangerous driving between 3 and 11 points). This is because if there happen to be special circumstances justifying not imposing the otherwise obligatory disqualification, the court then has open to it the power to impose a number of penalty points as an alternative.

It should be noted that where the defendant is convicted of two or more endorsable offences which arise out of offences committed on the same occasion then only the highest number of penalty points will be endorsed and not the cumulative total, unless the court thinks fit to order otherwise in which case it must state its reasons in open court. Thus suppose an offender commits the offence of uninsured driving (6 to 8 points) and speeding (3 to 6 points) he only acquires 8 penalty points and not up to 14.

18.3.4.3 For what period should the offender be disqualified?

If the offence carries obligatory disqualification then generally this is for at least 12 months. Above that period then the court must weigh a number of important factors. It has been stressed in many cases that the court should be careful not to impose too long a disqualification from driving. In the case of young offenders, particularly those who are 'car mad', the effect of over-lengthy disqualification is to make them lose all hope of recovering their driving licence and to merely invite them to commit offences of driving whilst disqualified. This is not to say however that very lengthy disqualifications may not in some situations be appropriate. Indeed disqualification for life is possible and in some cases may be rightly applied.

It should also be noted that an offender who has been disqualified for a longer period than two years may apply to the court after two years or the halfway date of the period, whichever is the longer, for the disqualification to be lifted. The prosecution must naturally be informed of the application and there is a hearing in open court at which the prosecution will describe the circumstances of the original offence and may put forward their objections.

Under the totting up system a disqualification is generally for at least six months. It may be for a longer period within the court's discretion.

It should also be noted that periods of disqualification now always run concurrently and not consecutively. Therefore if an offender is convicted of a number of offences, whether or not committed on the same occasion, and is liable to disqualification either under the totting up system and/or for the offences themselves, any disqualifications imposed must run concurrently. Of course the total length of the sentences imposed will affect the court's overall view of the gravity of the situation and thus whilst sentences of say 18 months' disqualification and six months' disqualification may be imposed for different offences it is the longer penalty which will reflect the court's overall view of what is appropriate for the whole 'disqualification package'.

Finally, it should be remarked that an offender cannot be disqualified unless he is given the opportunity to appear. Thus where an offender is invited to plead guilty by post, say to an offence of speeding, he will do so while sending his licence to the court as is required. If the points to be imposed for speeding take the points on his licence to a total of more than 12 then he is prima facie liable for disqualification. It does not inevitably mean that he will be disqualified because there may be circumstances in which the court will see fit not to impose that ultimate penalty, but certainly in such a case the matter will be adjourned to enable the defendant to attend court.

18.3.4.4 When may disqualification or endorsement not be imposed?

Where disqualification for the offence itself (rather than under the penalty points system) is obligatory, or endorsement of penalty points is obligatory, they must on the face of it be imposed. However in either case if the defendant can show 'special reasons' for either not disqualifying or for not imposing the endorsement at all, then the court may decline to do so. 'Special reasons' however in this context must relate to the circumstances of the offence itself *not* to the offender's personal circumstances and must not therefore be in the nature of mitigation generally. A good example of a reason which might justify non-disqualification is the case of a drink-driving offence where the offender's orange juice was 'laced' with vodka without his knowledge so that he is taken just over the legal limit (if of course he had any reason to suspect that he was drunk and his drink had been laced he could not argue this if he had continued to drive). Or that in the case of an offence of dangerous driving that the offender was driving someone to hospital in an emergency when the act occurred. Likewise, in the case of a speeding offence where endorsement of penalty points is obligatory, if the offender admitted the offence but was able to show that he was driving a dangerously ill passenger to hospital at high speed, the magistrates, whilst finding guilt proved, might well impose only an absolute discharge and no endorsement.

It must be said that the courts have not been eager to find special reasons established. Evidence on oath must be given by the offender in each case and it is not sufficient for these matters to be advanced merely in a plea in mitigation. The offender may well be subject to searching cross-examination by the prosecution. Although the prosecution do not generally concern themselves at all with sentence, this is one occasion where they do have an overriding duty to see that justice is done and that any reasons put forward as justifying non-endorsement or non-disqualification are thoroughly examined.

In the case of *discretionary* disqualification (e.g., careless driving) then *general mitigation* can be advanced in relation to any proper matter, either the circumstances of the offence or the offender's personal circumstances, with a view to avoiding disqualification entirely or of obtaining a reduction in the period imposed.

18.3.4.5 Disqualification under the penalty points system

If an offender is sentenced for an offence and penalty points are imposed which take his total to over 12 within the relevant period of three years he should in principle be disqualified for six months or longer. However an offender need not be disqualified if there are 'grounds for mitigating the normal consequences of the conviction'. This is not the same as the case previously described where there are *special reasons* for not imposing penalty points or an endorsement. In the former case the matters must concern the circumstances of the *offence* itself. However in connection with non-disqualification under the penalty points system the court may have regard to all the circumstances including the personal circumstances of the offender

Part II of the Road Traffic Offenders Act 1988 however provides that a court in deciding on this matter may only take into account hardship to the offender caused by loss of his licence where the hardship is 'exceptional'. Unfortunately there is no definition of 'exceptional hardship' and little guidance in case law. Circumstances which under previous law were considered appropriate for avoiding the consequences of disqualification often involved, for example: loss of a job because it depended on a driving licence, or where, because of the remoteness of the place of work, a car was necessary; the need to have a vehicle for important family reasons, e.g., transport of a disabled relative. Such things *might* still be sufficient. Hardship which is less than exceptional, e.g., for a private individual who does not need his motor vehicle for his job and who would be merely inconvenienced by having to use public transport, would not be an adequate reason for not imposing disqualification.

In addition the court may *not* take into account the triviality of the present offence. Thus the fact that the speeding offence concerned only involved exceeding the speed limit by, say, five mph would not in itself be a ground for mitigating the normal consequences. If three points imposed in this case takes the offender past a total of 12 then he ought still, in principle, to be disqualified.

It may well be that a person appears before the court and has penalty points imposed which takes his total over 12 but is able to persuade the magistrates that there is exceptional hardship and thus is not disqualified. What if a further offence is committed still within the period which would take his penalty points up by a further number? The 1988 Act provides that a person who has been excused disqualification because of mitigating circumstances on a previous occasion may not rely on any circumstances which the court took into account on that occasion. So for example one cannot avoid disqualification on two consecutive hearings merely by arguing that loss of a licence will involve loss of a job. In such a situation, if that is the only mitigating circumstance, disqualification will be imposed on the second occasion.

Accordingly the court should carefully record the mitigating factors it found present when dealing with an offender so that these are available in any future case. All too often these mitigating factors are recorded in extremely short summary form and it may well therefore be the case that one can give a fuller version of the reasons on the second occasion.

It also leads to the somewhat strange conclusion that if one has two separate excellent grounds for avoiding the normal consequences of the totting up system it would usually only be wise to put one of them forward. Suppose for example that a person desperately needed his car because he lived in a remote place and needed to transport a disabled relative to and from hospital, and that he needed his driving licence for his job. If his penalty points were taken over 12 he would be well advised to put forward only one of these cogent reasons so that in the event of him offending on a further occasion he could then use the other.

It ought finally to be repeated that in driving offences, disqualification and endorsement may be combined with most other penalties. Very commonly they are combined with fines. It should not be overlooked however that driving penalties may be imposed in addition to custodial sentences, for example in the case of causing death by dangerous driving where both a lengthy disqualification and a custodial penalty would be usual.

Below is a list outlining some of the more common endorsable offences and the relevant available penalty points:

	Penalty points
Causing death by dangerous driving	3–11
Dangerous driving	3–11
Careless driving	3–9
Failing to stop after an accident	5–10
Speeding	3–6
Disobeying traffic lights	3
Using uninsured motor vehicle	6–8
Driving when unfit through drink or drugs; or with excess alcohol in blood	3–11

18.4 Other Orders

The court may also consider the following orders which may be imposed on an offender either additionally to or instead of other forms of punishment.

18.4.1 COMPENSATION ORDERS

Under s. 35 of the Powers of Criminal Courts Act 1973 (as amended by s. 104 of the Criminal Justice Act 1988), a court may order compensation for any personal injury, loss or damage (including payment for funeral expenses or bereavement) resulting from any offence (including any offences taken into consideration) when imposing any other penalty, or instead of imposing any other penalty on an offender. However a court cannot make any order in respect of injury, loss or damage arising out of the presence of a motor vehicle on a road unless:

(a) the offence concerned was one under the Theft Act 1968 and damage occurred to the property in question whilst it was out of the owner's possession (e.g., damage to a motor vehicle which was taken away for joy-riding); or

(b) the offender was uninsured at the time and compensation is not payable under the Motor Insurers Bureau Schemes.

The court may make an order up to any amount in the Crown Court or a maximum of £5,000 in respect of any one offence in the magistrates' court but the court must have regard to the offender's means in the same way as they must have regard to those means in relation to imposing a fine.

A compensation order may be made as an alternative to dealing with the offender in any other way and if the offender has not got sufficient income to pay both the fine and compensation the court ought to impose a compensation order to ensure that the victim is compensated. Compensation orders are enforced by the court in the same way as a fine with the ultimate penalty of imprisonment for non-payment.

The Magistrates' Association Sentencing Guidelines (1992) set out guidelines for awards for common types of minor injury e.g.: loss of tooth £300–£500; sprain £100–£400; bruise (depending on size) £50–£75.

18.4.2 FORFEITURE ORDERS

Under s. 43 of the Powers of Criminal Courts Act 1973, where the court convicts an offender of an offence which is punishable on indictment with two years' imprisonment or more it may order forfeiture of any property which was in the offender's possession or control at the time of apprehension if the property was used for committing or facilitating any offence or was intended by the offender to be used for that purpose.

Thus for example the owner may be ordered to forfeit a car which has been used to transport stolen goods.

18.4.3 CONFISCATION ORDERS

Under s. 71 of the Criminal Justice Act 1988, a Crown Court may, in addition to dealing with a defendant in any other way, make a confiscation order in respect of the proceeds of the crime. In order for this provision to apply the defendant must have benefited from the relevant offence (including any offence taken into consideration) in a sum of at least £10,000. If he is convicted of more than one offence then the benefit of all the offences is taken into account. The amount that can be ordered is the benefit gained (i.e., at least £10,000 must be involved for this order to be made).

18.4.4 COSTS

A convicted offender may be ordered to pay costs to the prosecution as described earlier (see 2.4).

18.5 The Structured Approach to Sentencing under the Criminal Justice Act 1991 (as amended)

The Criminal Justice Act 1991 imposed a new structured approach to sentencing. As is well known, in its short life the Act has given rise to serious criticism and important reforms to it have already been introduced in the Criminal Justice Act 1993, in force in August 1993. The Act provided that the sentencing court should consider sentences in ascending order of severity. Thus the court should commence by considering whether any penalty beyond a discharge or fine is merited; if so then the court should first consider a 'community sentence' bearing in mind that these are said to be sentences of a serious nature. Only if the court considers that no community sentence is appropriate will it proceed to consider custodial sentences. The Act commences with the most serious matters and we shall therefore follow that order.

18.5.1 CUSTODIAL SENTENCES

Section 1(2) of the 1991 Act, as substituted by s. 66, Criminal Justice Act 1993, provides that a court:

. . . shall not pass a custodial sentence on the offender unless it is of the opinion—

    (a)   that the offence, or the combination of the offences and one or more offences associated with it was so serious that only such a sentence can be justified for the offence; or
    (b)   where the offence is a violent or sexual offence, that only such a sentence would be adequate to protect the public from serious harm from him.

In addition to this provision a custodial sentence may be passed if an offender refuses to consent to a community sentence proposed by the court of a kind which requires his consent.

The crucial change of emphasis here is away from consideration of the accused's previous criminal record and towards concentration entirely on the offence before the court and other offences associated with it.

18.5.1.1 The seriousness test

The court must have regard to the 'seriousness' of the offence and other associated offences at which it is looking. Thus notwithstanding that there are 10, or 50 offences dealt with at the same time, if they are all in themselves trivial, the court cannot conclude that the offender is simply such a pest that he ought to be given a custodial sentence. This requirement of 'seriousness' is said to provide a 'custody threshold requirement'.

18.5.1.2 Length of sentence

Section 2 of the 1991 Act deals with the length of custodial sentences and prescribes that the time imposed must be 'commensurate with the seriousness of the offence', or the combination of the offence and one or more *offences* associated with it; or in the case of violent or sexual offences for such longer term (not exceeding the maximum) as the court considers necessary to protect the public from serious harm.

18.5.1.3 Other important matters when imposing custody

(a)   Any court passing a custodial sentence is obliged by s. 1(4) of the 1991 Act to explain in open court that either or both paragraphs of s. 1(2) apply to the case and to explain why it has formed that view. The explanation must be in ordinary language so that the offender understands why he is receiving a custodial sentence.

(b)   *Pre-sentence reports*. Before giving the reason for selecting a custodial sentence, s. 3(1) of the 1991 Act requires that the court shall 'obtain and consider a pre-sentence report' in any case except where the offence is triable only on indictment. This latter provision avoids the court having always to have a pre-sentence report where the serious nature of the offence makes custody inevitable, though even in such a case the court has the option of obtaining a pre-sentence report.

(c)   Section 3(3)(a) of the 1991 Act provides that in addition to the pre-sentence report the court shall: 'take into account all such information about the circumstances of the offence (including any aggravating or mitigating factors) as is available to it.' This in turn imports consideration of ss. 28 and 29 of the 1991 Act which say in turn: 'Nothing in [the relevant part of the Act] shall prevent a court from mitigating an offender's sentence by taking into account any such matters as, in the opinion of the court, are relevant in mitigation of sentence.' (s. 28(1)). Section 29, as newly inserted by s. 66 of the Criminal Justice Act 1993 provides:

(1)   In considering the seriousness of any offence, the court may take into account any previous convictions of the offender or any failure of his to respond to previous sentences.

(2)   In considering the seriousness of any offence committed while the offender was on bail, the court shall treat the fact that it was committed in those circumstances as an aggravating factor.

In its short lived first incarnation, the original s. 29 of the 1991 Act, which was amended in August 1993 by the provision set out above, seriously constrained the right of the sentencing court to have regard to previous convictions. Indeed, it expressly said 'an offence shall not be regarded as more serious . . . by reason of any previous convictions of the offender'. A number of well publicised cases in early 1993 concentrated on the supposed inability of judges to pass harsh sentences on frequent offenders because of this section and following other criticism by politicians and the higher judiciary this led to the amendment in the terms set out above. The effect is now to give the court a wide power to consider the whole of the past record of the offender when sentencing and, in particular, to take into account failure to respond to previous sentences (i.e. apparently lenient sentences such as probation), and the fact that the offence was committed on bail, if that is the case, is to be treated as an aggravating factor.

As indicated previously, however, one still only reaches a consideration of custodial sentences as a last resort and the basic framework of the 1991 Act is not affected. That Act requires the court previously to have considered 'community sentences'.

18.5.2   COMMUNITY SENTENCES

The policy under the Criminal Justice Act 1991 is that more offenders should be punished 'in the community' and thus the concept of community sentence has substantially developed by certain changes in status of probation, which previously did not count as a 'sentence' or 'punishment' at all, and by other developments, e.g., of the combination order and the curfew order. The principle of the legislation is that community sentences will be viewed as serious forms of punishment and not an easy option for sentencers nor an agreeable alternative to prison for offenders. Because of the supposed seriousness of these sentences, by s. 6 of the 1991 Act the court must not pass a community sentence unless:

(a)   the offence (or the combination of the offence and one or more associated offences) is serious enough to warrant it; and

(b)   the court has considered which order or orders are most suitable for the offender; and

(c)   the restrictions on the offender's liberty imposed by the order or orders are commensurate with the seriousness of the offence or the combination of the offence and one or more offences associated with it.

In addition the court must obtain a pre-sentence report whenever it is considering:

(a)   a probation order which includes requirements additional to the standard conditions;

(b)   a community service order; or

(c)   a combination order.

A pre-sentence report is therefore *not* mandatory if the court is considering merely a probation order which does not include additional requirements, a curfew order or an attendance centre order, although in many cases it will be good practice for the court to obtain one.

The consent of the offender is required as we have seen in the case of probation orders, community service orders, combination orders and curfew orders.

18.5.3   DEVELOPMENTS BETWEEN THE 1991 ACT AND THE 1993 ACT

In its short life the relevant sections of the 1991 Act and the sentencing policy they encapsulated came in for a great deal of criticism as improperly tying the hands of sentencers, especially by the statutory limitations in the former s. 29 of the 1991 Act on the extent to which previous criminal behaviour could be taken into account. The 1993 amendments restore a wide discretion, as indicated above, to take past criminal behaviour into account when considering the seriousness of any offence. It remains to be seen whether the courts will interpret this requirement strictly, so that the present offence is only rendered more serious by the fact that it clearly forms a continuing pattern of specific criminal behaviour (as in the case of a persistent burglar), or whether the courts will feel free to take into account the whole history of criminality, even for offences very different from the one presently under consideration.

Some useful decisions were given in guideline cases under the 1991 Act in the Court of Appeal on 27 November 1992 and these were aimed at establishing sentencing policy under that Act. These cases are reported consecutively in the second volume of the 1993 All England Law Reports. They provide additional guidelines, some features of which will still be useful when considering sentencing under the 1993 amendments:

(a)   In *R* v *Cunningham* [1993] 2 All ER 15 the court observed that the purpose of the custodial sentence is primarily to punish and deter and therefore that the purpose of such a sentence must be commensurate with the punishment and deterrence required. The 'seriousness' of an offence means such things as the question of how many people it harms and to what extent. Thereafter, once a custodial penalty has been chosen, it would be a legitimate factor to take into account such matters as the prevalence of the type of offence.

(b)   In *R* v *Oliver* [1993] 2 All ER 9 the court considered to what extent regular dwelling-house burglary could be considered 'serious' and the relevance of the fact that some offences occurred in breach of a probation order.

(c) In *R* v *Cox* [1993] 2 All ER 19 the court observed that for the purposes of s. 1(2)(a) of the 1991 Act an offence is 'so serious that only a custodial sentence can be justified' if it is such as to make all right-thinking members of the public, knowing all the facts, feel that justice would not be done by the passing of anything other than a custodial sentence. The prevalence of a particular class of offence and public concern are relevant to the seriousness of an offence (the offence was one of reckless driving (now dangerous driving) including going at 30 miles an hour along the pavement for some part of the time).

(d) In *R* v *Bexley and others* [1993] 2 All ER 23 the court explained the interrelationship of subsections 29(1) and (2) of the 1991 Act and the extent to which circumstances of other offences may be taken into account. The court observed that only those which disclosed some aggravating factor in the instant offence or its combination with another offence (e.g., deliberately targeting or selecting elderly victims; or persistently using stolen credit cards to acquire large amounts of luxury goods) would fall within the section.

(e) In *R* v *Baverstock* [1993] 2 All ER 33 the court indicated that a sentencing court must be given details of the 'circumstances' of previous convictions for offences committed by the defendant and that it is not for the prosecution to decide what circumstances of other offences may be relevant nor should there be argument between prosecution and defence about the relevance and admissibility of the material to be placed before the judge. The established procedure in relation to previous convictions from before the 1991 Act remains appropriate. The fact that an offence was committed whilst on bail is an aggravating feature of the present offence.

18.6 Guideline Cases

Quite apart from the cases which we have just considered on the interpretation of ss. 1, 2 and 29 of the Criminal Justice Act 1991, for some years the Court of Appeal has provided sentencing guidelines in respect of serious offences. The object of these is to lead to a greater consistency in sentencing in such cases. There is no space in this text to set out in detail the principles from each of these guideline cases though regard must be had to them where the offence with which one is concerned in practice is one for which guidelines have been given. The guideline cases include the offences of rape (*R* v *Billam* [1986] 1 WLR 349); offences involving breach of trust (*R* v *Barrick* (1985) 7 Cr App R(S) 142); drug importation and supply (*R* v *Aramah* (1982) 4 Cr App R(S) 407); armed robbery (*R* v *Turner* (1975) 61 Cr App R 61); and social security fraud (*R* v *Stewart* (1987) 9 Cr App R(S) 135).

By way of example, extracts indicating the nature of these guidelines are given from two such cases.

18.6.1 *R* v *BARRICK* (1985) 7 Cr App R(S) 142

This case deals with persons in a position of trust, e.g., accountants, bank employees and solicitors, who have used that trusted position to defraud partners, clients or employers of sizeable sums of money. Usually such people will have previous good character and it is virtually certain that they will never offend again as they will never again in their lives be able to secure similar employment. There is likely to be substantial disgrace and hardship for the offender and his family.

In such cases the guidelines indicate that the case will attract immediate custody unless the circumstances are exceptional or the amount is small. If the amount is less than £10,000 imprisonment for a short term up to 18 months is appropriate; between £10,000 and £50,000 the term should be about two to three years; for larger sums the term of three and a half to four years may be appropriate. In the event of a guilty plea a discount should be given.

In addition the court should take into account the period over which the thefts were committed; the use to which the money was put; the effect upon the victims; the impact upon the public and public confidence; the effect upon fellow employees or business partners; the effect on the offender; the offender's history; matters of mitigation special to himself; any help given by him to the police.

18.6.2   *R v BILLAM* [1986] 1 WLR 349

This case deals with the offence of rape. For rape committed by an adult with no special features a figure of five years is the starting point if there was a plea of not guilty. For a rape committed by two or more, or rape by a burglar, or by a person who is in a position of responsibility towards the victim, or by a person who kidnaps the victim, the starting point is eight years.

At the top of the scale is a defendant who has carried out a campaign of rape on different victims for whom 15 years or more is appropriate. In addition to this if the defendant's behaviour has been perverted or psychopathic such that he is clearly a danger for an indefinite time, a life sentence will be appropriate.

The following factors may also aggravate the crime: violence over and above the force necessary to commit the crime; use of a weapon to frighten or wound; repeated rape; a carefully planned rape; previous convictions for sexual offences; victim is subjected to indignities or perversion; victim very old or very young; physical or mental effect upon the victim. In all these cases the sentence should be substantially higher than the starting point.

A plea of guilty, since it will relieve the victim of embarrassment and distress, should result in some reduction from the appropriate sentence. The fact that the victim may have been foolish (e.g., by accepting a lift in a car from a stranger) is not a mitigating factor and her previous sexual experience is also irrelevant. If the victim has behaved in a manner which indicated to the defendant that she would consent to sexual intercourse that is of some mitigation. The offender's previous good character is of minor relevance.

18.7   The Plea in Mitigation

We have now considered the total package of orders which may be made against a convicted defendant. We have considered penalties on the defendant, the making of compensation orders, and the question of costs has previously been discussed in connection with the financing of criminal litigation (see **Chapter 2**).

It is now appropriate to consider the plea in mitigation which will be made in an attempt to persuade the court to impose some lesser sentence than the tariff for the offence might appear to warrant. The task of an advocate making a plea in mitigation is to persuade the court to view the offender or the offence in the most favourable light possible. The ultimate purpose is, so to speak, to get the offender as light a penalty as possible. From this point of view an immediate custodial sentence would generally be regarded as the most drastic penalty that could be imposed and it will often be the primary concern to avoid this. However, even if a custodial sentence is inevitable it is still important to make a full plea in mitigation so that the term imposed may be as short as possible.

18.7.1   THE 1991 ACT AND 'TRADITIONAL' MITIGATION

Before the 1991 Act came into force, mitigation would generally have been aimed at the features which we shall consider below. Thus one would have looked to the realistic penalty which a court would be minded to impose and then attempted to persuade the court to impose some lesser penalty, or if imprisonment was inevitable, to have made the period as short as possible. Now however, mitigation will take on a more technical aspect because one will first have to attempt to persuade the court to look carefully at the 1991 Act and to consider potential penalties in ascending order from fines and discharges through community sentences and up to custodial sentences. The technical requirements of the Act at each of these stages will have to be carefully considered and it may be that whereas under the previous law a custodial sentence might have been feared as highly likely (e.g., a very persistent petty offender), that under the new Act such a penalty would be unlawful and therefore one will have to consider what penalties short of imprisonment the court would be minded to impose.

Even if imprisonment is a possibility there are technical arguments which may be mounted under the 1991 Act, e.g., as to the true meaning of the word 'seriousness' or the proper way in which the court should approach 'aggravating factors' and the like, as discussed above. The plea in mitigation therefore will commence with this kind of technical discussion which formerly would have been unnecessary.

Having considered the matters in the 1991 Act with a view to likely sentence, one can then turn to 'traditional' mitigation, the need for which is expressly preserved by s. 28 of the 1991 Act as we have seen, since s. 28(1) provides: 'Nothing . . . shall prevent a court from mitigating an offender's sentence by taking into account any such matters as, in the opinion of the court, are relevant in mitigation . . . .'

18.7.2 'KNOW THY JUDGE'

It is essential, when attempting to persuade a court towards a certain view of a penalty which it ought to impose, to make use of any knowledge of the personality or foibles of the sentencer. This is most easily done by counsel in the Crown Court where the same handful of circuit judges and recorders will appear in a given location time after time, and an experienced criminal barrister will be well aware that an argument which always appeals to judge A may be seen as positively aggravating by judge B. For solicitors the same may sometimes apply, bearing in mind that a solicitor has rights of audience on sentencing appeals from the magistrates' court to the Crown Court. However, in the context of the magistrates' court much will depend on local factors. In small rural courts it may indeed be that the same magistrates are seen time and time again. In larger urban courts the same stipendiary magistrate's predilections and preferences may become well known; in larger urban magistrates' courts however the rotating system by which lay magistrates sit in different combinations may make it unlikely that, save for those of the very strongest personality who live in the memory, the solicitor will be able to attribute known foibles to the faces before him. Where possible however it is vitally important to have regard to the personality of the sentencer. Thus, for example, to the writer's knowledge there are circuit judges who are sternly temperance minded and for whom any suggestion of drink being involved in the commission of an offence is not a mitigating factor showing impulsiveness, but an aggravating factor. Another Circuit Judge holds the apparently serious belief that the criminal classes should not be encouraged to procreate and thus the suggestion, which normally would be of some use in mitigation, that the offender's wife or girlfriend is pregnant will seriously irritate the judge (it goes without saying that a suggestion that both the offender's wife and his girlfriend are pregnant will be twice as bad). Similarly, different judges, or magistrates, take radically different views of the seriousness of offences involving cannabis. Some take the definite view that this is the first step on the rocky road to hard drugs; in another court, to the writer's knowledge, at least two of the magistrates, both of them practising doctors, take the view that cannabis is less harmful than tobacco and, both having strong personalities, impose their views on their colleagues such that in that court usually very lenient sentences indeed are passed for cannabis offences. Thus if one can obtain any knowledge of the sentencer it should be put to good use.

18.7.3 TRADITIONAL MITIGATION

Generally, it is best to divide a plea in mitigation into four sections and to treat these separately. This avoids putting forward a mishmash of unrelated matters which, albeit all favourable to a defendant, may give an unstructured impression. The four categories are:

(a) the offence itself;
(b) the offender;
(c) the offender's conduct in relation to the investigation of the crime and the proceedings; and
(d) the capacity to reform.

18.7.4   THE OFFENCE ITSELF

Here one should see what can be found in the immediate circumstances of the offence which makes it less serious than it might at first appear. A good example would be in the case of an assault where the offender had been subject to considerable provocation. One should not put forward one's mitigation so enthusiastically as to appear to indicate something which is in effect a defence, e.g., to suggest that it was self-defence rather than provocation. To do this is obviously to go behind either the plea of guilty and reopen the case or to impugn the jury's verdict. An example of something which might mitigate a dishonesty offence might be drink. This has to be advanced with some care. As mentioned above some sentencers have a view of drink which make them view it as an aggravating factor rather than as mitigation. It goes without saying of course that in any driving offence drink is unlikely to be a mitigating factor. It may well be, however, that on the facts of the case the element of drink can be presented in a favourable light, because as a general rule the court view it as some mitigation that an offence was committed on impulse rather than premeditatedly. Thus for example on a charge of say stealing £100, if the sum was left lying around and taken on a rash impulse, the offence would be regarded as rather less serious than for someone to procure the same amount by a cunning and premeditated plan. Since drink may well affect impulsiveness, to that extent it may be a mitigating factor.

18.7.4.1   Aggravation and mitigation

An advocate must be alive to the fact that some features in an offence may be *aggravating*. These features are usefully dealt with in some of the 'guideline cases' in the Court of Appeal referred to above. In addition, the Magistrates Association have issued a booklet of sentencing guidelines which features several 'seriousness indicators' which have an eye to the technical matters in the Criminal Justice Act 1991 but are also of general use. These 'seriousness' indicators deal with a number of matters which may aggravate an offence, e.g., breach of trust by person in authority; offence was cunning and premeditated; use of weapons; offence took place in a public place; the victim was particularly vulnerable; that it was an organised offence. Other common aggravating features are an element of professionalism in the crime; the use of excessive force; and gratuitous violence or destruction. By way of example, extracts from two pages of the Magistrates' Association Sentencing Guidelines are reproduced (see **18.8** and **18.9**) showing how magistrates should approach sentencing. The two examples chosen are those of an assault occasioning actual bodily harm under s. 47 of the Offences against the Person Act 1861 and dwelling-house burglary under s. 9 of the Theft Act 1968.

Ordinary mitigating features are those which tend to demonstrate impulsiveness, e.g., acting on the spur of the moment; reduced mental capacity; good motive in what was done; genuine ignorance of the law; personal or social pressure akin to duress; that the offender played a minor role in the crime; and the like.

In dealing with a crime one must therefore always have regard to aggravating features and attempt to deal with them rather than hoping that the court will not notice them. Thus for example if one is dealing with a senior employee who handles employer's money, such a person would be considered to have committed a much more serious offence if he stole that money than in the case of the same theft between strangers. Likewise if in the same instance the senior employee had involved another junior employee who was of previous good character in the crime this corruption would be a further aggravating feature. One must take instructions from the client and address oneself frankly to this kind of problem.

18.7.5   THE OFFENDER HIMSELF

This is the point at which the advocate has the opportunity to discuss at length and in detail the personal circumstances of the offender. It will be remembered that if there is a risk of a custodial sentence, by this stage probably a pre-sentence report will have been obtained. This may in itself set out a number of matters relevant to the plea in mitigation. It may lengthily rehearse the offender's upbringing, education and background, and family circumstances and deal with personal problems.

Bad advocates often merely parrot these, indeed sometimes actually reading them out despite the fact that the report is already before the magistrates. This is clearly boring and bad practice. One should seek to give the magistrates new information not already contained in the social enquiry report and if the social enquiry report is very full then one should refer the magistrates to it and stress or expand on the more favourable matters revealed. Matters which might be treated as being mitigation would be some of the following, if applicable.

18.7.5.1 Previous record

The best possible mitigation is no criminal record. It always gives a court pause for thought even in the case of a relatively serious crime that it is the offender's first offence. Thus, whilst previous criminal record may not inevitably be relevant in sentencing because of ss. 1 and 2 of the Criminal Justice Act 1991, absence of criminal record may still be particularly good mitigation. In addition to mere absence of criminal record however, positive features about the individual ought to be put forward such as any record of public service, service in the forces, good employment record, and settled family background. If the offence is one of dishonesty, reference to any positions of trust which the offender has had and faithfully carried out in the past, e.g., that he has handled a great deal of money for his employer for many years without shortages or discrepancies.

We have already considered the technical matters contained in the Criminal Justice Act 1991 and the way in which a previous record may be relevant to the present sentence. If an offender does have a criminal record then, bearing in mind the 1991 Act, it is important to deal with this so far as possible. For example, it may be possible to look back through the record and point to things which favour a particular course of action. Thus if for example there are lengthy gaps in the record and these correspond to periods of employment and the offender is presently in employment this might be a feature worth putting forward. It might tend to show that his offences are born out of frustration and financial hardship when he is unemployed. Equally, if he has received some particular kind of penalty in the past and this seems to have worked for him, e.g., a period of probation where he kept out of trouble for some time, this should be stressed. Another point worth making is that if the bulk of his criminal record is for one particular type of offence and the present offence is of a completely different type then under the 1991 Act one is entitled to suggest that the court ought to treat him as a first offender. Suppose, for example, that the offender has a bad criminal record for, say, offences of violence arising out of fights whilst under the influence of drink and the present offence is one of straightforward dishonesty. In such a case the court ought not to pay any attention to his record on the question of whether or not to choose a custodial sentence; and even if a custodial sentence is chosen there should be nothing in the previous conduct to aggravate it in terms of length.

18.7.5.2 Circumstances at the time of the crime

The offender's circumstances at the time of the crime should be described to the court if relevant. For example if the offence is one of dishonesty and occurred at a time of grave financial pressure on the defendant, especially if this was caused through circumstances beyond his own control, e.g., having been made redundant. Personal health problems or those of his loved ones may also be relevant, for example alcoholism or drug dependency, although the circumstances of this latter example must be treated with caution. Anything which in any way affected him at the time and made him more vulnerable or susceptible to pressures is worth stressing, such as bereavement or some personal tragedy. Perhaps connected to this is the next point.

18.7.5.3 The effect of his offence and punishment on others

The effect on others of his crime or potential punishment ought to be stressed. It is of course common place that if an offender goes to prison he will lose his job. Magistrates will hear this argument very often but it is still one worth putting forward. Another argument commonly advanced is that when considering the penalty to be imposed on the offender the court should have regard to its effect on society as a whole. Thus if he loses his job by being sent to prison it may be unlikely that he will easily obtain another one, so an additional point to make is that his family will be reduced to welfare benefits whilst he is there and indeed indefinitely afterwards. The cost to society of an individual being kept in prison has been variously estimated but the weekly cost of providing prison facilities alone is said to be over £400 depending on the type of institution in which he is detained. When one takes into account the additional cost to society of keeping his family the cost is a very significant one. It has indeed been pointed out by one leading criminologist that it would in purely financial terms be considerably better for the state to pay persistent offenders to take extended holidays abroad rather than to imprison them in England. A sentencing court is unlikely to take any specific notice of the financial argument when presented in these terms, though it will of course always bear in mind the undesirability in every case of imprisoning an individual in terms of prison overcrowding and cost.

18.7.5.4 Other penalties suffered

Linked to this point of the effect on his family, one should stress other penalties which the offence has occasioned of a non-judicial nature, such as personal humiliation in the light of publicity, loss of job or status, perhaps the break-up of his family if his wife has left him because of the offence, loss of earnings in the future and possibly the effect of being totally unemployable in his chosen job, e.g., where he was employed as a cashier and dishonesty has led to his dismissal, the certainty that he will never again obtain a position of trust (but see *R* v *Barrick* at **18.6.1** above).

Until the 1991 Act it was sometimes possible to urge the effect on a family, e.g., through loss of job, as a particularly powerful reason for suspending any sentence of imprisonment. This argument ought to be less successful than previously because it will be recalled that, expressly by the terms of s. 2(2)(b) inserted in the Powers of Criminal Courts Act 1973 by the 1991 Act, the exercise of the power to suspend must be 'justified by the exceptional circumstances of the case'. Since most criminals have familes who will be affected by their imprisonment, any given case can hardly be called 'exceptional'.

18.7.5.5 Time in custody

Finally, one might stress, if one hopes to avoid a custodial sentence, any period in custody which the accused has already spent in consequence of the investigation of the crime or remands. For example if he has already spent some weeks in prison before conviction it might be suggested that this is in itself sufficient penalty and represents sufficient of a shock to him to amount to an effective deterrent.

18.7.6 CONDUCT IN RELATION TO THE INVESTIGATION OF THE CRIME AND CRIMINAL PROCEEDINGS

It is always a potent feature in favour of an offender if he has co-operated in the prompt and efficient disposal of his case. This may take two aspects, as follows.

18.7.6.1 Co-operation with the police

The earlier that this co-operation commences the better. The best case of all would obviously be relatively rare, that is a person who was not even a suspect but walked into a police station and made a full confession. Whilst this is unlikely, prompt co-operation with the police from the onset of questioning is almost as good, for example an offender who makes a full confession leading to the recovery of stolen property at an early stage. The fact that property is recovered for the victim of the crime is a potent consideration in favour of an offender. So is giving evidence against, or giving information leading to conviction of, his associates in crime, e.g., a thief who names the handler or vice versa. When advising a client one should leave this matter very much up to the client. Obviously giving information leading to the arrest and conviction of criminal associates may lead to a lesser penalty from the court, but it may have certain undesirable consequences of a personal nature in relation to the behaviour of those former accomplices towards one's client, as and when they are all at large again.

18.7.6.2 Proceedings in court

A guilty plea at the earliest opportunity is also a powerful mitigating factor. It saves a great deal of the court's time, costs to public funds, and may also save embarrassment to the victims of the offence especially in sexual cases. In an appropriate case, a guilty plea is said to lead to a reduction in custodial sentence on the apparent tariff figure of up to one-third, and a guilty plea together with giving useful information about co-offenders may, in the case of serious crime anyway, lead to a reduction in sentence of more than 50 per cent (see *R* v *Lowe* (1977) 66 Cr App R 122, 11½ years reduced to five years on appeal because of such mitigating factors).

18.7.7 CAPACITY FOR REFORM

First it should be mentioned that the showing of contrition is an important factor. This can of course hardly be combined with conviction after a not guilty plea and must realistically only be urged in the case of a guilty plea. Factors which tend to show this might be that the offender has already made voluntary restitution to the victim in an appropriate case or has made a serious offer to do so by instalments and commenced paying them. Care should be taken to ensure that this is not seen as a sign of insincerity or an attempt to 'buy off' a sentence.

Other circumstances which show capacity to reform might be something in the offender's personal life which is about to change for the better to show that he is prepared to take on a more responsible role in society or in the family context. Factors which might be so regarded include finding a new job after a long period of unemployment; being about to get married; becoming pregnant in the case of a female offender; that a wife or cohabitee is pregnant in the case of a male offender.

The plea in mitigation should be structured and concise. It is better to avoid clichés, for example, the phrases 'victim of society' and 'he stands at the crossroads of his life' unless at least two of the magistrates have beards, wear sandals, or can otherwise be proved to be *Guardian* readers.

18.7.8 CHARACTER EVIDENCE

It is also open to the advocte to call character witnesses. The rules of evidence do not strictly apply at this stage and of course the accused's character is now known to the court. It is generally considered not of much use to call a close relative such as a mother or wife since she will inevitably say the same thing the sentencer has heard before, namely that the accused has always been a good, responsible and loving son/husband and deserves a last chance. There may be cases however where a suitably impassioned plea can have some effect and certainly does no harm. Much better is to call as a character witness someone such as an employer who is willing to hold the accused's job for him despite his knowledge of the conviction. The best of all of course and, perhaps surprisingly, by no means unknown, is to call as a character witness the employer against whom the theft was committed to say that notwithstanding this the employer will give the accused another chance. Where an employer is prepared to make this commitment it is a very powerful argument to put to the court that the court ought also to give the accused this further chance and not impose a custodial sentence.

Three final matters ought to be mentioned.

18.7.9 THE USE OF THE PRE-SENTENCE REPORT

As has been previously suggested, the pre-sentence report may often contain a great deal of useful background information. It is pointless to read this to the court and one should merely refer the court to the relevant passages. To an extent a report does a good deal of the mitigator's work for him. Commonly reports end with a recommendation for a particular type of sentence. There should be such a recommendation as to suitability for a community sentence where one is to be imposed. Where the probation officer who will have completed such a report does in fact make a recommendation for dealing with an offender by one or other particular type of sentence, and this is acceptable to the offender, then one may at the end of the plea in mitigation suggest that the court adopt the course recommended. Indeed the whole procedure of a plea in mitigation may in an appropriate case be short-circuited by an early enquiry of the court as to whether it would agree to adopt the recommendation of the probation officer. If it indicates that it will then no more need be said.

If the probation officer makes no particular recommendation for a type of sentence then in some courts this will be treated as equivalent to the probation officer saying that there appears to be no other method of dealing with the offender than custody. In such a case one needs to try even harder in a plea in mitigation to avoid the offender receiving a custodial sentence. It is fair to say that whilst most courts regard the contents of a pre-sentence enquiry report with great seriousness, it is a notorious fact that individual probation officers may on occasions recommend wholly unrealistic alternatives, e.g., in a very serious case may recommend probation where it is clearly inappropriate. If the advocate independently forms the view that the probation officer's recommendation is hopelessly optimistic then it may well not be enough simply to ask the court to adopt that recommendation but a full plea in mitigation stressing all possible factors in the defendant's favour may need to be made. It is sometimes good tactics in such a case to be seen to side with the sentencer against the probation officer and to indicate that one views the recommendation as optimistic. A striking opening to such a plea in mitigation might, for example, say:

> Contrary to the probation officer's suggestion most people might see this as a nasty spiteful crime by a man who for 10 years has made little contribution to society and whom it might appear that you would be highly justified in sending to prison immediately. On the other hand, despite that preliminary view I would urge you to consider the following . . .

18.7.10 SHOULD THE ADVOCATE RECOMMEND ANY PARTICULAR TYPE OF SENTENCE?

In cases where the probation officer in a report is not recommending any particular type of sentence there is nothing to stop the advocate from doing so, or indeed anyway from recommending one different to that recommended by the probation officer. Thus one may suggest to the court that a fine is an appropriate way of dealing with the offender and in that case details of the offender's means and outgoings should be given. Whilst one may recommend the type of sentence it is not generally considered appropriate to recommend a specific term or the amount of a fine. One would not for example suggest to a court that a case merited say nine months' imprisonment rather than some longer term or a fine of any particular amount. One merely recommends a type of sentence and asks the court to impose the minimum it sees fit. In this connection and in connection with mitigation generally it is appropriate to mention one further matter.

18.7.11 DEFERRED SENTENCE

Advocates who make pleas in mitigation often make some relatively optimistic claims on behalf of sex offenders concerning some change in lifestyle and capacity to reform. For example it may be suggested that a person will stay out of trouble if he is able to get a job and that he has an interview for a job in a few days' time. Likewise, claims may be made that an offender will pay compensation to the victim of the offence.

The court has a power under s. 1 of the Powers of Criminal Courts Act 1973 to defer passing any sentence for a period of up to six months. The main reason why a court might defer sentence is to enable it to take into account the offender's conduct after conviction and any change in circumstances that comes about.

When a court defers sentence the offender is released until the date when he is instructed to reappear, which should preferably be fixed by the court there and then. Moreover, in principle, the offender should return to be dealt with by the same judge or magistrates who have dealt with the case hitherto. When the offender does reappear before the court he or his advocate will be expected to explain what has occurred in the meantime, in particular with regard to any promises or undertakings given on the previous occasion. In principle if the offender has carried out his promise, e.g., to obtain a job or pay compensation and has not in the meantime reoffended, he should be safe from a custodial sentence. However merely staying out of trouble on its own is not sufficient to ensure that an offender will not be sent to prison. It is also important to consider whether the offender has done the best he can to change his lifestyle in the way suggested on his behalf at the mitigation stage. If the sentencing court does impose an immediate custodial sentence it should state precisely in what respect it considers there has been a failure to comply with the undertakings previously given.

18.8   The Magistrates' Association Sentencing Guidelines: Assault — Actual Bodily Harm

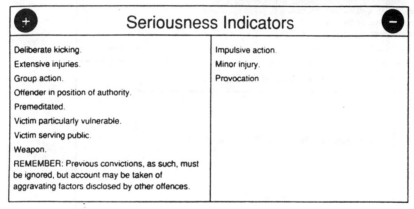

Offences Against The Person Act 1861 s. 47 Triable Either Way · See Mode of Trial Guidelines Penalty: Level 5 and/or 6 months	**Assault – Actual Bodily Harm**

⊕   Seriousness Indicators   ⊖

Deliberate kicking.	Impulsive action.
Extensive injuries.	Minor injury.
Group action.	Provocation
Offender in position of authority.	
Premeditated.	
Victim particularly vulnerable.	
Victim serving public.	
Weapon.	
REMEMBER: Previous convictions, as such, must be ignored, but account may be taken of aggravating factors disclosed by other offences.	

The Sentence

GUIDE	
Less serious cases	– is Discharge or **COMPENSATION** alone appropriate?
	– if not, consider **COMPENSATION** as a priority and/or Fine: the Guideline Fine is:-
	30 UNITS
Aggravating features (especially if police or public servant a victim) justifies at least a community sentence and in more serious cases, custody	– if too serious for fining, consider a Community Sentence.
	– if offence is serious enough to warrant a Community Sentence, consider what restrictions are appropriate.
	– if too serious for a Community Sentence, consider Custody.
	– if offence is so serious that only Custody can be justified, decide the length of the sentence.
	– if so serious that more than 6 months custody would be commensurate, commit for sentence.

18.9 The Magistrates' Association Sentencing Guidelines: Burglary (Dwellings)

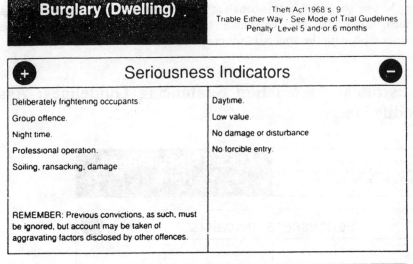

Burglary (Dwelling)

Theft Act 1968 s. 9
Triable Either Way · See Mode of Trial Guidelines
Penalty: Level 5 and/or 6 months

⊕ Seriousness Indicators ⊖

Deliberately frightening occupants.	Daytime.
Group offence.	Low value.
Night time.	No damage or disturbance
Professional operation.	No forcible entry.
Soiling, ransacking, damage	
REMEMBER: Previous convictions, as such, must be ignored, but account may be taken of aggravating factors disclosed by other offences.	

The Sentence

GUIDE	
Normally too serious for a fine (But walk-in burglaries as for theft)	– is Discharge or **COMPENSATION** alone appropriate?
	– if not, consider **COMPENSATION** as a priority and/or Fine: the Guideline Fine is:-
	<div align="center">30 UNITS</div>
Mitigating (eg young adult) and/or no aggravating features	– if too serious for fining, consider a Community Sentence.
	– if offence is serious enough to warrant a Community Sentence, consider what restrictions are appropriate.
Aggravating features	– if too serious for a Community Sentence, consider Custody.
	– if offence is so serious that only Custody can be justified, decide the length of the sentence.
	– if so serious that more than 6 months custody would be commensurate, commit for sentence.

NINETEEN

JUVENILES IN THE CRIMINAL PROCESS: THE YOUTH COURT

19.1 Introduction

In all other parts of this text we have dealt with the problem of adult offenders. It is inevitable however in the conduct of a criminal litigation practice that one will come across younger offenders. In the main, adults are persons of 18 or over and all are dealt with the same procedurally, except that for those between the ages of 18 and 20 inclusive there are certain kinds of *sentence* which may be available to the courts which are not available for those over 21. In this chapter we are concerned with those of 17 or younger who are collectively called 'juveniles', a non-technical term which encompasses 'children', aged 13 or under, and 'young persons', aged up to 17 inclusive.

19.2 At the Police Station

When a juvenile is kept at a police station, the Codes of Practice require (Code C, para. 1.7; Code D, para. 1.6) that 'an appropriate adult' should be present. In the case of a juvenile this means:

(a)   a parent or guardian or, if he is in care, a representative of the care authority or voluntary organisation; or
(b)   a social worker; or
(c)   failing either of the above, another responsible adult aged 18 or over who is not a police officer or employed by the police.

A solicitor himself however may not act as 'the appropriate adult'. The appropriate adult should also not be someone suspected of involvement in the offence. Similarly, if the parent or guardian has received admissions from the juvenile he should not be the appropriate adult. If the parent of a juvenile is estranged from him he should not be the appropriate adult if the juvenile does not want him. The police must use a good deal of initiative in this situation and the choice of the wrong 'appropriate adult' may invalidate any confessions subsequently made by the juvenile, e.g., as in *R* v *Blake* (1989) 89 Cr App R 179 where the accused did not want her father to be present but rather her social worker and the police proceeded nonetheless with the father; or *R* v *Morse* [1991] Crim LR 195 where the juvenile's father had an IQ of below 70 and was incapable of appreciating the situation, evidence of the confession was excluded because the father would have been of no use to his son.

A custody officer must, as soon as practicable after the detention of a juvenile, inform the appropriate adult of the grounds of detention and the juvenile's whereabouts and ask the appropriate adult to come to the police station. His function there is to ensure that there is an impartial adult to safeguard the rights of the juvenile. The appropriate adult may then exercise the juvenile's right to legal advice, but the juvenile may anyway consult a solicitor straightaway, and it is usually better to take instructions direct from the juvenile rather than the appropriate adult, although proper consultation is of course required. The juvenile has the final decision whatever his age. It is vital of course to ensure that the juvenile understands any allegations made and has given a full and coherent account. If the custody officer will not grant bail to the juvenile, the local authority should be contacted and the appropriate adult or parent/guardian informed.

Save in respect of the most serious offences, juveniles are not usually charged immediately but are bailed for a report to, and decision by, the Juvenile Bureau. It is vital to explain this procedure to the juvenile and discuss the possible outcomes, in particular the possibility of a caution. The importance of the juvenile admitting the crime, and only admitting it honestly, must be carefully explained.

19.3 Detention Pending First Appearance

By virtue of s. 38 of the Police and Criminal Evidence Act 1984 (as amended by s. 59 of the Criminal Justice Act 1991), a custody officer must now ensure that the juvenile is moved to local authority accommodation unless:

(a) it is impracticable for him to do so; or

(b) in the case of a juvenile aged 15 or older, no secure accommodation is available and keeping the juvenile in other local authority accommodation would not be adequate to protect the public from serious harm from him.

It should be noted that this latter provision is not confined to offences of violence or sexual offences and may be appropriate even in other cases since the phrase 'serious harm' is nowhere defined and could extend to the risk of property damage.

19.4 Courtroom Procedure

A juvenile is likely to make his first court appearance before magistrates. This is likely to be in the youth court unless he is charged jointly with an adult in which case both will come before the adult magistrates' court initially. The decision on whether a juvenile is tried summarily or on indictment is taken by the magistrates and the juvenile does not have the right to elect trial on indictment.

Section 24(1) of the Magistrates' Courts Act 1980 provides that a juvenile must be tried in a youth court (or in an adult magistrates' court if tried jointly with an adult) unless either:

(a) He is charged with homicide.

(b) He is charged jointly with an adult who is going to be tried on indictment *and* the magistrates consider that it is in the interests of justice to commit them both for trial.

In deciding whether to hold committal proceedings in respect of both an adult and a juvenile so as to send the juvenile for trial with the adult, the magistrates must consider the whole interests of justice, including the undesirability of putting a juvenile through the ordeal of Crown Court trial. The younger the juvenile is and the less serious the offence, the more likely it is that the magistrates will decide to commit only the adult to the Crown Court and allow the juvenile to plead to the charge in the magistrates' court. If the juvenile pleads not guilty the adult court will then remit him to the youth court to be tried. If he pleads guilty the adult court will consider sentence but its powers in this respect are limited and it will again usually remit the case for sentencing to the juvenile court.

(c) He has attained the age of 14, is charged with a grave offence (principally offences punishable with 14 years' imprisonment or more), and the magistrates consider that he could probably be sentenced under s. 53(2) of the Children and Young Persons Act 1933 if he were convicted. This power is concerned with the most serious kinds of offence and governs the case where a Crown Court may sentence a juvenile to detention for a term not exceeding the maximum prison term available in the case of an adult. A sentence under s. 53(2) is only possible where there has been a conviction on indictment. Thus even if a youth court commits a juvenile to the Crown Court for sentence under s. 37 of the Magistrates' Courts Act 1980 the Crown Court cannot then pass a s. 53(2) sentence because there has been no trial on indictment. Thus the magistrates must consider the possibility of committal for trial if they think the allegation is one of sufficient seriousness to warrant a substantial sentence of detention.

19.4.1 TRIAL OF JUVENILES IN AN ADULT MAGISTRATES' COURT

A juvenile who is to be tried summarily is to be tried in a youth court unless:

(a) he is charged jointly with an adult; or

(b) he appears before the magistrates together with an adult and has been charged separately but the charges are that he aided and abetted the commission of the offence alleged against the adult or vice versa; or

(c) he appears before the magistrates together with an adult, and the charge against him arises out of circumstances the same as or connected with the circumstances giving rise to the charge against the adult; or

(d) the trial has started against him in the erroneous belief that he was an adult (it may then be continued).

19.4.2 TRIAL OF JUVENILES IN A YOUTH COURT

The youth court (formerly known as the juvenile court) consists of magistrates drawn from a special youth court panel.

The following differences in procedure apply:

(a) A youth court must sit in a room which has not been used as an adult court within the last hour so as to avoid the mixing of juveniles and adult offenders.

(b) The general public have no right of admission to youth courts (where proceedings against juveniles take place in the adult courts this is however usually in open court).

(c) The bench of magistrates must include one of each sex.

(d) There is a certain change in terminology so that witnesses in the case 'promise' rather than 'swear' to tell the truth and if the magistrates decide that the juvenile is guilty they do not 'convict' but 'record a finding of guilt against him'. Likewise the term used after the finding of guilt is not 'sentence' but 'the making of an order upon a finding of guilt' (Children and Young Persons Act 1933, s. 59).

(e) The court may require the attendance before it of the parent or guardian of the child (Children and Young Persons Act 1933, s. 34).

(f) The media may not report the name or any other identifying details of the juvenile unless it is necessary in order to avoid injustice.

(g) There is no dock and the juvenile usually sits on a chair or bench facing the magistrates with his parents beside him. The magistrates are usually seated at the same level as the juvenile and will usually call him by his christian name.

19.5 Sentencing of Juveniles

19.5.1 THE CROWN COURT

The Crown Court may pass any sentence appropriate in the case of a juvenile. Section 56 of the Children and Young Persons Act 1933 provides that, except in cases of homicide, the Crown Court must remit a juvenile convicted on indictment to the youth court to be sentenced, unless satisfied that it will be undesirable to do so. However, guidelines given in leading cases indicate that a Crown Court judge need not remit for sentence if *inter alia* remitting would cause delay, unnecessary duplication of proceedings, and unnecessary expense; the effect of this is that in most cases, since he will be familiar with the facts, the Crown Court judge is likely to sentence a juvenile himself rather than remit the case to the youth court.

Where a juvenile of 15, 16 or 17 years is guilty of an indictable offence and the court considers that he should be sentenced to more than the six months' detention, which is the maximum available to a youth court by virtue of s. 37 of the Magistrates' Courts Act 1980, it may commit him to the Crown Court to be sentenced. The Crown Court may then pass a sentence of up to 12 months for the offence or deal with the offender in any way in which the youth court could have dealt with him.

19.5.2　THE ADULT MAGISTRATES' COURT

An adult magistrates' court's powers are limited in respect of juveniles. Apart from fines, and sentences of disqualification and endorsement, the adult court must remit a juvenile to the youth court to be sentenced by virtue of the Children and Young Persons Act 1969, s. 7. The adult magistrates' court cannot commit a juvenile to the Crown Court under s. 37 of the Magistrates' Courts Act 1980 but must remit him to the youth court which then does have the power of considering that option.

19.5.3　THE YOUTH COURT

The youth court has the following powers:

(a)　It may pass a sentence of detention in a young offender institution on those aged 15 and 16 for up to six months for any one offence; up to six months for any two or more offences which are purely summary; and up to 12 months for two or more either way offences.

(b)　It may fine up to £1,000 in the case of those aged 15, 16 or 17 and up to £250 in the case of an offender of 14 or younger. For obvious reasons it is highly unlikely that a fine will be appropriate for a juvenile in any event.

(c)　It cannot pass a sentence of detention under s. 53 of the Children and Young Persons Act 1953. These sentences are appropriate only in the minority of serious cases and in such cases clearly the case will be sent to the Crown Court.

(d)　By s. 34A of the Children and Young Persons Act 1933 (inserted by s. 56 of the Criminal Justice Act 1991) the parent or guardian of a juvenile is required to attend before a court when the juvenile appears. The parent or guardian may be required to enter into a recognisance to take proper care of him and exercise proper control over him and a sum of up to £1,000 may be ordered to be forfeited when that recognisance is breached. In addition, parents may be required to pay fines, costs or compensation orders imposed by the criminal courts on juveniles.

TWENTY

APPEALS IN CRIMINAL CASES

20.1 Appeals from the Magistrates' Court to the Crown Court against Conviction and/or Sentence: Magistrates' Courts Act 1980, ss. 108 to 110

A defendant who has been convicted in the magistrates' court following a plea of not guilty may appeal against either conviction or sentence or both to the Crown Court. This is done by giving notice of appeal in writing to the clerk of the magistrates' court concerned and to the prosecution within 21 days of sentence being passed. The notice of appeal need not go into any detail on the grounds and indeed it is usual to use a standard form of appeal which merely states that 'the defendant proposes to appeal on the grounds that the magistrates erred in fact and in law in convicting him', or 'the defendant appeals against sentence on the grounds that the sentence imposed was excessive in all the circumstances'.

There is no filtering mechanism, as with appeals to the Court of Appeal, so there is no discretion to refuse to accept the appeal nor is any application for leave to appeal necessary. If notice of appeal is not lodged within the prescribed time there is a discretion to extend the time for giving notice of appeal on application in writing to the Crown Court judge. Reasons for the lateness in appealing need to be supplied (Crown Court Rules 1982, r. 7(5)).

20.1.1 BAIL PENDING APPEAL

It should be remembered that if an immediate custodial sentence has been passed on a convicted person a bail application pending appeal may be made to the magistrates' court although the presumption in favour of bail does not apply. Accordingly in those circumstances a verbal notice of appeal should be given immediately sentence is passed, but this must still be supplemented by a written notice within the prescribed period. In similar circumstances an application to suspend a disqualification from driving pending appeal may also be made.

20.1.2 THE HEARING

The appeal is heard by a circuit judge or recorder sitting with an even number of magistrates (usually two) but with no jury (*Practice Direction (Crown Court Business: Classification)* [1987] 1 WLR 1671 and Supreme Court Act 1981, s. 74). The form of the appeal is a complete re-hearing. The parties may call the same evidence as in the court below in the hope that the higher court will take a different view of it or may call different evidence including not calling witnesses whom they did call in the court below. Matters of law may also be argued and new or different points of law may be raised.

20.1.3   APPEAL FOLLOWING PLEA OF GUILTY

A person who has pleaded guilty in the magistrates' court may appeal against sentence to the Crown Court following the same procedure as outlined above, but may not appeal generally against conviction. However it may be open to a person to argue that his plea of guilty was equivocal, that is to say that although he pleaded guilty, matters were put before the court then or subsequently, probably as mitigation, which actually undermined the plea. For example an accused who when charged with theft says 'guilty but I only took it because I thought it was mine'. In these circumstances the words which accompany the plea are such as to indicate a full defence and the plea should not have been accepted. In such a case an appeal against a conviction may be heard and the case will then be remitted by the Crown Court to the magistrates' court with the direction that the matter be treated as if a plea of not guilty had been entered. There will then be a retrial before the magistrates' court. It should be noted however that this jurisdiction only applies where there is something which occurs at the time which renders the plea clearly equivocal. If it later comes to light that the defendant had an arguable defence which was unknown to him at the time he is generally bound by his plea.

20.1.4   POWERS OF THE CROWN COURT

The powers of the Crown Court when hearing an appeal from a magistrates' court are contained in s. 48 of the Supreme Court Act 1981. The Crown Court may, having heard the appeal:

(a)   confirm, reverse or vary the decision appealed against; or

(b)   remit the matter with the court's opinion to the magistrates (for example where it found that the plea was equivocal); or

(c)   make any such other order as the court considers just, and by such order exercise any power that the magistrates might have exercised (e.g., make appropriate orders for costs); or

(d)   award any sentence whether lesser or greater than that which the magistrates actually awarded provided that the sentence is one which the magistrates' court had power to award. It should be noted therefore that there is a possibility of an *increase* in sentence which may act as some deterrent to frivolous appeals.

It is important not to confuse the procedure for appeals to a Crown Court with the powers of the Crown Court where magistrates commit an accused to the Crown Court for sentence under s. 38 of the Magistrates' Courts Act 1980 having tried the case summarily. Where this occurs the Crown Court has the power to impose any sentence up to the maximum sentence permitted by law for the offence in question.

Only the defence has a right of appeal from the magistrates' court to the Crown Court. If the prosecution thinks it has a basis for appeal on a point of law against an acquittal it must use the procedure next described.

20.2   Appeals from the Magistrates' Court to the Queen's Bench Division, Divisional Court

As we have previously seen, an appeal to the Crown Court may be on any matter of fact or law and may be brought by the defendant alone. There is an alternative avenue of procedure which is open to either side and this is by virtue of s. 111(1) of the Magistrates' Courts Act 1980 which provides that:

> Any person who was a party to any proceedings before a magistrates' court or is aggrieved by the conviction, order, determination or other proceeding of the court may question the proceeding on the ground that it is wrong in law or in excess of jurisdiction . . .

The appeal may therefore be made by either party, prosecution or defence, as long as it concerns a matter of law or an allegation of excess of jurisdiction. The procedure commences by requiring the magistrates to 'state a case' for the opinion of the High Court. The aggrieved party applies in writing to the magistrates within 21 days of the acquittal or conviction or sentence; the application may be by letter and should identify the question of law on which the High Court's opinion is sought. The application is sent to the magistrates' clerk. The kind of matters which may be raised by way of case stated are such things as whether the magistrates had power to try the case; whether they were right to find that there was a case to answer; whether inadmissible evidence was received or admissible evidence excluded, and the like.

A 'statement of case' is prepared by the court which will outline the facts called in question, state the facts which the magistrates found and then state the magistrates' finding on the points of law in question, listing any authority cited and finally posing the question for the High Court. The case is drafted by the magistrates' clerk in consultation with the magistrates. Drafts of the case are sent to the parties who may suggest amendments. The final form of 'case' is then sent to the appellant who must lodge it at the Crown Office of the Royal Courts of Justice in London. Notice must then be given to the respondent with a copy of the case.

The appeal is subsequently heard by the Divisional Court of the Queen's Bench Division in London in which at least two judges, but more usually three, sit. Evidence is not called and the appeal takes the form of legal argument for the appellant and respondent based solely upon the facts stated in the case.

The Divisional Court may reverse, affirm or amend the magistrates' decision or may remit the matter back to the magistrates with its opinion, e.g., with a direction that they continue the hearing, convict, acquit, or the court may remit the case to a different bench of magistrates. Costs may be awarded to either party out of central funds.

It should finally be noted that, where an individual has been convicted in the magistrates' court and appeals to the Crown Court by the procedure previously described, there is a subsequent appeal on a matter of law only by way of case stated from the Crown Court to the Divisional Court. This should not be confused with an appeal from the Crown Court after trial on indictment (i.e., before a jury) (for which, see **20.4**).

20.3 Application for Judicial Review

Instead of either of the methods of appeal previously mentioned, it may be open to a person to apply for judicial review of the decision of the magistrates' court, with the object of seeking the quashing of the magistrates' court decision. On making a decision by *certiorari* to quash the decision, the Divisional Court also has the power of remitting the case to the magistrates with a direction for them to proceed in an appropriate manner, in accordance with its own ruling. Alternatively the whole decision may be quashed so that and conviction and sentence are overturned.

Judicial review will generally lie where either:

(a) the order made by the magistrates' court was made in excess of jurisdiction; or
(b) where the magistrates' court acted in breach of the rules of natural justice. This is a vague and widening part of the principles of judicial review so that in recent cases examples of breach of the rules of nature justice have included the following: failure to give the accused reasonable time to prepare his defence (*R v Thames Magistrates' Court, ex parte Polemis* [1974] 1 WLR 1371; refusing to issue witness summonses (*R v Bradford Justices, ex parte Wilkinson* [1990] 1 WLR 692; or where the accused had pleaded guilty under a misapprehension as to the facts because blood samples given by them might have been contaminated by swabs containing alcohol used by police surgeons (*R v Bolton Justices, ex parte Scally* [1991] 1 QB 537). In all these cases the convictions were quashed by *certiorari*.
(c) Where there is an error of law on the face of the record the magistrates' court's decision may also be quashed by *certiorari*. This is relatively rare however because the error must be *on the face of* the record and magistrates do not, in the main, give reasons for their decision.

As an alternative to *certiorari*, the effect of which is to quash the decision, the other prerogative orders are available. These are *mandamus* and prohibition, which as their names imply, are orders requiring the magistrates' court to act, or not to act, in a certain way.

20.3.1   PROCEDURE

The procedure to apply for judicial review is in s. 31 of the Supreme Court Act 1981 and Rules of the Supreme Court, ord. 53. It is a two-stage procedure whereby:

(a)   The applicant must obtain leave to apply for review. This is obtained on affidavit with written grounds for review filed by the applicant and put before a single judge. It is possible for this to be supplemented by oral argument.

(b)   If leave to apply is granted, the application is dealt with by the Divisional Court which will hear argument from the applicant and anyone else affected by the outcome. Where the application is in effect brought against the magistrates' court, although the magistrates' court may supply any affidavit as to its reasoning or some other aspects, it is usual for the other party to be the CPS or the Home Office depending on the nature of the alleged error.

At the end of the hearing the court makes its decisions granting or refusing the order sought by the applicant and either bringing the case to an end or remitting the matter to the lower court for reconsideration. The grant of remedies by judicial review is always discretionary.

20.4   Appeals from the Crown Court to the Court of Appeal (Criminal Division)

A person convicted on indictment may appeal to the Court of Appeal against his conviction by virtue of s. 1 of the Criminal Appeal Act 1968. There is an appeal as of right on a matter of law alone (e.g., that the trial judge misinterpreted a statute). However where the ground of appeal is on a question of fact or of mixed fact and law (for example points of evidence are often mixed fact and law) then appeal can only be made either:

(a)   with the leave of the trial judge given at the end of the case; or
(b)   with the leave of the Court of Appeal.

In fact the leave of the trial judge is only rarely sought and most appeals to the Court of Appeal follow leave given by the Court of Appeal itself.

A convicted person who has legal aid for his trial is covered by legal aid for initial advice on appeal and the drafting of the grounds of appeal if his counsel recommends that an appeal be pursued. The procedure is as follows:

(a)   Within 28 days of conviction or sentence the appellant must serve on the Registrar of Criminal Appeals a notice of application for leave to appeal accompanied by draft grounds of appeal.

(b)   If the appeal is against conviction then there will probably need to be a transcript provided, either of the judge's summing up or perhaps of some part of the evidence at the trial. The court shorthand writer will then be asked by the Registrar of Criminal Appeals to transcribe the appropriate part of his notes, or a transcript will be made from the automatic recording equipment.

(c)   The papers are then put before a single judge who may be either a Lord Justice of Appeal or a High Court judge sitting as a member of the Court of Appeal. The papers will include the grounds of appeal, transcript and any other relevant documents.

This is a filtering stage at which the single judge considers whether leave ought to be given. There is no hearing and the matter will be decided simply on the papers. If he does grant leave to appeal he will grant legal aid (if necessary) for the hearing itself and the case then proceeds to the full court. If the single judge refuses leave to appeal the appellant has 14 further days in which to serve notice upon the Registrar if he wishes to continue with the case, that is to renew the application before the full court. The papers are then put before the full court. Again an oral hearing is not normal, at least in legal aid cases, and the full court reaches its decision by reading the papers in the case. The single judge is meant to act as a filtering mechanism and if he refuses leave to appeal and the appellant persists before the full court, the full court is empowered to give a so-called 'direction concerning loss of time' under s. 29 of the Criminal Appeal Act 1968. By virtue of this section and *Practice Direction (Crime: Sentence: Loss of Time)* [1981] WLR 270 the full court may direct that time in prison served between the single judge refusing leave and the full court refusing leave may not count as part of any custodial sentence imposed. Such a direction is normal unless the appellant received a written opinion from counsel that there were grounds for appeal. If the full court grants leave to appeal they may also grant legal aid for the hearing of the appeal proper.

As an alternative to the above procedure, if the Registrar of Criminal Appeals, after preliminary consideration of the grounds of appeal, considers that the appeal has a prima facie chance of success he may by-pass the single judge procedure, grant legal aid himself and list the application for leave to appeal for hearing by the full court. He will notify the prosecution and invite them to be represented and the court will then, whilst considering the issue of leave to appeal, usually treat the application for leave as the hearing of the substantive appeal.

20.4.1 THE HEARING OF THE APPEAL

At the hearing of an appeal against conviction the Court of Appeal will listen to argument and may exceptionally hear fresh evidence under s. 23 of the Criminal Evidence Act 1968 if that evidence:

(a) appears likely to be creditable; and
(b) would have been admissible at the trial on indictment; and
(c) it was not adduced at the trial on indictment but there is a reasonable explanation for failure to adduce it.

Thereafter, whether or not there is fresh evidence, the court will determine the appeal in accordance with s. 2 of the Criminal Appeal Act 1968 which provides three general grounds for allowing an appeal, namely that:

(a) the conviction should be set aside because, in all the circumstances of the case, it is unsafe or unsatisfactory; or
(b) the trial judge made a wrong decision on any question of law; or
(c) there was a material irregularity in the course of the trial.

Where the court considers that one or other of these grounds is satisfied it may allow the appeal, or, especially in fresh evidence cases, remit the case for a retrial before a different judge and jury so that the fresh evidence may be considered by the jury together with the original evidence.

Alternatively, the Court of Appeal may indicate that it would decide the point of appeal in favour of the appellant but 'apply the proviso'. The proviso (which is contained in s. 2 of the Criminal Appeal Act 1968) indicates that, notwithstanding that the point of the appeal might be decided in favour of the appellant, the court may dismiss the appeal if they are of the opinion that nonetheless no miscarriage of justice has actually occurred. Thus appeals on purely technical grounds are unlikely to result in the conviction being overturned.

20.4.2 APPEALS AGAINST SENTENCE

An appeal to the Court of Apepal is also possible against sentence but in such cases the leave of the court is always required. It will be necessary at the hearing of the appeal to indicate that the trial judge erred on a matter of principle; that the sentence is manifestly excessive; or that the sentence was wrong in law in some respect. Simply that the Court of Appeal might have imposed a different sentence within the appropriate range will not be sufficient for an appeal againt sentence to succeed. The Court of Appeal does not have the power to *increase* the sentence imposed by the court below by virtue of s. 11(3) of the Criminal Appeal Act 1968. This should however be distinguished from the relatively rare cases where the Attorney-General considers that the offender was dealt with unduly leniently in which case he may refer the sentence to the Court of Appeal for them to review it under s. 36 of the Criminal Justice Act 1988. In that specific case the Court of Appeal *does* have the power to increase the sentence.

20.5   Appeals to the House of Lords

Under s. 33 of the Criminal Appeal Act 1968, either prosecution or defence may appeal to the House of Lords from a decision of the Criminal Division of the Court of Appeal provided:

(a) the Court of Appeal certifies that the decision involves a point of law of general public importance; and

(b) either the Court of Appeal or the House of Lords gives leave to appeal. Such application for leave to appeal should be made immediately after the court's decision or at the latest within 14 days of the decision.

TWENTY ONE

THE EUROPEAN CONVENTION ON HUMAN RIGHTS

21.1   Introduction

The Council of Europe is an organisation of European states which is quite independent of the European Community and of any other political or economic body. At the time of writing, the membership is 27 strong and, in order to join, a State must demonstrate that it has a commitment to parliamentary democracy. Applications for membership are outstanding from a number of States which were formerly within the Eastern bloc.

The Council has permanent premises at Strasbourg and is organised into a number of divisions including a Directorate of Legal Affairs much of whose work is involved in the harmonisation of European law in a number of areas. The work of the Council of Europe which has the highest profile, however, is that of the European Commission of Human Rights and the European Court of Human Rights. The purpose of these bodies is to implement the European Convention for the Protection of Human Rights and Fundmental Freedoms ('The Convention').

The Convention was signed by the countries who were then members of the Council of Europe in November 1950. It was intended to be a statement made by the signatory governments who were said to share the common philosophical and democratic traditions of Western Europe.

Article 25 of the Convention provides that:

> The Commission may receive petitions . . . from any person, non-governmental organisation or group of individuals claiming to be the victim of a violation by one of the High Contracting Parties of the rights set forth in this Convention provided that the High Contracting Party against which the complaint has been lodged has declared that it recognises the competence of the Commission to receive such petitions . . .

The Convention thus was and remains unique in that, in cases where the contracting parties have accepted the *right of individual petition*, the European Commission and the European Court of Human Rights are given a competence to adjudicate on complaints made by individuals within the jurisdiction of the contracting States, whether those individuals are citizens or aliens, and irrespective of any other international agreement or treaty.

Of the 27 member countries of the Council of Europe, at the time of writing 25 have ratified the Convention and accepted the right of individual petition. The remaining two, Poland and Hungary, are widely expected to ratify in the immediate future. In considering present applications for membership from former Eastern bloc countries, the Council of Europe has made it clear that it will treat new States' willingness to ratify forthwith the European Convention and accept the right of individual petition as a crucial test of commitment to democracy, on which the success of an application for membership will depend.

21.2 The Effect of the Convention

The Convention therefore provides an opportunity for any individual within a member State to challenge the legal or political actions or institutions of the State concerned where he alleges that his rights under the Convention are breached. Apart from this right of individual petition, there is a possibility for applications to be brought *between States* although this has only happened in 18 cases since 1950. The overwhelming majority of applications (more than 21,000 by 1993) are brought by individuals against member States.

The Commission and Court cannot of course strike down national laws as such, but rulings may be given which must inevitably lead to the amendment or repeal of national laws or a change in administrative practices which have been found to have been in conflict with the principles of the Convention. In addition to the change in a State's laws or practices, compensation may be obtained by the individual adversely affected by the original breach.

In principle, a State cannot defy a ruling of the European Court and remain a member of the Council of Europe, and the political pressure to remain a member is very strong. Exceptionally, by virtue of Article 15:

> In time of war or other public emergency threatening the life of the nation, any High Contracting Party may take measures derogating from its obligations under this Convention to the extent strictly required by the exigencies of the situation. . . .

The effect of this is that if there is a genuine state of emergency a State may obtain a temporary reprieve from implementing a decision of the Court. The United Kingdom for example has made such a derogation in respect of some aspects of police powers in Northern Ireland.

In many of the countries within the Council of Europe, the Convention has been incorporated into their domestic constitutions. The effect of this is that the Convention rights become directly enforceable in the domestic courts of the country in question so that the first port of call for an aggrieved individual is the courts of his own country. Only if no satisfactory redress is obtained there need he take his case to Strasbourg. As is well known this is not the case in the United Kingdom. The status of the Convention in the UK will be discussed below but first it is appropriate to mention the UK's record in proceedings before the Commission and Court.

21.3 The 'League Table'

As is well known, the UK has been condemned by the Court for breaches of the Covnention on more occasions than any other European State. Very few, however, would consider that this in reality means that there are wholesale and flagrant breaches of human rights occurring on a daily basis as a matter of governmental practice in the UK. Whilst the UK is in many respects an undemocratic society and executive powers are often arbitrary, unaccountable and exercised in secrecy, it is transparent nonsense to suggest that the human rights of individuals are worse protected in the UK than in, say, Turkey. Our unfortunate position in the league table reflects the fact that we have accepted the right of individual petition for several decades whereas other member States of the Council of Europe have only accepted the right of individual petition relatively recently (e.g., Malta and Turkey). In addition, if one prepares a different league table based on population, then a very different position is shown. On this league table we do not come at the top, first place falling apparently to Austria. In addition, regard must be had to the competence of national lawyers in their imaginative uses of the Convention. There is no doubt that there is presently a high level of awareness in the UK of the potential of using the Convention as a further avenue of appeal. Press reports indicate that disgruntled complainants about almost every aspect of English life, legal or administrative, claim to be 'taking their cases to the European Court' although the press reports, and indeed the disgruntled parties themselves, are usually unclear about whether they mean the European Court of Justice or the European Court of Human Rights. The fact, moreover, that the Convention is not directly applicable in the UK courts whereas it is in other countries means that disputes involving the rights guaranteed under the Convention inevitably take place on a European stage in UK cases whereas they may well be litigated to a satisfactory conclusion in the domestic courts of other countries who have incorporated the Convention.

21.4   The Status of the Convention

A much discussed current question is the extent to which the Convention affects English law directly. The use of the Convention as an aid to interpretation of English authorities or to resolve problems of conflicting authorities in the common law has been problematic. Thus in an early case, *Ostreicher* v *Secretary of State for the Environment* [1978] 1 All ER 591, the High Court said that one article of the Convention '. . . was of little assistance . . . it is in vague terms'. The Convention was better received by Lord Denning in *R* v *Chief Immigration Officer Heathrow Airport ex parte Salamat Bibi* [1976] 3 All ER 843:

> The position as I understand it is that if there is any ambiguity in our statutes or uncertainty in our law, then the courts can look to the Convention as an aid to clear up the ambiguity and uncertainty . . . but I would dispute altogether that the Convention is part of our law.

Later, in *Ahmed* v *ILEA* [1978] QB 36 he said:

> The Convention is not part of our English law but . . . we will always have regard to it. We will do our best to see that our decisions are in conformity with it. But it is drawn in such vague terms that it can be used for all sorts of unreasonable claims and provoke all sorts of litigation. As so often happens with high sounding principles they may have to be brought down to earth. They have to be applied in a work-a-day world.

The status of the Convention has been partly resolved in the context of statutory interpretation by the House of Lords in *R* v *Secretary of State for the Home Office ex parte Brind and others* [1991] AC 696. The House of Lords held that, although in general terms in construing domestic legislation which was ambiguous in that it was capable of a meaning which either conformed to or conflicted with the Convention the courts would presume that Parliament intended to legislate in conformity with the Convention, there was no corresponding presumption that, as a matter of domestic law, the courts would review the exercise of an administrative discretion on the basis that such discretion had to be exercised in conformity with the Convention. Accordingly, the Convention could not be a source of rights and obligations in English law and resort could not be had to it for the purpose of construction unless there was an obvious ambiguity in the relevant statute. In the Court of Appeal in that case the Convention received an even less warm reception, Lord Donaldson indicating that it was up to the government of the day whether or not to ensure that new statute law was consistent with the Convention and Ralph Gibson LJ indicating that a court should only apply the English rules of construction of statutes and that only if no ordinary rule of construction assisted could the Convention be used.

The Convention received a somewhat warmer reception in *Derbyshire CC* v *Times Newspaper and Others, The Times,* 20 February 1993 where the House of Lords referred to Article 10 of the Convention (which guarantees freedom of speech) but noted with satisfaction that the common law was consistent with the Convention in any event.

Despite these cases the Convention continues to be cited with enthusiasm by some judges as at least a highly persuasive authority. For example, the Court of Appeal in *Middlebrook Mushrooms Ltd* v *Transport and General Workers Union, The Times,* 18 January 1993 adverted favourably to Article 10 of the Convention in support of their judgment notwithstanding that that article had not been relied on by either party in the appeal.

21.5   The Style of the Convention

Although British lawyers played a prominent part in its drafting, the Convention is drafted in a somewhat 'European style' as Lord Denning's earlier criticism indicates. Thus, for example, Article 8 of the Convention prescribes:

(1)   Everyone has the right to respect of his private and family life, home and correspondence . . .

(2)   There shall be no interference by a public authority with the exercise of this right except such as is in accordance with the law and is necessary in a democratic society in the interests of national security, public safety or the economic well being of the country, for the prevention of disorder or crime, or for the protection of health or morals and for the protection of the rights and freedom of others.

This comprehensive article, usually described as the 'right of privacy' article, has provoked a vast volume of applications to the European Commission in matters to do with, *inter alia*, telephone tapping; a claimed right to privacy; illegal search; abortion; the refusal of abortion; the right to a homosexual relationship; the right to refuse medical examination; the right to refuse blood testing; contraception; the refusal of contraception; divorce; custody; child care; immigration; deportation; and in a large number of cases to do with the rights of prisoners, including the right to refuse to wear prison clothing, to receive daily visits and to free correspondence. The article is so widely framed both in the statement of the right and in the acceptable derogation from it as to appear not much more than a pious exhortation. It is so wide that it is meaningless in the strict sense that no individual would know whether his own case was within or outside the protection conferred but for the very considerable jurisprudence which the Commission and Court have developed in applying the article.

In general, however, when construing Article 8 or any other article, it is fair to say that rights which are guaranteed in the Convention are to be construed in the broadest sense and any restrictions on those rights in the narrowest. Thus it is always for a State which maintains that a particular restriction is necessary under Article 8(2) (or any other article) to demonstrate why that is so and to show that the restriction on the right is proportional to the mischief envisaged. This is clearly likely to be a nice balance.

21.6   Procedure under the Convention

The most important kind of case brought under the Convention is an individual application against a member State. An application must be sent in writing and is usually initially by letter; thereafter an application form is sent to the applicant or his representative and the application is registered. A report is then prepared by the Secretariat of the Commission of Human Rights and presented by a member of the Commission (the rapporteur) to the Commission itself or sometimes to a committee of three members. There will then be an opportunity for the respondent government to provide written observations. The Commission, or a chamber of at least seven members, possibly with the benefit of an oral hearing for which it may grant legal aid to the applicant, will then go on to decide whether the application is *admissible*. There are four important aspects to this:

(a)   An application must not be *incompatible* and thus only the rights guaranteed by the provisions of the Convention can be invoked. Thus in past case law it has been established that the Convention does not provide, e.g., a right to a university degree; a right to asylum; a right to start a business; a general right to free legal aid; a right to a passport; or the right to a promotion. Nonetheless one must also bear in mind that although no article protects any of the aforementioned rights, a right which is not set forth expressly in the Convention may still be protected indirectly via one of the provisions in it.

Thus, for example, although the Convention does not recognise a right to a pension, violation of an existing right to a pension may be contrary to Article 1 of the First Protocol, in which the right to enjoyment of possessions is protected.

(b) An applicant must have sufficient *locus standi*, that is he must in some sense be a victim of the act complained of and not merely an officious bystander who would like administrative practices or legal rulings changed as a point of principle. The Commission has however given a generous construction to the concept of 'indirect' victim, e.g., the complaint of a mother about the treatment of her detained son (*Y* v *Austria* (case 898/60)) and even someone who complained that a perfectly lawful act by a Convention country might expose him to a breach of the Convention outside Europe has been held to have *locus standi* (*Kirkwood* v *United Kingdom* (case 10479/83), where the applicant was objecting to extradition to California where he would be likely to receive the death sentence). Although the Convention expressly permits the death penalty, Kirkwood successfully argued that the 'death row' phenomenon of excessive delay would constitute inhuman and degrading treatment contrary to Article 3.

(c) By virtue of Article 26: 'The Commission may only deal with the matter after all domestic remedies have been exhausted, and within a period of 6 months from the date on which the final decision was taken'. We shall now consider both elements of this principle:

(i) 'Exhausting domestic remedies'. This rule in essence means that an applicant must have taken his case to the highest relevant tribunal or administrative authority in the country concerned before he may even commence proceedings in Strasbourg. Thus there may well have been a very considerable delay whilst a case is taken to the highest court of appeal. It is fair to say that respondent governments commonly and quite shamelessly take the preliminary point that the appellant has not exhausted every conceivable route of appeal and challenge through all the judicial and administrative processes available. In one case which the writer observed in Strasbourg, which had to do with the improper revocation of a planning permission thus depriving the owner of the land affected of a substantial sum of money, the respondent government complained before the Commission (and repeated its complaint before the Court) that the applicant had not exhausted domestic remedies because there were no less than eight alternatives routes through the various judicial and administrative planning appeal processes in the country concerned, and the applicant had only exhausted five of them. (The Court considered this spurious.) It is fair to say that latterly the Commission and Court have taken a more relaxed view of this requirement and have said in particular in the case of *Cardot* v *France* (case 24/1990/215/277) that this requirement must be applied with some degree of flexibility and without excessive formalism. Thus the unavailability of legal aid for an appeal or the existence of binding case law against an appellant from the highest court in the country (see also *Boschet* v *Belgium* (case 10835/84), have been held to be adequate reasons not to have attempted to take the case to the very highest tribunal.

(ii) 'The application must have been submitted within a period of six months from the date on which the final national decision was taken.' This means the decision of the highest court or highest administrative body. Occasionally however there is no available administrative challenge. For example, in the case of *Christians Against Racism and Fascism* v *the United Kingdom* (case 8440/78) the applicants complained about a regulation prohibiting public processions during a certain period. The Commission decided that as there was no way of challenging that regulation before any court the relevant date was the date when the applicants were actually affected by the measure concerned.

(d) An application must not be '*manifestly ill-founded*'. This ground of inadmissibility really indicates that the Commission is a filtering mechanism. The word 'manifestly' is clearly a nonsense because many of the cases which have been rejected as 'manifestly ill-founded' are very close to the borderline indeed and certainly could have gone either way. In many cases the Commission does not differentiate very sharply between the question of manifestly ill-founded and the question of incompatibility with the Convention and the case law is far from consistent.

21.6.1 THE PROCEDURE AFTER AN APPLICATION HAS BEEN DECLARED ADMISSIBLE

After the Commission has declared an application admissible, it subjects the complaint therein to an examination of the merits. The application is initially examined by a *rapporteur* and there will be an attempt to try to achieve a 'friendly settlement' which shows respect for human rights. Often this involves a monetary payment with or without an amendment to the domestic legal order. The parties are invited to make written observations and subsequently to submit oral arguments at one or several hearings. Usually these will be supplementary rather than essential because the fundamental arguments will have been put forward during the admissibility stage. At such a hearing any member of the Commission may, with the consent of the President, put questions to the parties.

Article 31 of the Convention provides:

> If a solution is not reached the Commission shall draw up a report on the facts and state its opinion as to whether the facts found disclose a breach by the State concerned of its obligation under the Convention. . . .

Thus if a friendly settlement is not obtained the Commission will give its decision in an 'Article 31' report.

21.6.2 THE PERSONNEL OF THE COURT AND COMMISSION

The European Commission is comprised of a number of members, one from each of the Convention countries. They are in effect nominated by their member governemnts although there is a notional election by the 'Committee of Ministers' that is the foreign ministers of each of the member States or their deputies. The members of the Commission are elected for a period of six years but may be re-elected. The members are invariably lawyers and although each country nominates one, the members of the Commission are most certainly *not* there to put the case for their own country. Indeed, on appointment, members of the Commission must swear an oath that they: 'will exercise their powers and duties honourably, impartially and conscientiously'.

The members of the Court 'shall be of high moral character and must either possess the qualification required for appoitnment to High Judicial office or be jurisconsults of recognised competence'. Members of the Court are elected for a period of nine years but may be re-elected. Whereas the Commission works in Strasbourg, full-time members of the Court work only part-time, typically about ten days each month. There is no requirement for a member State to appoint its own nationals as its chosen judge and indeed Liechtenstein for some years has appointed a Canadian academic as its judge, the rest of Liechtenstein lawyers presumably being fully engaged in secreting the assets of sundry Third World despots.

All Article 31 reports are forwarded to the Committee of Ministers which is an organ of the Council of Europe which has certain functions under the Convention and is comprised of foreign ministers of the member States or their deputies. The case may within three months be sent to the Court by the Commission or by a government involved. If the case is not sent to the Court the Committee of Ministers will pass a resolution as to whether or not the Convention has been violated and compensation can be awarded at this stage. This procedure is however extremely rare, and what we shall consider is the procedure when the case comes to the Court.

Before the case goes before the Court there is often a further exchange of 'memorials' (i.e., written submissions) and there is then an oral hearing. The Court has a registrar who deals with preliminary procedural matters and convenes the hearing. The quorum of judges is 12. The current President of the Court is Norwegian and the other judges are chosen by lot except that the judge from the member State affected must be one of them. As indicated before, he is expected to exercise an impartial jurisdiction, and is most assuredly not there to look after the interests of his own country. The judge of the member State is in essence there in order to provide the other judges with any necessary expertise about his domestic legal system. The Court sits in semi-circular formation in the 'Human Rights building' with the President at the centre. The other judges sit in no particular order save that the German judge may well come down the evening before and put his towel over the chair of his choice.

21.6.3 PROCEDURE BEFORE THE COURT

The European Commission attends the hearings and acts as a sort of *amicus curiae*, introducing its own findings in the case and making observations upon them and upon any other matter arising. The respondent government is invariably represented by very senior lawyer and the appellant by his own lawyer who may be either a practitioner, or in some cases an academic.

The proceedings are subject to simultaneous translation for the judge by the interpreters of the Court and headphones are also provided for those in the public gallery. The interpreters, whilst technically perfect, all appear to be on secondment from the planet Vulcan and most wear long hair to conceal their pointed ears. They chant their interpretations in a mesmeric robotic way, often in a slight assumed American accent. Even if one speaks French sufficiently to be able to follow the proceedings without interpretation, it remains the best free entertainment in Strasbourg to listen in on the headphones to the English version.

The proceedings will be introduced by the European Commission and thereafter the respondent government will speak with the applicants speaking last. The proceedings are remarkably swift, quite substantial cases being over in well under a day.

Considering that this, in a real sense, is the most important and effective court in the world, the quality of advocacy is extremely variable. Indeed, the writer was told by a member of the staff of the European Court that the reason why so many British cases reach the Court is that the Court likes to see British advocates because of their competence. (The advocates of Holland and Italy were singled out for particularly unfavourable mention.)

The proceedings are somewhat unstructured and the judges exercise little control over the advocates. Often even preliminary facts appear not to have been clearly established and the advocates sometimes lapse in to giving evidence themselves. In one case involving Sweden, which the writer observed, the Swedish Government's counsel began asserting that the applicant was wrong about some material matter in terms that 'I spoke to the Ombudsman about this only last week and he told me . . .'. At a later stage the applicant's representative, an academic lawyer, sought to put in evidence his own Ph.D thesis to demonstrate the essentially fascistic nature of the Swedish state.

In cases where compensation for the individual is sought, there appears to have been no pre-hearing discovery or production of documents and very little formal proof, the advocate often merely stating the sum which his client thinks would be fair recompense. Questions from the judges are extremely rare. The Court invariably reserves its decision.

21.7 Articles of the Convention

The subject matter of the articles of the Convention of major importance are as follows:

(a) Article 2 The right to life.
(b) Article 3 The right not to be subject to torture or inhuman or degrading treatment or punishment.
(c) Article 4 The right not to be held in slavery or servitude or to be required to form compulsory labour.
(d) Article 5 The right to liberty and security of the person.
(e) Article 6 The right to a fair trial.
(f) Article 7 The right not to be prosecuted retrospectively.
(g) Article 8 The right to respect for private and family life.

(h)   Article 9   The right to freedom of thought, conscience and religion.
(i)   Article 10   The right to freedom of expression.
(j)   Article 11   The right to freedom of peaceful assembly and free association.
(k)   Article 12   The right to marry and found a family.
(l)   Article 13   The right to an effective remedy before a national authority.
(m) Article 14   The right to have one's other rights under the Convention secured without discrimination on the grounds of sex, race, language, religion, national origin, property or birth.
(n)   Protocol 1   The right to peaceful enjoyment of possessions; the right to education; the right to free elections.

21.8   The Convention and Criminal Justice

There is no space in this book to consider the case law under all the articles of the Convention. For the criminal justice system the important articles are Article 13 and Articles 5, 6 and 7. The text of these articles appears below:

Article 5

1.   Everyone has the right to liberty and security of person. No one shall be deprived of his liberty save in the following cases and in accordance with a procedure prescribed by law;
   (a)   the lawful detention of a person after conviction by a competent court;
   (b)   the lawful arrest or detention of a person for non-compliance with the lawful order of a court or in order to secure the fulfilment of any obligation prescribed by law;
   (c)   the lawful arrest or detention of a person effected for the purpose of bringing him before the competent legal authority on reasonable suspicion of having comitted an offence or when it is reasonably considered necessary to prevent his committing an offence or fleeing after having done so;
   (d)   the detention of a minor by lawful order for the purpose of educational supervision or his lawful detention for the purpose of bringing him before the competent legal authority;
   (e)   the lawful detention of persons for the prevention of the spreading of infectious diseases, of persons of unsound mind, alcoholics or drug addicts or vagrants;
   (f)   the lawful arrest or detention of a person to prevent his effecting an unauthorised entry into the country or of a person against whom action is being taken with a view to deportation or extradition.
2.   Everyone who is arrested shall be informed promptly, in a language which he understands, of the reasons for his arrest and of any charge against him.
3.   Everyone arrested or detained in accordance with the provisions of paragraph 1(c) of this Article shall be brought promptly before a judge or other officer authorised by law to exercise judicial power and shall be entitled to trial within a reasonable time or to release pending trial. Release may be conditioned by guarantees to appear for trial.
4.   Everyone who is deprived of his liberty by arrest or detention shall be entitled to take proceedings by which the lawfulness of his detention shall be decided speedily by a court and his release ordered if the detention is not lawful.
5.   Everyone who has been the victim of arrest or detention in contravention of the provisions of this Article shall have an enforceable right to compensation.

Article 6

1.   In the determination of his civil rights and obligations or of any criminal charge against him, everyone is entitled to a fair and public hearing within a reasonable time by an independent and impartial tribunal established by law. Judgment shall be pronounced publicly but the press and public may be excluded from all or part of the trial in the interest of morals, public order or national security in a democratic society, where the interests of juveniles or the protection of the private life of the parties so require, or to the extent strictly necessary in the opinion of the court in special circumstances where publicity would prejudice the interests of justice.
2.   Everyone charged with a criminal offence shall be presumed innocent until proved guilty according to law.

3.   Everyone charged with a criminal offence has the following minimum rights;

(a)   to be informed promptly, in a language which he understands and in detail, of the nature and cause of the accusation against him;

(b)   to have adequate time and facilities for the prepration of his defence;

(c)   to defend himself in person or through legal assistance of his own choosing or, if he has not sufficient means to pay for legal assistance, to be given it free when the interests of justice so require;

(d)   to examine or have examined witnesses against him and to obtain the attendance and examination of witnesses on his behalf under the same conditions as witnesses against him;

(e)   to have the free assistance of an interpreter if he cannot understand or speak the language used in court.

Article 7

1.   No one shall be held guilty of any criminal offence on account of any act or omission which did not constitute a criminal offence under national or international law at the time when it was committed. Nor shall a heavier penalty be imposed than the one that was applicable at the time the criminal offence was committed.

2.   This Article shall not prejudice the trial and punishment of any person for any act or omission which, at the time when it was committed, was criminal according to the general principles of law recognised by civilised nations.

Article 13

Everyone whose rights and freedoms as set forth in this Convention are violated shall have an effective remedy before a national authority notwithstanding that the violation has been committed by persons acting in an official capacity.

21.8.1   ARTICLE 13

It is worth dealing first with Article 13 which *appears* to be of vital general importance.

It provides that there should be an effective remedy before a national authority even if the violation of the Convention has been committed by persons acting in an official capacity. In short this requires a national political system to have effective courts or other bodies capable of making decisions and providing remedies for violations. Article 13 is usually seen as ancillary to other violations of the Convention and very often in cases where breaches of Article 13 with some other article have been brought, if there is a finding of a violation of that other article, the court does not go on to consider Article 13. Thus, for example, in the case of *Malone* v *United Kingdom* (judgment 26 April 1984; A95) which had to do with unlawful telephone tapping and a violation of Article 8, the Court, having found that there was a violation of Article 8, did not go on to consider the violation of Article 13 alleged.

A further problem is the question of whether Article 13 guarantees a remedy which allows a contracting State's laws to be challenged before a national authority on the ground of being contrary to the Convention. The case of *Leander* v *Sweden* (judgment of 26 March 1986; A116) decided, in a very confusing judgment, that Article 13 does not guarantee any such remedy and therefore it is not incumbent upon member States to provide mechanisms for adjudication on Convention rights within their domestic legal system. Article 13 viewed alone is therefore virtually without effect.

21.8.2   ARTICLE 7

We will now turn to the articles more directly relevant to criminal justice, taking first Article 7. This is relatively uncontroversial and provides a prohibition on retrospective prosecution in respect of acts which were not criminal at the time they were committed. It remains to be seen how this article will be applied in a case such as *R* v *R* [1991] 4 All ER 481 under which the crime of marital rape has on one view been 'created' after centuries during which it was no crime. The language used by the Law Lords seems quite clear in that they recognise that they are creating a new offence rather than merely negating a previous defence. On the face of it the defendant's success in the European Court would appear assured under Article 7 but matters under the Convention are rarely so straightforward. In deciding whether there has been a breach of Article 7 one has to have regard also to Article 7(2) which provides that 'this article shall not prejudice the trial and punishment of any person for any act or omission, which at the time when it was committed, was criminal according to the general principles of law recognised by civilised nations'. One can therefore see a good deal of argument about the extent to which 'civilised nations', whoever they may be, have recognised that marital rape is or is not a crime, should this case ever reach the European Court.

21.8.3   ARTICLE 5

Article 5 deals with the right to liberty and security for the person and allows six different situations where that right may be restricted. Not surprisingly, the right to restrict liberty after conviction and while on remand pending trial are the most important provisions. In relation to the latter there are limits on the power to remand in custody, which is permitted only 'when it is reasonably considered necessary to prevent his committing an offence or fleeing after having done so'. Thus in decided cases the Commission and Court frequently had to consider such matters as reasonableness of grounds for arrest; length of detention on remand; the imposition of restrictions or conditions on bail. The rights in the article are further enforced by Article 5(3) which guarantees a right to be brought before a judge for a trial within a reasonable time or to release pending trial. The case law shows that even in the case of detention for remarkably long periods, no breach of the Convention may exist. Some of these delays are quite extraordinary by English standards, remands in custody of up to four years having been found acceptable on various grounds including the complexity of the case and the difficulties of collecting evidence. The reasoning in these decisions, which naturally reflect the domestic legal experience of the relevant members of the Commission or Court, appear highly questionable given that Article 6 provides a presumption of innocence until conviction.

It must nonetheless be conceded that, in balancing the various factors and the interests of continuity in the criminal justice systems in its many different States, the Commission and Court have been faced with an extremely difficult task. As a balance of what is politically acceptable and what is achievable it does nonetheless sometimes seem that the Commission and Court have shrunk from a proper application of the Convention. If even within the much criticised British criminal justice system it is possible to have a section of a statute (s. 22, Prosecution of Offences Act 1985) which in principle guarantees a period of not longer than 182 days between first appearance in the magistrates' court and commencement of Crown Court trial, then there is no reason why that as a norm should not be sought elsewhere. In the UK the prosecution do of course have the right to apply to extend these time limits, but at least there is then a judicial process for investigating the merits of delay.

This criticism of the case law under the Convention must however be subject to the consideration that the greatest single group of all applications to the European Commission are persons involved in the criminal justice process who often see such applications as a further route of appeal, or just an opportunity to embarrass the officers of the criminal justice system concerned. Many such applications are utterly frivolous but still require a good deal of work from the Commission at the preliminary stage.

The other relevant parts of Article 5 need no further discussion. The Commission and Court have been inclined to accept that 'the right to have the lawfulness of deprivation of liberty by arrest or detention decided speedily and by a court' is susceptible of a wide variety of interpretations throughout the member countries and there is certainly no requirement that an accused on remand need be produced at frequent intervals to a court for them to reconsider his position. Nothing in the English criminal justice system is likely to offend these provisions.

21.8.4   ARTICLE 6

It is Article 6 which contains the most important and wide-ranging provisions governing the criminal trial. This article is closely modelled on the Sixth Amendment to the Constitution of the United States of 1791 but is rather more extensive than that amendment. When framing this article in particular, the authors of the Convention obviously faced enormous practical and theoretical problems. The eventual text needed to be a minimum statement of the rights of persons in the criminal justice system having regard to the very different conditions prevailing in Europe in 1950. It also required the accommodation of the different legal traditions of all the original signatories to the Convention. The principle that the proper purpose of criminal justice is to apprehend, convict and punish criminals is not a controversial one. Nonetheless the differences in procedures and indeed substantive law throughout Europe in ensuring this reasonable objective are considerable. These differences were a very important constraint on the degree of precision with which the relevant articles of the Convention could be drafted and thus the Convention does not deal at all with a number of very central matters.

In particular there is no consideration of what 'crimes' are as such. The Court has always held it inappropriate for it to decide whether a certain activity should or should not be criminalised in an individual country provided that there is no attempt merely to sidestep the Convention (e.g., by reclassifying the matter concerned so as to give what is really being prosecuted as a crime, the appearance of a civil or administrative dispute, for example between an individual and a local authority by a change in nomenclature).

The regimes in particular in the case of 'victimless' crimes such as drugs, prostitution, pornography, gambling and insider trading vary tremendously throughout the member States with these activities attracting substantial penalties in some and not amounting to crimes at all in others.

21.8.4.1 Criminal procedure in Europe

As is well-known, European criminal justice systems have at least one fundamental difference from the common law system.

This is the inquisitorial nature of part of the process; this usually (at least in serious crimes) involves the existence of an '*instruction*' stage during which a dossier on the crime is prepared by a judge, sometimes with his own independent police force under his control with whose assistance he embarks upon an independent investigation. There is little real similarity to the committal process in England. In particular the judge may embark on comprehensive interrogation of the suspect with no lawyer present and no right of silence; may arrange confrontations between the suspect and witnesses or the victim; and can even undertake detailed reconstructions of the crime at the scene, often with the press or even television cameras in attendance. At this stage the rights of the accused appear very different to those in the English process. The nature of remands and criteria for the grant of bail may likewise be dramatically different.

There are equally striking differences in courtroom procedures. The judge usually runs the case and conducts much of the examination of witnesses himself; also the deference traditionally shown by English barristers to judges is usually lacking and it is a considerable culture shock to witness the often open hostility or contempt between the advocates and the sometimes young and inexperienced members of the professional judiciary. The procedures in multi-defendant trials also often contrast dramatically with English trials which are usually split so as to ensure manageable proportions. It would be unthinkable in England, as occurred in Italy in the Red Brigade and Mafiosi trials, that up to 80 defendants would be cooped up in a giant cage at the back of the court, often engaged in what seemed to be some kind of party whilst the proceedings in front of them dragged on for years. Another important difference is the intervention of the so-called 'civil party' (i.e., the victim) who often has the right to be represented at certain stages of the criminal trial and to argue for compensation, or even for the specific penalty to be imposed on the accused.

Courtroom procedure may arguably be a question of style, though inevitably the trier of fact must be influenced by such things. Of greater importance are evidential or procedural rules which must directly bear on the outcome of the trial. Thus for example in many countries the accused's criminal record is brought out at the start of the proceedings and placed before the trier of fact. As was discussed in **Chapter 13**, complex English rules in the main prevent this happening on the basis that the trier of fact would be so dramatically influenced by his knowledge of the accused's criminal record as to make the so-called 'forbidden connection' between criminal record and present guilt. Similarly the UK system goes to considerable trouble by a variety of procedural rules backed by the ultimate sanction of contempt of court to ensure a minimum of pre-trial publicity. Other jurisdictions (and even the other main common law jurisdiction, the USA) have no such rules and give no attention at all to the risk of eventual jurors being prejudiced, so that press speculation, and worse, about the identity of the malefactor is very common. So for example in a much publicised French case the 'Villemin Affair' to do with the murder of a young boy in France, the Goncourt-prize-winning novelist Marguerite Duras published a novel before the trial had started purporting to describe the crime and naming the murder. Other extraordinary developments in that case include the fact that the young examining magistrate, whose inexperience was said to have contributed to some of the problems, resigned and wrote a sensational book concerning his view of the case and his admiration for one of the leading suspects in it.

There is a wealth of case law on the application of Article 6 of the Convention and aspects of individual State's criminal justice systems have been subjected to the most minute scrutiny. Although the existence of a proper appeal procedure does not in itself remedy undesirable institutional aspects of a State's legal system, the Court has usually tended to look at the net outcome of the case rather than merely examining the trial at first instance. In considering what is a 'fair trial' the Court applies a variety of concepts, some of which are relatively vague, such as *proportionality* (a balance between remedy and wrong addressed), *equality of arms* (the concept that both parties are entitled to equal rights and adequacy of representation — a matter which cannot be too closely adhered to in some contexts), and '*margin of appreciation*' which allows that member States must have discretions in certain areas, amongst them criminal procedure.

21.8.4.2 Article 6 and the law of evidence

It is clear that the Court will not impugn individual State laws of evidence where these laws have to do with competence of witnesses or the actual assessment of evidence, for example the absence of corroboration requirements. The only strict requirements of Article 6 are 'a fair and public hearing by an independent and impartial tribunal', 'a presumption of innocence', and provisions in Article 6(3) which have to do with proper time to prepare and proper means to conduct a defence.

There is a great deal of case law, some of it confusing and contradictory, about various aspects of the conduct of a trial. Much recent case law has been under Article 6(3)(d) and as to whether the requirement that a person should have the minimum right 'to examine or have examined witnesses against him . . .' indicates that hearsay by the production of out-of-court witness statements is inevitably contrary to the Convention. Even the interpretation of this apparently straightforward phrase has given rise to grave dfficulties. The court often retreats behind a general formula that 'the assessment of evidence is a matter for national courts' and has declined to rule that statements from absent witnesses are contrary to the Convention (see *Isgro* v *Italy* (case 1/1990/192/252) and *Asch* v *Austria* (case 30/1990/221/283). In other cases on virtually indistinguishable facts the court has held that the introduction of hearsay evidence from out-of-court witnesses was in breach of the Convention (see *Kostovski* v *Netherlands* (case 10/1988/154/208) and *Unterpertinger* v *Austria* (case 1985/87/134).

The difficulty in such cases could again be interpreted as indicating that the Court shrinks from the apparently straightforward application of the clear wording of the Convention, which does indeed seem to prohibit hearsay, in the light of the possible political consequences of interfering so drastically in the criminal justice systems of the many European countries which appear to permit hearsay in the criminal trial (as of course does the UK under the many exceptions to the hearsay rule, e.g., ss. 23 and 24, Criminal Justice Act 1988).

21.9 Practical Use of the Convention

Challenges to the outcome of English cases are likely to prove increasingly popular. Articles 5 and 6 are both sufficiently vague as to leave a good deal of scope for interpretation and notwithstanding a great deal of case law (though some of it is inaccessible) on criminal justice systems there are usually individual features which make cases distinguishable. At present, legal aid is unlikely to be granted from Strasbourg until a reasonable amount of work has been done on a case and it is apparently the view of the Legal Aid Board that the Green Form cannot be used for work on applications to Strasbourg since such applications are not 'a question of English law'. One is however more likely to receive realistic instructions to take a case to Strasbourg in cases involving public law rights, for example under the more general articles such as Articles 8 and 10 where the scope for interpretation is even greater than in the case of criminal justice.

Nonetheless it may be an important last resort to take a client's case to Strasbourg. In the most high profile of cases this is likely to result, at best, only in a change to the domestic legal order and monetary compensation because the delay in taking cases to Strasbourg is extreme, a period between the wrong complained of and the decision of the Court of several years being the norm. Thus if your client is subject to a period of imprisonment he is most likely to have served his sentence before any ruling is obtained from Strasbourg. The Commission does in fact have the power under rr. 27 and 28 of the Rules of Procedure in urgent cases to give precedence to a particular complaint and under r. 36 to 'indicate to the parties any interim measure the adoption of which seems desirable in the interest of the parties or the proper conduct of the proceedings before it' but this kind of recommendation (which is anyway not legally binding on the contracting States) is most unlikely to be used so as to procure the release from custody of a person pending his application to the Commission and Court.

INDEX

INDEX

INDEX